MW00768164

21ST CENTURY NURSING LEADERSHIP

Edited by
Mary Magee Gullatte, PhD, RN, ANP-BC, AOCN®, FAAN

To Sergio
Thanks for your
transformational leadership
Mary Gullatte 11/27/2017

Oncology Nursing Society
Pittsburgh, Pennsylvania

ONS Publications Department

Publisher and Director of Publications: William A. Tony, BA, CQIA
Senior Editorial Manager: Lisa M. George, BA
Assistant Editorial Manager: Amy Nicoletti, BA, JD
Acquisitions Editor: John Zaphyr, BA, MEd
Associate Staff Editors: Casey S. Kennedy, BA, Andrew Petyak, BA
Design and Production Administrator: Dany Sjoen
Editorial Assistant: Judy Holmes

Copyright © 2018 by the Oncology Nursing Society. All rights reserved. No part of the material protected by this copyright may be reproduced or utilized in any form, electronic or mechanical, including photocopying, recording, or by an information storage and retrieval system, without written permission from the copyright owner. For information, visit www.ons.org/sites/default/files/Publication%20Permissions.pdf, or send an email to pubpermissions@ons.org.

Library of Congress Cataloging-in-Publication Data

Names: Gullatte, Mary Magee, editor. | Oncology Nursing Society, issuing body.
Title: 21st century nursing leadership / edited by Mary Magee Gullatte.
Description: Pittsburgh, Pennsylvania : Oncology Nursing Society, [2018] |
  Includes bibliographical references and index.
Identifiers: LCCN 2017028957 (print) | LCCN 2017029575 (ebook) | ISBN
  9781635930092 | ISBN 9781635930047 (pbk.)
Subjects: | MESH: Leadership | Nursing, Supervisory | Nurse Administrators |
  Nurse's Role | Ethics, Nursing | Vocational Guidance
Classification: LCC RT82 (ebook) | LCC RT82 (print) | NLM WY 105 | DDC
  610.7306/9--dc23
LC record available at https://lccn.loc.gov/2017028957

Publisher's Note

This book is published by the Oncology Nursing Society (ONS). ONS neither represents nor guarantees that the practices described herein will, if followed, ensure safe and effective patient care. The recommendations contained in this book reflect ONS's judgment regarding the state of general knowledge and practice in the field as of the date of publication. The recommendations may not be appropriate for use in all circumstances. Those who use this book should make their own determinations regarding specific safe and appropriate patient care practices, taking into account the personnel, equipment, and practices available at the hospital or other facility at which they are located. The editor and publisher cannot be held responsible for any liability incurred as a consequence from the use or application of any of the contents of this book. Figures and tables are used as examples only. They are not meant to be all-inclusive, nor do they represent endorsement of any particular institution by ONS. Mention of specific products and opinions related to those products do not indicate or imply endorsement by ONS. Websites mentioned are provided for information only; the hosts are responsible for their own content and availability. Unless otherwise indicated, dollar amounts reflect U.S. dollars.

ONS publications are originally published in English. Publishers wishing to translate ONS publications must contact ONS about licensing arrangements. ONS publications cannot be translated without obtaining written permission from ONS. (Individual tables and figures that are reprinted or adapted require additional permission from the original source.) Because translations from English may not always be accurate or precise, ONS disclaims any responsibility for inaccuracies in words or meaning that may occur as a result of the translation. Readers relying on precise information should check the original English version.

Printed in the United States of America

Innovation • Excellence • Advocacy

This book is dedicated in loving honor and memory of my parents:
Bilbo Magee, 1915–2002, WWII Veteran
and Hazel Magee, 1929–2008

For the many blessings I have received from two wonderful parents who always inspired us to dream big and reach for the stars. To my loving and supportive husband, Rodney Gullatte, Sr.; our son, Rodney Gullatte, Jr., his wife, Iris Rivera Gullatte, and our granddaughters, Mary Carmen and Tatiana Isabella Gullatte; and our daughter, Ronda Gullatte Broome, and her husband, Ryan Broome. Family, you are my strength and my joy. To all my brothers and sisters: Selma, Billy, Lester, Amanda (deceased), Winnie, Willace, Hope, Donna, and Sue Ann, thank you for your unconditional love and unwavering support.

Contributors

Editor

Mary Magee Gullatte, PhD, RN, ANP-BC, AOCN®, FAAN
Corporate Director, Nursing Innovation and Research
Emory Healthcare
Atlanta, Georgia
Adjunct Clinical Faculty
Nell Hodgson Woodruff School of Nursing
Emory University
Atlanta, Georgia
Chapter 1. Leading From the Evolving Future; Chapter 11. Balancing Multiple and Competing Priorities; Chapter 21. Professional Nursing Association Membership and Board Leadership; Chapter 22. Mentoring Current and Future Nurse Leaders; Chapter 23. Reinventing Yourself for Future Leadership

Authors

Nancy Howell Agee, MN, RN
President and Chief Executive Officer
Carilion Clinic
Roanoke, Virginia
Chapter 20. Journey From Bedside to Boardroom

Nancy M. Albert, PhD, CCNS, CHFN, CCRN, NE-BC, FAHA, FCCM, FHFSA, FAAN
Associate Chief Nursing Officer, Nursing Research and Innovation
Cleveland Clinic
Clinical Nurse Specialist, Heart Failure
Kaufman Center for Heart Failure, Cleveland Clinic Main Campus
Cleveland, Ohio
Chapter 19. Leading Clinical Nurse Engagement in Research

Angela Adjetey Appiah, MSN, MPH, MA, RN, FAACM
Senior Administrative Director, Oncology Services
Northwell Health Cancer Institute at Phelps
Phelps Hospital Northwell Health
Sleepy Hollow, New York
Chapter 22. Mentoring Current and Future Nurse Leaders

Laurie Badzek, LLM, JD, MS, RN, FAAN
Director and Professor
University of North Carolina Wilmington
Wilmington, North Carolina
Chapter 15. Ethics and Nursing Leadership

Katherine Bell, MSN, APRN, ACNS-BC
Advanced Practice Nurse
Head and Neck Surgery
MD Anderson Cancer Center
Houston, Texas
Chapter 18. Health Policy and Advocacy for Nurse Leaders

Carol Boston-Fleischhauer, JD, MS, RN
Managing Director and Chief Nursing Officer
The Advisory Board Company
Washington, DC
Chapter 7. Leading and Sustaining a Robust Workforce

Jeannine M. Brant, PhD, APRN-CNS, AOCN®, FAAN
Oncology Clinical Nurse Specialist and Nurse Scientist
Billings Clinic
Billings, Montana
Chapter 17. Leading the Global Transformation of Health Care

Mary Bylone, RN, MSM, CNML
President
Leaders Within LLC
Colchester, Connecticut
*Chapter 6. Leading and Sustaining a Healthy Work
    Environment*

Connie Carson, PhD
Healthcare Consultant
Carson Consulting
Littleton, Colorado
*Chapter 8. Communication Strategies in the
    Multigenerational Workforce*

Christina Cone, DNP, APRN, ANP-BC, AOCNP®
Nurse Practitioner, Administrative Director
Duke University Medical Center, Duke Cancer Institute,
    Preston Robert Tisch Brain Tumor Center
Durham, North Carolina
*Chapter 10. Interprofessional Team Collaborations in
    Improving Patient Outcomes and Value-Based Care*

Jane Englebright, PhD, RN, CENP, FAAN
Chief Nurse Executive and Senior Vice President
HCA Healthcare
Nashville, Tennessee
Chapter 13. Executive Leadership Acumen

Rhonda R. Foster, EdD, MPH, MS, RN, NEA-BC
Leadership Consultant
The Grace Consulting Group
Santa Rosa, California
Principal Consultant
Stamp and Chase
St. Louis, Missouri
Chapter 2. Leadership Blueprint for Nursing's Future

Vicki Good, DNP, RN, CENP, CPPS
System Director of Quality and Clinical Safety
Cox Health
Springfield, Missouri
*Chapter 6. Leading and Sustaining a Healthy Work
    Environment*

Tracy Gosselin, PhD, RN, AOCN®, NEA-BC
Chief Nursing and Patient Care Services Officer
Duke University Hospital
Duke University Health System
Durham, North Carolina
*Chapter 10. Interprofessional Team Collaborations in
    Improving Patient Outcomes and Value-Based Care*

Lisa Hardman, DNP, RN, CDE, VHA-CM
Clarksburg, West Virginia
Chapter 15. Ethics and Nursing Leadership

Marsha Hughes-Rease, BSN, MSN, RN, MSOD, PCC
Executive Coach, Consultant, and Educator
American Nurses Association Nursing Knowledge
    Center
Silver Spring, Maryland
Chapter 2. Leadership Blueprint for Nursing's Future

Dianne M. Jacobs, MSN, RN
Healthcare Consultant
CoMass Group, LLC
Atlanta, Georgia
Chapter 5. Leading a Culture of Civility

Sultan Kav, PhD, RN
Professor of Nursing
Baskent University Faculty of Health Sciences,
    Department of Nursing
Ankara, Turkey
*Chapter 17. Leading the Global Transformation of Health
    Care*

Brittany Lively, BS, PA-C
General Oncology Physician Assistant
Rocky Mountain Cancer Centers
Denver, Colorado
*Chapter 8. Communication Strategies in the
    Multigenerational Workforce*

Kathy Malloch, PhD, MBA, RN, FAAN
President, MKLS, LLC
Professor of Practice, College of Nursing and Health
    Innovation
Arizona State University
Glendale, Arizona
Clinical Professor, College of Nursing
The Ohio State University
Columbus, Ohio
Chapter 3. Quantum Leadership for a New Age of Nursing

Patricia J. Maramba, DNP, RN
Senior Lecturer
West Virginia School of Nursing
Morgantown, West Virginia
Chapter 15. Ethics and Nursing Leadership

**Jane M. McCurley, DNP, MBA, RN, NEA-BC, CENP,
FACHE**
Assistant Chief Nurse Executive
HCA Healthcare
Nashville, Tennessee
Chapter 13. Executive Leadership Acumen

Patricia Reid Ponte, RN, DNSc, NEA-BC, FAAN
Nurse Scholar in Residence
Phyllis F. Cantor Center for Research in Nursing and
    Patient Care Services
Dana-Farber Cancer Institute
Boston, Massachusetts
Chapter 4. Thriving in a Time of Continuous Change

Tim Porter-O'Grady, DM, EdD, ScD(h), APRN, FAAN, FACCWS, GCNS-BC, NEA-BC, CWCN, CFCN
Senior Partner, Health Systems; Tim Porter-O'Grady
    Associates, Inc.
Atlanta, Georgia
Clinical Professor, Leadership Scholar, College of Nursing
The Ohio State University
Columbus, Ohio
Professor of Practice, College of Nursing and Health
    Innovation
Arizona State University
Tucson, Arizona
Adjunct Professor, School of Nursing
Emory University
Atlanta, Georgia
Chapter 3. Quantum Leadership for a New Age of Nursing

Ninfa M. Saunders, DHA, MBA, MSN, FACHE
President and Chief Executive Officer
Navicent Health: Georgia Health System and
    The Medical Center of Central Georgia
Macon, Georgia
Chapter 20. Journey From Bedside to Boardroom

Linda J. Shinn, MBA, RN, FASAE, CAE
President and Chief Executive Officer
Consensus Management Group
Indianapolis, Indiana
*Chapter 12. Project Management and Business Planning
    for Nurse Leaders*

Alec Stone, MA, MPA
Director of Health Policy
Oncology Nursing Society
Pittsburgh, Pennsylvania
Chapter 18. Health Policy and Advocacy for Nurse Leaders

LeAnn Thieman, LPN, CSP, CPAE
Self-Employed
Founder of SelfCare for HealthCare™
Fort Collins, Colorado
Chapter 9. Compassionate Care Begins With Self-Care

Ronnie Ursin, DNP, MBA, RN, NEA-BC, FACHE
Chief Nursing Officer
Northern Louisiana Medical Center-Community Health
    Systems
Ruston, Louisiana
*Chapter 21. Professional Nursing Association
    Membership and Board Leadership*

Deborah Kirk Walker, DNP, FNP-BC, NP-C, AOCN®, FAANP
Associate Professor and Nurse Practitioner
University of Alabama at Birmingham School of Nursing
Birmingham, Alabama
Chapter 16. Leading Future Innovations in Nursing Education

Les Wallace, PhD
President
Signature Resources, Inc.
Aurora, Colorado
*Chapter 14. Executive Competencies for a Disruptive
    Healthcare Future*

Deidre Walton, JD, MSN, RN
Immediate Past President
National Black Nurses Association
Scottsdale, Arizona
*Chapter 21. Professional Nursing Association
    Membership and Board Leadership*

Nancy P. Wingo, PhD, MA
Assistant Professor
University of Alabama at Birmingham School of Nursing
Birmingham, Alabama
Chapter 16. Leading Future Innovations in Nursing Education

Reviewers

Megan Allen, MAJ
Publications Coordinator
Navicent Health
Macon, Georgia

Jeanne S. Armentrout
Executive Vice President and Chief Administrative Officer
Carilion Clinic
Roanoke, Virginia

W. Jason Atkins, MBI, RN-BC
Chief Nursing Information and Quality Officer
Emory Healthcare
Atlanta, Georgia

Kathleen Bartholomew, RN, MN
Healthcare Consultant, International Speaker, and
    Author
San Juan Island, Washington

Kathryn Boorer, PhD
Scientific Communications
NantHealth
Culver City, California

Ronda G. Broome, MS, CTR
Project Coordinator, Oncology Services
Oncology Analytics
Piedmont Healthcare
President, Georgia Tumor Registrars Association
Atlanta, Georgia

Brenda R. McCune Brown, BS, MS, APRN-BC
Nurse Practitioner (Retired)
Marietta, Georgia

Deborah L. Cox, MBA, MS-CM, MT (ASCP)
Principal
CoMass Group
Atlanta, Georgia

Kerri A. Dalton, MSN, RN, AOCNS®
Associate Director, Education
Duke Cancer Network, Network Services
Durham, North Carolina

Christy Dempsey, MSN, MBA, CNOR, CENP
Senior Vice President and Chief Nursing Officer
Press Ganey Associates
South Bend, Indiana

Nancye R. Feistritzer, DNP, RN
Vice President, Patient Care Services, and Chief Nursing
  Officer
Emory University Hospital and Emory University
  Hospital at Wesley Woods
Atlanta, Georgia

Firma IT Solutions
Specializing in IT and Cybersecurity
Rodney Gullatte, Jr., Owner
www.firmaitss.com

William Fleck, MPA
Corporate Director, Enterprise Staffing
Emory Healthcare
Atlanta, Georgia

Beth Kantz, RN, MS
Cofounder and President
Corrigan Kantz Consulting
Brookline, Massachusetts

Richard Lamphier, RN
Clinical Program Manager
Project S.A.V.E.
Children's Healthcare of Atlanta
Atlanta, Georgia

Jacqueline Moss, PhD, RN, FAAN
Professor and Assistant Dean for Clinical Simulation
  and Technology
University of Alabama at Birmingham School of Nursing
Birmingham, Alabama

Sérgio Mota, MSN, RN, CCRN-CSC
Unit Director, 7E Medical Oncology
Emory University Hospital
Atlanta, Georgia

Brenda Nevidjon, MSN, RN, FAAN
Chief Executive Officer
Oncology Nursing Society
Pittsburgh, Pennsylvania

Patricia L. Peterson, BSN, JD
President and Chief Executive Officer
Colorado Cancer Research Program
Denver, Colorado

Anna Marie Richardson
Executive Assistant, Office of the President,
  Administration
Carilion Clinic
Roanoke, Virginia

Linda Riley, PhD, RN
Director, Nursing Research and Evidence-Based Practice
Children's Healthcare of Atlanta
Atlanta, Georgia

Hui Tan, MPH, RN
Nursing Manager
Hunan Cancer Hospital
Changsha, People's Republic of China

Qi Wang, BSN, RN
Head Nurse
Nursing Department
Tianjin Medical University Cancer Hospital
Tianjin, People's Republic of China

Lynn Whelan, DNP, RN, NEA-BC, ONC
ACNO Cardiac and Procedural Areas and Enterprise
  Staffing Pool
Emory University Hospitals
Atlanta, Georgia

Disclosure

Editors and authors of books and guidelines provided by the Oncology Nursing Society are expected to disclose to the readers any significant financial interest or other relationships with the manufacturer(s) of any commercial products.

A vested interest may be considered to exist if a contributor is affiliated with or has a financial interest in commercial organizations that may have a direct or indirect interest in the subject matter. A "financial interest" may include, but is not limited to, being a shareholder in the organization; being an employee of the commercial organization; serving on an organization's speakers bureau; or receiving research funding from the organization. An "affiliation" may be holding a position on an advisory board or some other role of benefit to the commercial organization. Vested interest statements appear in the front matter for each publication.

Contributors are expected to disclose any unlabeled or investigational use of products discussed in their content. This information is acknowledged solely for the information of the readers.

The contributors provided the following disclosure and vested interest information:
Jeannine M. Brant, PhD, APRN-CNS, AOCN®, FAAN: Genentech, Insys, honoraria
Deborah Kirk Walker, DNP, FNP-BC, NP-C, AOCN®, FAANP: Alabama Cancer Congress, Oncology Nursing Society Foundation, leadership position; Coosa Valley Hospital, Hematology Oncology Associates, LLC, St. Vincent's Health System, honoraria; Beeson Presbyterian Church, Dean's Scholar Award, research funding
Deidre Walton, JD, MSN, RN: National Black Nurses Association, leadership position

Contents

Foreword
by Sharon Krumm

21st Century Nursing Leadership provides nurses in management and leadership roles with specific information and guidance that is based on the most current research, knowledge, and demonstrated best practices. It is the "go-to" resource for nurses in every practice setting and in every aspect of the continuum of care. The novice and the most experienced nurse leader/manager will find this resource invaluable.

While the world of health care is forever changing, the one constant is the need for effective nurse leaders to successfully guide the nursing workforce through these changes. Additionally, as our world expands, not only must we keep up with the expansion, but we have a responsibility to provide expert leadership to ensure that patients affected by our care and practice standards receive the highest possible quality of care, regardless of the part of the world in which they live. It is appropriate and exciting to read the chapters in this book that address issues related to the leadership of the globalization of nursing practice.

This book contains essential chapters on the topics of project management, business planning, managing priorities, and interprofessional collaboration. These chapters are well supported by chapters of equal importance, including those on civil, ethical, and healthy, multigenerational work environments. Visioning for the future is vital to steering the course for healthcare and nurse leaders to help shape that future.

One of the many contributions that the authors made is to address all facets of leadership. This includes leaders in clinical roles and those who lead educational innovations and research efforts and initiatives.

Unfortunately, although we remain the largest healthcare workforce, nurses' voices are far too often absent from discussions and decisions related to health policy and are limited or missing in boardrooms. The chapters on health policy and advocacy, the journey from the bedside to the boardroom, mentoring, managing multiple priorities, association leadership, and reinventing oneself should be read, reread, and highlighted by every nurse leader.

Dr. Gullatte, the authors of each chapter, and the Oncology Nursing Society have provided an invaluable service in writing this book for nurses at every level and in every setting and specialty nursing practice. This book will be an essential resource for nurses in the years ahead as it provides a captivating look at the issues that matter most to experienced and emerging leaders.

Sharon Krumm, PhD, RN
Administrator and Director of Nursing
Sidney Kimmel Comprehensive Cancer Center
Johns Hopkins Hospital
Assistant Professor
Johns Hopkins University School of Nursing and
Johns Hopkins University Department of Oncology
Baltimore, Maryland

Foreword

by Roy L. Simpson

In my more than 40 years of practice, leadership has been key to safe patient care and advancing the profession at the patient care level. As we advance nursing practice and leadership, association leadership and membership have become paramount to patient care above and beyond our employer and employee relationship. Professional association leadership and membership are core to a profession. One cannot be an informed professional today in the climate of care without membership in a professional association.

Dr. Gullatte has assimilated a renowned cadre of authors with stellar and exemplary qualities who come from different spaces to drive the profession. When patients, consumers, the general public, and many of our colleagues are asked about nurses, I am not sure they get it. I am not sure that they have a true understanding of the dedication, education, and critical knowledge that nurses possess and apply to patient care.

The authors in this book are the *crème de la crème* of leadership for setting your sails for the future in true professional nursing leadership. From Connie Curran and Therese Fitzpatrick's book *Claiming the Corner Office* to my articles and books on technology—the linchpin is knowledge—our future leadership is key to success. From Margaret McClure and Muriel Poulin, we saw where the Magnet® blueprint of the 14 forces led the way to Gail Wolf's transformation leadership guiding us as a profession in practice, administration, and research. Tomorrow's future is with middle managers who require authors and contributors to health care to forge a path for future leaders. We need runways for future nurse leaders to fly from. This book provides a guide and blueprint for inspiring and applying words of wisdom and experiences of the chapter authors to share a vision for nursing leadership in navigating the future of health care. Some authors share wisdom through their personal journey, which may resonate with your own. Wisdom from past experiences helps to shape future leaders.

Health care of the future will challenge many things, which requires leadership. Expect to be challenged on licensure—from institutional and compact licensure to federal licensure versus state licensure. Laying a path for workplace advocacy, professional governance, and self-regulation of practice at every level, leaders must be lifelong learners, with the courage to remove those from professional status who are not lifelong learners as identified over time through observation and documentation of practice and education.

Dr. Gullatte and the authors take the readers to new heights and requirements of leadership to navigate new healthcare opportunities and threats and challenge us to embrace a new paradigm in healthcare leadership. As Drs. Porter-O'Grady and Malloch take us to quantum leadership, we are reminded of our core as nurses and presented with a runway for the best to transform quantum practices in nursing. Others address critical topics such as mentorship, self-care, clinical inquiry, managing priorities, change, creating and sustaining healthy work environments, reinventing oneself, and many more issues that are important in preparing future nurse leaders at every level.

Nurses have the capacity to lead the transformation of health care from diverse venues. One of the most important duties of the U.S. president is to make appointments to the Supreme Court when vacancies exist. So here is an analogy for you to ponder: There are more than 3.4 million nurses and 1.3 million attorneys, yet we have no nurses on the Supreme Court. With more than 450 million people in the United States, we have no nurse even as a district judge in 2,758 districts. There is no evidence of a judge or justice who has a healthcare background, yet they make rulings on matters that affect the profession and consumers of health care. When we talk about leadership, we need to think broadly about our values and culture penetrating the everyday life of health care in the global world in which we practice. Envision nursing leadership without borders. Let's envision bold change and go for the Supreme Court in leadership. The U.S. Constitution does not specify qualifications for justices such as age, education, profession, or citizenship. A justice does not have to be a lawyer or a law school graduate, nor does a judge. So why not a nurse? Now we get to vision, which is what leaders do. There has to be a vision of our future and nurses ready to lead with the vision. Helen Keller has been quoted as saying, "The only thing worse than being blind is having sight but no vision."

To be a leader, one must have a vision or be destined to take any road. Only through advancing education, thoughtful reflection, and practical and lived experiences does one craft and achieve a vision. To advance the vision, one needs skills, an action plan, resources, and incentives to realize the vision. Today's world is complex. Complexity management requires tools and knowledge to achieve a vision. While pundits and TV ads go for snippets and sound bites, complexity management is never about pundits or sound bites; it is about having these tools and being smart and knowledgeable.

Without a shared personal and professional vision, chaos, disorder, and confusion are likely to ensue. Feel the pulse of colleagues and people with whom you work. One can walk the halls and feel the confusion. It is real, and there must be clarity of a shared vision to advance change.

This new leadership book is so important to today's leaders. It addresses many topical areas along with firsthand experiences and knowledge to develop leaders and advance the profession. Read it, digest it, find yourself a mentor, and brand yourself as a leader. Remember, leaders change positions and roles often in order to create climate and culture. Today's world is mobile, and this creates different values and needs for leadership.

I wish you continued success in your leadership accolades for the future. Remember that change is inevitable, and be clear about the change you want to be associated with for your future. It is a great future when nurse leaders step up to the table of leadership, from the Supreme Court to executive boards of for-profit and nonprofit organizations.

Enjoy the read. Learn, grow, and remember that from data to information to knowledge, we are all part of the continuum of wisdom driving our profession. Step up and be a leader today with newfound knowledge generated in this exciting book on 21st-century nursing leadership.

Roy L. Simpson, DNP, RN, DPNAP, FAAN, FACMI
Clinical Professor, Doctoral Program
Nell Hodgson Woodruff School of Nursing
Emory University
Atlanta, Georgia

Acknowledgments

I wish to express special thanks to the colleagues and mentors who have had a positive impact on helping to shape my professional growth and practice and for encouraging me to pursue personal and professional goals with persistence and determination:

Nurses: Mary Beth McDowell, Mary Huch, Charlotte McHenry, Laura Porter Kimble, Marla Salmon, Brenda Brown, Linda McCauley, Pat Stanfil Edens, Carrie Gullatte, Edith Folsom Honeycutt, Mary F. Woody, Nelza Levine, Janice Phillips, Pearl Moore, Clara Jenkins, Jessie Anderson, Cynthia Crank, Ryan Iwamoto, Kevin Sowers, Sharon Krumm, Melba Hill-Paschel, Marjorie Kagawa-Singer, Roberta Strohl, Deborah McGuire, Catherine Futch, Ann Belcher, Brenda Nevidjon, Rhonda Scott, Paula Rieger, Kathi Mooney, Susan Beck, Mary Scott, Mildred Sawyer, Barbara Powe, Sultan Kav, Sheldon Sloan, Laura Hurt, Patti Owen, Hui Tan, Selinza Mitchell, Qi Wang, Veronica Tasker, Randy Crawford, Wan-min Qiang, Cecile Pena, Linda Burns-Bolton, Annette Tardy Morgan, Deborah Mayer, Lisa Alexander, Ayda Nambayan, Jeannine Brant, Norissa Honea, Peggy Joyce, Sandra Mitchell, Lisa Kennedy Sheldon, Ellen Smith, Susan Tavernier, Liu Yang, Susan Grant, Delcina Brown, Guadalupe Palos, Tim Porter-O'Grady, Yongyi Chen, Joan Lockhart, Debbie Wujcik, and countless other colleagues with whom I have worked, including Eddie Liukai and those who have coached and mentored me throughout my professional nursing education and career.

Physicians: James Bennett, James Fisher, Imani Vannoy, Douglas Murray, Daniel Nixon, David Lawson, Harold Freeman, Charles Huguley, James Steinberg, Leonard Heffner, Elliot Winton, Toncred Styblo, Kamal Mansour, William Wood, Louis Sullivan, Tina Jones, Robert Hermann, Edmund Waller, Amy Langston, Christopher Flowers, Carl Washington, and Navee Zhang.

I also wish to express sincere gratitude to my employers at Emory Healthcare for their support of my professional growth. To my Emory Healthcare Nurse Executive Team colleagues and other coworkers, managers, staff, colleagues, and friends across all departments of Emory Healthcare who have contributed in some measure to my professional growth, love of people, and passion for nursing.

Special thanks to the staff of the Oncology Nursing Society Publications Department for their work on this publication. A sincere note of gratitude to all of the patients and their families who have guided my nursing practice and leadership throughout my career.

Special Thanks to the Chapter Authors and Reviewers

My sincere appreciation and thanks to all of the contributing authors, consultants, and reviewers of this book. Special thanks to a wonderful and caring, dedicated, and committed team of local, national, and international nursing healthcare professionals and leaders.

CHAPTER 1

Leading From the Evolving Future

Mary Magee Gullatte, PhD, RN, ANP-BC, AOCN®, FAAN

The past is behind—learn from it; the future is ahead—prepare for it; the present is here—live it.

—Thomas S. Monson (1989)

Introduction

Imagine having the opportunity to transport 10–15 years into the future. Think about what your experience would look like, particularly in health care. Ponder the following: What will be the nursing and patient care needs? Where and how will health care be delivered? What will be the competencies and skills needed by nurse leaders to meet the patient care needs? Having the opportunity to get a firsthand view of the future is not reality, nor can anyone predict the future. However, as a nurse leader, one can look at lessons from the past and current environmental healthcare scans to draw inferences and forecast future directions. This chapter will serve to unlock the boundaries of the imagination and thinking in a different way to prepare for leading in an unknown and ever-evolving future of health care.

Examining information from public, private, government, and global data sources, one can use the information to begin defining goals and strategies to help shape and lead the future of health care. Nurses make up the single largest group of healthcare professionals in the United States. The public continues to rate nurses as the most honest and ethical of professionals (Norman, 2016). Hence, it is our professional duty to help lead the transformation of the future of health care.

This chapter, as well as the entire book, was written to be a guide to leadership knowledge building and inspiration for nurses who desire to prepare themselves for the 21st century and beyond by leading from the emerging and dynamic future in health care. As you read, take the time to imagine, dream, and envision a better and stronger healthcare future—a future that you personally seize the opportunity to actively lead. Use your futuristic imagination to inspire yourself and empower others to a new level of leadership. Think and imagine what can be. The power of positive and possibility thinking will help you achieve your desired outcomes. Futuristic leaders expect positive outcomes and are confident in their ability to engage themselves and others in a shared vision to make it so (Feather, 2004).

Leading Change, Advancing Health

In 2010, the Institute of Medicine (IOM, now called the Health and Medicine Division of the National Academies of Sciences, Engineering, and Medicine) published *The Future of Nursing: Leading Change, Advancing Health*. The IOM committee formulated four key strategic messages:
- Nurses should practice to the full extent of their education and training.
- Nurses should achieve higher levels of education and training through an improved education system that promotes seamless academic progression.
- Nurses should be full partners, with physicians and other health professionals, in redesigning health care in the United States.
- Effective workforce planning and policy making require better data collection and an improved information infrastructure. (IOM, 2011, p. 4)

These key messages resulted in eight recommendations. For the purposes of this chapter, the focus will be on "Recommendation 7: Prepare and enable nurses to lead change to advance health":
- Nurses, nursing education programs, and nursing associations should prepare the nursing workforce to assume leadership positions across all levels, while public, private, and governmental health care decision makers should ensure that leadership positions are available to and filled by nurses.
- Nurses should take responsibility for their personal and professional growth by continuing their education and seeking opportunities to develop and exercise their leadership skills.
- Nursing associations should provide leadership development, mentoring programs, and opportunities to lead for all their members.
- Nursing education programs should integrate leadership theory and business practices across the curriculum, including clinical practice.
- Public, private, and governmental health care decision makers at every level should include representation from nursing on boards, on executive management teams, and in other key leadership positions. (IOM, 2011, p. 14)

This recommendation from the IOM report focuses on nursing leadership as key to shaping the future of health care through personal development, continuous learning, and leadership. The overall outcome from strengthening leadership development results in improved patient care outcomes.

One national strategy put forth by the Nurses on Boards Coalition, a group of national nursing organizations, is a campaign to place 10,000 nurses on governing boards by 2020 (American Nurses Association, 2014). This effort is in direct response to one of the IOM recommendations to advance nursing leadership. Realization of such a vision will require nurses prepared for a different and higher level of leadership. Strength of leadership requires personal will and passion to excel at skills such as communication, negotiation, and building positive relationships.

Sanborn (2006) identified five behavioral acts of a leader: believing they can positively shape their careers; leading through relationships; leading from a mindset of collaboration versus control; gaining followers through persuasion and influence rather than coercion; and getting others to follow through a shared vision rather than fear. Are you ready to lead a healthcare future that is complex and constantly evolving? To lead from the future requires a belief in the future and a vision of that future that is shared by others. Think and imagine differently.

The Power of Futuristic Thinking

Chris Arkenberg (2013), a research and strategy lead at Orange Silicon Valley, wrote that future thinking is not about the future as much as it is about the present. The allure of future thinking is to be able to predict with some element of certainty that what one can forecast will happen (Arkenberg, 2013). Health care includes predictions about patient volume, quality patient care outcomes, revenue, expenses, staffing, and other key metrics. The ability to interpret data sources from past and present sources is necessary to make business forecasts in dynamic and diverse healthcare systems. Prospects of the future can seem daunting at times. A sense of comfort exists in the known versus the unknown.

What role does imagination play in future thinking? Hall (2013) espoused that the power of imagination is essential to prospective thought and enables the mind to view the future. The author wrote that exemplars of an *imagine–think* cycle are brainstorming and free thinking (Hall, 2013). This concept embodies the notion of letting one's imagination run free to imagine and dream without restrictions. What emerges from this kind of thinking is a new vision of the future.

Nurse leaders challenged with trying to stay ahead of the present may devote little time on what the long-range future will require. One example of this complexity is staffing across practice settings. Predictions assert a future shortage of nurses to meet demands across the domains of academia, research, and service. The number of nurses who will be retiring from the active workforce in practice, research, administration, and academia presents a real concern for healthcare leaders. The U.S. Department of Labor (2015) projected a 16% growth in RN employment for 2014–2024. Despite the projected growth of nurses entering the workforce, more than half of a million nurses are expected to retire over the next five to eight years (Ramachandran, 2014).

The current environmental scan includes an ever-increasing workforce shortage for both current and future demands across all sectors of practice, academia, and research and inclusive of diverse professional specialties and subspecialties. Areas of particular concern and complexity are related to increasing competition for dwindling research funds; personalized/individualized health care with increased use of targeted therapies and immunotherapies for disease management; tightening of the reimbursement belt from government and private payers; adjusting to the transition to the International Classification of Diseases, 10th Revision (ICD-10); embracing top-of-license practice; and testing new models of care for efficiency and effectiveness in achieving desired patient outcomes.

Futuristic thinking and forecasting based on past and present data are key leader strategies in planning and leading in the future healthcare environment. Therein lies the path to futuristic thinking and planning. Louis Pasteur has been credited with the quote that "chance favors the prepared mind." How does one prepare for leading from the future? The next section will review leader competencies required to lead from the emerging future.

Leader Competencies for the Future

Navigating and leading in a complex and ever-transforming and emerging healthcare future requires knowledge, talent, and skills of the nurse leader. Several chapters in this book address the skills and competencies required for nurse leaders to be successful in leading change and advancing health care for the 21st century. Chapter 14 explores and outlines the executive leader competencies for the healthcare future. The Oncology Nursing Society developed leadership competencies in 2012, which are available at www.ons.org/sites/default/files/leadershipcomps.pdf. These competencies are an example of how some professional nursing associations are educating and preparing their association members for higher levels of leadership needed for the future.

The American Organization of Nurse Executives (AONE) has a number of leader competencies across various care settings and levels of leadership. The AONE competencies identify five key domains needed in all nurse leaders: communication and relationship building, knowledge of the healthcare environment, leadership, professionalism, and business skills (AONE, n.d., 2015). More information about the AONE leader competencies can be found at www.aone.org/resources/nurse-leader-competencies.shtml.

Although these competencies are referred to as executive competencies, they embody the overall competencies for nurse leaders at different levels. The depth and breadth of the competencies, as well as the level of required business acumen, are dependent on the leadership level and position of the nurse in the health system. To be a successful futuristic leader, one must have a level of mastery of the leader competencies and a vision regarding the direction of health care and one's role in leading the transformation.

An emerging theory for leader competency is that of relational coordination, which also espouses the concept of relational leadership. Gittell (2016) describes these theoretical concepts in her book *Transforming Relationships for High Performance: The Power of Relational Coordination*. At the core of coordination is communication. It is widely accepted that the simplistic forms of communication are bidirectional, two-dimensional spans, with a sender and receiver. Now and in the future, for communication to be effective and lead to successful transformational outcomes, leaders must recognize it has to be multidimensional and multidirectional. Communication does not occur in a vacuum but instead is analogous to a busy beehive, with multiple parties sending and receiving in many directions simultaneously. Similar to the work in the beehive, communication must be organized, thoughtful, and with purpose and vision.

The energizing theory of relational coordination is lending a framework to how and what constitutes the bases of successful, organized, purposeful, and visionary communication. Relational coordination is constantly engaging inter- and intraprofessional peers and colleagues across disciplines to engage in conversation to problem solve, create new directions, and forge shared decisions. The power of positive relationships should not be underestimated and is foundational to the future transformation of healthcare and organizational stability.

Relational leadership is creating an environment that is transformative in breaking down silos and barriers to strengthen the bonds of coming together for a common purpose to achieve desired organizational outcomes. Forging open and honest relationships across departments and disciplines with a shared understanding of work will support the accomplishment of strategic organizational goals fostering improved communication, which is reflective of the high-performing organizations needed for a healthy and sustainable healthcare future.

Professional Leader Development

To become a futuristic and visionary nurse leader, nurses need a level of academic preparation, experience, vision, talent, and a willingness to take risks. To start personal development as a nurse leader, one should complete a self-assessment to reveal personal characteristics that can help guide decisions and actions about leadership style.

Kouzes and Posner (2012) identified the five practices of exemplary leadership: model the way; inspire a shared vision; challenge the process; enable others to act; and encourage the heart. Having the courage to act on one's vision does not mean being ruthless or heartless. Regardless of your preferred leadership style, you must develop a wide repertoire of decision-making approaches that allow you to be directive when seeking compliance and collaborative when seeking commitment.

As a leader with a vision for the future, learn to use the head (coupled with data, past experiences, and instinct) to make difficult decisions and to use the heart to implement them in ways that speak to the needs of those affected by the decision. No one style fits all people or all situations. Taking a tough, directive stance all the time will cause one to ultimately lose the trust and support of people as they begin to feel like victims and who may attempt to sabotage well-intentioned efforts. Conversely, always taking a conciliatory and "touchy-feely" style risks losing the very respect one seeks, as one risks being perceived as spineless or unable to handle tough decisions. It is a delicate balance. The challenge lies in knowing when to be tough-minded and firm and when to be a follower, negotiator, collaborator, and compromiser seeking guidance and input from others. It is easy to fall back on the familiar and comfortable personality or preferred leadership style. Although the transformational leadership style is one that most people strive to practice most often, in reality, a successful leader will use a combination of styles based on the situation. It takes courage to modify the approach in different situations and with different people to achieve the desired managerial outcomes.

Tap into the expertise and wisdom of other leaders and seek their counsel and mentorship and engage others in a process of shared leadership, where appropriate. This allows an opportunity to get commitment, or buy-in, from others and align a shared vision to support and lead change. Multiple contributors usually generate better ideas for implementation than a single leader can. One key to leading from the future is knowing how and when to engage others in creating the vision and sharing in the decision making.

Another of the five leader characteristics espoused by Kouzes and Posner (2012) is creation of a shared vision. How does one create a shared vision of the future and possibilities? This occurs in two parts: (a) imagining the future by looking forward based on lessons from the past and an informed environmental scan (i.e., having a vision of what could be and sharing it with others), and (b) enlisting others by developing a shared sense of destiny in what the future can hold (i.e., appealing to the shared aspirations of others and giving life to the vision and dream). As a futuristic leader, it is important to seize authority and apply leader strengths. *Authority* means to influence that which commands respect and confidence ("Authority," n.d.). Believe in yourself and approach your dreams with authority. This includes conquering personal and professional doubts and fears. Dare to make a difference and take a risk.

Leading From an Emerging Future

In their book *Leading From the Emerging Future*, Scharmer and Kaufer (2013) cited two modes of learning: (a) learning from the past and (b) learning from the emerging future. Scharmer and Kaufer proposed that the single most important leader capacity is "the ability to shift from reacting against the past to leaning into and presencing an emerging future" (p. 3), which requires one to suspend personal judgments, redirect attention, let go of the past, lean into the future, and let it come.

Leading from the future requires risk taking—stepping out into the unknown, but not blindly. Scharmer and Kaufer espoused that three *deep learning cycles* are at play in visioning an emerging future (see Figure 1-1). Leaders draw on data from the past and present when making decisions about the future.

As you prepare to gaze into the looking glass of the future, take time to pause and be thoughtful and reflective as you take in all the data elements from the past and present. As the predictions and forecasting take shape, you have the assurance in knowing that the predictive models of the future you desire to create were based on best data and experiences.

The deep learning cycles are based on the concept of *consciousness-based* thoughts and behaviors. Nurse leaders are engaged in visioning and preparing for an emerging healthcare future. What will this future hold? What are the resource needs for that future? What will the patient and family needs be in the emerging healthcare future? Thinking will need to be at a level higher than where we currently stand. Do you have the courage to transcend the mind, heart, and will to transform the future? Infinitely more questions exist that can only be explored and answered by you as a leader. However, take caution not to try to define the answers on your own. The emerging future in health care requires collaboration and partnership with an interprofessional team. The collective wisdom and vision will be necessary to prepare and lead from the healthcare emerging future. The metaphor of "thinking outside of the box" has been used in the past to encourage transcendent thinking. Conscious awareness of what is versus what could be will direct futuristic thinking and leadership. Reliable data also are required in the equation to lend credibility to the leader's visioning process.

Planning With a Purpose

Visioning and planning without a defined purpose is like dreaming in black and white when the future is in vivid color. Learning from the past to lead from the emerging future involves

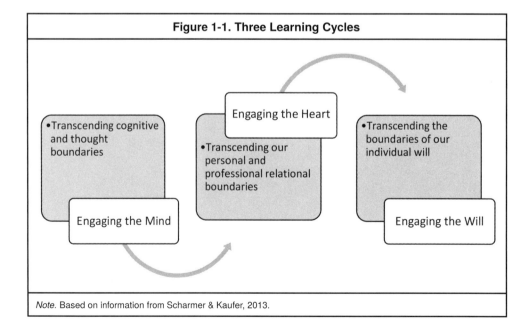

Figure 1-1. Three Learning Cycles

- Transcending cognitive and thought boundaries

Engaging the Mind

Engaging the Heart
- Transcending our personal and professional relational boundaries

- Transcending the boundaries of our individual will

Engaging the Will

Note. Based on information from Scharmer & Kaufer, 2013.

transcending three boundaries: cognitive, relational, and personal will (Scharmer & Kaufer, 2013). According to this theory, emergence from these boundaries requires the leader to pause and take time to observe, reflect, and act (Scharmer & Kaufer, 2013). One can learn from the past while taking the time to observe the present. Pause and reflect on the current state while envisioning a better future.

To embrace the concept of leading from the future and act on your vision, you must plan with a purpose and be prepared to take a risk. Planning is not a solo act. The leader must have the support and engagement of the team. Identify partners with whom you can share your vision and gain their support to work with you in further shaping the vision and developing goals and tactics to actualize the vision. Listen to the collective wisdom of the team and watch as your vision gains more strength and takes form. Know that the development to a new vision for the future is an iterative process and not a one-and-done process. Dr. Anil Kumar Sinha (n.d.) said, "When a plan is given wings of action, it culminates into positive result."

Summary

Being a leader is not just about a title; it is about *influence* (Sanborn, 2006). Do not limit the leader that is inside you. Be an emerging leader to embrace the future and plan to be part of the leadership that will shape the future of health care. Create a shared vision of what the healthcare future can be and lead from your vision, placing high importance on the partnerships and relationships with your followers and those around you who can contribute to your success. The power of imagination and dreaming is a key factor in shaping possibility thinking. Imagination is the mind's ability to create a vision for what could be; it takes leadership to act on that vision and engage others to follow. This is your time—your time and your moment to step up and lead from that vision of the future; seize it now! Prepare for the unexpected while you expect the best. As Sam Walton, founder of Walmart stores, said, "High expectations are the key to everything" (Feather, 2004, p. 30).

References

American Nurses Association. (2014, November 17). *National coalition launches effort to place 10,000 nurses on governing boards by 2020* [News release]. Retrieved from http://www.nursingworld.org/FunctionalMenuCategories/MediaResources/PressReleases/2014-PR/Effort-to-Place-Nurses-on-Governing-Boards.html

American Organization of Nurse Executives. (n.d.). Nurse leader competencies. Retrieved from http://www.aone.org/resources/nurse-leader-competencies.shtml

American Organization of Nurse Executives. (2015). *AONE nurse executive competencies.* Retrieved from http://www.aone.org/resources/nurse-leader-competencies.shtml.

Arkenberg, C. (2013). Future thinking isn't about the future, it's about the present. Retrieved from https://www.fastcoexist.com/2682713/future-thinking-isnt-about-the-future-its-about-the-present

Authority. (n.d.). In *Merriam-Webster's online dictionary* (11th ed.). Retrieved from https://www.merriam-webster.com/dictionary/authority

Feather, F. (2004). *Futuristic leadership A-Z.* Toronto, Canada: Motivated Publishing Ventures.

Gittell, J.H. (2016). *Transforming relationships for high performance: The power of relational coordination.* Stanford, CA: Stanford University Press.

Hall, J.N. (2013). *Futurlogics: A system of prospective thinking* (2nd ed.). West Jordan, UT: Self Teaching Publications.

Institute of Medicine. (2011). *The future of nursing: Leading change, advancing health.* Washington, DC: National Academies Press.

Kouzes, J.M., & Posner, B.Z. (2012). *The leadership challenge: How to make extraordinary things happen in organizations* (5th ed.). San Francisco, CA: Jossey-Bass.

Monson, T.S. (1989, May). Go for it! *Ensign.* Retrieved from https://www.lds.org/ensign/1989/05/go-for-it

Norman, J. (2016, December 19). Americans rate healthcare providers high on honesty, ethics. Retrieved http://www.gallup.com/poll/200057/americans-rate-healthcare-providers-high-honesty-ethics.aspx

Ramachandran, V. (2014, May 7). The new nursing shortage. Ozy.com. Retrieved from http://usat.ly/1kXZn42

Sanborn, M. (2006). *You don't need a title to be a leader.* New York, NY: Doubleday Broadway.

Scharmer, O., & Kaufer, K. (2013). *Leading from the emerging future: From ego-system to eco-system economies.* San Francisco, CA: Berrett-Koehler.

Sinha, A.K. (n.d.). Retrieved from http://www.searchquotes.com/quotes/author/Dr_Anil_Kr_Sinha

U.S. Department of Labor. (2015). *Occupational outlook handbook, 2016–17 edition.* Retrieved from http://www.bls.gov/ooh/healthcare/registered-nurses.htm

CHAPTER 2

Leadership Blueprint for Nursing's Future

Marsha Hughes-Rease, BSN, MSN, RN, MSOD, PCC, and
Rhonda R. Foster, EdD, MPH, MS, RN, NEA-BC

> *People get trapped by using patterns of behavior to protect them-*
> *selves against threats to their self-esteem and confidence and to*
> *protect groups, intergroups, and organizations to which they be-*
> *long against fundamental, disruptive change.*
>
> —Chris Argyris (2010, pp. 17–18)

Introduction

The purpose of this chapter is to explore how nurse leaders can use five disciplines to adapt to an increasingly demanding and unpredictable external environment. The disciplines are personal mastery, mental models, shared vision, team learning, and systems thinking, which will be explored in more detail. The authors have framed this chapter as the blueprint for nursing leadership using the concepts of a learning organization and systems thinking. Case scenarios are included to illustrate actual leader blueprint tactics, although the names used do not represent actual individuals. The national environment has become increasingly volatile, uncertain, complex, and ambiguous (VUCA). In other words, leaders are living and working in a VUCA world with no industry exempt, including health care. Subsequently, the demand for change in the healthcare sector is unrelenting, and healthcare leaders are finding themselves at the epicenter of the impact of these changes and charged with navigating through it.

An *epicenter* is usually thought of as the focal point of a difficult or unpleasant situation. However, the nursing profession, especially nurse leaders, have an opportunity to turn what might be considered a difficult situation into a learning journey. Petrie (2014) observed that leaders who are equal to the task of taking on this VUCA environment have developed more complex and adaptive thinking abilities.

Transformational nurse leaders have moved from the one-heroic-leader–centric approach to building a more shared and integrated *vertical* (refers to the ability to think in more complex, systemic, strategic, and interdependent ways) and *horizontal* (refers to the adding of more knowledge, skills, and competencies) leadership capacity to respond to increasingly complex challenges. However, a fundamental shift in mindset and attitude is required to make this transition. The authors believe that a framework for learning organizations introduced more than 25 years ago may be even more relevant in the 21st century in leading healthcare organizations.

In 1990, Peter Senge's book, *The Fifth Discipline*, created a new conversation about organizational behavior and leadership development. Recognizing a *discipline* as a "developmental path for acquiring certain skills or competencies," Senge (2006) introduced five disciplines that he asserted provide a foundation for building learning organizations: personal mastery, mental models, team learning, shared vision, and systems thinking. As Raines (2009) pointed out, Senge's conceptual framework collectively mapped out a rich and comprehensive terrain of how to lead a learning organization. Raines pointed out that "a leader or coach can explore any of the five disciplines first. Each discipline is whole unto itself and part of a more complex and larger whole" (p. 1).

What is a learning organization? Just what constitutes a robust definition of a learning organization has been up for debate for a number of years. According to Senge (2006), it is an organization "where people continually expand their capacity to create the results they truly desire, where new and expansive patterns of thinking are nurtured, where collective aspiration is set free, and where people are continually learning how to learn together" (p. 3). Garvin (1993) and Garvin, Edmondson, and Gino (2008) suggested that a learning organization is an organization that is skilled at creating, acquiring, and transferring knowledge and at modifying its behavior to reflect new knowledge and insights. Perhaps one of the more user-friendly definitions comes from BusinessDictionary.com:

> Organization that acquires knowledge and innovates fast enough to survive and thrive in a rapidly changing environment. Learning organizations (1) create a culture that encourages and supports continuous employee learning, critical thinking, and risk taking with new ideas, (2) allow mistakes, and value employee contributions, (3) learn from experience and experiment, and (4) disseminate the new knowledge throughout the organization for incorporation into day-to-day activities. ("Learning Organization," n.d.)

Maguire and McKelvey (1999) pointed out that a more distributed leadership approach increases accountability of individuals and groups for their actions and increases responsibility for working toward a shared vision, exploring possibilities, and taking initiatives that are aligned with the organizational strategic direction. Mitleton-Kelly (2003) agreed that organizational environments with characteristics associated with a learning organization tend to promote learning and leadership at all levels (distributed leadership) and have more accountability for actions because individuals tend to more readily accept responsibility for their actions. The concepts of a learning organization and systems thinking are not new.

Personal Mastery

In his original work, Senge (2006) pointed out that personal mastery goes beyond competence and skills. He identified the characteristics of individuals who have a high level of personal mastery. These characteristics included having a sense of purpose behind their visions and goals, as well as being able to use their sense of inquisitiveness to clearly decipher their current reality, and being committed to seeing reality more and more accurately. Individuals with a heightened sense of personal mastery have also learned how to perceive and work with forces of change instead of resisting. They feel connected to others but have a clear sense of self-differentiation. Senge emphasized that people with a high level of personal mastery are acutely aware of their own ignorance, incompetence, and growth areas. Most importantly, they are willing to go on a learning journey that will never end.

According to Senge, Kleiner, Roberts, Ross, and Smith (1994), the central practice of personal mastery involves learning to hold both a personal vision and a realistic grasp of the current reality. A creative tension results from experiencing the gap between current reality and desired outcomes. One's natural inclination is to decrease discomfort by seeking the path of easiest resolution. The essence of personal mastery is having a compelling vision and the discipline to close the gap between current reality and the new vision.

Case Study: Articulating a Personal Vision to Mobilize Others

In the past two weeks, Carol started her new position as chief nursing officer (CNO) at a safety net hospital located in a large urban community in the Northeast United States. A safety net hospital or health system provides a significant level of care to low-income, uninsured, and vulnerable populations. Carol sat in her office contemplating her first meeting with the clinical nurses and reflecting on how she had gotten to this point in her career. Carol realized that this move had been the realization of a compelling vision she had a few years ago. Carol had held two prior CNO positions in smaller community hospitals located in affluent midwestern communities. Although she felt comfortable with her overall effectiveness as a nurse executive at both hospitals, she had also felt restless. It was only during a session with her executive coach that Carol was able to begin to articulate a vision about what she wanted as a nurse executive. As Carol prepared her remarks for the meeting with the clinical direct care nurses, she decided it would be important for them to hear her learning journey.

She started her presentation with this personal disclosure: "My personal vision was to work in a hospital whose mission was to serve vulnerable populations. I realized that this vision stemmed from a deeply held commitment to social change and healthcare equity. I could potentially realize that vision as a nurse leader working in a different type of healthcare setting. However, I also realized that my leadership experiences in community hospitals serving a homogeneous population really would not prepare me. I spent two of the past five years working as a healthcare administrator in a large U.S. Agency for International Development–supported hospital located in southern India. Recently, I worked in the Office of Minority Health at the Department of Health and Human Services on public policy addressing healthcare disparities. I come to this role with a keener insight and more passion on how we can work together to serve our community."

Although Carol's journey took a somewhat circuitous route, she recognized that she needed a different type of competence to realize her vision. She had the technical skills and knowledge to be a nurse executive. However, her breakthrough thinking was that she needed a different type of development experience from the traditional approach of acquiring more knowledge.

One of the key concepts for developing the discipline of personal mastery can be found in the growing body of research on vertical development, also known as adult development. It focuses on an individual's way of making meaning and understanding of oneself and the world. McCauley, Drath, Palus, O'Connor, and Baker (2006) identified as one of the basic propositions of adult development theory that individuals' development influences what they notice or can become aware of—in other words, what they can describe, reflect on, and change. In interviews with more than 30 experts in vertical leadership development, Petrie (2015a) was able to summarize three opportunities for building vertical leadership capacity: (a) disruptive experiences, (b) exposure to new perspectives, and (c) opportunities to make sense of things.

Petrie (2015b) advocated that *heat experiences* can disrupt habitual ways of thinking and cause leaders to search for new and better ways to make sense of the challenges they face. He describes a *heat experience* as a complex situation that disrupts and disorients a leader's habitual way of thinking. The leader discovers that current ways of making sense of the world are inadequate. This can open the mind to search for new and better ways to make sense of the challenge.

In the case study, Carol was fortunate that she was able to leverage all three opportunities identified for building vertical leadership capacity to create a rich developmental experience based on a creative tension between her current reality and a very compelling vision. She was also able to use this vision to inspire her staff to deliver excellent nursing care. Other recommendations for closing the gap between the current reality and desired future include the following:

- Create a support system, for example, an executive coach or mentor, to help you move toward a desired vision.
- Assess your current reality, including both strengths and limitations, which often requires seeking constructive feedback from others.
- Identify "heat experiences" that will disrupt your habitual ways of thinking and challenge assumptions and mental models; this may include a stretch assignment, making a horizontal move, or even taking on a new initiative that demands a growth mindset.
- Be open and transparent with people who have different worldviews, opinions, and backgrounds.
- Try something new and be prepared to use failure as a developmental opportunity.

Mental Models

One approach to understanding human reasoning is use of mental models. Senge (2006) and others (Magzan, 2012; Senge et al., 1994) have described mental models as deeply held or ingrained beliefs, images, assumptions, and stories one carries in the mind about oneself, other people, and every aspect of the external reality. Mental models are powerful because they not only affect what one may see or perceive, but they also consequently influence what is done because, as it is often said, perception is reality.

Leaders' mental models develop from socialization, education and training, reward, influence, and personal experience and can be unconscious or tacit. Senge (2006) pointed out that when models exist below the leader's level of awareness, they remain unexamined and, thus, unchanged. Unfortunately, leaders can get locked into their own tacit mental models or mindsets that filter out new opportunities as threats and potentially impede innovative thinking. To be more effective as change champions, leaders need to be willing to expose the limitations in their own thinking. This may require giving others permission to challenge their reasoning and perceived reality.

Case Study: Challenging Personal Reasoning

Randy had been appointed as the interim chief nurse executive (CNE) for a newly created seven-hospital system for four months. He was previously the CNO of the largest hospital in the system prior to the merger. In anticipation of assuming a broader scope of leadership responsibility, Randy had attended several executive leadership courses, received his graduate degree in Nursing Administration, and acquired an advanced certification in nursing administration. During graduate school and in some of the courses, he had received significant feedback via various assessment tools. Most of his feedback from peers and direct reports was positive. However, he noted a recurring theme concerning his need to be action oriented. The feedback suggested that Randy sometimes made decisions too quickly without all the information and was perceived as reluctant to receive input from others who might think differently.

Randy recognized that he had learned to be action oriented while working as a clinical nurse in critical care. As a CNO, he had also been recognized by members of the executive team for being able to make quick decisions resulting in positive outcomes. However, Randy knew that the complexity of the challenges at the systems level demanded a different leadership strategy. He needed to slow down his thinking if he was going to be effective in his new role. Randy also knew that the CNOs at the seven hospitals had very different mindsets and often viewed problems in different ways. He decided to create a CNE advisory council and appointed the seven CNOs as members. The sole purpose of the group was to challenge him (and each other) to think about complex issues in a different way. The group soon learned to have crucial conversations that surfaced assumptions and created the opportunity to reframe issues from different perspectives. The result: Randy and the other nurse leaders were able to design more innovative strategies as a team than they would have created as individuals.

Many innovative ideas fail to be translated into meaningful strategic organizational actions simply because such ideas do not match dominant mental models (Berger, 2012; Heifetz, Grashow, & Linsky, 2009; Kegan & Lahey, 2009, 2016; Magzan, 2012). In the case study, Randy learned to balance his strong tendency toward advocacy by creating a diverse group that forced him to slow down and examine his mental models. Ross and Roberts (n.d.) observed that as people rise in an organization, they are forced to deal with more complex and interdependent issues where no one individual knows the answer. It may be a situation where the only viable option is for groups of informed and committed individuals to think together to arrive at new insights. At this point, they need to learn to skillfully balance advocacy with inquiry.

In addition to learning to balance advocacy and inquiry, other recommendations for improving the discipline of examining mental models include the following:

- Assess the current way of taking in information and use that information to make decisions, including using tools such as the Myers-Briggs Type Indicator®, StrengthsFinder, and Insights Discovery to provide information about personal preferences for decision making, communication, and performance.
- Enlist executive and peer coaching to help surface and challenge your own assumptions and mental models.
- Identify "heat-seeking experiences" that will disrupt habitual ways of thinking and challenge assumptions and mental models.
- Create experiences that allow for exposure to people with different worldviews, opinions, and backgrounds.
- Provide a safe environment to engage organizational members with diverse mindsets in deep conversations that help to surface assumptions, implicit biases, and beliefs that may be hindering change.

Team Learning

Senge (2006) pointed out that team learning is the process of aligning and developing the capacity of a team to create its desired outcomes and builds on the discipline of shared vision. Kayes and Burnett (2006) distinguished team learning from team performance and indicated that team learning in organizations (a) involves interaction among team members related to gathering, sharing, processing, and acting on knowledge, (b) requires a level of agreement among team members about acceptable patterns of behavior for knowledge sharing, and (c) results in performance improvement (or deterioration) for the team.

Edmondson (2004, 2012) suggested that errors and problems in care delivery processes present learning opportunities. She advocated "executive-as-learning" as a way of operating an organization that combines continuous learning with high performance. Her research suggested that organizational learning occurs through a team-based learning infrastructure. Further, her research suggested that collective learning must be led by dedicated, learning-oriented, frontline leaders such as nurse managers.

Case Study: Creating an Environment for Team Learning

Donna is the nurse leader for two busy medical-surgical units. She has established shared decision-making councils on both units to evaluate the delivery of nursing care and to make changes in nursing practice. Initially, she did not participate in the unit meetings because she thought her presence would inhibit the council members from engaging in open and honest dialogue. She later realized that members of both groups lacked the skills to think and learn together to address unit issues. The clinical nurses were becoming increasingly frustrated with the meetings. The recurring complaint was, "We keep addressing the same issues and not getting anywhere." Dispelling her own mental model that nurse leaders should not be involved in the unit shared governance council meetings, Donna decided that she would become the facilitator of both councils. During her first meetings, she challenged the staff council members to share what was working and what was not working about their meetings. It soon became apparent that the nurses were behaving and thinking in certain ways to "protect" or "defend" themselves. The staff perceived they were being blamed for a deviation of care or felt guilty about not providing a certain standard of care. Donna was able to facilitate a conversation to help council members identify what was needed to have effective unit councils. The conversation included how they could create an environment of psychological safety needed to have open and honest conversations about the quality of patient care. Not only did they identify what they needed from her, but they also identified what they needed from each other. They developed ground rules to help build trust and create a supportive environment allowing members to explore the "undiscussables," surface assumptions or inferences, and share relevant information. Additionally, they agreed that prior to making a decision, they needed to identify the decision-making rule that would generate the degree of commitment needed for successful implementation. With a lot of practice and commitment, Donna began to see both teams become more skilled at generating new learning that resulted in creative and sustainable changes. These changes resulted in increased alignment with the nursing and organizational strategic plan and improved unit quality indicators, nurse satisfaction, and patient satisfaction. Through team learning, the overall performance of the councils improved, and the desired outcomes of the unit councils were realized.

In order to change an unproductive mindset of a team, Schwarz (2013) suggested the team leader and team members have to change their basic assumptions and values about how team members interact with each other, as well as the role of the team leader and members of the team. Donna was able to create an environment of psychological safety that allowed team members to acknowledge basic assumptions and values that were undermining team performance and to create new agreements for working together more effectively. Besides creating an environment of psychological safety, some other recommendations for increasing the team learning include the following:

- Use an outside facilitator or team coach who is trained in techniques for building reflection and inquiry skills.
- Create a cadre of individuals who facilitate and enable team members to have a discussion with a balance of advocacy and inquiry.
- Provide team members with the opportunity to gain more insight into their individual strengths, as well as personality and learning preferences they bring to the team.
- Encourage team members to share and reinforce behaviors that benefit and enhance the team's skills and strengths.
- Ensure that team members have the opportunity to examine and address behaviors that interfere with the mutual learning of all team members.

Shared Vision

Most organizations, particularly those in health care, have an organization or system vision. In a learning organization, it is important to have a shared vision. Senge (2006) stated that a shared vision is the answer to the question, "What do we want to create?" He added that it is more than an idea but something that is palpable and creates a sense of commonality that permeates the organization and gives coherence to diverse activities. It is the picture that people throughout an organization carry. A shared vision is vital for the learning organization because it provides the focus and energy for organizational learning (Senge, 2006).

Senge (2006) noted that shared visions can be extrinsic or intrinsic. Extrinsic shared visions focus on achieving something relative to an outsider, such as a competitor. The problem with this type of shared vision is that it can be transitory once achieved and rarely calls forth the creativity and excitement of building something new. Conversely, a shared vision that is intrinsic uplifts people's aspirations. It focuses on the greater or larger purpose that is embodied in the organization's products or services.

The discipline of shared vision exists to integrate a deep sense of involvement between the members of an organization in developing "shared images of the future they want to create for it, that is, values, objectives, and mission" (Fillion, Koffi, & Ekionea, 2015, p. 81). Fillion et al. (2015) identified that when the members of an organization truly share a vision, they become involved and connected, linked together by a common aspiration and identity reflecting their own personal vision.

According to Senge et al. (1994), a successful strategy for building a shared vision comprises several key precepts. First, every organization has a destiny. It often can be found in the mission or purpose statement. Second, clues to understanding an organization's deeper purpose often can be identified in the founders' aspirations and the reason the industry came into being. Third, not all visions are equal. To be genuinely shared, such visions must emerge from many people reflecting on the organization's purpose. The fourth precept is the need to design and evolve ongoing processes in which people at every level of the organization, and in every role, can speak from the heart about what really matters to them and be heard by senior management and each other. Fifth, there is an organizational equivalent to the personal mastery concept of "creative tension." It is the innate pull that emerges when one holds clear pictures of a vision juxtaposed with the current reality. That energy can be described as the excitement, anticipation, or urgency that provokes a leader to take the actions required to close the gap between their vision and their current reality.

Case Study: Building a Shared Vision

During a consultation, members of the organization's senior leadership team were asked by a consultant to share their organizational vision, mission, and values. Each member of the senior leadership team articulated the mission, vision, and values without hesitation and seemed very proud of their shared understanding. This same question was asked of management and staff throughout the organization. They stated the organization's mission and values but were unable to articulate the vision as eloquently as the members of the senior team. In a follow-up meeting, Larry, the CNE, voiced surprise, and the other team members said they were embarrassed that the staff and leaders could not "speak to it," especially because the executive leader team had the vision printed on the back of employees' identification badges.

After a lengthy discussion, the senior leaders realized that they had a shared vision statement, but it stopped at the executive suite. They also realized that although they had engaged physicians, board members, managers, and directors, the staff had not been involved. The result was a lack of an *articulated* shared vision. Although somewhat discouraged, they felt it was a unique opportunity to build shared meaning and garner commitment of individuals throughout the organization and start over with shared decision making.

The shared-vision discipline is essentially focused on building shared meaning, potentially where none existed before (Senge et al., 1994). According to Senge et al. (1994), in traditional organizations, the only meaning most members know has been handed to them from above—from a tactic hierarchy of meaning embedded in the organization's authority structure. The importance of shared meaning is that it represents a collective sense of what is important and why. According to Senge (2006), a vision is truly shared when people are bound together by a common aspiration and a sense of commonality permeates the organization and gives coherence to diverse activities. Shared visions emerge from personal visions, as they are rooted in personal values, beliefs, aspirations, and concerns. Therefore, it is also important to consider other recommendations for increasing a shared vision:

- Involve more members of the organization in the development process. This means giving up the traditional hierarchical perspective that the vision comes only from the executive suite or the board retreat.
- Provide team members with the opportunity to share their personal visions. This allows you to gain more insight into what the members of the team or organization really care about and aspire to be. It is important to share and listen to the organizational dreams of employees and team members.
- Provide employees the opportunity to proactively enroll themselves in the process, as opposed to the leader persuading them to buy in. Enrollment gives individuals a choice, and you gain more commitment and engagement.
- Be mindful that vision is merely the "what" of work to be done. However, it is critical to connect or align the "what" with purpose, governing principles, mission, and values.

- Test the level of excitement for the vision. Does it create excitement or apathy? It can be tested by simply asking, "What about this vision generates excitement, and what about this vision does not generate excitement?"

Systems Thinking

As organizations are become increasingly competitive and complex, it is of paramount importance that systems thinking be applied. Meadows (2008) defines systems as "an interconnected set of elements that is coherently organized in a way that achieves something" (p. 11). Therefore, according to this definition, "a system must consist of three kinds of things: *elements, interconnections*, and a *function* or *purpose*" (Meadows, 2008, p. 11). Many organizations are organized as a system and want to operate as a system but continue to think in pieces, parts, and silos. Organizational learning in healthcare systems is central to managing the learning requirements in complex interconnected dynamic systems where all have to know common background knowledge along with shared meta-knowledge of roles and responsibilities to execute their assigned functions, communicate and transfer the flow of pertinent information, and collectively provide safe patient care (Ratnapalan & Uleryk, 2014).

Senge (2006) defined systems thinking as a discipline for seeing wholes or a framework for seeing interrelationships rather than as things and for seeing patterns of change rather than static snapshots. He further stated that complexity can undermine confidence and responsibility. It can become all too easy to say, "There is nothing I can do about it" or "It is the system that is causing the problem." According to Senge (2006), *systems thinking* is actually the fifth discipline because it is the conceptual cornerstone that underlies all of the five learning disciplines. He adds that without systems thinking, there is neither the incentive nor the means to integrate the learning disciplines once they have come into practice. Senge (2006) further noted that the five disciplines must develop as an ensemble, and that this prevents them from being viewed as gimmicks or the latest organizational fad.

Systems thinking encompasses a large and fairly amorphous body of methods, tools, and principles, all oriented to working at the interrelatedness of forces and seeing them as a part of a common process (Senge et al., 1994). According to Senge et al. (1994), a good systemic thinker in the organizational context can see four levels operating simultaneously: the events, the behavioral schemes, the systems, and the mental models.

In systems thinking, it is also important to consider systemic structures (Senge et al., 1994). The authors noted that they are often invisible until someone points them out, are not always built consciously, and are built out of choices made by people in organizations consciously and unconsciously over time.

According to Senge (2006), the objective is to recondition one's perceptions such that it is possible to see not only the structures involved, but also the influence of these structures and resulting patterns. The degree of learning organization denotes the way an organization is structured, and the routines followed will have a major effect on the rate of learning that takes place (Dias & Escoval, 2015).

Organizations need to enhance the capacity to transform themselves in a creative way (Dias & Escoval, 2015). Organizational learning in health care is not a onetime intervention, but a continuing organizational phenomenon that occurs through formal and informal learning. It has a reciprocal association with organizational change. Subsequently, organizational changes accompanied with systems thinking can elicit organizational learning that results in new knowledge and practices (Ratnapalan & Uleryk, 2014). Fillion et al. (2015) identified the last step in systems thinking as the leverage effect. The *leverage effect* refers to the concept that making small shifts in one thing can produce big changes in everything. A leverage point is usually the identification of specific actions and changes in systemic structures that will produce significant and durable improvements. However, the highest leverage interventions are the ones that create a shift in mental models and alignment in shared vision to produce the most sustainable change in culture. The assertions of Edmondson (2004) and Senge (2006) suppose that the best results are not necessarily coming from large-scale efforts, but rather from well-directed small actions.

Case Study: Integrating Systems Thinking

Judy has accepted a position as associate CNO. She is primarily responsible for operations, which includes nursing operations, ancillary services, and ambulatory services. Judy tries to get a sense of the organization by conducting interviews with each department. Each department meeting goes well, as they have an opportunity to discuss what is working and what is not. After months of meetings, Judy begins to develop a list of actions that need to be addressed immediately and long term. She wants to make an impact soon and appear responsive. Her first priority is to address issues that seem simple and would improve employee satisfaction. Because Judy was new to the organization, she did not realize the downstream effect connected to each issue. Therefore, each issue solved created a problem in another area because of invisible and visible structures or "work-arounds" that had been created to achieve departmental results, and problems she thought were solved resurfaced. Judy soon realized that processes and structures were connected to one another and that she needed to incorporate systems thinking to truly identify how every issue affected another.

The healthcare delivery system is responsible for providing safe and quality patient care. How that is accomplished is dependent on the system and its thinking. Senge (2006) believes that nonsystemic ways of thinking are very harmful because the focus is on low-effect changes. Leaders tend to focus on symptoms where the pain and tension is greatest and tend to repair or improve symptoms, rather than the underlying cause. They often fail to acknowledge patterns of behavior over time and that their current problems may be the unintended consequences of remedying past problems. Such efforts may improve the situation in the short term but make it worse in the long term.

Besides learning how to incorporate systems thinking and looking at the 50,000-foot view, other recommendations for improving the discipline of systems thinking include the following:

- Consider what is in the best interest of the whole organization.
- Pay close attention to the official and unofficial structures and the processes at the point of care in the organization and how they function. Ask about the "work-arounds" and why they exist.
- When you do not know something, do not hesitate to ask questions and learn.
- Avoid the urge to repair symptoms without looking at the system for more data to help define the real problem.
- Consider the dots that need to be connected, which may be a circuitous pattern and not a straight line. This may be a limitation for linear thinkers, which often is a barrier to solution finding.

Summary

It is important for nurse leaders to note that the five disciplines, although discrete, actually function as an ensemble (Senge, 2006). It is not a gimmick, fad, or a new thing to do. The principles of *The Fifth Discipline* can serve as a blueprint for improving organizational learning that may have been ahead of its time. It provides leaders with a way to solve problems, engage staff, and nurture creativity and innovation while increasing organizational learning.

Oftentimes, leaders take principles from other disciplines and apply them to organizations in pieces and parts. Yet, they are responsible for the whole. It is imperative that leaders integrate the five disciplines to engage employees, solve problems, innovate, and redesign structures and processes to achieve the desired outcomes. To be competitive in this VUCA healthcare environment, it is equally important to think differently, function differently, and expect different and better results. It is no longer a reasonable nor effective strategy to fix parts of the organization or some areas and not others; they are too interconnected. *The Fifth Discipline* offers a framework for leaders to apply while building their leadership capacity in constantly changing and demanding times.

References

Argyris, C. (2010). *Organizational traps: Leadership, culture, organizational design.* New York, NY: Oxford University Press.

Berger, J.G. (2012). *Changing on the job: Developing leaders for a complex world.* Stanford, CA: Stanford University Press.

Dias, C., & Escoval, A. (2015). Hospitals as learning organizations: Fostering innovation through interactive learning. *Quality Management in Health Care, 24,* 52–59. doi:10.1097/QMH.0000000000000046

Edmondson, A.C. (2004). Learning from failure in health care: Frequent opportunities, pervasive barriers. *Quality and Safety in Health Care, 13*(Suppl. 2), ii3–ii9. doi:10.1136/qshc.2003.009597

Edmondson, A.C. (2012). *Teaming: How organizations learn, innovate, and compete in the knowledge economy.* San Francisco, CA: Jossey-Bass.

Fillion, G., Koffi, V., & Ekionea, J.-P.B. (2015). Peter Senge's learning organization: A critical view and the addition of some new concepts to actualize theory and practice. *Journal of Organizational Culture, Communications and Conflict, 19*(3), 73–102.

Garvin, D.A. (1993, July–August). Building a learning organization. *Harvard Business Review.* Retrieved from https://hbr.org/1993/07/building-a-learning-organization

Garvin, D.A., Edmondson, A.C., & Gino, F. (2008). Is yours a learning organization? *Harvard Business Review.* Retrieved from https://hbr.org/2008/03/is-yours-a-learning-organization

Heifetz, R., Grashow, A., & Linsky, M. (2009). *The practice of adaptive leadership: Tools and tactics for changing your organization and the world.* Boston, MA: Harvard Business Press.

Kayes, D.C., & Burnett, G. (2006). *Team learning in organizations: A review and integration.* Retrieved from http://www2.warwick.ac.uk/fac/soc/wbs/conf/olkc/archive/olkc1/papers/177_kayes.pdf

Kegan, R., & Lahey, L.L. (2009). *Immunity to change: How to overcome it and unlock the potential in yourself and your organization.* Boston, MA: Harvard Business School Publishing.

Kegan, R., & Lahey, L.L. (2016). *An everyone culture: Becoming a deliberately developmental organization.* Boston, MA: Harvard Business School Publishing.

Learning organization. (n.d.). In *Business dictionary.* Retrieved from http://www.businessdictionary.com/definition/learning-organization.html

Maguire, S., & McKelvey, B. (1999). Complexity and management: Moving from fad to firm foundations. *Emergence, 1*(2), 19–61.

Magzan, M. (2012). Mental models for leadership effectiveness: Building future different than the past. *Journal of Engineering Management and Competitiveness, 2,* 57–63. Retrieved from http://www.tfzr.rs/jemc/files/Vol2No2/V2N22012-03.pdf

McCauley, C.D., Drath, W.H., Palus, C.J., O'Connor, P.M.G., & Baker, B.A. (2006). The use of constructive-developmental theory to advance the understanding of leadership. *Leadership Quarterly, 17,* 634–653. doi:10.1016/j.leaqua.2006.10.006

Meadows, D.H. (2008). *Thinking in systems: A primer.* White River Junction, VT: Chelsea Green Publishing.

Mitleton-Kelly, E. (2003). Ten principles of complexity and enabling infrastructures. In E. Mitleton-Kelly (Ed.), *Complex systems and evolutionary perspectives of organisations: The application of complexity theory to organisations* (pp. 23–50). Bingley, United Kingdom: Emerald Group Publishing Limited.

Petrie, N. (2014). *Vertical leadership development—part 1: Developing leaders for a complex world.* Retrieved from http://insights.ccl.org/wp-content/uploads/2015/04/VerticalLeadersPart1.pdf

Petrie, N. (2015a). *A how-to guide for vertical leadership development.* Retrieved from https://trainingmag.com/how-guide-vertical-leadership-development

Petrie, N. (2015b). *The how-to of vertical leadership development—part 2.* Retrieved from http://insights.ccl.org/wp-content/uploads/2015/04/verticalLeadersPart2.pdf

Raines, L. (2009). *Looking both ways through the windows of Senge's five disciplines.* Retrieved from http://integral-focus.com/pdf/Senge.pdf

Ratnapalan, S., & Uleryk, E. (2014). Organizational learning in health care organizations. *Systems, 2,* 24–33. doi:10.3390/systems2010024

Ross, R., & Roberts, C. (n.d.). Balancing inquiry and advocacy. Retrieved from https://www.solonline.org

Schwarz, R. (2013). *Smart leaders, smarter teams: How you and your team get unstuck to get results.* San Francisco, CA: Jossey-Bass.

Senge, P. (1990). *The fifth discipline: The art and practice of the learning organization.* New York, NY: Currency.

Senge, P.M. (2006). *The fifth discipline: The art and practice of the learning organization* (Rev. ed.). New York, NY: Doubleday.

Senge, P.M., Kleiner, A., Roberts, C., Ross, R.B., & Smith, B.J. (1994). *The fifth discipline fieldbook: Strategies and tools for building a learning organization.* New York, NY: Currency.

CHAPTER 3

Quantum Leadership for a New Age of Nursing

Tim Porter-O'Grady, DM, EdD, ScD(h), APRN, FAAN, FACCWS, GCNS-BC, NEA-BC, CWCN, CFCN, and Kathy Malloch, PhD, MBA, RN, FAAN

Creativity is allowing yourself to make mistakes. Art is knowing which ones to keep.

—Scott Adams (2015)

Introduction

What we have learned about leadership over the past 30 years has eclipsed all we have known about leadership for the previous 5,000 years. The study of leadership has changed as the understanding of human dynamics and quantum realities have advanced and changed our understanding of how people and organizations work. This change is a result of the growth in research on complex adaptive and responsive systems recognizing that systems operate more successfully when understood as networks of convergence, energy, and synthesis (Donaldson, 2017; Griffin & Stacey, 2005; Miller & Page, 2007). This chapter looks at the development of leaders and provides insights on new leadership essentials, professional role accountability, generational considerations, mentoring, professional governance, and communicating direction.

Understanding Leadership

Historically, the greatest of leaders have been identified (Kets de Vries, 2003). We have had less success, however, in enumerating specific characteristics of leadership that can be universally replicated and form a firm foundation for identifying the full range of leadership characteristics in complex organizations (Daft, 2015; Ismuratova & Shalgynbayeva, 2013; Kotter, 2001).

According to Gill (2011), 92 categories of leadership, 276 definitions of leadership, and more than 1,000 constructs or statements related to leadership exist.

Still, the fundamental characteristics remain central to the expression of the role of leader. Even in networked organizations, the pivotal role of the leader remains unchanged even though the content and expression of that role require a shifting mix of competencies (Alberts, 2013; Archibald & Archibald, 2016) (see Figure 3-1).

Over the past 40–60 years, the academic and business communities have dedicated much effort to assessing characteristics of leadership (Bolman & Deal, 2013; Heifetz & Laurie, 2001). Great leaders have been studied in detail, and leadership traits have been defined, researched, and explicated as a way of finding fundamental numerators that conform to the foundations of our understanding and become the content of formalized programs directed toward teaching leadership (Drucker, 1998). Leadership is known to be a valid and mean-

Figure 3-1. Leadership Characteristics
• Vision
• Determination
• Personality
• Self-knowledge
• Vulnerability
• Energy
• Identification
• Communication

ingful part of the human experience. Leaders have surfaced under all kinds of circumstances, from war, great political and social change, religious and moral foundations, and cultural and social transformations (Ferris, 1889; Gill, 2011).

The idea of leadership has remained constant throughout the ages. Even as social changes occurred, human evolution progressed, and new knowledge emerged, the role of leadership has been heralded and celebrated as essential to advancing the human experience. Each age of human experience has produced a leader who represented the characteristics of the times. In reviewing the course of human experience, it becomes clear that leadership changes and adjusts depending on demand, social circumstances, and the particular needs of the time. Indeed, each generation of human interaction created the conditions from which leadership would emerge. These conditions are fundamental circumstances within which any model of leadership responds to the demands of the time. Leadership operates through the expression of vision, determination, and force of personality and will, converging to create a significant change in the order of things (Sorcher & Brant, 2002).

Leadership is more than personality traits and characteristics. Leaders are both born and made. Leaders are born insofar as they are influenced by the genetic characteristics of their heredity. Leaders are made insofar as social development, circumstances, and personal experience converge to create the conditions and context within which specific leaders could emerge. Leadership "happens" at the point of convergence where there is a good fit among the times, the demand, and the individual's personal characteristics (Alberts, 2013; Pearman, 1998).

A shift in circumstance can be significant in creating opportunities for leadership. The news is filled with individuals who, driven by circumstances, took a risk, rose to the occasion, took charge, and were able to exemplify real leadership. Individuals who are otherwise seen as average and ordinary, in extraordinary circumstances, step up and excel in the expression of leadership capacity and skills. This is a clear example of critical, or situational, leadership. This type of leadership has many of the characteristics of learned leadership but often is devoid of the content and elements necessary to sustain leadership over a long period of time and in a wide variety of circumstances (Gill, 2011). The literature is just as replete with exemplars of critical leadership and hero behavior in immediate circumstances that simply failed to stand the test of time in a wide variety of other circumstances. The learned leadership of which we speak in this chapter is one that responds to the wide variety of conditions and circumstances found in work life, creating a sustainable frame for leadership that represents a growing and progressive dynamic that ultimately broadens and enhances both the capacity for and the exercise of good leadership (Owen, 2012).

Some generic and identifiable characteristics of leadership can be learned and replicated. Although these characteristics can be taught, the circumstances and knowledge in which leadership characteristics can be expressed are important considerations for the success of specific leadership traits. A good leader recognizes this convergence of forces and conditions and responds to them with such clarity and appropriateness that the actions undertaken are congruent with the demand for them, and a meaningful transformation occurs or valued outcomes are achieved.

New-Age Leader

The remainder of this book focuses on pursuing the characteristics of leadership and enumerating the basic elements and traits of leadership that create good leaders in the digital times. Critical to this process is that the elements of development are congruent with the needs and circumstances of the time. The emerging circumstances are necessarily embedded in digital realities in which communication pathways have increased exponentially, the speed of interaction possibility is global and real-time, and data can be accessed instantaneously. This increase in communication, timing, and data dynamics has rendered the healthcare environment unbelievably complex. Many of the characteristics that enabled successful leadership in a 20th-century "Newtonian" model of social organization and work (vertical, structural, institutional, fixed, and finite) will not transfer into the 21st century, which is driven by "quantum" models of work and workplace and exemplified by complexity, chaos, mobility, and the need for fast-paced responses (Bleich, 2014; Malloch & Porter-O'Grady, 2009; Wheatley, 1999).

The emerging 21st-century workplace demands a different kind of leader with a different set of skills than those that were successful in the past. Developing this leader calls for a novel mix of strategies. This new landscape for work creates conditions within which the leader must incorporate the emerging sociopolitical realities, shifting economics, and the technologic revolution. This reality creates the foundation for a unique and dynamic role for the leader. Increased globalization and the communication competencies are influenced by the elements of interaction, communication, and relationships (Anderson, 2001; Myatt, 2014). The leader must be able to thrive and engage both the role and people in a way that best fits these challenging and changing circumstances. To thrive, awareness and adoption of new mindsets and behaviors is needed. The following mindsets and behaviors are presented in detail to facilitate adaptation to the emerging circumstances:

- Awareness of changes and implications. Understanding the quantum context changes the foundational understanding of leadership. In the 21st century, recognizing the signposts of change and the forces of integration and connectedness creates a context for leadership that demands an updated expression of leadership skills. The leader in the workplace must be fast, fluid, and flexible in personal style, orientation, and role expression.
- Active engagement of different types of workforce members. The leader in the 21st century must be able to engage a diverse workforce within a wide variety of work circumstances (see Figure 3-2).
- Leading outsourced work and workers. As outsourcing in short-term work arrangements becomes increasingly popular, the leader

Figure 3-2. New-Age Leader Characteristics
• Quantum models • High complexity • Highly mobile • Professional • Fast changing • Portable services • Outsourced work • Technologic

must enforce a different set of leadership skills than those used when a workforce is directly employed (Drucker, 2002). The leader must be able to deal with an ever-widening range of role and personality characteristics in employees. Because of the span of generations employed in the workplace, blending and managing multifocal, multigenerational workers in a highly transforming work environment is a critical requirement for effective leadership (Lancaster & Stillman, 2002). Different from the 20th-century focus on stability and process, the focus for leaders in the 21st century is on agility, adaptability, relevance, and value.

- Expectations for value. In a technologically advanced world, outcome and value become increasingly important. The 20th century focused on "give" service technologies, whereas the 21st century emphasizes "get" service technologies. However, the differences extend beyond that focus (Porter-O'Grady & Afable, 2002). Technology makes it possible for outcomes to be more clearly delineated than in the past. We can identify outcomes and then determine the most appropriate processes directed at obtaining them. In past processes, orientation and work were the primary emphases of effort, often at the expense, certainly in the service environment, of having identified unachievable service deliverables. Through the use of technology and service algorithms, we can identify desirable outcomes and "back into" specific processes that can directly advance these outcomes (Evans & Wurster, 2000).

- Thriving in the "AND" space. Changing circumstances often shift the expectations to the opposite end of a spectrum. The drive for ironclad standardization within a high-reliability orientation has now been challenged with the need for user personalization to achieve user satisfaction as well as safe practices. New leadership requires leaders to recognize both standardization of the infrastructure *and* personalization of the application of care to the user. The AND approach is applicable to the provider–user dichotomy. Similarly, the provider's position as leader of the team now needs to shift to users (called "patients" in the 20th century) as the leaders of their personal health and health plan. Technology acquisitions have also created an untenable divide between effective care processes and software engineering. The use of information technology models in health care provides the user with a choice of processes based on desired skills and specifically customized outcomes. This user-driven, mass-customized approach to service delivery emphasizes customer ownership rather than unilateral provider-controlled changes. These new rules alter the foundations of healthcare service (Miller, 2014). This dramatic move away from provider-driven orientation in clinical work toward more customer-driven and value-based clinical activities changes the conditions and circumstances of health care with which leaders must now contend at every level of service activity.

- Human caring, compassionate leadership, AND technology. Human caring drives technology adoption and implementation. Clinicians must drive the co-creation of new practices using technologic enhancements such as electronic records and monitoring devices. New practices that emerge from technology adoption often interfere with effective and efficient practices and must necessarily be course-corrected by clinicians. The unacceptable primacy of technology at the expense of effective patient care processes, and compassionate leadership that embraces positive employee engagement, needs to shift to an AND approach; patient care processes *and* supporting people and technology must be the approach. To be sure, the intent of an electronic health record is not to further complicate the delivery of health care but rather to streamline the documentation of care.

- Evolution of language with the new work. For any transformation, new words and concepts emerge that better reflect the new ideas and expectations. Moving to new leadership models in which empowerment, portability, openness, complexity, uncertainty, energy, and vulnerability are expected requires clarification of words and meanings. Table 3-1 includes examples of emerging and more reflective words for new leadership to better communicate essential ideas, as well as words to avoid.

- Advancing movement. The development of effective managers for this transforming work is a creative process. While a new workplace unfolds, management and leadership must be continuous and dynamic. The challenge in this situation is recognizing that both leadership and the circumstances within which it is applied need to change together at precisely the same rate. The difficulty in developing leaders in this context is that much of what one would develop a

Table 3-1. New Leadership Language: Supporting Concepts and Concepts to Avoid		
Concepts or Ideas	**Supportive Language and Mindsets**	**Language and Mindsets to Avoid**
Leadership that is changing as new circumstances emerge and a new kind of leadership is needed; leading in complex adaptive systems is the overall work of the leader	**Leadership** is expressed through **visioning**, determination, recognition of **complexity**, and **alignment** with current circumstances. **Complex adaptive systems** are based on **complexity science**, which recognizes the interwoven parts of a system (unit, department, or organization), self-organization, and empowerment. Complex systems will self-organize, especially where professionals make up a large percentage of the workforce. **Vulnerable** or **vulnerability** infers recognition of the extent and limitations of one's knowledge and abilities. Recognizing one's limitations encourages dialogue and new relationships.	Leading by directing and controlling others. **Directing** is about one individual telling another what to do and removes the opportunity for input from that person. **Controlling** also removes the opportunity for input from the other person. Move away from command and control and rely on the skills of facilitating, envisioning, transforming, and leveraging talents.
Being open to new ideas. In the best of all worlds, this could happen . . . Focusing on potential new approaches and/or **opportunities**	**Opportunities** exist to . . . Being optimistic, thoughtful, and creative encourages positive, useful solutions.	"That will not work here; we have tried that." **Resistance** to change infers purposeful nonparticipation or nonsupport rather than lack of knowledge.
Teamwork to **facilitate** dialogue and assist others in achieving and refining the work of the organization through critique and synergy	**Engagement, inclusivity, setting the table** **Facilitation and valuing** of others to embrace ideas and support for identified work Setting the table infers collection of content experts, opinion leaders, culture resources, and experienced and novice individuals to create an exceptional experience and outcomes that are wider, deeper, and more informative.	**Individual, diversity** Diversity emphasizes differences while inclusivity focuses on including the key stakeholders and content experts. **Motivation** comes from within a person and not from the will of another.
Learning from other individuals, projects, disciplines, or cultures; coming together to gain input, refinement, consensus, and new ideas	**Networking, relationships, linkages, collaboration, key stakeholders** Working together aggregates available knowledge, expertise, and experience to use in solution finding.	Ex officio. Participants represent positions rather than content expertise or stakeholder role.

(Continued on next page)

Table 3-1. New Leadership Language: Supporting Concepts and Concepts to Avoid (Continued)		
Concepts or Ideas	**Supportive Language and Mindsets**	**Language and Mindsets to Avoid**
Learning from things that did not work out as intended	**Failure** indicates that the processes of work did not result in desired improvement. Failure provides essential information and is a tool of progress considered normative in life's journey of learning and adaptation.	**Error** infers that something or someone did something wrong or negative. In fact, the human interactions resulted in a failure of processes rather than an error and can be more appropriately attributed to system dynamics rather than an individual, purposeful error. Finding errors often involves affixing blame on an individual or individuals. **Problems** are about something to be fixed rather than something to learn from.
Getting the desired result that makes a difference	**Valued results** The results make a positive difference compared to the initial position.	**Output/outcomes** refers to unqualified/fixed results or products that may or may not result in sustainable improvements for key stakeholders.
Leading to **strengthen** and **grow**; being open to future possibilities	**Transformation** is fluid and dynamic and infers **empowerment**. **Visioning** with **principles** to guide activity. Principles provide direction and allow for unique strategies based on circumstances.	**Transaction** refers to an exchange of content not always associated with positive value. **Strategic planning** is fixed and not dynamic; guided by rules. **Rules** are specific and nonnegotiable and do not allow for adjustment based on circumstances.

leader for is shifting before the leader has an opportunity to act. This dynamic means, more specifically, that leadership development must occur within the context of a changing and transforming view that will shift and adjust the leadership skills and expectations at the same time the leader plays out the role. In short, to thrive in uncertainty, leaders must learn on the run. Rather than leading people, leaders now lead movement (Porter-O'Grady, 2010).

Knowledge and the Professional

As the leader must adjust to the constant state of change in the workplace, the worker also is challenged to adapt to these changes. The interplay between worker and workplace changes because of the complexity of the workplace and the demand for high-level skills. As the workplace comes to depend more on the knowledge and skills of the worker, the locus of control shifts from workplace to worker (Cristofoli, Markovic, & Meneguzzo, 2014). In 21st-century organizational circumstances, the workplace is more dependent on the skills and talents of the worker than the worker is dependent on the resources and rewards of the workplace. This shift in locus of control creates more dependence on knowledge workers and creates more mobility and value for knowledge work (see Figure 3-3). Work is itself now more mobile and portable and accelerates the portability and value of the worker. As a result, the traditional worker value expressed in commitment to the workplace has shifted to commitment to the work, wherever value is attached to it. The

Figure 3-3. Knowledge Workers
• Own work
• Self-directed
• Noncompliant
• Seek life balance
• Technologic
• Independent
• Value focused

emerging reality now across health care is that nursing work can now be done anywhere. Nurses are recognizing the inherent value of their knowledge and the application of it. The worker no longer must be committed to a specific workplace for a long period of time to claim the kinds of rewards or remunerations that this knowledge worker has now come to expect (Dzotsi, 2014) (see Figure 3-4).

Leading the knowledge worker requires that leaders recognize that they are leading a worker over whom they fundamentally have no ownership or long-term control. This mobility in the worker and a fluid relationship of the worker to the workplace creates a change in the dynamic between leader and worker. It changes the conditions and circumstances of leadership itself. Vertical and controlling models of leadership and decision making are no longer effective. Leadership is moving from mechanisms of control over work and the worker to processes of partnership and co-ownership in relationship to performance, expectations, and work outcomes. Managing and leading a partnership is considerably different from controlling and directing employees (Bennis & Sample, 2015).

Leadership by influence instead of control requires a unique skill set. Control mechanisms usually more represent parental behaviors in the parent–child relationship and interchange than represents adult-to-adult respect and communication. Influence also implies a stronger collective wisdom and the use of team mechanisms for problem solving and decision making. Leaders often claim that such activities lengthen the amount of time it takes to make decisions or take action. While this is true when referring to the dynamic of decision making and implementation, it is not true when applied to the process. When leaders decide unilaterally from a position of control and attempt to get compliance and cooperation, the amount of time involved in actually achieving alignment, congruence, compatibility, agreement, support, acquiescence, and

Figure 3-4. Leading Professionals Is Different
Professionals do not by definition owe their allegiance to institutions or organizations. They are instead directly aligned with those they serve. Professionals are not committed to the workplace; they are, instead, committed to the work of the profession. To the professional, it is the obligation of leadership to see to it that the professional can do his or her work well with the requisite resources and the level of quality both the professional and those they serve expect. If this "balance" of variables affecting professional work is not achieved and maintained, the relationships between the leader and the professional and the organization and profession break down. When that happens, it is very difficult to reconstruct.

performance is several times more intense and longer than the use of a more engaging approach (Aarons, Ehrhart, Farahnak, & Hurlburt, 2015).

As the nursing profession assumes more accountability for the outcome of its members, organizational leaders must change their relationship to the profession and the professional. Professions are composed of knowledge workers with specific skills and expectations for performance. In any mature profession, the expectation of the professional will be that he or she fulfills the obligations for the activities of the profession and will meet the standards of performance and practice exemplified through the profession's values (Porter-O'Grady, 2001). Here again, the professional model of work parallels the work conditions of the knowledge worker. The need for interdependence, accountability, clarity of expectations, and commitment to defined outcomes for all practices are common values between the profession and its members. In this professional frame of reference, knowledge workers have a right to expect that they will have ownership over their work but that ownership will be disciplined by clear expectations, well-delineated accountability, and enumeration and clarity of work outcomes (Northouse, 2015).

Clearly, exercising the role of leader now requires the structure of empowerment and partnership that had not existed in organizations over most of the 20th century. Newer models of shared leadership and decision making, which engage the profession in a partnership model, create a different set of expectations for organizational leaders (Wilhelm, 2017). This professional partnership calls into play more adult-to-adult relationships and intersections between the organization and the professional (knowledge worker). Now, the leader must exhibit both content and context skills. The content of leadership is disciplined by the context of partnership, accountability, equity, and ownership, all characteristics of a professional organization (Porter-O'Grady, 1992). These contextual characteristics create the format through which the nurse leader must operate. These characteristics help to form the framework within which the leader must develop the role and skills necessary to provide meaningful and viable leadership within the professional organization.

Creating the Vessel for Leadership

It is difficult to develop leadership in others if the context for the expression of leadership and learning is not appropriate. Too often, leaders focus on skill development in others without recognizing that the contextual framework for leadership is as important as the skill content. Creating a safe place for potential leaders to learn and develop is an important corollary to building excellent leadership skills (Fetterman, 2001; Porter-O'Grady & Malloch, 2016) (see Figure 3-5).

The changing context for work does not lend itself well to creating a stable and calm environment within which to develop leadership skills. The challenge for the leader, mentor, and teacher is to be able to evidence good leadership skills in a context of high mobility and constantly shifting change in the workplace. A part of the dynamic that this represents creates a mosaic of opportunities and experiences that the emerging leader must recognize and be able to unfold potential leadership skills within it. This real-world orientation to the expression and experience of leadership is a critical value in the developing and maturing of leadership skills (Murphy, 2002).

Figure 3-5. Current Work Context

- Uncertain
- Ever changing
- High-technology based
- Complex
- Adaptive
- Innovative
- High patient turnover
- Nonresidential
- Short term
- User driven

In a contemporary professional workplace, leaders must recognize that they are managing and leading a practice environment. The expectations emerging in the practice environment are requiring higher levels of interdependent judgments, better skills in relationship building, greater interaction in goal proficiency, and greater individual maturity and self-management. It is within this frame of reference that the emerging leader confronts the development of personal leadership skills.

Empowerment means recognizing the power already present in a situation or a person and allowing this power to be legitimately expressed (Miller, 2013). The emerging leader, therefore, must have a clear commitment to individual empowerment and the ability to build a context for empowerment that supports the growing interdependence and independence of individual practitioners in the expression of their nursing practice. Those responsible for educating the new leader must recognize that creating an appropriate and valid context for the expression of leadership gives a frame of reference for the empowered skills that will be necessary within the emerging complex work environment. Development of appropriate leadership skills helps to focus the emerging leader on the abilities that best fit the emerging conditions and circumstances influencing nursing practice. If this context or framework for leadership expression is established and a better fit is created between the leadership learned and that expressed, the greater the potential for ensuring the appropriate, meaningful, and valid expression of nursing practice (see Figure 3-6).

Figure 3-6. Empowerment

The leader does not give empowerment to anyone.
Empowerment is the recognition of the power already present in a role and allowing it to be legitimately expressed. For true empowerment to exist, both leader and staff must know what the expectations of the practice role are and give it all it needs to ensure that the expected outcomes are achieved. The best expression of empowerment in any role is the successful and satisfying achievement of the expectations of the role.

This situation calls for a high level of maturity within the expression of leadership (Warner, 2002). The nursing profession is now moving out of its historical adolescence into an adulthood requiring a different level of behavior and intersection with others in the healthcare system. As nurses begin to coordinate, facilitate, and integrate care across the broader spectrum of service environments, the interface with other disciplines and people in the delivery of healthcare services will grow in volume and intensity. This situation now calls the individual nurse to a higher level of skill with regard to communication, interaction, and goal achievement. Leaders must represent in their own practice a commitment to this understanding and a willingness to advance it in the role of all those they lead. In developing this next generation of leaders, the educator and/or mentor will need to be alert to the following circumstances:

- The ability of the emerging leader to conceptualize complexity
- The leader's potential for handling future conflict
- The ability of the new leader to engage others' issues without owning them
- The leader's skill with group process management
- The emerging leader's sense of self and personal confidence in the face of conflict, aggression, and negativity
- The ability of the leader to envision the direction of the changing journey within the cultural, social, and economic realities of a given organization

Creating Synergy: Professional Governance

Professional, disciplinary, and interdisciplinary relationships and integration are receiving increasing attention as organizations begin to see themselves operating as complex adaptive systems (CAS) (Hazy, Goldstein, & Lichtenstein, 2007). This more systems-based view of human enterprise and work is beginning to drive a whole new conceptualization of the interaction and relationship between people in the workplace. In predominantly professional environments such as law, engineering, architecture, medicine, and nursing, it is increasingly apparent that the principles that govern successful delineation, distribution, and application of professional work are considerably different from other more functionally defined work environments (Shaw, Walker, & Hogue, 2008). From a CAS perspective, sustainable clinical outcomes and evidentiary processes demand an interdisciplinary interface operating at a level of confluence much higher than has been traditionally apparent or expected (Davis, 2015).

This need for interdisciplinary synergy requires that several elements in the organization act in concert and operate in a way that reflects the unique characteristics of each professional group in the enterprise and yet demonstrates the expectation that individual disciplinary effort will, at some point, converge with the work of others to represent a synergy of effort that demonstrates an impact on outcome (Sikma, 2006). Two fundamental elements are necessary for this synergy to be evident: (a) each discipline is clear regarding its unique role and contribution, and (b) this unique disciplinary work will coalesce and converge with the work of other disciplines to create a composite whole whose alignment represents the achievement of a sustainable value or outcome.

In health care, for the past century, the disciplines have been busy at work identifying the unique character and content of their role and the boundaries that definitively circumscribe competencies and actions that characterize their role. This emphasis on discipline-specific identity establishment, boundary fixing, and role characteristics has caused each of them to focus primarily within. Although this has done much to establish the contribution that each makes and the value that each has, it has done little to focus on the essential interface between them where value is obtained and outcomes are sustained. As health care moves to a more systems view and develops a CAS framework for understanding the nature of work and contribution, it is no longer tenable for the disciplines to solely focus on their own role, function, and contribution. As systems understanding clearly enumerates, the real value of contribution is both determined and found at the intersections in the system (Edgren, 2008). In the case of the professions, this synergy is found at the interface of their work, not within the unilateral boundaries of their own function. This synergy is demonstrated at the points of convergence between the efforts of the various contributors, and this coalescence of action and value aggregates to demonstrate the locus of real evidence of viability and positive difference for patients (Geer-Frazier, 2014).

However, the journey to integration and synthesis cannot simply be driven by desire and good management. Collaboration is not achieved merely because one wants it. Collaboration is achieved when the structural and processing imperatives necessary to it have been carefully attended to and the infrastructure necessary to support it has been competently created (Porter-O'Grady & Malloch, 2015). For disciplines to speak with each other and to value the contribution each has to make, a common frame of reference is necessary, an organizational structure within which a relationship can be built and an operating milieu that represents the character of deliberation, decision making, and action representative of professional behavior. And it is here where the rub exists. For physicians, a professional model and a pattern of interacting structures have been developed over the decades and operate at a level of relative maturity. Although this model has challenges, it is predominantly an effective model that clearly articulates the role, position, and activities of the profession in relationship to its members and to the profession's relationship to other stakeholders. Because of physicians' success in creating this kind of a model, they have a classical professional infrastructure that parallels much of the same patterns of professional behavior in other disciplines that have done essentially the same work in building their professional infrastructures. Although evidencing different constructs, the principles of professional direction and ownership are as clearly articulated within each professional frame.

This is not so, however, with the nursing profession. Because of its traditions—predominantly women, historically subservient and arguably oppressed, primarily institutionally controlled, employee-based, and more functionally than relationally delineated—it has been slow to mature its professional infrastructure to parallel those of other disciplines (Ashley, 1976). Although the research is replete with reasons and circumstances for this condition, it has been a slow journey to professional equity for the largest professional body in health care (Hall, 1993). The advance of shared governance systems in nursing in the early 1980s was a seminal attempt to both mature and actualize the infrastructure necessary to configure the nursing profession in a way that represents the professional decision-making and work-organizing characteristics of other professional disciplines (Porter-O'Grady, 1992). While respecting the unique characteristics of nursing as a profession, shared governance has recognized the essential structural design and decisional, relational, and process foundations upon which professional decision making and action taking are grounded (Clavelle, O'Grady, Weston, & Verran, 2016; Porter-O'Grady, 2009).

A first principle in effective interdisciplinary synergy is an understanding that each discipline must be competent to act equitably and with a capacity to act and to relate comparably with a clear understanding of the value of the contribution it makes to the relationship. If this does not occur, regardless of the table at which the disciplines meet, the role, interaction, relationship, and communication that occur there are uneven, inequitable, and necessarily unbalanced, thereby impeding any potential for true relational synergy (Kritek, 2002). Here is where the principles and structural properties of professional governance become critical to the discipline. Professional governance creates an infrastructure that requires an operating framework for accountability, interaction, clinically driven ownership and decision making, and the creation of internal professional equity that represents and expects the requisites of ownership, investment, and personal engagement. These varied expectations and the competencies associated with them are expected to operate effectively at the interdisciplinary table, without which the conversation is skewed, unbalanced, and unilaterally controlled. In the case of nursing, professional governance is a developmental infrastructure that provides the vehicle for the profession to grow its internal patterns of behavior, relationship, ownership, and decision making to parallel and represent the same kinds of professional behavioral expectations of other mature professions at the table. Synergy cannot occur in the presence of inequity; indeed, synergy implies equity.

It is not the point of this chapter to outline the principles and structural elements of professional governance, as that has been done more thoroughly in other texts. What is important to note within the context of leadership development is the centrality of the structural imperative to developing professional behavior. Without an infrastructure that demands an operational process of professional behaviors associated with accountability, ownership, and engagement, those activities become random, incidental, and irregular. As a result, a wide variety of both appropriate and inappropriate discipline-specific behavior emerges in individuals and in the organization. This creates the conditions that limit other more mature professions from seeing nursing as mature, equitable, and comparably competent. Consequently, the interaction between disciplines, most notably physicians and nurses, is not well developed and is frequently inequitable. Going forward, nurses primarily will need to deal with the language and relationships of equity, value, and contribution as they begin to demonstrate important clinical contributions to value-based clinical processes such as bundles, the interprofessional continuum of care, and interprofessional decisions related to the management of episodic and long-term care. The issue for nursing will be to clearly define for itself and others what its value and contribution is, followed by clear demonstration of the competencies reflecting that value contribution.

Once individual professions demonstrate the capacity for horizontal, relational, accountable, and interactional professional frames for behavior, the principles of shared decision making cross disciplinary boundaries and create a mechanism and methodology for effectively building synergistic interdisciplinary relationships (Porter-O'Grady, 2009). These relationships are built around common frames of reference related to competency, contribution, and clinical efficacy. Ultimately, this means that each discipline, aware of its contribution to the whole, joins in the collaborative dialogue and effort to integrate the unique activities of each discipline in a way that advances valuing and evaluation of their mutual efficiency, effectiveness, and efficacy. This convergence reflects the patients' need to evaluate the value and impact not based on the unique contribution of a particular discipline, but instead on the synergistic integration of the contribution of all stakeholders who have an impact on the quality of the patient experience and the outcome of the clinical event. For example, nursing's predominant role in this equation will likely be expressed in the coordination, integration, and facilitation of the relationship between team members, of the contribution each team member makes, the consolidation and integration of the sum contribution of each of these members, and, ultimately, the impact on the patient experience and on positive clinical outcomes. This is the role that nurses bring to the table and that provides the contextual framework for their contribution to the deliberations and the decisions made at that table.

In evidence-based practice (evidentiary systems), synergy and synthesis of interdisciplinary relationships are essential underpinnings. In fact, true evidence-based practice cannot be sustained without this interdisciplinary synthesis having been well established both structurally and operationally (Porter-O'Grady, 2010). From this broader CAS understanding of organizational integrity and professional relationship, professional shared governance is no longer an option. Call it what you will, an infrastructure for professional accountability, integration, application, and evaluation of clinical practice is simply no longer optional. Effective clinical leaders need to see their own competency in light of an operating professional infrastructure and recognize in their skill development a need for stronger emphasis on collaborative leadership, staff accountability and ownership, and more horizontally delineated methods of management in partnership within a professional clinical environment. Intradisciplinary and interdisciplinary synergy simply cannot occur without those corollary leadership capacities. Keep in mind that nursing is at the center of this emerging value equation. And now the options for behaving in any way other than that grounded on value are increasingly limited regardless of the discipline. Integration and coordination of the care expressed in value bundles, care continuums, or comprehensive episodic care now requires a clear agreement regarding the contribution of each of the stakeholders and evidence of a heightened goodness-of-fit between each and all their work efforts in a way that demonstrates the value of good resource use and a positive impact on both clinical processes and outcomes.

Mentoring Leaders

To "create" effective new leaders, current leaders must recognize that the development of leadership in others is an outflow of the leadership present in themselves. The mentoring process involves setting an example from personal experiences that others can emulate, build upon, and incorporate into their own practice. The mentor provides both framework and format within which the emerging leader can safely develop skills and ensure that opportunities exist for the individual's own leadership expression. Mentors, through their own behavior, set patterns of process and skill that, when emulated, produce meaningful outcomes and advance the value of the expression of leadership in those being mentored.

The mentor must be aware of the significant value of that role in the life of others. Mentors are not free of flaws; instead, they honestly recognize the content of their character and use this knowledge for their personal growth and development, as well as their own accommodation to the realities inherent in their personal and professional journey. The journey is not perfect for the mentor, but the mentor actualizes the adjustment to personal imperfection, accommodates for it, and practices moving beyond its limitations. The mentor exemplifies the imperfections of human expression and acknowledges them. The mentor then adjusts leadership style and skill to compensate for the negative potential that personal human frailty may have on the expression of competent leadership. By exemplifying the conflicts inherent in this personal and professional journey of leadership, the mentor creates a safe and meaningful opportunity for the recognition of deficits in the emerging leader, allows for the celebration of human frailties, and exemplifies the challenge and excitement in the human effort to triumph over adversity and limitation. The mentor sees leadership as a journey of growth and a sign of commitment to one's personal advancement. Finally, this commitment to movement within the role of leader serves as a signpost to others of the willingness and ability to engage in and embrace the challenges of clinical practice in the face of the vagaries and contradictions of the human work environment (see Figure 3-7).

Figure 3-7. Traits of the Mentor
• Vulnerable
• Open
• Flawed
• Clear
• Firm
• Insightful
• Experienced
• Practical
• Strategic
• Empathetic
• Patient
• Available

Most mature leaders have suggested the specific contribution of their mentors during their personal leadership journey and developmental process. Mentoring for the learner provides an opportunity to identify with solid leadership skills and to be able to access another individual who is mature in the experience of leadership, with the frank and open discourse related to any developmental issue associated with growing and maturing as a leader. The mentor serves as a demarcation between one level of behavior and another in the developing role of leader. Furthermore, the mentor serves as an evaluator of the growing level of skill in the emerging leader (Brown, 2001). The mentor sometimes is the parental replacement in an "adult-to-adult" relationship, creating a much stronger and equitable foundation for interaction and communication as an adult. Still embedded in the mentoring relationship are the safety and support necessary for effective growth and development, thus creating an interchange of value, meaning, and support for the emerging leader in experimenting with new facets of the leadership experience. From the mentor, the new leader gets a better understanding of the circumstances and the conditions of effective leadership and a political and contextual frame for the ever-present challenges inherent in the pathway from emergent to mature leader (Miller, 2017).

As this shift in role accountability continues, the collection and management of leadership wisdom becomes a priority. Historically, the wisdom of individual sages and organizations was treated informally and anecdotally. The availability of sophisticated digital communication vehicles and data storage advances the need for a more formal process in documenting and sharing wisdom across generations. Engaging in wisdom sharing also shifts this process from simply a career handoff process to a dynamic process in which individuals from all generations identify wisdom that is classic across all circumstances and always useful compared to wisdom that is relevant only in designated circumstances (Malloch & Porter-O'Grady, 2016). Determining what is valued and what can be left behind also brings emphasis to nursing that will be more visible and more available to all generations. Sharing journeys, writing experiences, values, failures, and successes serves all nurses in professional role development. The dialogue about nursing work guides us to determine what really matters as professional work. Accomplished professionals often believe all of their work should be saved for the ages; collaborating with younger generations gives new light to the work that fully fits with emerging circumstances. The values and perceptions of each generation support a living dynamic rather than career-ending memorials. See Chapter 22 for more information on mentoring and succession planning.

Communicating Direction

All leaders must have a vision of the direction of change and the change journey for the organization. Leaders are consistently managing mobility and movement; however, neither one is inherently valuable. The value of movement is disciplined by the direction in which one is moving and the meaning that movement has in achieving specified and clear outcomes for all participants. The leader, in this role, is essentially a signpost reader. This means that the leader constantly lives in the *potential* of the journey as it moves toward goals and outcomes that have value for the organization and the people in it (Coffman & Gonzalez-Molina, 2002). The leader must be able to see the direction of the journey and then translate that direction into a language that followers can understand. The leader can break down the direction of change into increments and elements, allowing staff members to slowly incorporate the changes into their work.

The leader is a translator of organizational goals and priorities, economic and financial realities that must be accommodated, and the ultimate work requisites of driving a competitive and complex healthcare environment. Although nurses recognize the reality associated with these issues, they often have a difficult time incorporating these realities into the practices and processes of nursing care. Through translation, the leader assists the staff in accommodating and incorporating changes into their own practice experience (see Figure 3-8).

Figure 3-8. Translation Skills
• Clear vision
• Broad view of the issues
• In the language of staff
• What does it mean to me?
• What do I do?
• Impact of the act
• Ensuring competence

Summary

The leader is forever learning. Effective leaders live within a developmental context. This is no less true for nursing. An important difference for the nurse leader, or at least an important emphasis, is related to providing a leadership language that fits the unique circumstances of a profession predominated by women and historically represented by institutional employment. Also, the long history of strong vertical, authority-based, and subordinate relationships in the medical paradigm has created issues in nursing related to self-image and value. However, much of the justification for this is quickly evaporating in an interdisciplinary framework and with nurses increasingly having a broader-based and deeper academic background. Nurse leaders must deal appreciatively with the unique historic experience of nursing and nurses yet accelerate the expectations of full membership in engagement in healthcare decision making, delivery, and evaluation. The expectation of the nurse leader should be that each nurse fully engages and embraces the role of the nursing profession in an increasingly interprofessional paradigm. In that exercise, all of the challenges of leadership found in any arena will require the competencies and skills of leaders in any environment.

The work of learning and leadership never ends. All leaders must be as committed to their own development as they are to their role. Leadership is a living journey that represents a personal commitment to individual growth and development. The effective leader joins in the effort to not only develop the roles of the professional staff, other workers, and the organization, but also to ensure the wisdom of contributions of individuals within the organization. The maturity and growth of the leader serve as an exemplar to those who are in an earlier stage of their leadership journey. The obligations of mentorship and the development of other leaders are inherent in the role. Growing in leadership competence is a shared experience, the expectation of which is communicated from one leader to another. Those who are leaders have an opportunity and an obligation to extend to each other what has been learned through experience and the development of the role—the sharing of wisdom across generations. All leaders must realize that they are on a life journey that will not end as long as they are in the role. The most viable and successful leaders always know that they are not fully competent in the expression of leadership. They know that competence is not completely obtainable and understand that leadership is a journey, not an event. The significance and joy of leadership are in its continuing dynamic and ever-challenging call to personal mastery and entry into the never-ending mystery of human growth and relationship.

Adapted from "Leading the Profession" (pp. 21–44), by T. Porter-O'Grady in M.M. Gullatte (Ed.), Nursing Management: Principles and Practice *(2nd ed.), 2011, Pittsburgh, PA: Oncology Nursing Society. Copyright 2011 by Oncology Nursing Society.*

References

Aarons, G.A., Ehrhart, M.G., Farahnak, L.R., & Hurlburt, M.S. (2015). Leadership and organizational change for implementation (LOCI): A randomized mixed method pilot study of a leadership and organization development intervention for evidence-based practice implementation. *Implementation Science, 10*(11), 1–12. doi:10.1186/s13012-014-0192-y

Adams, S. (2015, June 21). The famous quote I never said. *Scott Adams' Blog.* Retrieved from http://blog.dilbert.com/post/122081192901/the-famous-quote-i-never-said

Alberts, B. (2013). On effective leadership. *Science, 340,* 660. doi:10.1126/science.1239927

Anderson, W.T. (2001). *All connected now: Life in the first global civilization.* Los Angeles, CA: Westview Press.

Archibald, R.D., & Archibald, S.C. (2016). *Leading and managing innovation: What every executive team must know about project, program, and portfolio management* (2nd ed.). Boca Raton, FL: CRC Press.

Ashley, J.A. (1976). *Hospitals, paternalism, and the role of the nurse.* New York, NY: Teachers College Press.

Bennis, W., & Sample, S.B. (with Asghar, R.). (2015). *The art and adventure of leadership: Understanding failure, resilience and success.* Hoboken, NJ: Wiley.

Bleich, M.R. (2014). Developing leaders and systems thinkers—part I. *Journal of Continuing Education in Nursing, 45,* 158–159. doi:10.3928/00220124-20140327-13

Bolman, L.G., & Deal, T.E. (2013). *Reframing organizations: Artistry, choice, and leadership.* San Francisco, CA: Jossey-Bass.

Brown, B.L. (2001). *Mentoring and work-based learning* (Trends and Issues Alert No. 29). Columbus, OH: ERIC Clearinghouse on Adult, Career, and Vocational Education.

Clavelle, J.T., O'Grady, T.P., Weston, M.J., & Verran, J.A. (2016). Evolution of structural empowerment: Moving from shared to professional governance. *Journal of Nursing Administration, 46,* 308–312. doi:10.1097/NNA.0000000000000350

Coffman, C., & Gonzalez-Molina, G. (2002). *Follow this path: How the world's greatest organizations drive growth by unleashing human potential.* New York, NY: Warner Books.

Cristofoli, D., Markovic, J., & Meneguzzo, M. (2014). Governance, management and performance in public networks: How to be successful in shared-governance networks. *Journal of Management and Governance, 18,* 77–93. doi:10 .1007/s10997-012-9237-2

Daft, R.L. (2015). *Management* (12th ed.). Farmington Hills, MI: Cengage Learning.

Davis, H. (2015). Social complexity theory for sense seeking: Unearthing leadership mindsets for unknowable and uncertain times. *Emergence: Complexity and Organization, 17*(1), 1–14. Retrieved from https://journal .emergentpublications.com/article/social-complexity-theory-for-sense-seeking

Donaldson, W. (2017). *Simple_complexity: A management book for the rest of us: A guide to systems thinking.* New York, NY: Morgan James.

Drucker, P.F. (1998). *Peter Drucker on the profession of management.* Boston, MA: Harvard Business School Press.

Drucker, P.F. (2002). They're not employees, they're people. *Harvard Business Review, 80*(2), 70–77.

Dzotsi, E. (2014). *How to manage remote workers.* Palm Bay, FL: Qomlavy Networks.

Edgren, L. (2008). The meaning of integrated care: A systems approach. *International Journal of Integrated Care, 8*(4). doi:10.5334/ijic.256

Evans, P., & Wurster, T.S. (2000). *Blown to bits: How the new economics of information transforms strategy.* Boston, MA: Harvard Business School Press.

Ferris, G.T. (1889). *Great leaders: Historic portraits from the great historians.* New York, NY: Appleton.

Fetterman, D.M. (2001). *Foundations of empowerment evaluation.* Thousand Oaks, CA: Sage.

Geer-Frazier, B. (2014). Complexity leadership generates innovation, learning, and adaptation of the organization. *Emergence: Complexity and Organization, 16*(3), 105–116.

Gill, R. (2011). *Theory and practice of leadership* (2nd ed.). Los Angeles, CA: Sage.

Griffin, D., & Stacey, R. (Eds.). (2005). *Complexity and the experience of leading organizations.* New York, NY: Routledge.

Hall, B.A. (1993). Time to nurse: Musings of an aging nurse radical. *Nursing Outlook, 41,* 250–252.

Hazy, J.K., Goldstein, J.A., & Lichtenstein, B.B. (Eds.). (2007). *Complex systems leadership theory: New perspectives from complexity science on social and organizational effectiveness.* New York, NY: ISCE Publishing.

Heifetz, R., & Laurie, D.L. (2001). The work of leadership. *Harvard Business Review, 79*(11), 131–140.

Ismuratova, S., & Shalgynbayeva, K. (2013). Leadership in the future experts' creativity development with scientific research activities. In S.S. Ercetin & S. Banerjee (Eds.), *Chaos, complexity, and leadership* (pp. 305–314). New York, NY: Springer.

Kets de Vries, M.F.R. (2003). *Leaders, fools and impostors: Essays on the psychology of leadership* (Rev. ed.). Lincoln, NE: iUniverse.

Kotter, J.P. (2001). What leaders really do. *Harvard Business Review, 79*(11), 85–96.

Kritek, P.B. (2002). *Negotiating at an uneven table: Developing moral courage in resolving our conflicts* (2nd ed.). San Francisco, CA: Jossey-Bass.

Lancaster, L.C., & Stillman, D. (2002). *When generations collide.* New York, NY: HarperBusiness.

Malloch, K., & Porter-O'Grady, T. (2009). *The quantum leader: Applications for the new world of work* (2nd ed.). Burlington, MA: Jones & Bartlett Learning.

Malloch, K., & Porter-O'Grady, T. (2016). *The career handoff: A healthcare leader's guide to knowledge and wisdom transfer across generations.* Indianapolis, IN: Sigma Theta Tau International.

Miller, A. (2014). *Redefining operational excellence: New strategies for maximizing performance and profits across the organization.* New York, NY: American Management Association.

Miller, J.H., & Page, S.E. (2007). *Complex adaptive systems: An introduction to computational models of social life.* Princeton, NJ: Princeton University Press.

Miller, M. (2013). *The heart of leadership.* San Francisco, CA: Berrett-Koehler.

Miller, M. (2017). *Leaders made here.* San Francisco, CA: Berrett-Koehler.

Murphy, J. (Ed.). (2002). *The educational leadership challenge: Redefining leadership for the 21st century.* Chicago, IL: University of Chicago Press.

Myatt, M. (2014). *Hacking leadership: The 11 gaps every business needs to close and the secrets to closing them quickly.* Hoboken, NJ: Wiley.

Northouse, P.G. (2015). *Leadership: Theory and practice* (7th ed.). Thousand Oaks, CA: Sage.

Owen, H. (2012). *The spirit of leadership: Liberating the leader in each of us* (16th ed.). San Francisco, CA: Berrett-Koehler.

Pearman, R.R. (1998). *Hard wired leadership: Unleashing the power of personality to become a new millennium leader.* New York, NY: Davies-Black.

Porter-O'Grady, T. (1992). *Implementing shared governance: Creating a professional organization.* Baltimore, MD: Mosby.

Porter-O'Grady, T. (2001). Profound change: 21st century nursing. *Nursing Outlook, 49,* 182–186. doi:10.1067/mno .2001.112789

Porter-O'Grady, T. (2009). *Interdisciplinary shared governance: Integrating practice, transforming health care* (2nd ed.). Burlington, MA: Jones & Bartlett Learning.

Porter-O'Grady, T. (2010). A new age for practice: Creating the framework for evidence. In K. Malloch & T. Porter-O'Grady (Eds.), *Introduction to evidence-based practice in nursing and health* (2nd ed., pp. 1–30). Burlington, MA: Jones & Bartlett Learning.

Porter-O'Grady, T., & Afable, R. (2002). Reforming the health care structure: Physicians and hospital leaders must come together in a genuine partnership. *Health Progress, 83*(1), 17–20.

Porter-O'Grady, T., & Malloch, K. (2015). *Quantum leadership: Building better partnerships for sustainable health* (4th ed.). Burlington, MA: Jones & Bartlett Learning.

Porter-O'Grady, T., & Malloch, K. (2016). *Leadership in nursing practice: Changing the landscape of health care* (2nd ed.). Burlington, MA: Jones & Bartlett Learning.

Shaw, L., Walker, R., & Hogue, A. (2008). The art and science of teamwork: Enacting a transdisciplinary approach in work rehabilitation. *Work, 30,* 297–306.

Sikma, S.K. (2006). Staff perceptions of caring: The importance of a supportive environment. *Journal of Gerontological Nursing, 32*(6), 22–29.

Sorcher, M., & Brant, J. (2002). Are you picking the right leaders? *Harvard Business Review, 80*(2), 78–85, 128.

Warner, J. (2002). *Aspirations of greatness: Mapping the midlife leader's reconnection to self and soul.* New York, NY: Wiley.

Wheatley, M.J. (1999). *Leadership and the new science: Discovering order in a chaotic world* (2nd ed.). San Francisco, CA: Berrett-Koehler.

Wilhelm, T. (2017). *Shared leadership: The essential ingredient for effective PLCs.* Thousand Oaks, CA: Corwin.

CHAPTER 4

Thriving in a Time of Continuous Change

Patricia Reid Ponte, RN, DNSc, NEA-BC, FAAN

Introduction

Today's healthcare environment is remarkable for its state of continuous change. Each day brings news of research breakthroughs, new care modalities, innovative technologies, and revisions to healthcare policies and regulations. Relationships within healthcare systems and communities are also in a constant state of flux. As nurse leaders, we are challenged to stay on top of these and other changes to anticipate their implications for the profession and practice of nursing. We are further challenged to use the changes to advance the healthcare value proposition of improving population health, reducing costs per capita, and improving the patient experience of care and the work life of healthcare providers (Berwick, Nolan, & Whittington, 2008; Sikka, Morath, & Leape, 2015).

The challenges and opportunities facing nurse leaders are not confined to nurses in formal leadership positions. Leadership is a professional imperative for every nurse and, as such, transcends nursing roles and institutional and geographic boundaries. Given the diversity of nurse leader roles, there is no single "right" way to lead during times of constant change. Rather, the goals nurse leaders establish and the decisions they make are necessarily informed by multiple factors, including many that are unique to the leader's organization and practice setting. As nurse leaders gain experience, they find themselves drawing on leadership principles or commitments that have proved helpful in guiding their own actions and the actions of leaders whom they most respect. This chapter examines six leadership commitments that many nurse leaders have found valuable in their leadership practice and presents examples illustrating how the commitments can be put into action in today's healthcare environments.

Commitment 1: Build Trust With Self and Others

Committing to building trust is perhaps the most important commitment a leader can make. Trust is fundamental to forming effective relationships and influencing and enacting change.

Leaders who are trusted inspire confidence; those who work with them are confident in the leader's integrity and abilities (Covey, 2006), and confident that the leader will treat them fairly and respect their contributions and perspectives. In contrast, as noted by Stephen R. Covey in the foreword to Stephen M.R. Covey's (2006) book, low trust exacts a hefty price by encouraging the development of hidden agendas, interpersonal conflict, interdepartmental rivalries, and defensive communication. In a low-trust environment, a leader's ability to effect change slows and, in the worst case, breaks down altogether.

Covey (2006) identified four qualities or "cores" that are vital to establishing credibility and trust. Two of the qualities, a leader's *capabilities* and the *results* a leader produces, relate to competence. The other two, a leader's *integrity* and a leader's *intent* or motivations, relate to character. Covey noted that these qualities work together to influence how others perceive us as leaders. Equally important, they also influence the degree to which we trust ourselves.

Self-trust involves believing that your contributions are important and that you have what it takes to be a good leader. Leaders who doubt their own capabilities and the value of their own contributions have a difficult time representing and inspiring the confidence of those who report to them. While some amount of self-doubt can be useful in promoting self-reflection and personal growth, it can be a problem for those of us who are less confident about who we are and what we bring to the table. The advancement of cultures of safety that emphasize the value and importance of each person's perspective and contributions has been helpful in reducing this phenomenon. However, even in such environments, nurse leaders can benefit from daily reminders to be true to themselves and mindful of the unique insights, gifts, and abilities they have to offer, as this may give them courage to speak out and take action.

The following example involving the chief nursing officer (CNO) of a large healthcare institution illustrates how a lack of self-trust can inhibit effective leadership. Two years ago, the chief medical officer (CMO) of the organization transitioned to another prominent institution after working with the CNO for more than 13 years. An organizational redesign positioned the new CMO in a partnership with another nurse leader, a change that the CNO fully supported, given the needs of the organization. As time went on, however, the CNO realized she was not forging an effective relationship with the new CMO. This compromised the strength of the CNO–CMO leadership model and the ability of the two to collaborate on leading the clinical enterprise across the continuum. Rather than discussing the situation with the new CMO and her boss, the chief executive officer, the CNO became riddled with self-doubt and decided to try solving the problem on her own. As the months went by and the situation continued, she became less communicative and engaged with the medical staff than she should have been. On some level, she also lost her organizational voice as she turned her focus inward to the nursing department and nursing practice issues only.

In time, the CNO realized that to be effective, she needed to express her concerns about the leadership structure and work toward changing it and fully integrating the CNO role into the organization once again. As she began meeting regularly with the CMO, the new organizational structure became normalized, and the CNO and CMO were able to partner to carry out their roles as the clinical executives accountable for the entire clinical enterprise. This experience illustrates the importance of trusting oneself and the danger of retracting in the face of a challenge. It also brings to mind the words of the poet, philosopher, and cancer survivor, Mark Nepo, who cautioned that "what is not expressed is depressed" (Nepo, 2000, p. 52) and may work against us by preventing our authentic selves from being at work in our lives.

Commitment 2: Ensure Inclusive Decision Making, Healthy Debate, and Proactive Communication

Dialogue and healthy debate, as well as shared or inclusive decision making, are widely recognized as essential for a healthy work environment (American Association of Critical-Care Nurses, 2016), continuous improvement (Langley et al., 2009), and organizational and team learning (Edmondson, 2012). Many nurse leaders come to realize through experience that if they do not include the right stakeholders in a decision, they often make a wrong decision and need to go back, develop a different plan, and do the work of building consensus again. Even if they make the right decision the first time, they risk losing the trust of those who were left out of the decision-making process.

Shared decision making is facilitated by an organizational climate that encourages the free exchange of ideas and by governance and committee structures that engage individuals who represent different perspectives, expertise, and knowledge in the decision-making process. Even with such structures in place, leaders must continually send the message that every person and point of view is valued. Without this, groups have a tendency to seek harmony and consensus at the expense of considering a full range of solutions and options.

Although keeping the lines of communication open with immediate work groups is critical, communicating with departments and leaders outside one's normal circle is just as important and can be more of a challenge. One approach to maintaining open communication is to take time at the beginning of each year to identify individuals with whom you need to stay connected for strategic and operational purposes and schedule communication "touchpoints." If your primary goal is to share updates, the touchpoints might involve quarterly 30-minute meetings. If more frequent interaction is needed, you might consider scheduling monthly or weekly phone or face-to-face meetings. For some external stakeholders, an annual lunch or dinner might be the right approach. Although email is an option for some levels of relationships, telephone conversations and face-to-face meetings are often far more effective if the goal is to further understand and share perspectives and ideas. Before sitting down at your keyboard, take a moment to consider whether the better plan is to back away from the computer and speak with a colleague in person.

Commitment 3: Recognize Your Power and Use It in a Positive Way

Leadership expert and Harvard Business School professor Abraham Zaleznik once observed, "Whatever else organizations may be . . . they are political structures. This means that organizations operate by distributing authority and setting a stage for the exercise of power" (Zaleznik, 1970, para. 2). Thus, power dynamics such as competition and conflicts of interest are a natural part of any organization. While they are to be expected, power dynamics can become a problem if left unchecked, as an organization's success hinges on cooperation and a commitment to common purposes among organizational leaders.

All nurse leaders who participate in organizational priority setting, resource deployment, and decision making must accept the role they hold as power brokers and become agile and effective in power politics. "Managing up" and networking are key to using one's power base effectively (Pfeffer, 2010). Knowing this, nurse leaders must prioritize working effectively with their organization's executive management team and board members and must network internally and externally to ensure they are "known" and trusted.

Most importantly, nurse leaders must commit to using their power to advance the organizational and nursing missions and patients, families, and communities rather than personal ambition. Researcher and author Jim Collins (2001) offered a model for leaders in his book *Good to Great*, which described the attributes of "level 5" leaders, or leaders who perform at the highest level of executive capabilities. Collins noted that such leaders are driven not by their own ego and quest for personal renown, but by what is best for the organization and will ensure its success in the future, long after the leader has moved on.

An example that profoundly illustrates the value of basing actions and decisions on what is best for patients and the organization occurred at Dana-Farber Cancer Institute (DFCI) in the mid-1990s, when DFCI was thrust into the spotlight following medication errors that resulted in the death of one patient and grave complications in another. Rather than resorting to blame and punishment for those involved, the organization's nursing, medical, and administrative leaders and board of trustees launched an exhaustive investigation into the complex systems that contributed to the errors (Connor, Ponte, & Conway, 2002). The leaders' actions heralded a new approach to error management that emphasized transparency and error prevention and led to improved organizational systems and structures. Their actions also had a far-reaching effect, as they helped fuel the national patient safety movement that continues to shape care delivery practices today.

Commitment 4: Design and Execute Strategic and Operational Plans With Well-Defined Success Metrics and Role Accountability

Given the number of demands confronting nurse leaders, it is understandable that leaders are sometimes tempted to put off strategic planning and instead spend their time on more immediate tasks. This is a mistake. A strategic plan that specifies department goals, priorities, and metrics can transform the performance of a leadership team (Ponte et al., 2016). With such a plan in place, team members move from pursuing their own priorities and pulling in separate directions to focusing their energies and resources on achieving a shared set of goals. A well-crafted strategic plan serves as a road map for nurse leaders by charting a course for the next three to five years and providing a framework for annual operating plans and priorities. As with any map, some elements of the plan may change over time, but the compass points remain the same.

To be truly useful, a strategic plan should reflect organizational goals and trends in health care that are likely to affect nursing, as well as the department's own priorities and needs (Drenkard, 2001; Ponte et al., 2016). The best strategic plans are achieved through an inclusive process in which each member of the nursing leadership team participates in examining the department's strengths, gaps, and opportunities for improvement and helps define goals and priorities for the future. In addition to consulting experts about future trends in health care, the team should seek input on department priorities from direct care nurses, interdisciplinary colleagues, organizational leaders, and other stakeholders. By using such an inclusive process, nurse leaders ensure that the plan aligns with organizational goals and also garner support for strategic nursing initiatives.

A key step often overlooked in strategic planning involves translating the goals and priorities specified in the plan into actionable initiatives with identified owners and performance metrics. This level of detail helps the plan move off the page and drive action: identifying owners clarifies individual accountability for key elements of the plan, and the metrics become tools for monitoring progress. Beyond this, the overall plan, with its specified goals, timelines, and metrics, becomes a gauge of leadership performance that the leadership team can use to assess its own productiveness and efficiency (Ponte et al., 2016).

Commitment 5: Support Creativity, Innovation, and Effective Collaborative Leadership Through Professional Development of Self and Others

In his classic book *The Fifth Discipline*, Peter Senge observed, "The organizations that will truly excel in the future will be the organizations that discover how to tap people's commitment and capacity to learn" (Senge, 1990, p. 4). Although Senge's book was published in 1990, his message still rings true today. Indeed, it is particularly applicable to healthcare organizations and other knowledge-intensive settings that are subject to constant change and where ongoing learning by individuals and teams is essential for staying competitive (Edmondson, 2012). In such settings, the onus is on leaders to create environments that support and promote ongoing learning and the sharing and application of new ideas and knowledge.

Prioritizing leadership development for oneself and for nurses at all levels of the organization positions nurse leaders and those they mentor or supervise to be at their best while striving for greater effectiveness. Offering formal leadership development programs at regular intervals is a good way to ensure that individuals have the time and space needed to reflect on personal characteristics and behaviors and learn strategies for improving performance effectiveness. Furthermore, helping leaders at all levels to become aware of their unique attributes, confident in their strengths, and clear about opportunities for improvement frees them to be their most creative and innovative selves. For some, ascribing to a particular leadership theory or model is helpful in framing situations, making decisions, and taking action and further increases their confidence in the capabilities, knowledge, and expertise they bring to each challenge.

Efforts to foster creativity and innovation in the workplace are greatly aided by nurses' inherent creativity. Evidence of this creativity can be found each day in the way nurses partner with patients and families to develop strategies for coping with illness or staying healthy. Nurses also are masterful in identifying solutions to problems in care delivery. Evidence of this can be found by observing groups of nurses in action. An example is provided by one hospital's Nursing Practice Committee. The committee is a key component of the hospital's nursing governance structure and consists of frontline clinical nurses and nurse leaders from different practice areas. At a recent meeting, the group sought to address a lack of standardization in the way patients were weighed prior to chemotherapy treatments. Through discussion, the committee members determined that each clinical area used a slightly different process, and they then brainstormed ideas for a uniform strategy. Many techniques were shared, including some that even the most experienced nurses had not considered. By the end of the meeting, the group agreed on a standardized process and created a plan for disseminating it across the organization.

As this example suggests, innovation is a team sport. Nurse leaders can take advantage of this by engaging others in their own efforts to find solutions to problems and by creating a climate and structures that promote learning and the dialogue and give-and-take that lead to creative solutions.

Commitment 6: Foster a Mindful Nursing Practice for Self and Others

I want to share a personal experience that was an epiphany for me. Some years ago, I experienced a series of difficult events that involved a major loss of trust in a critical relationship and the loss of a close family friend to suicide. The events happened at a time when I was immersed in a busy career, and I convinced myself that at least some of what occurred was because of my lack of attention to the home front. With time and reflection, I was able to appreciate that my career focus was part of the context, but not the impetus, for the events. At the same time, I began to question how I distributed my attention and energy. It was through this line of questioning that I discovered mindfulness.

As described by mindfulness expert Jon Kabat-Zinn, mindfulness is the awareness of "what arises when you pay attention, on purpose, in the present moment, non-judgmentally, and as if your life depended upon it" (Kabat-Zinn, 2012, p. 17). Mindfulness can be nurtured through practices such as meditation, mindful movement, and other practices that enhance one's aware- ness of the moment. Research has shown that the consistent use of such practices can be help- ful in reducing stress and burnout and in managing chronic physical and mental health condi- tions (Bohlmeijer, Prenger, Taal, & Cuijpers, 2009; Chiesa & Serretti, 2009; Foureur, Besley, Burton, Yu, & Crisp, 2013; Goyal et al., 2014; Mackenzie, Poulin, & Seidman-Carlson, 2006; Moody et al., 2013).

Mindfulness techniques can be helpful in managing the day-to-day stress that is part of lead- ership practice and also can help leaders achieve greater clarity during challenging situations. A simple but effective technique involves stopping and taking a moment to focus on your breath- ing and observe what is happening inside—your thoughts, feelings, and physical reactions. By freeing the mind of distractions, this practice allows you to listen more attentively and to more carefully consider and respond to the situation at hand.

Mindfulness practices can be similarly helpful to clinical nurses as they care for patients in today's stressful and fast-paced work environments. In a recent account, nurse leaders described how they implemented programs to help nurses learn and adopt mindfulness practices that benefit how they care for patients, as well as themselves (Ponte & Koppel, 2015). The nurse leaders also took steps to incorporate mindfulness principles into nursing practice more broadly by adopting integrative nursing (Koithan, 2014) as a key component of the organization's nursing philosophy and framework for practice. Integrative nursing is guided by a set of core principles (see Figure 4-1) that identify human beings as whole sys- tems that are inseparable from the environment and have an innate capacity for health and healing. The principles also emphasize nursing's holistic focus on patients and nurses' use of a full range of therapeutic, evidence-based modalities to support and augment healing. With its focus on holism and person-centeredness, integrative nursing has much in common with mindfulness and also provided the organization's nurses with an invaluable framework for supporting and practicing interdisciplinary and patient- and family-centered relationship- based care.

Figure 4-1. Integrative Nursing Core Principles

- Human beings are whole systems inseparable from their environments.
- Human beings have an innate capacity for health and well-being.
- Nature has healing and restorative properties that contribute to health and well-being.
- Integrative nursing is person centered and relationship based.
- Integrative nursing practice is informed by evidence and uses the full range of therapeutic modal- ities to support and augment the healing process, moving from the least intensive and invasive to more, depending on need and context.
- Integrative nursing focuses on the health and well-being of caregivers, as well as those they serve.

Note. Based on information from Koithan, 2014.

Summary

Although nurse leaders may identify additional commitments that guide their practice, the six described in this chapter are in many respects foundational. In addition to being timeless, the commitments apply to leaders in every role and practice setting. Taken together, they position leaders to not merely survive, but to flourish and thrive during times of continuous change.

The author would like to thank Beth Kantz, RN, MS, for her writing and editing support.

References

American Association of Critical-Care Nurses. (2016). *AACN standards for establishing and sustaining healthy work environments: A journey to excellence* (2nd ed.). Retrieved from http://www.aacn.org/wd/hwe/docs/hwestandards.pdf

Berwick, D.M., Nolan, T.W., & Whittington, J. (2008). The Triple Aim: Care, health, and cost. *Health Affairs, 27,* 759–769. doi:10.1377/hlthaff.27.3.759

Bohlmeijer, E., Prenger, R., Taal, E., & Cuijpers, P. (2010). The effects of mindfulness-based stress reduction therapy on mental health of adults with a chronic medical disease: A meta-analysis. *Journal of Psychosomatic Research, 68,* 539–544. doi:10.1016/j.jpsychores.2009.10.005

Chiesa, A., & Serretti, A. (2009). Mindfulness-based stress reduction for stress management in healthy people: A review and meta-analysis. *Journal of Alternative and Complementary Medicine, 15,* 593–600. doi:10.1089/acm.2008.0495

Collins, J. (2001). *Good to great: Why some companies make the leap . . . and others don't.* New York, NY: HarperCollins.

Connor, M., Ponte, P.R., & Conway, J. (2002). Multidisciplinary approaches to reducing error and risk in a patient care setting. *Critical Care Nursing Clinics of North America, 14,* 359–367. doi:10.1016/S0899-5885(02)00017-5

Covey, S.M.R. (with Merrill, R.R.). (2006). *The speed of trust: The one thing that changes everything.* New York, NY: Simon & Schuster.

Drenkard, K.N. (2001). Creating a future worth experiencing: Nursing strategic planning in an integrated healthcare delivery system. *Journal of Nursing Administration, 31,* 364–376. doi:10.1097/00005110-200107000-00008

Edmondson, A.C. (2012). Teaming: How organizations learn, innovate, and compete in the knowledge economy. San Francisco, CA: Jossey-Bass.

Foureur, M., Besley, K., Burton, G., Yu, N., & Crisp, J. (2013). Enhancing the resilience of nurses and midwives: Pilot of a mindfulness-based program for increased health, sense of coherence and decreased depression, anxiety and stress. *Contemporary Nurse, 45,* 114–125. doi:10.5172/conu.2013.45.1.114

Goyal, M., Singh, S., Sibinga, E.M.S., Gould, N.F., Rowland-Seymour, A., Sharma, R., … Haythornthwaite, J.A. (2014). Meditation programs for psychological stress and well-being: A systematic review and meta-analysis. *JAMA Internal Medicine, 174,* 357–368. doi:10.1001/jamainternmed.2013.13018

Kabat-Zinn, J. (2012). *Mindfulness for beginners: Reclaiming the present moment—and your life.* Boulder, CO: Sounds True.

Koithan, M. (2014). Concepts and principles of integrative nursing. In M.J. Kreitzer & M. Koithan (Eds.), *Integrative nursing* (pp. 3–16). doi:10.1093/med/9780199860739.003.0001

Langley, G.J., Moen, R.D., Nolan, K.M., Nolan, T.W., Norman, C.L., & Provost, L.P. (2009). *The improvement guide: A practical approach to enhancing organizational performance* (2nd ed.). San Francisco, CA: Jossey-Bass.

Mackenzie, C.S., Poulin, P.A., & Seidman-Carlson, R. (2006). A brief mindfulness-based stress reduction intervention for nurses and nurse aides. *Applied Nursing Research, 19,* 105–109. doi:10.1016/j.apnr.2005.08.002

Moody, K., Kramer, D., Santizo, R.O., Magro, L., Wyshogrod, D., Ambrosio, J., … Stein, J. (2013). Helping the helpers: Mindfulness training for burnout in pediatric oncology—A pilot program. *Journal of Pediatric Oncology Nursing, 30,* 275–284. doi:10.1177/1043454213504497

Nepo, M. (2000). *The book of awakening: Having the life you want by being present to the life you have.* San Francisco, CA: Conari Press.

Pfeffer, J. (2010). *Power: Why some people have it—and others don't.* New York, NY: HarperBusiness.

Ponte, P.R., Berry, D., Buswell, L., Gross, A., Hayes, C., Kostka, J., … West, C. (2016). Transforming oncology care: Developing a strategy and measuring success. *Seminars in Oncology Nursing, 32,* 110–121. doi:10.1016/j.soncn.2016.02.005

Ponte, P.R., & Koppel, P. (2015). Cultivating mindfulness to enhance nursing practice. *American Journal of Nursing, 115*(6), 48–55. doi:10.1097/01.NAJ.0000466321.46439.17

Senge, P.M. (1990). *The fifth discipline: The art and practice of the learning organization.* New York, NY: Currency.

Sikka, R., Morath, J.M., & Leape, L. (2015). The Quadruple Aim: Care, health, cost and meaning in work. *BMJ Quality and Safety, 24,* 608–610. doi:10.1136/bmjqs-2015-004160

Zaleznik, A. (1970, May). Power and politics in organizational life. *Harvard Business Review.* Retrieved from https://hbr.org/1970/05/power-and-politics-in-organizational-life

CHAPTER 5

Leading a Culture of Civility

Dianne M. Jacobs, MSN, RN

A crucial measure of our success in life is the way we treat one another every day of our lives.

—P.M. Forni (2002, p. 4)

Introduction

"Nurses eat their young." Mention this phrase, and most nurses will know exactly what you are talking about. Some will share personal or witnessed experiences. Even student nurses are aware of the behavior and can identify the units in the hospital they should avoid if possible. How can it be that nurses, recognized by the American public as the most trusted and ethical profession (Gallup, 2015), treat each other with such disrespect and unkindness, especially its newest members? This is a paradox the nursing profession has struggled with for a long time and one that has a serious impact on patient safety, the delivery of quality patient care, and the well-being of nurses. Studies in the past two decades link preventable medical errors to a culture of incivility and bullying among nurses and other healthcare providers (Joint Commission, 2008; Kohn, Corrigan, & Donaldson, 2000). Leading a culture of civility has never been more critical than now. This chapter will examine the culture of incivility that exists in nursing, demonstrate steps leaders can take to address such a culture, and recommend strategies to bring qualities of civility into the workplace.

What We Tolerate, We Teach

Lacking consensus, numerous terms are used to describe the behavior, such as incivility, disruptive behavior, horizontal hostility, lateral violence, horizontal violence, and bullying. The distinction with bullying is the existence of a real or perceived power differential between the people involved (Bartholomew, 2014; Vessey, DeMarco, & DiFazio, 2010). Regardless of what we call it, the behavior is toxic and needs to be addressed. Naming it is the first step (Bartholomew,

2014; Griffin & Clark, 2014). Specific behaviors include gossiping, spreading rumors, refusing to assist a colleague, not returning calls, backstabbing, undermining, failing to keep promises, and scapegoating. Many of these behaviors might at first seem to be a result of normal conflict, and not all conflict is bad. Differences of opinion and disagreement often lead to healthier solutions, eliminate bias, improve problem solving, and reach better solutions when the conflict is addressed appropriately. However, the behaviors named here have the opposite effect and can lead to both psychological and physical harm when they are accepted as normal in a work environment (Bartholomew, 2014; Griffin & Clark, 2014; Vessey et al., 2010).

Cynthia Clark's "Continuum of Incivility" illustrates the importance of early detection and intervention to prevent the progression of these negative behaviors to avoid the worst-case scenario of increasing psychological trauma and physical violence (see Figure 5-1).

The most common targets of these behaviors are people new to an area, especially newly licensed nurses, but also experienced nurses who travel between institutions or who float to different units (Bartholomew, 2014; Griffin & Clark, 2014; Upstate Area Health Education Center [AHEC] Lateral Violence in Nursing Project, 2007–2009).

How Did We Get Here?

Most nurses enter the profession for truly altruistic reasons and are very caring. What happens? Culture happens. Health care by nature is hierarchical, and this influences how professionals relate to each other. Research suggests that nurses display characteristics of an oppressed group (Griffin & Clark, 2014; Vessey et al., 2010). Dominated by a medical profession whose values and behaviors are identified as the "right ones," nurses feel powerless to speak up, fearing retaliation and humiliation. Failing to take action, known as *self-silencing*, is behavior attributed to administrators, nurse

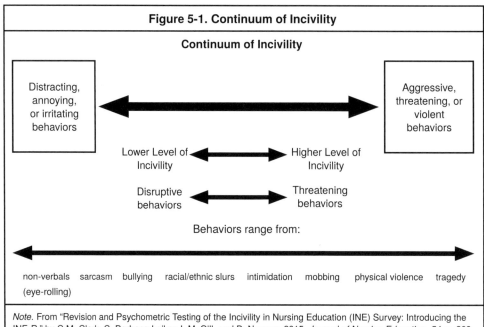

Figure 5-1. Continuum of Incivility

Note. From "Revision and Psychometric Testing of the Incivility in Nursing Education (INE) Survey: Introducing the INE-R," by C.M. Clark, C. Barbosa-Leiker, L.M. Gill, and D. Nguyen, 2015, *Journal of Nursing Education, 54,* p. 309. Copyright 2009 by C.M. Clark; revised 2013, 2014. Reprinted with permission.

managers, and senior nurses that occurs when there is awareness of the problem but it is ignored. This reaction perpetuates nonreporting by staff because of the belief that "nothing is ever done to address the issue, so why risk my involvement?" Not speaking up perpetuates the behavior (American Nurses Association [ANA], 2015b; Bartholomew, 2014; Vessey et al., 2010). Other contributing factors include generational differences, cultural differences, and the highly stressful healthcare environment (Joint Commission, 2008; Kohn et al., 2000; Vessey et al., 2010).

The good news is that the majority of nurses are not perpetrators of the behavior. However, many may witness or fall victim to it. In either situation, the behavior is toxic and can have devastating effects, affecting nurses' ability to be fully present and engaged in the care of their patients. Research shows that simply witnessing rude behavior significantly impairs our ability to perform cognitive tasks (Porath & Erez, 2007). Distraction and disengagement are integrally linked to unsafe practices and preventable medical errors (Joint Commission, 2008; Kohn et al., 2000; Porath & Erez, 2007).

Field Testing and Lessons Learned

Lateral Violence Among Nurses—Let's Get Rid of It! (Upstate AHEC Lateral Violence in Nursing Project, 2007–2009), a federally funded practice grant, provided training to more than 3,000 nurses, nurse managers, student nurses, and faculty to recognize and address lateral violence. Feedback from program participants revealed that lateral violence behavior existed in every participating hospital and school of nursing and confirmed that anyone new to a unit, particularly newly licensed nurses, were most often the victims and the experienced nurses most likely the perpetrators. The behavior was rarely reported, and the most common reaction by management was to ignore it. Many of the participants had been victims of the behavior, and almost all had witnessed it at some point in their career. Their stories revealed the disruptive, and even devastating, effects these toxic behaviors have on the well-being of nurses and their ability to care for patients (Upstate AHEC Lateral Violence in Nursing Project, 2007–2009).

Strategies for Promoting Civility in the Workplace

Be the change. Despite the pervasive existence of incivility in health care, change is possible and begins with you and your commitment to do what is necessary to create a culture of civility. Start by taking an honest look at your own behavior. Even the best of us have behaviors or habits we can improve. Use the principles of civility as your guide: respect, empathy, flexibility, cultural sensitivity, authenticity, and a genuine care for self and others (Forni, 2002). Align personal leadership skills with the ANA Code of Ethics (ANA, 2015a).

Ask for feedback from your team. This includes what they like best about your leadership style and what they would like more of. Be authentic. Be visible. These behaviors demonstrate your commitment to real, positive change. As a leader in your organization, your behavior sets the tone and significantly influences the behaviors of others. Civility is leadership.

Identify the existing culture. An important step for creating sustainable change is to identify the existing culture. This can be accomplished by conducting a formal workplace environment survey such as the American Association of Critical-Care Nurses (AACN) Healthy Work Environment Assessment Tool (AACN, n.d.). Also, a simple survey such as the Culture of Regard can provide a snapshot of the culture of a unit or team (Bartholomew, 2014).

Be proactive. Set zero-tolerance expectations. Uncivil behavior needs to be addressed as vigorously as any other identified threat to patient and employee safety. Training is necessary to recognize and address incivility when it occurs and should be part of onboarding for new employees, as well as annual competency review once everyone is trained. Classes need to include a definition of the behavior, discussion of its impact, identification of professional behavioral standards, a commitment to make necessary changes, and practice with a communication model for directly addressing the behavior when it occurs. Creating a "Commitment to My Coworkers" during the class is an effective way to identify professional behavioral standards and unify staff (Bartholomew, 2014). Practicing the communication model is integral to hardwiring this critical skill and the success of creating a culture of civility (Griffin & Clark, 2014). To reinforce training and hardwire the technique, include crucial conversation examples, such as addressing gossip or inappropriate communication and behaviors and other scenarios offered by the group, at the beginning of each staff meeting for at least a year.

Address the behaviors before and when they occur. A culture of civility requires nurses to be as proficient in relational skills, especially skilled communication, as they are in technical skills (AACN, 2012; Griffin & Clark, 2014). Skilled communication allows for open conversation, civil discourse, and conflict resolution. As illustrated by Clark's Continuum of Incivility, ignoring uncivil behavior can lead to serious consequences. Both staff and leaders need to be prepared to respond when confronted with uncivil behavior just as they would for any situation that threatens the safety of patients and staff. Merely speaking up can stop the behavior (Griffin & Clark, 2014). Rehearsing responses before you need them is key to success and should be introduced in the initial education session. Cognitive rehearsal, or practicing saying the words out loud as if you were talking directly to the person, allows for building "muscle memory" and the confidence to respond in emotionally charged interactions with a colleague (Griffin & Clark, 2014).

This can be done through role play and simulation tools. Using an assertive communication technique, such as the DESC Assertive Communication Model (Bower & Bower, 2004), participants construct responses to scenarios of uncivil behaviors. The four steps of the model are as follows:

- **Describe** the situation: "Jane, I overheard you tell Sallie I must be the manager's pet because I always get the schedule I request."
- **Express** feelings and **explore** intent: "It felt like a put-down and I was embarrassed. Was that your intent?" [Pause.] Most likely the person will deny the intent, but proceed anyway.
- **Specify** what you want to happen: "Well, it felt like one to me. Please don't do that again."
- State the positive **consequences** of working together to solve the issue: "It is important that we be able to work as a team. Have you spoken with the manager about your schedule?"

Once everyone has been trained, continue to hardwire this important skill by practicing examples in staff meetings and include them in annual competency review. There is even a board game, called *Can We Talk?* (Upstate AHEC, 2007), for practicing scenarios. Just talking about the behavior and giving it a name brings hope that something will be done. Dedicating time for practice builds confidence and gets results. Establishing respectful, professional communication competency in all healthcare environments is essential for better outcomes for patients and the well-being of nurses (AACN, 2016; Griffin & Clark, 2014). Another resource is the book *Crucial Conversations* (Patterson, Grenny, McMillan, & Switzler, 2012). This book has practical tips and tools on how to talk with someone when the situation is important for strengthening relationships and improving productivity.

Primary prevention: Hire for civility. One of the most effective ways to maintain and support a culture of civility is to hire civil people. Thoroughly check references. Gather as much information as possible from reliable sources in addition to the ones provided by the candidate

(Pearson & Porath, 2005). Use behavioral interviewing techniques and professional behavioral standards to measure performance during the interview and the probationary period before hiring. Listen to personal intuition and get feedback from staff.

Stay vigilant. Even with a zero-tolerance policy and proactive hiring for civility, there will be employees who refuse to get on board. Noncompliance with established norms and professional behavioral standards must be addressed in a timely manner and apply to everyone regardless of position and power in the organization. Behaviors need to be well documented. Policies and procedures must be in place for appropriate disciplinary action, including firing the employee (Pearson & Porath, 2005). No one gets a "pass" on patient safety.

Reward excellence. To maintain a culture of civility, it is important to recognize and reward employees who model civility. Ask them what type of recognition makes them feel appreciated. Although monetary rewards are most often at the top of the list, personal recognition, such as a handwritten note or "lunch with the boss," is a close second (Pearson & Porath, 2005). One of the most impactful actions as a leader is to give genuine, specific feedback that recognizes and praises excellence.

Summary

Be the change. Embrace the journey. Incivility among healthcare providers has been integrally linked to preventable medical errors and higher costs of health care and threatens the well-being of nurses. Change is possible. Dr. Forni is right: "A crucial measure of our success in life is the way we treat one another every day of our lives" (Forni, 2002, p. 4). An adage derived from the teachings of Mahatma Gandhi is to "be the change that you wish to see in the world," while Mary Gullatte said, "Live the change you wish to see in the workplace and lead others." Are you willing to do what is necessary to lead a culture of civility? If so, your staff will follow.

References

American Association of Critical-Care Nurses. (n.d.). AACN healthy work environment assessment tool. Retrieved from https://www.aacn.org/nursing-excellence/healthy-work-environments/aacn-healthy-work-environment-assessment-tool

American Association of Critical-Care Nurses. (2016). *AACN standards for establishing and sustaining healthy work environments: A journey to excellence (2nd ed.): Executive summary.* Retrieved from https://www.aacn.org/-/media/aacn-website/nursing-excellence/healthy-work-environment/execsum.pdf?la=en

American Nurses Association. (2015a). *Code of ethics for nurses with interpretive statements.* Silver Spring, MD: Author.

American Nurses Association. (2015b). Incivility, bullying, and workplace violence [Position statement]. Retrieved from http://www.nursingworld.org/Bullying-Workplace-Violence

Bartholomew, K. (2014). *Ending nurse-to-nurse hostility: Why nurses eat their young and each other* (2nd ed.). Danvers, MA: HCPro.

Bower, S.A., & Bower, G.H. (2004). *Asserting yourself: A practical guide for positive change* (Updated ed.). Cambridge, MA: Da Capo Press.

Forni, P.M. (2002). *Choosing civility: The twenty-five rules of considerate conduct.* New York, NY: St. Martin's Press.

Gallup. (2015). Honesty/ethics in professions. Retrieved from http://www.gallup.com/poll/1654/honesty-ethics-professions.aspx

Griffin, M., & Clark, C.M. (2014). Revisiting cognitive rehearsal as an intervention against incivility and lateral violence in nursing: 10 years later. *Journal of Continuing Education in Nursing, 45,* 535–542. doi:10.3928/00220124-20141122-02

Joint Commission. (2008, July 9). *Sentinel event alert: Behaviors that undermine a culture of safety.* Retrieved from https://www.jointcommission.org/assets/1/18/SEA_40.PDF

Kohn, L.T., Corrigan, J.M., & Donaldson, M.S. (Eds.). (2000). *To err is human: Building a safer health system.* Washington, DC: National Academies Press.

Patterson, K., Grenny, J., McMillan, R., & Switzler, R. (2012). *Crucial conversations: Tools for talking when stakes are high* (2nd ed.). New York, NY: McGraw-Hill.

Pearson, C.M., & Porath, C.L. (2005). On the nature, consequences and remedies of workplace incivility: No time for "nice"? Think again. *Academy of Management Perspectives, 19*(1), 7–18. doi:10.5465/ame.2005.15841946

Porath, C.L., & Erez, A. (2007). Does rudeness really matter? The effects of rudeness on task performance and helpfulness. *Academy of Management Journal, 50,* 1181–1197. doi:10.2307/20159919

Upstate Area Health Education Center. (2007). *Can we talk? Lateral violence training toolkit.* Retrieved from http://www.upstateahec.org

Upstate Area Health Education Center Lateral Violence in Nursing Project (C. Luciano, PD). (2007–2009). Department of Health and Human Services, Health Resources and Services Administration, Bureau of Health Professions, Nurse Education, Practice and Retention grant (Award No. D11HP08361).

Vessey, J.A., DeMarco, R., & DiFazio, R. (2010). Bullying, harassment, and horizontal violence in the nursing workforce: The state of the science. *Annual Review of Nursing Research, 28,* 133–157. doi:10.1891/0739-6686.28.133

CHAPTER 6

Leading and Sustaining a Healthy Work Environment

Mary Bylone, RN, MSM, CNML, and Vicki Good, DNP, RN, CENP, CPPS

> *In the long run there is no more liberating, no more exhilarating experience than to determine one's position, state it bravely, and then act boldly. Action brings with it its own courage, its own energy, a growth of self-confidence that can be acquired in no other way.*
>
> —Eleanor Roosevelt, *Tomorrow Is Now*

Introduction

Research, technologic advances, and change in the healthcare environment continue to proliferate at a rate greater than ever predicted with the goal of delivering safer, higher quality care. As healthcare settings implement the latest technology, often the fundamental elements critical for leading and sustaining a healthy work environment (HWE) are given less priority. Since the release of the *To Err Is Human* report (Kohn, Corrigan, & Donaldson, 2000), healthcare institutions and professionals have strived to establish a culture that supports safe and high-quality care. The American Association of Critical-Care Nurses (AACN) conducted a study on the critical care work environment in 2008. The findings were concerning in that most nurses described a work environment hampered by poor communication, lack of teamwork, staffing concerns, and moral distress. In 2013, a follow-up study was performed and, unfortunately, the findings indicated that the environment had further declined (Ulrich et al., 2006, 2009; Ulrich, Lavandero, Woods, & Early, 2014). These findings were validated by a group of healthcare leaders in 2015 assembled by the National Patient Safety Foundation. The leaders declared that health care had made small progress toward the efforts of improved safety and quality primarily related to lack of establishing and sustaining a culture and work environment that supports healthcare clinicians (National Patient Safety Foundation, 2015).

In the resource-constrained healthcare environment, is devoting resources to leading and sustaining an HWE of value? Absolutely. Research has linked the effects of a poor working environment and culture to negative patient outcomes such as length of stay, mortality rates, and hospital-acquired conditions (Aiken et al., 2011; Huang et al., 2010; Kelly, Kutney-Lee, Lake, & Aiken, 2013; Laschinger & Leiter, 2006; Rossi & Edmiston, 2012). Additionally, lack of an HWE has negative consequences to nurses' overall health. Nurses working in unhealthy work environments have demonstrated higher rates of burnout, lower retention rates to their position and the profession, and higher rates of moral distress (Lucian Leape Institute, 2013; Rushton, Batcheller, Schroeder, & Donohue, 2015; Sacco, Ciurzynski, Harvey, & Ingersoll, 2015; Ulrich et al., 2014).

In response to these overwhelming concerns with the goal of providing safe and high-quality care to critical care patients, AACN published standards for establishment of an HWE in 2005 and updated the standards in 2015. AACN defined six fundamental standards for establishing and sustaining HWEs (see Figure 6-1). The standards are merely the foundation for creating an HWE. Nurse leaders also must consider clinical practice, patient outcomes, and regulatory requirements to ensure an optimal environment (AACN, 2016; Good, 2009).

The six standards are interdependent and rarely stand alone. For example, to have effective decision making, competencies within skilled communication must be mastered. Therefore, all standards should be considered essential, none more important than another. By embracing all six standards, the likelihood of enhancing clinical excellence and achieving optimal patient outcomes increases (AACN, 2016; Good, 2009) (see Figure 6-2).

As healthcare leaders, leading and sustaining an HWE must be a key priority. This chapter will review methods to assess the existing healthcare environment, implementation strategies for each of the standards, and conclude with information on how to monitor the journey to an HWE.

Creating a Healthy Workplace

As discussed earlier, over the past few decades, small steps of progress have occurred in creating a healthy workplace. To accelerate changes, progressive actions must occur. However, giving up the past, even when it is not producing desired results, is far more difficult for some than continuing doing what they have always done and complaining about

---

Figure 6-1. American Association of Critical-Care Nurses Standards for Establishing and Sustaining Healthy Work Environments

- Skilled communication: Nurses must be as proficient in communication skills as they are in clinical skills.
- True collaboration: Nurses must be relentless in pursuing and fostering true collaboration.
- Effective decision making: Nurses must be valued and committed partners in making policy, directing and evaluating clinical care, and leading organizational operations.
- Appropriate staffing: Staffing must ensure the effective match between patient needs and nurse competencies.
- Meaningful recognition: Nurses must be recognized and must recognize others for the value each brings to the work of the organization.
- Authentic leadership: Nurse leaders must fully embrace the imperative of a healthy work environment, authentically live it, and engage others in its achievement.

Note. From *AACN Standards for Establishing and Sustaining Healthy Work Environments: A Journey to Excellence* (2nd ed., p. 10), by American Association of Critical-Care Nurses, 2016, Aliso Viejo, CA: Author. Copyright 2016 by American Association of Critical-Care Nurses. Reprinted with permission.

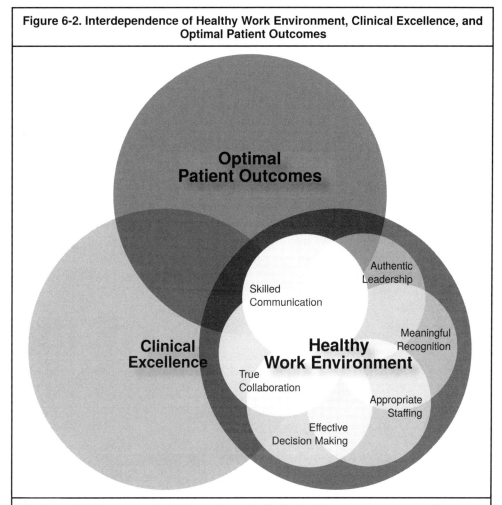

Figure 6-2. Interdependence of Healthy Work Environment, Clinical Excellence, and Optimal Patient Outcomes

Optimal Patient Outcomes

Clinical Excellence

Healthy Work Environment

Skilled Communication

Authentic Leadership

Meaningful Recognition

True Collaboration

Appropriate Staffing

Effective Decision Making

Note. From *AACN Standards for Establishing and Sustaining Healthy Work Environments: A Journey to Excellence* (2nd ed., p. 11), by American Association of Critical-Care Nurses, 2016, Aliso Viejo, CA: Author. Copyright 2016 by American Association of Critical-Care Nurses. Reprinted with permission.

the results or hoping for better days. Remember, hope is not a strategy. Making changes requires tremendous effort and stamina, and it is a journey best begun by identifying a reason to do it differently this time. The decision to break the cycle of the past can come from many sources. It can be leader led or come from the team members, or it may be an obvious solution discovered when reviewing an untoward event. There is rarely one clear event that sparks the need to take a step in the direction of creating a healthier workplace. Many times, action does not take place until the accumulation of toxicity reaches a point where people are leaving, morale is low, and patients suffer. A breakdown in communication occurs. People use positions of power to influence others and decisions are made without enough information or the necessary voices at the table.

In contrast, other organizations have foundations for a healthy workplace in place and the team wants to make it better yet. Any of these scenarios, whether coming from a need to end a suboptimal situation or to improve upon existing success, all start by identifying opportunities.

The process is best accomplished by observing the current health of the workplace and comparing it to the desired work environment.

Gap Analysis

Performing a gap analysis of the work environment can provide the leader with the information necessary to inspire others to try a new approach. When done correctly, it uses the data to answer most people's initial reaction to change: "But this is the way we have always done it. Why should we do it differently now?" Let those words inspire the leader or team member to bravely move forward. After all, when the work environment is a healthy one, everyone is the winner; patients, families, nurses, organizations, insurance companies, and society are all in a better place when everyone is working toward a common goal, built on evidence-based practice and teamwork. Getting people to agree on the areas presenting opportunities may be more challenging. Tools are available to perform a gap analysis. AACN (n.d.) provides a tool specific for assessing the health of the workplace. The beauty of the tool is that it is web-based and anonymous and produces a report with suggested resources for working on the weaker areas. The foundation of the tool is the six AACN (2016) standards for building and sustaining an HWE: skilled communication, true collaboration, effective decision making, appropriate staffing, meaningful recognition, and authentic leadership. The assessment tool can be used for a single unit or an organizationwide assessment. Whatever tool is selected, use it to begin the journey and repeat it again after some great work has been accomplished. It will provide an assessment of the efforts and help leaders to better understand if adjustments need to be made or if the current plan is hitting the mark and should continue with little change.

Leading and Sustaining a Healthy Workplace

The completed gap analysis is a crucial step in understanding what is and is not working within the work environment. It provides information to prioritize and focus as the plan is implemented. This is key moving forward. Sometimes, energies can be directed to improve things that are already working and trying to take them to the next level. Because a healthy workplace is so important to patient outcomes, beginning efforts must be directed to the areas in need of the most improvement. The AACN HWE standards work together, not in isolation. Although a unit might score very high in a few of the standards, if there are areas in need of work, the total unit does not benefit from the average of the good and the not-so-good. The areas in need of improvement, if not addressed, will chip away at the behaviors that were once outstanding.

Priorities of focus are best placed on the areas with the largest opportunity for improvement. Once opportunities are identified, going about making changes to improve the environment is the next step. Again, many choices may be present. For example, if a unit has an equal opportunity identified in skilled communication and meaningful recognition, the unit must decide whether to address one opportunity at a time or both at the same time. Regardless of the decision, the first step is to take the report, celebrate the successes, identify the opportunities, and figure out how to make it better. If the AACN tool is used, the report will be broken into six categories aligning with each of the standards. One of two ideas can be used. One method is to make the lowest-scoring area the focus of the next few months of work and convene a team to meet and discuss strategies for improvement. It will take approximately four to six months, perhaps even longer, to make meaningful headway in changing behaviors. The other method is to assemble several teams and assign a low-scoring standard to each of the teams so that the work happens in parallel instead of sequentially. Which method to choose can depend on the amount of resources available for this project and the number of standards in need of work. Another consideration would involve the situation where one standard is far below the others, which are clumped together in the results. As discussed earlier, success in creating a healthy workplace does not lie in the averaging of scores but in bringing all the scores up to a satisfactory level. This concept bears additional thought. The goal is not mediocrity. Settling for good enough or average will not create a workplace where people feel valued and patients achieve optimal outcomes. Average workplaces do not attract and retain talented staff, nor do they wow patients with extraordinary care. Units working on reaching HWEs are aiming for an A+, not a B.

The leader should also consider opportunities to assign frontline staff in the leadership role to influence change in the work environment. Managing teams of peers can be challenging, and, in some instances, these teams will also include physicians and administrators, depending on the opportunities that arise in the gap analysis. Not every frontline staff member has the desire or skills to lead teams. If frontline staff leadership on the unit is limited, the number of teams that can be active at any given time may need to be adjusted to the leadership resources available at the time. The desire to lead the team is key. Some staff may see that the path to success requires quite a bit of rocking the boat on the status quo and may decide to opt out. The desired frontline leader will possess effective communication skills, ability to hold crucial conversations, project management skills, and a desire to hold the team accountable to the defined team outcomes. With a team led by a person who does not possess effective leadership skills, results may be delayed or absent. In instances where frontline staff leadership is immature or absent, the formal unit leader will need to take on the role of team lead.

When the HWE standards were developed, the authors believed that no one standard was more important than another and that each standard had equal importance in the health of the work environment (AACN, 2016). However, it is easy to see that without skilled communication, it will be hard to have true collaboration on teams, to embrace data for effective decision making, to provide meaningful recognition, or to be an authentic leader. If the assessment identifies skilled communication as a weakness, it is logical to begin working on that aspect of the environment.

Once priorities have been established, it helps to select some of the lighter-lifting projects to begin. Determining the opportunity, putting a plan in place, and achieving success will give the team a great start. When these tasks can be accomplished in a short time, it enables the team to celebrate an early win, which can inspire others to join in and catapult the team to the next milestone. It might seem like a good idea to take on the biggest problem at the start; however, it is better to leave that one until later. Get some wins on the chart. Increase engagement from other team members and build enthusiasm. Additionally, using visible signs to plot progress and provide recognition goes a long way to keeping people involved in moving forward, as some of the necessary changes can take six months or more.

Keeping team members engaged over the longer haul can be challenging. There are many avenues to engaging teams. Engagement and communication methods can range from simple bulletin boards to several electronic methods. Perhaps posting the problem standards along with a bulleted list of suggested solutions will help to keep everyone aware of the work being done and the progress being made. Another great visual is a large poster with a pledge by all staff (nurses and non-nurse team members) to participate in building a healthy workplace. Many electronic tools are available to engage team members. Examples include blogs that discuss opportunities, shared websites where team members can discuss opportunities, and social media sites established for the team to engage with one another.

Many medical associations and other healthcare organizations, including the Joint Commission, have endorsed the AACN standards for an HWE. Having a physician show engagement through endorsing the commitment statement or participating in communication sites sends a loud and clear message to staff. Do not forget to include administration. The buy-in for success needs to come from and be supported at all levels in the organization. That is when real change can take place.

Healthy Work Environment Standards

Skilled Communication

Per the HWE standards, nurses must be as proficient in communication skills as they are in clinical skills (AACN, 2016) (see Figure 6-3). The clinical environment often does not support this principle, as greater time is spent ensuring competency in clinical skills versus competency in communication. Communication occurs in many forms, including written, spoken, and nonverbal, as well as silence. Silence is the most challenging and often has the highest consequences (Maxfield, Grenny, Lavandero, & Groah, 2010; Maxfield, Grenny, McMillan, Patterson, & Switzler, 2005). Silence plagues the work environment, primarily related to fear due to lack of respectful, effective communication (Lucian Leape Institute, 2013; Ulrich et al., 2014).

Figure 6-3. Critical Elements of Skilled Communication

- The health care organization provides team members with support for and access to interprofessional education and coaching that develop critical communication skills, including self-awareness, inquiry/dialogue, conflict management, negotiation, advocacy, and listening.
- Nurses and all other team members are accountable for identifying personal learning and professional growth needs related to communication skills.
- Skilled communicators focus on finding solutions and achieving desirable outcomes.
- Skilled communicators seek to protect and advance collaborative relationships among colleagues.
- Skilled communicators invite and hear all relevant perspectives.
- Skilled communicators call upon goodwill and mutual respect to build consensus and arrive at common understanding.
- Skilled communicators demonstrate congruence between words and actions, holding others accountable for doing the same.
- Skilled communicators have access to appropriate communication technologies and are proficient in their use.
- Skilled communicators seek input on their communication styles and strive to continually improve.
- The health care organization establishes zero-tolerance policies and enforces them to address and eliminate abuse and disrespectful behavior in the workplace.
- The health care organization establishes formal structures and processes that ensure effective and respectful information sharing among patients, families, and the health care team.
- The health care organization establishes systems that require individuals and teams to formally evaluate the impact of communication on clinical and financial outcomes, and the work environment.
- The health care organization includes communication as a criterion in its formal performance appraisal system, and team members demonstrate skilled communication to qualify for professional advancement.

Note. From *AACN Standards for Establishing and Sustaining Healthy Work Environments: A Journey to Excellence* (2nd ed., p. 14), by American Association of Critical-Care Nurses, 2016, Aliso Viejo, CA: Author. Copyright 2016 by American Association of Critical-Care Nurses. Reprinted with permission.

Silence must be addressed by establishing a culture that supports psychological safety of staff when they speak up and equipping nurses with the skills to effectively communicate. An environment where a nurse knows that leadership support will be given when critical events must be addressed leads to psychological safety for the nurse. Psychological safety is built after time, and trust develops when consistent support is given to bedside clinicians (Drescher, Korsgaard, Welpe, Picot, & Wigand, 2014). Effective communication is most successful when standardized communication approaches are used to ensure consistent message delivery and when focus on crucial conversations occurs between team members. Use of standardized tools gives every team member the same framework and methodology. Unfortunately, each discipline within the healthcare environment is educated differently. This often leads to challenges when communicating key concerns. Including the entire interprofessional team during training, team meetings, and simulation exercises allows team members to better understand one another and provides opportunities to discuss and clarify language differences.

Communication is a cycle in which information is sent by one person to another individual or group and the message is correctly received. Effective communication should be complete, clear, brief, and timely (Agency for Healthcare Research and Quality [AHRQ], n.d.). In the chaotic healthcare environment, disruptions occur, interrupting the communication cycle and resulting in communication failures. To ensure skilled communication, TeamSTEPPS® 2.0, which was developed by AHRQ and the Department of Defense, addresses overall team performance, including strategies to enhance team communication. Instructor training, content, teaching materials, and cases studies are all available free of charge from the TeamSTEPPS 2.0 website (www.ahrq.gov/teamstepps/index.html) for use by any healthcare system.

The four strategies suggested by AHRQ (n.d.) to standardize communication are SBAR, callout, check-back, and handoffs. SBAR (Situation, Background, Assessment, Recommendation) provides a standardized method for the healthcare team to communicate crucial information (see Figure 6-4). An "i" has been added at the beginning of SBAR (iSBAR), which represents making an introduction before the SBAR conversation begins. By using a standardized approach, key information is communicated. Research has demonstrated improvements in information communicated, as well as overall safety culture, when SBAR is consistently used (Randmaa, Mårtensson, Swenne, & Engström, 2014).

The second strategy recommended is the callout (AHRQ, n.d.). This is used in urgent or emergent situations to ensure all information is communicated to the team. During intense situations, often the team assumes to know the next step or assumes a step has been completed in the process. When assumptions are made, mistakes are made. During the callout, the team members verbalize every critical piece of information even when the information may seem obvious.

The third strategy recommended to ensure skilled communication is the check-back (AHRQ, n.d.). The check-back ensures closed-loop communication. Remembering that communication is when information transfers from the sender to receiver, an opportunity needs to exist to ensure that the receiver comprehended the message sent. During the check-back process, the sender sends the

---

Figure 6-4. Elements of iSBAR

i: Introductions
S: Situation—What is happening with the patient?
B: Background—What is the clinical background?
A: Assessment—What do I think the problem is?
R: Recommendation—What would I recommend?

Note. Based on information from Agency for Healthcare Research and Quality, 2013.

message and the receiver receives the information, and the receiver then checks back with the sender, closing the communication loop when the receiver verbalizes the intended message. For example: During a phone conversation, the leader states that she will change the RN's scheduled day off to Friday, and the RN closes the communication loop by stating, "My day off will now be Friday."

The last strategy to improve skilled communication in health care is the handoff (AHRQ, n.d.). An effective handoff must include an opportunity to ask questions to clarify the message and confirm receipt of the information. Nurse leaders must ensure effective handoffs in all transitions of care of patients (e.g., shift to shift, transfer to a different department, transfer to an outside facility). Handoffs remain an area of concern for all providers. Methods for effective handoffs have included checklists, electronic medical record forms, and prepopulated lists. Each facility must develop a handoff method that works best for its environment and culture.

Healthcare conversations are frequently considered "crucial" because of high stakes, hierarchical boundaries, and emotional content. According to VitalSmarts (Maxfield et al., 2005), a conversation is considered crucial when a discussion occurs between two or more individuals, stakes are high, opinions vary, and emotions run strong. This definition aligns closely with the complex healthcare environment. Seven areas that affect crucial conversations include broken rules, mistakes, lack of support, incompetence, poor teamwork, disrespect, and micromanagement (Maxfield et al., 2005). Addressing these areas can be even more challenging when nurses are faced with hierarchical differences when advocating for their patients or themselves. When these areas arise, the environment must be conducive to allow open communication to prevent negative outcomes to the patients or nurses. VitalSmarts (www.vitalsmarts.com) provides numerous resources including books, research, and structured training for teams to develop strong communication skills surrounding crucial conversations. Refer to Chapter 8 for more information on communication strategies.

True Collaboration

Nurses must be relentless in pursuing and fostering true collaboration. True collaboration is a process that is developed over time (see Figure 6-5). Collaboration can only occur once skilled communication, trust, and respect are established within the team. Collaboration is a process whereby individuals and groups come together to make plans and decisions for the betterment of patient care (Muller-Juge et al., 2013). In 2011, the Interprofessional Education Collaborative (IPEC) Expert Panel convened to define competencies for interprofessional collaborative practice. In today's complex healthcare environment, interprofessional teams must work collaboratively to meet the needs of patients. In 2003, the Institute of Medicine (now called the Health and Medicine Division of the National Academies of Sciences, Engineering, and Medicine) defined key processes in teamwork, which included communication, cooperation, coordination, and collaboration, but the key competencies were not defined. The IPEC Expert Panel (2016) advanced the work on collaboration by defining the key competencies to ensure effective collaboration. The competencies include providing a climate of mutual respect and shared values, roles and responsibilities to address the care needs of patients and to promote health of populations, interprofessional communication, and teams and teamwork. Underpinning these competencies is the ability to form positive relationships.

The IPEC competencies provide a framework for initial and ongoing curriculum content, as well as a collaborative framework for patient care. Despite a defined framework, translation of the framework in the clinical care setting is not consistently realized. Role confusion and lack of shared goals for patient care lead to diminished teamwork among healthcare team members (Muller-Juge et al., 2013). Research conducted by Muller-Juge et al. (2013) demonstrated that nursing and hospital resident physicians had conflicting perceptions of each discipline's roles,

---

Figure 6-5. Critical Elements of True Collaboration

- The health care organization provides team members with support for and access to interprofessional education and coaching that develop collaboration skills.
- The health care organization creates, uses, and evaluates processes that define each team member's accountability for collaboration and how unwillingness to collaborate will be addressed.
- The health care organization creates, uses, and evaluates operational structures that ensure the decision-making authority of nurses is acknowledged and incorporated into the norm.
- The health care organization ensures unrestricted access to structured forums, such as ethics committees, and makes available the time and resources needed to resolve disputes among all critical participants, including patients, families, and the health care team.
- Every team member embraces true collaboration as an ongoing process and invests in its development to ensure a sustained culture of collaboration.
- Every team member contributes to the achievement of common goals by giving power and respect to each person's voice, integrating individual differences, resolving competing interests, and safeguarding the essential contribution each makes in order to achieve optimal outcomes.
- Every team member acts with a high level of personal integrity and holds others accountable for doing the same.
- Team members master skilled communication, an essential element of true collaboration.
- Each team member demonstrates competence appropriate to his or her role and responsibilities.
- Nurse and physician leaders are equal partners in modeling and fostering true collaboration.

Note. From *AACN Standards for Establishing and Sustaining Healthy Work Environments: A Journey to Excellence* (2nd ed., p. 18), by American Association of Critical-Care Nurses, 2016, Aliso Viejo, CA: Author. Copyright 2016 by American Association of Critical-Care Nurses. Reprinted with permission.

---

responsibilities, and patient care goals, hindering their ability to work as a unified team. Similar findings were discovered by Chong, Aslani, and Chen (2013), with the addition that the healthcare team struggles on how to effectively collaborate with the patient.

Three primary forms of collaboration are needed to foster an HWE. First, strong *nurse-to-physician* collaboration must exist. Demonstration of positive nurse–physician relationships through mutual respect and collaboration leads to nurse retention and empowerment (Leape et al., 2012a, 2012b). The second form of collaboration needed is *nurse-to-nurse*. Collaboration between nurses is essential from the bedside to the leader's office. When nurses at the bedside have relationships that facilitate nurse–nurse collaboration, nurses are more confident in decision making (Bucknall, 2003). Despite the synergy that can be achieved with nurse–nurse collaboration, disrespectful behavior between bedside nurses continues to exist. Lastly, collaboration must exist between the *nurse and the patient and family*. Positive patient outcomes such as decreased length of stay, increased patient satisfaction, and decreased comorbid conditions result in the presence of strong collaboration between the patient, family, and healthcare staff (Revta, 2004).

Collaboration does not just occur; it must be developed. Structured methods are needed to bring the team together to foster the collaborative relationship. Two tools in the TeamSTEPPS 2.0 program facilitate teamwork and collaboration: briefing and huddling. Briefing is a tool used to develop both short- and long-term plans with the team to ensure that goals are understood throughout the team and that all roles are identified and defined. Briefings can be used at scheduled times or as needed. For example, the operating room may elect to conduct a briefing before every case. During the briefing, the entire team introduces themselves and the role and responsibilities they will have during the case; the surgeon discusses any potential issues he or she may expect; and the team makes plans for how the case will proceed and the resources needed to complete the case (AHRQ, n.d.). The key to effective briefings is efficiency—most should be performed within one minute.

A huddle differs slightly from the briefing, as the huddle is used when adjustments to the existing plan of care need to be made because of changes within the team, patient condition, or resource allocation. During the huddle, a team leader is designated who facilitates collaboration within the team to raise situational awareness and determine how adjustments need to be made to meet patient needs. For example, in the middle of the shift, an RN becomes ill and needs to leave, and three admissions are due to arrive from the postanesthesia care unit in the next 90 minutes. The charge nurse calls a huddle with the team to establish a plan of action to ensure that all patients receive the care needed (AHRQ, n.d.). Use of both briefings and huddles has resulted in reduced interruptions, prevention of errors and harm, increased empowerment, and overall facilitation of collaboration (Goldenhar, Brady, Sutcliffe, & Muething, 2013; Jain, Jones, Simon, & Patterson, 2015; Ricci & Brumsted, 2012). Read more about team collaboration in Chapter 10.

Effective Decision Making

The third AACN standard emphasizes that nurses must be valued partners in making policy, directing and evaluating clinical care, and leading organizational operations in making effective decisions (AACN, 2016) (see Figure 6-6). Effective decision making is linked to several of the other HWE standards. To have effective decision making within the healthcare setting, the team must have skilled communication and respectful collaboration for success (van Schaik, O'Brien, Almeida, & Adler, 2014). The complexity of the healthcare environment continues to magnify, which necessitates that all clinicians work collaboratively to make the most effective decisions to support cost-effective, high-quality patient care.

Shared leadership principles have shown positive impact on effective decision making and positive patient outcomes across health care. Initially, shared leadership focused on nurses affecting key decisions on the unit. Research demonstrated that nurses who participate in decision making within their units are more likely to have higher job satisfaction and higher retention rates (Choi, Bakken, Larson, Du, & Stone, 2004). Recently, application of shared leadership has expanded to the entire interprofessional team across all levels of the organization.

Figure 6-6. Critical Elements of Effective Decision Making

- The health care organization clearly articulates organizational values, and team members incorporate these values when making decisions.
- The health care organization ensures that nurses in positions from the bedside to the boardroom participate in all levels of decision making.
- The health care organization provides team members with support for and access to ongoing interprofessional education and development programs focusing on strategies that ensure collaborative decision making. Program content includes mutual goal setting, negotiation, facilitation, conflict management, systems thinking, and performance improvement.
- The health care organization has operational structures in place that ensure the perspectives of patients and their families are incorporated into decisions affecting patient care.
- Individual team members share accountability for effective decision making by acquiring necessary skills, mastering relevant content, assessing situations accurately, sharing fact-based information, communicating opinions clearly, and inquiring actively.
- The health care organization establishes systems, such as structured forums involving appropriate departments and health care professions, to facilitate data-driven decisions.
- The health care organization establishes deliberate decision-making processes that ensure respect for the rights of every individual, incorporate all key perspectives, and designate clear accountability.
- The health care organization has fair and effective processes in place at all levels to objectively evaluate the results of decisions, including delayed decisions and indecision.

Note. From *AACN Standards for Establishing and Sustaining Healthy Work Environments: A Journey to Excellence* (2nd ed., p. 22), by American Association of Critical-Care Nurses, 2016, Aliso Viejo, CA: Author. Copyright 2016 by American Association of Critical-Care Nurses. Reprinted with permission.

To ensure success, interprofessional teams should be given specific expectations and desired outcomes. For many team members, being a part of a decision-making body and reaching a consensus is a new experience and skill for development. Within the team, leadership responsibilities may change from one task to the next based on the skills and competency needed for the leader. When teams are asked to come together to make shared decisions, the overall effectiveness of the team increases, leading to optimal patient outcomes and high team satisfaction (Drescher et al., 2014; Mathieu, Kukenberger, D'Innocenzo, & Reilly, 2015; Wang, Waldman, & Zhang, 2014).

To facilitate team effectiveness, structure is a must. Teams should have designated times to meet in person with an established meeting agenda and goals. Bringing the team together to meet face-to-face, versus relying on conference calls or emails, facilitates skilled communication and collaboration, leading to more effective consensus building and team decision making (Bergman, Rentsch, Small, Davenport, & Bergman, 2012; van Schaik et al., 2014). Consider the following as an example of effective decision making: A unit is asked to consider implementing new dressing materials and dressing protocols to reduce costs and improve patient outcomes. To reach an effective decision, the team membership represents surgeons, ostomy nurses, bedside nurses, and pharmacists. The team meets once a week at designated times facilitated by the assistant head nurse. Consensus is reached after a few meetings, and a new dressing is selected that results in lower costs and excellent clinical outcomes.

To avoid rash decision making, teams can adopt systematic approaches to help solve problems. One such example is the Lean methodology, which is an evidence-based decision-making approach that originated in Japan with the Toyota Production System. Many consider Lean as a methodology to save money and reduce waste, but one of its key strengths is the stepwise approach that is applied to decision making. One of the fundamentals of Lean is that those closest to the decision should be involved in the decision making. The methodology encourages all people involved in a decision to enter the *gemba*, or the place where care is delivered, to best understand the problem and potential solutions. Using the tools of Lean methodology brings structure to reach effective decisions for interprofessional teams (Johnson, Patterson, & O'Connell, 2013; Kimsey, 2010). Lean projects can be scaled from simple to highly complex decisions, making the tool very valuable.

Appropriate Staffing

The AACN HWE standard concerning appropriate staffing begins by saying that staffing must match the nurse's competencies with the patient's needs. The standard serves to address both the patient's needs and who (nurse competency) needs to do the work. Every patient has care that must be completed; this is referred to as the *acuity* of the patient. However, acuity does not speak to the competency required to perform the work. It only addresses the number of minutes or hours required to provide the care. Some work can be accomplished by assistive personnel, whereas other work requires an RN. Some care requires a respiratory therapist. Do not confuse acuity with how sick a patient is at any given moment in time. Acuity merely identifies the amount of work that must be done to provide the amount of care that the patient requires. The competency necessary to provide that care dictates who gives the care. Appropriate staffing occurs when synergy exists between the two. To have the knowledge to make these decisions, leaders must seek input from the nurse caring for the patient. This caregiver is the person who best understands the needs of the patient in that moment and can assist in determining the best allocation of the resources available. When assignments are made without this consideration, as in using geographic location only, the best fit is hit-or-miss, and competent care may be compromised.

It is equally important to plan for staffing using historical trends to secure the appropriate number and skill mix in advance, making adjustments in real time based on newly gained information. Nurses should be assigned work that is at the top of their license and not tasks that could be done by another member of the team. Nurses should do nursing, plain and simple. When nurses are busy running around looking for equipment or transporting specimens to the laboratory, they are not available for assessments and interventions that depend on their expertise. Often, nurses will get caught up in the numbers game where they attempt to match census with staffing numbers. This strategy often falls short of the goal for this standard. The strategy would work if every patient were the same and all nurses possessed the same level of expertise in every area. Unless those parameters can be ensured, patients' needs are best met when matched to the competencies of the caregivers assigned (see Figure 6-7). Read about workforce strategies in Chapter 7.

Meaningful Recognition

Feeling valued should be a fundamental right. Scores are higher in units where staff are recognized in a meaningful manner. This seems like a simple concept. However, the AACN (2016) standard calls out a few specifics. First, recognition should be measured not by quantity, but quality. And it must take into consideration that the needs of each individual are different; something that holds value to one staff member may not be as valuable to the next. Some of the most meaningful recognition comes from fellow team members, second only to the thanks expressed by patients and families. A great recognition program includes an ongoing and consistent process. It focuses on providing timely acknowledgment of actions that make a difference and can be accomplished with very little financial expenditure. A genuine "thank you" where the connection is made eye to eye and the tone is sincere can go much further than a blanket thank-you letter in template format containing a gift card. Meaningful recognition needs to be personalized and given for behavior that goes above the expectation. It also needs to align with the action being acknowledged. Overdoing praise for performing regular job duties will quickly be identified by the team and will water down the impact when recognition is given the next time (see Figure 6-8).

Figure 6-7. Critical Elements of Appropriate Staffing

- The health care organization has staffing policies in place that are solidly grounded in ethical principles and support the professional obligation of nurses to provide high-quality care.
- Nurses participate in all organizational phases of the staffing process from education and planning—including matching nurses' competencies with patients' assessed needs—through evaluation.
- Nurses seek opportunities to obtain knowledge and skills required to demonstrate competence to ensure an effective match with the needs of patients and their families.
- The health care organization has formal processes in place to evaluate the effect of staffing decisions on patient and system outcomes. This evaluation includes an analysis when patient needs and nurse competencies are mismatched and how often contingency plans are implemented.
- The health care organization has a system in place that facilitates team members' use of staffing and outcomes data to develop more effective staffing models.
- The health care organization provides support services at every level of activity to ensure nurses can optimally focus on the priorities and requirements of patient and family care.
- The health care organization adopts technologies that increase the effectiveness of nursing care delivery. Nurses are engaged in the selection, adaptation, and evaluation of these technologies.

Note. From *AACN Standards for Establishing and Sustaining Healthy Work Environments: A Journey to Excellence* (2nd ed., p. 26), by American Association of Critical-Care Nurses, 2016, Aliso Viejo, CA: Author. Copyright 2016 by American Association of Critical-Care Nurses. Reprinted with permission.

Figure 6-8. Critical Elements of Meaningful Recognition

- The health care organization has a comprehensive system in place that includes formal processes and structured forums that ensure a sustainable focus on recognizing all team members for their contributions and the value they bring to the work of the organization.
- The health care organization establishes a systematic process for all team members to learn about its recognition system and how to participate by recognizing the contributions of colleagues and the value they bring to the organization.
- The health care organization's recognition system reaches from the bedside to the boardroom, ensuring individuals receive recognition consistent with their personal definition of meaning, fulfillment, development, and advancement at every stage of their professional career.
- The health care organization has processes in place to nominate team members for recognition in local, regional, and national venues.
- The health care organization's recognition system includes processes that validate the recognition is meaningful to those being acknowledged.
- Team members understand that everyone is responsible for playing an active role in the organization's recognition program and meaningfully recognizing contributions.
- The health care organization regularly and comprehensively evaluates its recognition system, ensuring effective programs that help move the organization toward a sustainable culture of excellence that values meaningful recognition.

Note. From *AACN Standards for Establishing and Sustaining Healthy Work Environments: A Journey to Excellence* (2nd ed., p. 30), by American Association of Critical-Care Nurses, 2016, Aliso Viejo, CA: Author. Copyright 2016 by American Association of Critical-Care Nurses. Reprinted with permission.

Authentic Leadership

Authentic leadership is the final standard in the AACN HWE standards (AACN, 2016). The intention of the standard is multifaceted but boils down to a few simple concepts. First, leadership is not about a position. It is not about a title. It is meant to apply to every team member when put in a position to lead anything. RNs are logical leaders. They lead teams to care for patients. They lead patients and their families to achieve goals and progress toward outcomes. They lead, by example, newer, less experienced nurses and nursing students. Most RNs do not have a formal title that contains the word *leader*, yet this standard applies to them. And the reason leadership does apply, regardless of position of assigned authority, is this: to be a good leader of anything or anybody, the leader must be authentic. Authentic leaders must walk the talk; they must be real. Behaviors of authentic leaders must align with the core values held important by the leader. The authentic leader must believe that the standards of the HWE cannot be compromised. The authentic leader cannot tolerate team members who do not live up to the intentions of the critical elements listed for each standard and hold themselves and team members accountable. The authentic leadership standard has the same expectation for each team member whether in a formal or informal leadership position (see Figure 6-9).

Certain styles of leadership lend themselves naturally to being authentic. One example is servant leadership (Blanchard & Barrett, 2011). This style of leadership involves connecting with people on a personal level and caring for them as more than just someone who is performing a job. This style does not infer giving over authority to the team members, although it would not prohibit it, but instead creates an environment of partnership with team members to accomplish the work, which perfectly aligns with the HWE standards (Shirey, 2009). In addition, servant leadership also lays the foundation for succession planning. This style allows the leader to invest in staff to assist with their professional and personal growth and development. Servant leaders lead through inspiration and fewer directives. People want to follow, want to emulate, and, therefore, are more likely to embrace the work required to promote teams and communication.

Working in partnership creates environments where staff are encouraged to grow and where they feel safe to take risks and even fail.

Evaluating Progress

Everyone enjoys a celebration, especially following hard work. And making necessary changes in behaviors, leaving the past behind, and embracing a new way of thinking is hard work. The best way to evaluate success starts at the beginning of the journey. When the work is identified, identify a metric to determine when the work has been accomplished. When possible, break down that journey into manageable chunks that can be accomplished within four to six weeks to be able to celebrate frequently to keep momentum going. Since the publication of *Silence Kills* (Maxfield et al., 2005), patient outcomes such as mortality, hospital-acquired infections, and length of stay have been linked to the presence of an HWE (Kelly et al., 2013; Laschinger & Leiter, 2006). This is a great example of evidence-based practice. It also makes it easier to associate the progress to metrics that are accepted by all disciplines. Now, core measure compliance

---

Figure 6-9. Critical Elements of Authentic Leadership

- The health care organization provides support for and access to education and coaching to ensure that nurse leaders develop and enhance knowledge and abilities in authentic leadership, skilled communication, effective decision making, true collaboration, meaningful recognition, and appropriate staffing.
- Nurse leaders demonstrate an understanding of the requirements and dynamics at the point of care and within this context successfully translate the vision of a healthy work environment.
- Nurse leaders excel at generating visible enthusiasm for achieving the standards that create and sustain healthy work environments.
- Nurse leaders ensure the design of systems necessary to effectively implement and sustain standards for healthy work environments.
- The health care organization ensures that nurse leaders are appropriately positioned in their pivotal role in creating and sustaining healthy work environments. This role includes participation in key decision-making forums, access to essential information, and the authority to make necessary decisions.
- The health care organization facilitates the efforts of nurse leaders to create and sustain a healthy work environment by providing the necessary time and financial and human resources.
- The health care organization makes a formal mentoring program available for all nurse leaders. Nurse leaders actively engage in the mentoring of nurses in all roles and levels of experience.
- Nurse leaders role model skilled communication, true collaboration, effective decision making, meaningful recognition, and authentic leadership.
- The health care organization includes the individual's influence on creating and sustaining a healthy work environment as a criterion in each nurse leader's performance appraisal. Nurse leaders demonstrate leadership in creating and sustaining healthy work environments in order to achieve professional advancement.
- The health care organization ensures progress toward creating and sustaining a healthy work environment is evaluated at regular intervals using tools designed for that purpose. The AACN Healthy Work Environment Assessment tool is available at www.aacn.org/hwe.
- Nurse leaders and team members mutually and objectively evaluate the impact of leadership processes and decisions on the organization's progress toward creating and sustaining a healthy work environment.

Note. From *AACN Standards for Establishing and Sustaining Healthy Work Environments: A Journey to Excellence* (2nd ed., p. 34), by American Association of Critical-Care Nurses, 2016, Aliso Viejo, CA: Author. Copyright 2016 by American Association of Critical-Care Nurses. Reprinted with permission.

means something to every member of the team, to management, to executive leadership, and to the board of directors. Make sure to include these core measure values as part of the dashboard constructed to account for the progress and the effects of the hard work done by all. Earlier, the impact of unhealthy environments on morale, retention, engagement, and cost was discussed (Aiken et al., 2011; Huang et al., 2010; Kelly et al., 2013; Laschinger & Leiter, 2006; Rossi & Edmiston, 2012). Therefore, it makes sense to use these accepted measures when determining progress.

Summary

Often, the most difficult work requires the simplest of solutions. The AACN (2016) HWE standards lay the foundation for work that is common sense; it is just not common practice. For too long, unhealthy situations have been tolerated. Certain behaviors have become a rite of passage, and people were told to develop a tougher skin or get out. The measure of a skilled healthcare provider had everything to do with technical skills and little to do with the ability to treat others with respect, much less consider them as partners in caring for patients. Fortunately, those days are falling into yesteryear in many places, but tremendous work remains to be done. Who does this work belong to? This work belongs to everyone. Each and every member of the team needs to call out the imperative to live the standards necessary to create a healthy workplace. It is no longer a feeling in our gut that says we need to look at doing things according to these fundamental principles. Research now exists that calls it out as a requirement. Leadership must ensure the smooth and safe passage of all team members as they journey toward this deserved accomplishment. Everyone is needed to make this happen. Nurses closest to the patients, managers in the middle, and nurse executives at the top each have a role to play. And although the jobs may be different, the goals are the same. This is not an idea waiting for the right time. This is the right idea, and the time is right now.

References

Agency for Healthcare Research and Quality. (n.d.). TeamSTEPPS. Retrieved from https://www.ahrq.gov/teamstepps/index.html

Aiken, L.H., Cimiotti, J.P., Sloane, D.M., Smith, H.L., Flynn, L., & Neff, D.F. (2011). Effects of nurse staffing and nurse education on patient deaths in hospitals with different nurse work environments. *Medical Care, 49,* 1047–1053. doi:10.1097/MLR.0b013e3182330b6e

American Association of Critical-Care Nurses. (n.d.). AACN Healthy Work Environment Assessment Tool. Retrieved from http://www.hweteamtool.org

American Association of Critical-Care Nurses. (2016). *AACN standards for establishing and sustaining healthy work environments: A journey to excellence* (2nd ed.). Retrieved from https://www.aacn.org/wd/hwe/docs/hwestandards.pdf

Bergman, J.Z., Rentsch, J.R., Small, E.E., Davenport, S.W., & Bergman, S.M. (2012). The shared leadership process in decision-making teams. *Journal of Social Psychology, 152,* 17–42. doi:10.1080/00224545.2010.538763

Blanchard, K.H., & Barrett, C. (2011). *Lead with LUV: A different way to create real success.* Upper Saddle River, NJ: FT Press.

Bucknall, T. (2003). The clinical landscape of critical care: Nurses' decision-making. *Journal of Advanced Nursing, 43,* 310–319. doi:101046/j.1365-2648.2003.02714.x

Choi, J., Bakken, S., Larson, E., Du, Y., & Stone, P.W. (2004). Perceived nursing work environment of critical care nurses. *Nursing Research, 53,* 370–378. doi:10.1097/00006199-200411000-00005

Chong, W.W., Aslani, P., & Chen, T.F. (2013). Multiple perspectives on shared decision-making and interprofessional collaboration in mental healthcare. *Journal of Interprofessional Care, 27,* 223–230. doi:10.3109/13561820.2013.767225

Drescher, M.A., Korsgaard, M.A., Welpe, I.M., Picot, A., & Wigand, R.T. (2014). The dynamics of shared leadership: Building trust and enhancing performance. *Journal of Applied Psychology, 99,* 771–783. doi:10.1037/a0036474

Goldenhar, L.M., Brady, P.W., Sutcliffe, K.M., & Muething, S.E. (2013). Huddling for high reliability and situation awareness. *BMJ Quality and Safety, 22,* 899–906. doi:10.1136/bmjqs-2012-001467

Good, V.S. (2009). The critical care environment. In K.K. Carlson (Ed.), *AACN advanced critical care nursing* (pp. 3–21). St. Louis, MO: Elsevier Saunders.

Huang, D.T., Clermont, G., Kong, L., Weissfeld, L.A., Sexton, J.B., Rowan, K.M., & Angus, D.C. (2010). Intensive care unit safety culture and outcomes: A US multicenter study. *International Journal for Quality in Health Care, 22,* 151–161. doi:10.1093/intqhc/mzq017

Interprofessional Education Collaborative Expert Panel. (2016). *Core competencies for interprofessional collaborative practice: 2016 update.* Washington, DC: Interprofessional Education Collaborative.

Jain, A.L., Jones, K.C., Simon, J., & Patterson, M.D. (2015). The impact of a daily pre-operative surgical huddle on interruptions, delays, and surgeon satisfaction in an orthopedic operating room: A prospective study. *Patient Safety in Surgery, 9,* 8. doi:10.1186/s13037-015-0057-6

Johnson, P.M., Patterson, C.J., & O'Connell, M.P. (2013). Lean methodology: An evidence-based practice approach for healthcare improvement. *Nurse Practitioner, 38,* 1–7. doi:10.1097/01.NPR.0000437576.14143.b9

Kelly, D., Kutney-Lee, A., Lake, E.T., & Aiken, L.H. (2013). The critical care work environment and nurse-reported health care–associated infections. *American Journal of Critical Care, 22,* 482–488. doi:10.4037/ajcc2013298

Kimsey, D.B. (2010). Lean methodology in health care. *AORN Journal, 92,* 53–60. doi:10.1016/j.aorn.2010.01.015

Kohn, L.T., Corrigan, J.M., & Donaldson, M.S. (Eds.). (2000). *To err is human: Building a safer health system.* Washington, DC: National Academies Press.

Laschinger, H.K.S., & Leiter, M.P. (2006). The impact of nursing work environments on patient safety outcomes: The mediating role of burnout engagement. *Journal of Nursing Administration, 36,* 259–267. doi:10.1097/00005110-200605000-00019

Leape, L.L., Shore, M.F., Dienstag, J.L., Mayer, R.J., Edgman-Levitan, S., Meyer, G.S., & Healy, G.B. (2012a). Perspective: A culture of respect, part 1: The nature and causes of disrespectful behavior by physicians. *Academic Medicine, 87,* 845–852. doi:10.1097/ACM.0b013e318258338d

Leape, L.L., Shore, M.F., Dienstag, J.L., Mayer, R.J., Edgman-Levitan, S., Meyer, G.S., & Healy, G.B. (2012b). Perspective: A culture of respect, part 2: Creating a culture of respect. *Academic Medicine, 87,* 853–858. doi:10.1097/ACM.0b013e3182583536

Lucian Leape Institute. (2013). *Through the eyes of the workforce: Creating joy, meaning, and safer health care.* Boston, MA: National Patient Safety Foundation.

Mathieu, J.E., Kukenberger, M.R., D'Innocenzo, L., & Reilly, G. (2015). Modeling reciprocal team cohesion-performance relationships, as impacted by shared leadership and members' competence. *Journal of Applied Psychology, 100,* 713–734. doi:10.1037/a0038898

Maxfield, D., Grenny, J., Lavandero, R., & Groah, L. (2010). *The silent treatment: Why safety tools and checklists aren't enough to save lives.* Retrieved from http://www.silenttreatmentstudy.com

Maxfield, D., Grenny, J., McMillan, R., Patterson, K., & Switzler, A. (2005). *Silence kills: The seven crucial conversations for healthcare.* Retrieved from https://www.aacn.org/nursing-excellence/healthy-work-environments/~/media/aacn-website/nursing-excellence/healthy-work-environment/silencekills.pdf?la=en

Muller-Juge, V., Cullati, S., Blondon, K.S., Hudelson, P., Maître, F., Vu, N.V., … Nendaz, M.R. (2013). Interprofessional collaboration on an internal medicine ward: Role perceptions and expectations among nurses and residents. *PLOS ONE, 8*(2), e57570. doi:10.1371/journal.pone.0057570

National Patient Safety Foundation. (2015). *Free from harm: Accelerating patient safety improvement fifteen years after To Err Is Human.* Boston, MA: Author.

Randmaa, M., Mårtensson, G., Swenne, C.L., & Engström, M. (2014). SBAR improves communication and safety climate and decreases incident reports due to communication errors in an anaesthetic clinic: A prospective intervention study. *BMJ Open, 4*(1), e004268. doi:10.1136/bmjopen-2013-004268

Revta, B. (2004). NICU—The "I" stands for integrated. *Journal of Neuroscience Nursing, 36,* 174–176.

Ricci, M.A., & Brumsted, J.R. (2012). Crew resource management: Using aviation techniques to improve operating room safety. *Aviation, Space, and Environmental Medicine, 83,* 441–444. doi:10.3357/ASEM.3149.2012

Rossi, P.J., & Edmiston, C.E., Jr. (2012). Patient safety in the critical care environment. *Surgical Clinics of North America, 92,* 1369–1386. doi:10.1016/j.suc.2012.08.007

Rushton, C.H., Batcheller, J., Schroeder, K., & Donohue, P. (2015). Burnout and resilience among nurses practicing in high-intensity settings. *American Journal of Critical Care, 24,* 412–420. doi:10.4037/ajcc2015291

Sacco, T.L., Ciurzynski, S.M., Harvey, M.E., & Ingersoll, G.L. (2015). Compassion satisfaction and compassion fatigue among critical care nurses. *Critical Care Nurse, 35*(4), 32–42. doi:10.4037/ccn2015392

Shirey, M.R. (2009). Authentic leadership, organizational culture, and healthy work environments. *Critical Care Nursing Quarterly, 32,* 189–198. doi:10.1097/CNQ.0b013e3181ab91db

Ulrich, B.T., Lavandero, R., Hart, K.A., Woods, D., Leggett, J., & Taylor, D. (2006). Critical care nurses' work environments: A baseline status report. *Critical Care Nurse, 26*(5), 46–50, 52–57. Retrieved from http://ccn.aacnjournals.org/content/26/5/46.long

Ulrich, B.T., Lavandero, R., Hart, K.A., Woods, D., Leggett, J., Friedman, D., … Edwards, S.J. (2009). Critical care nurses' work environments 2008: A follow-up report. *Critical Care Nurse, 29*(2), 93–102. doi:10.4037/ccn2009619

Ulrich, B.T., Lavandero, R., Woods, D., & Early, S. (2014). Critical care nurse work environments 2013: A status report. *Critical Care Nurse, 34*(4), 64–79. doi:10.4037/ccn2014731

van Schaik, S.M., O'Brien, B.C., Almeida, S.A., & Adler, S.R. (2014). Perceptions of interprofessional teamwork in low-acuity settings: A qualitative analysis. *Medical Education, 48,* 583–592. doi:10.1111/medu.12424

Wang, D., Waldman, D.A., & Zhang, Z. (2014). A meta-analysis of shared leadership and team effectiveness. *Journal of Applied Psychology, 99,* 181–198. doi:10.1037/a0034531

CHAPTER 7

Leading and Sustaining a Robust Workforce

Carol Boston-Fleischhauer, JD, MS, RN

To win in the marketplace . . . you must first win in the workplace.

—Doug Conant

Introduction

To say that today's chief nurse executives (CNEs) wear many hats is an understatement. Regardless of organization type or size, be it a freestanding community hospital, a multihospital healthcare system, or a cross-continuum, clinically integrated network, the CNE's accountabilities include strategy, quality, safety, patient experience, operations, finance, and human resources. While the argument could be made that all the CNE's responsibilities require equal time and attention, the vexing and unique challenges posed by today's practice environment suggest a heightened focus on the nursing workforce—in particular, the professional nurse workforce. The CNE bears full accountability for the strength of nursing; therefore, the CNE must take steps to build a professional nursing workforce prepared to meet the challenges that lie ahead. This chapter will outline the CNE's and other nurse leaders' roles in leading and sustaining a robust nursing workforce, with the specific focus on RNs who are fully engaged to support the needs of patients and families in our transforming healthcare system.

Adding to the challenge of workforce leadership are trends highlighted by ever-changing workforce analytics, which are informative to both the public and private sector about the supply and demand of healthcare workers. The Health Resources and Services Administration (HRSA) and the U.S. Department of Health and Human Services provide data on the state of the nurse workforce in America (AMN Healthcare, 2013; HSRA, 2017). The RN workforce has grown by nearly 1 million since 2008, with a reported 3.7 million RNs (including advanced practice RNs) in the U.S. workforce (HRSA, 2013). The majority of RNs are providing inpatient or outpatient (ambulatory) care in hospital settings. The most recent data (2008–2010) indicate that the average age of RNs is 44.6 years, with a large portion older than age 50 years (HRSA, 2013). There will continue to be variation by state of supply and demand for RNs; however, the projected net growth of RNs is an additional 1,089,500 FTEs by 2030. The latest HRSA modeling projects an excess of about 8% of demand for RNs and 13% deficit of LPNs by 2030 (HRSA, 2017). This modeling takes into account various future factors such as insurance reform, value-based models of care, shift to more community- and home-based care, preventive care, and population health (HRSA, 2017). The aging of the nursing workforce will have a major impact, not only on the supply of nurses over the next 10–15 years but also in the knowledge and skills of the years of experience that will be lost. Notably, concerns remain as to whether this increasing supply will meet the ever-changing demand as more and more care sites are added to cross-continuum care delivery expectations, new roles are created, and the competition for nurses, especially experienced nurses in key specialties, is growing exponentially. Further, recent statistics reflect increased RN turnover rates exceeding 25% (Duffield, Roche, Homer, Buchan, & Dimitrelis, 2014). Increased RN turnover represents an additional concern for the CNE who is challenged to ensure workforce stability, as well as tight control of direct and indirect labor costs, in light of overall resource limitations.

Confirmation of key working assumptions is necessary for this discussion. First, the CNE is already working closely with the chief human resource executive and other nurse leaders and key clinical nurses in the organization to design a workforce blueprint for the future, including anticipated roles and competencies needed in all care settings. Beyond a traditional recruitment plan, this workforce blueprint needs to mirror the anticipated changes that the organization or system will design in response to changing reimbursement patterns and the assumption of clinical and financial risk. In particular, this workforce planning equation must account for anticipated expansion of services beyond acute/tertiary care to ambulatory services, home care, community-based care models, patient-centered medical homes, and the like.

Second, the system has a comprehensive recruitment plan in place that addresses immediate staffing needs and cultivates a strong candidate pipeline (both internal and external) for new roles being created in and across the entire care network. The plan also must include the presence of baseline drivers for qualified candidates to accept employment positions throughout the nursing enterprise as they are offered, for example, competitive wages and benefits, support for professional development, and a work environment that supports top-of-license practice. Indeed, these baseline drivers must also be locally competitive, sensitive to any generational and cultural differences, and responsive to root causes of increased RN turnover.

Finally, tools and mechanisms exist to support effective decisions regarding staffing models and schedules. These tools are evidence based and used throughout the entire nursing enterprise to ensure safe, appropriate staffing levels according to the care needs of patients, individual units, and the organization overall.

Defining a Robust Nursing Workforce

The term *robust* is quite straightforward. Merriam-Webster defines it as that which is "strong and healthy, strongly formed or built, not likely to fail or weaken" ("Robust," n.d.-b). Macmillan defines a robust organization as one that is "strong and successful" ("Robust," n.d.-a). Applying those broad definitions to the nursing workforce suggests that the CNE must examine and have a plan to ensure that the nursing enterprise is both strong and successful in achieving measures for which the nursing enterprise is accountable. A quick review of the success measures and outcomes that a typical organization's nursing workforce needs to advance is helpful to emphasize the scope of this ambition.

For starters, success measures exist in the pay-for-performance terrain from the public and private payers' perspectives, for example, the Centers for Medicare and Medicaid Services. Annually, nursing-sensitive outcome measures related to care processes and team-based outcomes such as patient experience, efficiency, mortality, readmissions, and hospital-acquired conditions increase both in number as well as overall targets. Second, given nursing's direct and indirect impact on an organization's overall cost structure, success with cost and resource management is vital. Additionally, success measures exist related to the profession itself that serve not only to advance the nursing enterprise, but also to further contribute the organization's overall effectiveness. For example, higher nurse engagement is strongly correlated with higher patient experience levels, resulting in better care outcomes, as well as lower costs related to a more stable nurse workforce (Dempsey & Reilly, 2016). Finally, success measures related to the stability and sustainability of the entire nursing enterprise, given its pivotal role in organizational success, must be addressed as well.

Designing a Strategic Framework for a Robust Nursing Workforce

Although many strategies could be examined to address the ultimate ambition of this discussion, today's transforming healthcare environment elevates three strategies as core to an overarching framework in terms of both immediate relevance and cumulative impact. First, a principled approach is needed to address the key drivers of nurse engagement. Second, renewed efforts must be taken to cultivate a positive work environment for nursing practice. Third, steps must be in place to ensure that nurse managers have the development and mentoring, as well as the organizational and executive support, they need to be effective in their roles. Beyond the cumulative effect of these three strategies, the interdependencies are equally significant. Without a solid plan in place to address all these strategies in tandem, the CNE and other nurse leaders will be limited in their ability to sustain a nursing workforce at levels strong enough to ensure the degree of organizational success that is now required.

Strategy 1: Nurse Engagement

The study of nurse engagement, including its impact on organizational outcomes, is not new. Citations abound in the literature that directly link increased nurse engagement to an enhanced patient experience, improved clinical outcomes, and increased financial performance. Likewise, direct linkages exist between nurse engagement and commonly measured workforce variables, including absenteeism, burnout, and turnover (Adler, Virkstis, Stuart, & Berkow, 2014; Dempsey, Reilly, & Buhlman, 2014; McHugh, Kutney-Lee, Cimiotti, Sloane, & Aiken, 2011; Press Ganey, 2015).

With this wealth of studies come numerous survey options and associated analytics to guide one's efforts. Of note, despite the plethora of tools and methods available to measure engagement, the core attributes of what constitutes an engaged nurse are widely accepted by healthcare industry experts. For example, Strumwasser and Virkstis (2015) reported three core attributes believed to be important to identify an engaged employee: inspired to do their best work, willing to exceed the expected level of effort, and personally motivated to help the organization succeed.

Notably, an *engaged* employee or nurse is different than an employee or nurse who is *satisfied*. With the latter, the nurse's line of sight, focus, and motivation is largely focused on his or her job at the operating unit that he or she is working in, day in and day out. An engaged nurse is one who, beyond being satisfied with his or her immediate job responsibilities, is equally as motivated to ensure that the organization succeeds. Given the significant priorities that organizations face and the direct alignment of nurse engagement to the achievement of organizational outcomes, job satisfaction is baseline, but no longer enough. It is the engaged nursing workforce that will propel the nursing enterprise forward, contributing to organizational success and supporting better patient outcomes.

The Advisory Board and its Survey Solutions (known as ABSS) has been measuring nurse and employee engagement for years through its Employee Engagement Survey. In its work, the top drivers of nurse engagement have been identified. From the most recent survey results of more than 343,000 employees representing 575 healthcare organizations and systems, Strumwasser and Virkstis (2015) isolated the five best opportunities for improving nurse engagement:

- Clarifying the linkage between executive actions and the mission and vision of the healthcare organization
- Reducing stress and burnout
- Demonstrating that the organization values nurse input
- Ensuring that nurse recognition is professionally meaningful to the nurse
- Broadening access to innovative and nontraditional professional development opportunities

Another example comes from a white paper published by Press Ganey (2015), in which five recommendations for improving the nurse work environment that affect nurse engagement were identified. Here, the individual components are based on composite variables that reflect different aspects of the work environment and include the following (Press Ganey, 2015):

- Robust shared governance structure (including RN autonomy and control over practice)
- Support for excellent communication and positive interprofessional relationships
- Consistent and adequate staffing and balanced skill mix
- Development of a highly educated nursing workforce
- Appropriate, strong, and consistent leadership support

These components align well with the recommendations from the 2011 *Future of Nursing: Leading Change, Advancing Health* report from the Institute of Medicine (now called the Health and Medicine Division of the National Academies of Sciences, Engineering, and Medicine).

A comprehensive nurse engagement strategy is an essential component of the nurse executive team's strategy for leading and sustaining a robust nursing workforce. Beyond confirmation of the overall level of nurse engagement that exists at the organizational level, more specific, unit-based data are needed. Further, any data that suggest unique employee populations needing more customized attention—for example, new hires within the first year of employment, new graduates, and the 25–35-year-old employee group—need to be analyzed as well. In fact, given the increasingly diverse employee population in terms of age and culture, attention to both multigenerational and multicultural engagement needs is now required (HRSA, 2010). Action plans led by nurse managers can address unit-specific needs. Likewise, strategies that cut across units for high-risk populations, as well as strategies fundamentally anchored to advancing improvement opportunities under the direct control of the CNE team, must be fully developed.

How does this look in practice? Consider the engagement improvement opportunity related to nurses perceiving that the organization values their input. The shared governance concept has evolved into a broader concept of professional governance. Professional governance has four primary tenets: accountability, professional obligation, collateral relationship, and effective decision making (Clavelle, O'Grady, Weston, & Verran, 2016; Joseph & Bogue, 2016). At the organizational level, support for a professional governance framework represents a strong foundation, and notably, the overwhelming majority of U.S. hospitals have some form of professional governance in place. Putting a framework in place is one thing; leveraging its potential aligned with this engagement improvement opportunity is another matter. The challenge is determining whether the approach to professional governance is truly one that ensures broad clinical nurse input into priorities and action plans, along with consistent feedback regarding ideas that have been shared. Further, determination also is needed as to whether the model is functional across the system versus highly variable depending on the unit. Functionality can be measured by observation and national surveys that identify staff engagement in a culture of trust, professional accountability, ownership of practice, intra- and interprofessional collaboration, competency, and an environment of peer review. More information on professional governances is found in Chapter 3.

Beyond shared or professional governance, numerous other mechanisms exist for staff involvement in both the identification of priorities and the creation of solutions—things as simple as the hosting of weekly brown bag lunches with the CNE, extensive staff participation on process improvement teams, and unit-based huddle boards to encourage timely suggestions for change, to name a few. What is most important is ensuring that whatever mechanism is in place for staff idea generation is functioning at a high level and that staff witness clear and consistent demonstration of their ideas being heard, and acted upon, whenever feasible. So, a solid nurse engagement strategy is the first of three strategies essential for the CNE leading and sustaining a robust workforce.

Strategy 2: Strengthening the Work Environment

The daunting pressures that staff face in today's incredibly complex care environments, coupled with continued resource constraints, require CNEs to renew their efforts by ensuring a positive work environment for nursing practice. Chapter 6 outlines strategies to lead and sustain a healthy work environment. Over the years, the impact of the work environment on various outcomes has been studied, and various frameworks have been employed to improve the environment within which nurses practice. For example, the American Nurses Credentialing Center's (ANCC's) five Forces of Magnetism provide a strong organizing construct for evaluating and advancing the work environment for nursing. Hospitals and healthcare systems use this framework for the pursuit of Magnet® designation, which is considered the highest recognition of nursing excellence (Broom & Tilbury, 2007). The five components of the new Magnet model are based on the original 14 Forces of Magnetism and are as follows (ANCC, 2013):

- Transformational leadership
- Structural empowerment
- Exemplary professional practice
- New knowledge, innovation, and improvements
- Empirical quality results

ANCC's Pathways to Excellence® program and its 12 practice standards provides another organizing framework for improving the work environment for nurses. The standards focus on the workplace, a balanced lifestyle for nurses, and policies that support nurses on the job. To earn Pathway designation, a healthcare organization must demonstrate the integration of the 12 standards into its operating policies, procedures, and management structure.

Admittedly, both programs involve significant effort on the part of the CNE and the entire nursing enterprise. In fact, one could argue that the value of pursuing either program lies more in the journey than the destination (Broom & Tilbury, 2007). However, a large body of evidence demonstrates a direct relationship between the work environments that these programs foster and clinical, patient experience, and job satisfaction measures (Bormann & Abrahamson, 2014; Friese, Xia, Ghaferi, Birkmeyer, & Banerjee, 2015; Laschinger, Almost, & Tuer-Hodes, 2003). Therefore, the guiding principles of these two programs should at least be considered by all CNEs working to advance a positive work environment.

Beyond the Magnet and Pathways programs, consider the National Database of Nursing Quality Indicators® Practice Environment Scale and its six environmental components (Warshawsky & Havens, 2011):

- Recognition and praise for a job well done
- Opportunities for advancement
- Preceptor programs
- Collaboration between physicians and nurses, and teamwork
- Administration that listens and responds to employee concerns
- CNE who is highly visible and accessible to staff

This scale is used for measurement versus designation, but it provides additional guidance for CNEs in terms of what drives a positive work environment for nursing practice.

Further, results from the global RN4Cast study (Sermeus et al., 2011) demonstrated greater correlation in hospitals with positive work environments and mortality, compared to those hospitals that only added nursing staff without attention to Practice Environment Scale work environment components (Aiken et al., 2011). That finding provides CNEs and nurse leaders with some evidence to refute the long-standing argument that the only way to combat a poor work environment is through the addition of staff; rather, a more deliberate approach toward shoring up the overall work environment for nursing practice is the better alternative.

A related and increasingly concerning theme regarding the health or lack thereof of the work environment is the level of stress and burnout being reported. Although nursing has always been a demanding profession, the unprecedented expectations being placed on the nursing enterprise for efficiency, effectiveness, achievement of outcomes, and the like are taking their toll. Technology, particularly electronic health records, must also be factored into this analysis (Adler et al., 2014; Bodenheim & Sinsky, 2014; McHugh et al., 2011).

The Institute for Healthcare Improvement has recently suggested that its Triple Aim initiative should be expanded (Sikka, Morath, & Leape, 2015). The Institute and other experts have suggested that the Triple Aim, which includes enhancing patient experience, improving population health, and reducing costs, cannot be achieved without attention to the work life of healthcare providers as well, including the stressful work environment in which clinicians are practicing. Indeed, to expand from the Triple Aim to a Quadruple Aim acknowledges that the backbone of any effective organization is its workforce—one that is engaged and productive, capable of finding joy and meaning in work, versus one experiencing excessive stress that mitigates human capability for enjoying the experience of care delivery (Bodenheimer & Sinsky, 2014).

Organizations and systems have increased their efforts to support employee health through various types of stress reduction programs, employee wellness initiatives, and employee assistance programs, if needed. Likewise, it is best practice for organizations to clearly support employees whenever an adverse event occurs, in part to support the emotional trauma that clinicians experience whenever an untoward or unexpected clinical event occurs. The question that CNEs must answer is whether the organization's stress management and reduction efforts are largely reactionary in nature, rather than preemptive. Organizations that have mechanisms in place to both acknowledge how stressful the practice environment always is and to provide routine outlets for better stress management versus those that react to employee stress after extreme symptoms are manifested are in a much better position to combat this core driver of unhealthy work environments. So, ensuring proactive support of staff with stress-reducing opportunities as opposed to reacting after either a stressful event has occurred or extreme signs of staff burnout are apparent can serve to improve the work environment for nurses. However, overall engagement of the workforce is simultaneously improved as well (Adler et al., 2014).

A number of organizations are experimenting with more intensive approaches to mitigating the excessive stress that clinicians of all disciplines experience, including nurses. One such example comes from the Schwartz Center for Compassionate Healthcare at Massachusetts General Hospital and its Schwartz Rounds™. As background, Kenneth Schwartz was a patient diagnosed with lung cancer in 1994 and treated aggressively at Massachusetts General Hospital. Despite valiant efforts, he ultimately died of his cancer in 1995. However, he recognized and clearly articulated the direct impact of his compassionate caregivers on his experience. His experience and personal belief in the power of compassionate care is commemorated through the Schwartz Center. Organizations that seek to use its tools can offer Schwartz Rounds to its clinicians. Schwartz Rounds are regular, interdisciplinary discussions conducted by trained facilitators that focus on a range of practice topics that drive emotional stress. During these rounds, clinicians are provided a safe and confidential opportunity to explore their emotional reactions to specific patient experiences and work through their stress with their colleagues. Results from those who participate in Schwartz Rounds include an increased perception of a positive work environment and decreased work-related stress. More than 425 U.S. and Canadian healthcare organizations participate in Schwartz Rounds, and international use of this practice is increasing as well (Lown & Manning, 2010; Schwartz Center for Compassionate Healthcare, n.d.; Thompson, 2013).

While supporting a positive work environment for nursing practice is not new in and of itself, the complexities of contemporary health care require CNEs to renew their efforts in this area. Increasing support for the work environment responsive to today's unique challenges represents the second strategy that CNEs must employ to lead and sustain a robust nursing workforce.

Strategy 3: Support for the Nurse Manager

Although the CNE is ultimately accountable for leading and sustaining a robust nursing workforce, the impact that the frontline leadership (nurse managers) has with this overall ambition is extraordinary. Research consistently correlates the direct relationship between an effective nurse manager on nurse satisfaction and engagement, turnover, and the overall health of the work environment (Anthony et al., 2005; Kath, Stichler, & Ehrhart, 2012; Yu, Harter, & Agrawal, 2013). For example, through a multivariate regression analysis of key management effectiveness indices and employee engagement levels, staff who perceive their managers as being effective are five times more likely to be engaged than staff who perceive their managers as being ineffective (Dempsey & Reilly, 2016; Dempsey et al., 2014; Rothenberger, 2014). Of note, this is from the perspective of staff versus the CNE, but the data are significant. Prior discussion in this chapter has already confirmed the link between workforce engagement and the strength of the workforce in successful achievement of organizational outcomes. Therefore, a close look at what shapes a staff nurse's perception of effectiveness is important. The Advisory Board Survey Solutions, through interviews and survey analyses, created a Management Effectiveness Index, which consists of survey variables scored by staff, including the following (Rothenberger, 2014):

- I have helpful discussions with my manager about my career.
- I receive regular feedback from my manager about my performance.
- My manager communicates messages that my coworkers need to hear, even when the information is unpleasant.
- My manager helps me balance my job and personal life.
- My manager helps me learn new skills.
- My manager is open and responsive to staff input.
- My manager stands up for the interests of my department.

Looking at RN turnover through the lens of nurse manager effectiveness is important to this discussion. As noted earlier, nurse turnover is increasing and for a variety of reasons. For new graduates, upward of 17.5% of newly licensed RNs are turning over within one year of employment, and approximately 33% are turning over within three years (Kovner, Brewer, Fatehi, &

Jun, 2014), and more recent anecdotal data suggest much higher rates. However, concern over turnover should not be limited to new graduates. Experienced nurse turnover is increasing as well, with recent statistics for overall nurse turnover, regardless of age, hovering at approximately 16.5% (Yarbrough, Martin, Alfred, & McNeill, 2017). Although the root causes of turnover for new graduates versus experienced nurses may vary, the overall concern is what RNs are looking for in the practice environment, which is directly within the control of the nurse manager (Yarbrough et al., 2017). Fundamentally, increased nurse turnover plays havoc on overall business unit stability and the ability to remain productive and efficient despite shortages. Likewise, the impact of increased nurse turnover on the bottom line is significant for the CNE, given the costs associated with replacement. However, the larger issue for this discussion is the cost to the organization in terms of achieving organizational outcomes if the nurse manager is not equipped, prepared, or supported to ensure a positive work environment for the staff that she or he is managing, with turnover as the corresponding measure.

A comprehensive approach to ensuring that the nurse manager and other frontline leaders are effectively supported should include hiring for fit; achievement of manager competencies; structural options for comanagement, especially in larger units; spans of control in keeping with evidence-based benchmarks; and access to much-needed business, financial, and ancillary services to free up nurse manager time to be present on the unit. However, for purposes of this discussion, three important themes rise to the top: the power of nurse manager competencies and leadership styles, the impact of increased spans of control, and attention to nurse manager engagement.

For development purposes, numerous competency models exist for nurse managers. One example is the nurse manager competency model developed by the American Organization of Nurse Executives (AONE), which acknowledges the nurse manager role as vital to the creation of work environments that support the work of the care team. Nurse manager competencies according to this model are organized into three domains: the science (managing the business), the art (leading people), and the leader within (creating leadership within oneself) (AONE, 2015).

The issue here is not so much which competency model a CNE is using, but rather having a principled approach to ensure that all nurse managers are assessed for competency strengths and development needs, both at the time of appointment and at regular intervals. Likewise, resources must be in place to ensure that where deficiencies lie, the nurse manager has access to effective professional development opportunities aligned with the identified needs.

Beyond competencies, however, the nurse manager's leadership traits have also been found to affect numerous metrics related to a positive work environment, including retention and job satisfaction. In particular, transformational leadership styles have been cited as being particularly relevant to this correlation (Bormann & Abrahamson, 2014; Force, 2005). For example, in a study by Bormann and Abrahamson (2014), not only was transformational leadership styles of nurse managers positively correlated with nurse satisfaction, but passive-avoidant leadership styles were negatively correlated with the same measures. That transformational leadership is also one of the five components associated with the Magnet Recognition Program is of secondary consequence but nonetheless important to acknowledge.

Discussions of how frontline nurse leaders support positive work environments for their staff frequently cite the importance of staff empowerment. However, for nurses to work in practice environments that promote autonomy and control over the practice environment, the nurse manager must be supported to put the necessary systems in place. One of the most widely recognized structural mechanisms for cultivating control over one's practice at the unit level is shared or professional governance, as has been mentioned earlier in this chapter. However, beyond structure, manager behaviors to support nurse empowerment are important as well. A study conducted by MacPhee, Skelton-Green, Bouthillette, and Suryaprakash (2012) and others have suggested that empowering behaviors demonstrated by nurse managers positively correlate to nurses feeling empowered and, consequently, improved clinical outcomes. To truly enable a positive work environment, nurse managers must be skilled to focus less on the control of nurse work and more on the coordination and facilitation of nurse work. Indeed, nurse leaders' empowering behaviors can influence how nurses perceive their work environment, thereby increasing overall work environment effectiveness (Laschinger et al., 2003).

Span of control for the nurse manager continues to threaten the manager's ability to be effective regardless of function, but in particular as it relates to staff engagement and empowerment. With unreasonable spans of control, nurse managers' ability to use their skills to ensure that staff are functioning to the full scope of their professional practice, thereby contributing to organizational outcomes, is compromised (Jones, McLaughlin, Gebbens, & Terhorst, 2015). Furthermore, managers' ability to ensure they have the time to ensure sufficient attention to the core elements of the Practice Environment Scale for nurses can be eroded with increased spans of control (Ausserhofer et al., 2014). Research consistently suggests that every effort should be made to ensure that spans of control are realistic to the needs of the unit, including but not limited to patient acuity and preparation of staff. Employing evidence-based tools and recognized benchmarks to assess for vulnerability is key.

However, in light of overall resource constraints and the high improbability of adding more nurse managers to the leadership structure, CNEs are evaluating alternatives to provide focused nurse manager support. In particular, examples are increasing of strategies employed by CNEs to augment the skills and responsibilities of nurse managers by creating administrative support roles and human resources business partners, as well as financial analytic support. In most cases, these strategies are full-time position or budget neutral for the department, with role realignment occurring in collaboration with the centralized support departments (Chubbs, 2013). Additionally, organizations continue to demonstrate creativity in the development of unit-based dyad or triad leadership models, with unit leadership shared equally between an RN manager and a physician. Likewise, CNEs are experimenting with the integration of either expert RNs or clinical nurse leaders into unit operations, again, fundamentally to address the expanding workload and responsibilities of nurse managers with large spans of control. However, the employment of adjunct support roles for the nurse manager along with creative management models ultimately frees up some time during the nurse manager's day to attend to the needs of the practice environment generally, and specifically to address the core components of the Practice Environment Scale as identified earlier in this chapter.

Finally, CNEs must prioritize nurse manager and other nurse leader engagement. While this chapter started with a discussion of the importance of prioritizing frontline/clinical nurse engagement to ensure that the workforce is poised to support the achievement of organizational outcomes, the simultaneous need to attend to engagement of all the nurse leaders within the organization cannot be overemphasized. Correlations have been cited throughout this chapter regarding the direct linkage between nurse managers and key work environment enablers. Strategies to support manager skills and competencies, along with ensuring support for increasing spans of control, are baseline. The nurse manager's practice environment is characterized by a dizzying array of organizational outcomes. Absent strong engagement by managers in outcome achievement, the CNE's ambition of leading and sustaining a robust nursing workforce will fail.

Three CNE strategies are key in this terrain. First is a breakdown of existing employee engagement data for the entire organization, to include a look at various manager categories within the leadership structure. At the very least, an analysis of frontline manager engagement should be conducted, which is defined here as those individuals having 24-hour clinical and operational accountability for a specific unit or units. If possible, further dissecting engagement data to examine any trends with assistant nurse managers and charge nurses would be advantageous as well. Although national data demonstrate that healthcare managers overall are more engaged than frontline staff, clearly there is room for improvement (Vonderhaar & Simmons, 2016).

The second CNE strategy is to become knowledgeable regarding the core drivers of frontline nurse leader engagement. This is an area studied far less than engagement drivers for staff but equally important in terms of our broader ambition. Some examples of core drivers for consideration include the following (Vonderhaar & Simmons, 2016):
- Executive actions reflect the organization's mission and values.
- Training and development helps me improve.
- I am supported in promotion opportunities.
- Executives respect the contributions of my department.
- My manager has helpful discussions with me about my career.
- I am kept informed of the organization's plans.
- My organization recognizes employees for a job well done.
- My ideas and suggestions are valued.
- My organization helps me deal with stress and burnout.
- My performance reviews help me improve.
- I have a manageable workload.

Admittedly, several of the drivers of manager engagement are comparable to staff engagement drivers. However, the specific tactics to address the drivers are different and should be identified accordingly.

Third, do not underestimate the impact of manager stress on overall manager effectiveness. Although manager stress and burnout are also cited among the manager engagement drivers, the significance of manager stress levels warrants special focus by the CNE (Shirey, 2006). Evidence clearly links increased manager stress levels with a variety of indicators, including the overall health of the unit-based work environment. Indeed, a stressed nurse manager, by adversely affecting the unit's work environment and nurse retention, can influence overall organizational performance as a result (Kath et al., 2012).

While most research on job stress among nurses focuses on the frontline/clinical nurse, a body of information is emerging to guide CNEs on ways to support nurse leader-related stress and resilience. One such example comes from a study conducted by Kath and others, who focused on not only the extent of nurse manager stress and its effects, but also key moderators. Key strategies noted to mitigate nurse manager job stress included the extent to which CNEs support nurse manager autonomy, access to information that allows nurse managers to be effective in autonomous roles, and enhanced participation in decision making throughout the nursing leadership enterprise (Kath et al., 2012).

This finding is further supported by new research demonstrating that new nurse manager retention is directly related to the manager's involvement in decision making throughout the entire nursing enterprise, as well as senior leadership transparency (Djurkic, Jun, Kovner, Brewer, & Fletcher, 2017). Therefore, how the CNE involves nurse managers in decision-making processes and ensures transparency about how nursing enterprise decisions are being made is vital to nurse manager retention. Such retention serves to stabilize the unit's workforce, increasing the unit's capability to focus on unit-based goals and objectives led by the nurse manager.

Warshawsky, Rayens, Lake, and Havens (2013) have suggested the need for creating a Practice Environment Scale for nurse managers similar to that which has been developed for staff. These researchers defined the nurse manager's practice environment as the organizational context that affects the nurse manager's ability to achieve optimal staff, patient, and organizational outcomes. Data collected from a tool that measures the nurse manager's practice environment could then guide the CNE in determining the elements essential to maximizing the effectiveness of the manager while concurrently mitigating manager stress levels and increasing overall manager engagement (Warshawsky et al., 2013).

Support for the frontline nurse leaders within the organization is critical for the entire nurse executive team, led by the CNE, committed to leading and sustaining a robust nursing workforce poised to support the achievement of clinical practice, quality, experience, and safety outcomes. Beyond hiring for fit and ensuring that nurse managers are properly coached and equipped with tools to support core responsibilities, the immediate need exists to focus support on developing nurse manager competencies and leadership styles, attending to span of control, and manager engagement. Aspects of these and other leader competencies are covered in Chapters 2, 3, 13, and 14. Further, Chapter 22 outlines opportunities and benefits of mentoring for managers.

Summary

A robust RN workforce is defined as one that is strong and poised to work with other care team members in the achievement of organizational outcomes. This is no easy feat, and the nurse executive team faces several formidable barriers. Notwithstanding the core mission to ensure highly reliable and high-quality patient care that is both patient centric and cost-effective, barriers include competing priorities, scarce resources, increasing organizational uncertainty, and the accelerated pace of change.

In addition, rising concerns about dramatically declining retention rates, increased RN turnover and vacancies, particularly in tough-to-fill positions, and an aging workforce, as well as expanded challenges to even recruit nurse talent into the organization, let alone retain and engage them, permeate nearly every executive conversation. Further, as acute care organizations and systems integrate with ambulatory, post-acute, home health, and community services, the CNE's span of workforce control is likely to increase across the care continuum as well. Given that organizational measures increasingly span the continuum, this means deeper understanding of the unique needs of the nursing workforce in a variety of settings, above and beyond what is needed in acute care, if the cross-continuum workforce is to be strong and successful.

Reported increases in lateral violence and bullying within the profession confound even the best and the brightest nursing leadership team who is committed to leading and sustaining a robust nursing workforce across the continuum. Given its unique organizational impact, the issue of lateral violence is addressed in Chapter 5.

The CNE and nurse executive team leaders lead the largest workforce in health care, and the workforce is viewed by the best and the brightest as the backbone of healthcare organizations. With a principled set of strategies to address nurse engagement, the work environment for nursing practice, and nurse manager effectiveness, the CNE is poised to partner with their colleagues in leading and sustaining a robust workforce—one that is strong and successful in achieving outcomes essential for the broader organization's success.

References

Adler, K., Virkstis, K., Stuart, J., & Berkow, S. (2014). *The national prescription for nurse engagement: Best practices for enfranchising frontline staff in organizational transformation.* Washington, DC: Advisory Board Company.
Aiken, L.H., Cimiotti, J.P., Sloane, D.M., Smith, H.L., Flynn, L., & Neff, D.F. (2011). The effects of nurse staffing and nurse education on patient deaths in hospitals with different nurse work environments. *Medical Care, 49,* 1047–1053. doi:10.1097/MLR.0b013e3182330b6e

American Nurses Credentialing Center. (2013). *2014 Magnet® application manual.* Retrieved from http://www .nursecredentialing.org/MagnetApplicationManual.aspx

American Organization of Nurse Executives. (2015). *AONE nurse manager competencies.* Retrieved from http://www .aone.org/resources/nurse-manager-competencies.pdf

AMN Healthcare. (2013). *2013 clinical workforce survey: A national survey of hospital executives examining clinical workforce issues in the era of health reform.* Retrieved from http://www.amnhealthcare.com/industry -research/2147484558/1033

Anthony, M.K., Standing, T.S., Glick, J., Duffy, M., Paschall, F., Sauer, M.R., … Dumpe, M.L. (2005). Leadership and nurse retention: The pivotal role of nurse managers. *Journal of Nursing Administration. 35,* 146–155. doi:10.1097/00005110-200503000-00008

Ausserhofer, D., Zander, B., Busse, R., Schubert, M., De Geest, S., Rafferty, A.M., … Schwendimann, R. (2014). Prevalence, patterns and predictors of nursing care left undone in European hospitals: Results from the multi-country cross-sectional RN4Cast study. *BMJ Quality and Safety, 23,* 126–135. doi:10.1136/bmjqs-2013-002318

Bodenheimer, T., & Sinsky, C. (2014). From Triple to Quadruple Aim: Care of the patient requires care of the provider. *Annals of Family Medicine, 12,* 573–576. doi:10.1370/afm.1713

Bormann, L., & Abrahamson, K. (2014). Do staff nurse perceptions of nurse leadership behaviors influence staff nurse job satisfaction? The case of a hospital applying for Magnet® designation. *Journal of Nursing Administration, 44,* 219–225. doi:10.1097/NNA.0000000000000053

Broom, C., & Tilbury, M.S. (2007). Magnet status: A journey, not a destination. *Journal of Nursing Care Quality, 22,* 113–118. doi:10.1097/01.NCQ.0000263099.21558.ec

Chubbs, K. (2013). Business acumen in nursing management. *Nursing Leadership, 26*(4), 13–16. doi:10.12927/cjnl .2013.23635

Clavelle, J.T., O'Grady, T.P., Weston, M.J., & Verran, J.A. (2016). Evolution of structural empowerment: Moving from shared to professional governance. *Journal of Nursing Administration, 46,* 308–312. doi:10.1097/NNA .0000000000000350

Dempsey, C., & Reilly, B.A. (2016). Nurse engagement: What are the contributing factors for success? *Online Journal of Issues in Nursing, 21*(1), 2. doi:10.3912/OJIN.Vol21No01Man02

Dempsey, C., Reilly, B., & Buhlman, N. (2014). Improving the patient experience: Real-world strategies for engaging nurses. *Journal of Nursing Administration, 44,* 142–151. doi:10.1097/NNA.0000000000000042

Djurkic, M., Jun, J., Kovner, C., Brewer, C., & Fletcher, J. (2017). Determinants of job satisfaction for novice nurse managers employed in hospitals. *Health Care Management Review, 42,* 172–183. doi:10.1097/HMR .0000000000000102

Duffield, C.M., Roche, M.A., Homer, C., Buchan, J., & Dimitrelis, S. (2014). A comparative review of nurse turnover rates and costs across countries. *Journal of Advanced Nursing, 70,* 2703–2712. doi:10.1111/jan.12483

Force, M. (2005). The relationship between effective nurse managers and nursing retention. *Journal of Nursing Administration, 35,* 336–341. doi:10.1097/00005110-200507000-00005

Friese, C.R., Xia, R., Ghaferi, A., Birkmeyer, J.D., & Banerjee, M. (2015). Hospitals in 'Magnet' program show better patient outcomes on mortality measures compared to non-'Magnet' hospitals. *Health Affairs, 34,* 986–992. doi:10 .1377/hlthaff.2014.0793

Health Resources and Services Administration. (2010). *HRSA study finds nursing workforce is growing and more diverse.* Retrieved from https://www.hrsa.gov/about/news/pressreleases/2010/100317_hrsa_study_100317_finds_nursing _workforce_is_growing_and_more_diverse.html

Health Resources and Services Administration. (2013). *The U.S. nursing workforce: Trends in supply and education.* Retrieved from https://bhw.hrsa.gov/sites/default/files/bhw/nchwa/projections/nursingworkforcetrendsoct2013.pdf

Health Resources and Services Administration. (2017). *National and regional supply and demand projections of the nursing workforce: 2014–2030.* Retrieved from https://bhw.hrsa.gov/sites/default/files/bhw/nchwa/projections/ NCHWA_HRSA_Nursing_Report.pdf

Institute of Medicine. (2011). *The future of nursing: Leading change, advancing health.* Washington, DC: National Academies Press.

Jones, D., McLaughlin, M., Gebbens, C., & Terhorst, L. (2015). Utilizing a scope and span of control tool to measure workload and determine supporting resources for nurse managers. *Journal of Nursing Administration, 45,* 243–249. doi:10.1097/NNA.0000000000000193

Joseph, M.L., & Bogue, R.J. (2016). A theory-based approach to nursing shared governance. *Nursing Outlook, 64,* 339–351. doi:10.1016/j.outlook.2016.01.004

Kath, L.M., Stichler, J.F., & Ehrhart, M.G. (2012). Moderators of the negative outcomes of nurse manager stress. *Journal of Nursing Administration, 42,* 215–221. doi:10.1097/NNA.0b013e31824ccd25

Kovner, C.T., Brewer, C.S., Fatehi, F., & Jun, J. (2014). What does nurse turnover rate mean and what is the rate? *Policy, Politics, and Nursing Practice, 15*(3–4), 64–71. doi:10.1177/1527154414547953

Laschinger, H.K.S., Almost, J., & Tuer-Hodes, D. (2003). Workplace empowerment and magnet hospital characteristics: Making the link. *Journal of Nursing Administration, 33,* 410–422.

Lown, B.A., & Manning, C.F. (2010). The Schwartz Center rounds: Evaluation of an interdisciplinary approach to enhancing patient-centered communication, teamwork, and provider support. *Academic Medicine, 85,* 1073–1081. doi:10.1097/ACM.0b013e3181dbf741

MacPhee, M., Skelton-Green, J., Bouthillette, F., & Suryaprakash, N. (2012). An empowerment framework for nursing leadership development: Supporting evidence. *Journal of Advanced Nursing, 68,* 159–169. doi:10.1111/j.1365-2648.2011.05746.x

McHugh, M.D., Kutney-Lee, A., Cimiotti, J.P., Sloane, D.M., & Aiken, L.H. (2011). Nurses' widespread job dissatisfaction, burnout, and frustration with health benefits signal problems for patient care. *Health Affairs, 30,* 202–210. doi:10.1377/hlthaff.2010.0100

Press Ganey. (2015). *Nursing special report: The influence of nurse work environment on patient, payment and nurse outcomes in acute care settings.* South Bend, IN: Author.

Robust. (n.d.-a). In *Macmillan online dictionary.* Retrieved from http://www.macmillandictionary.com/us/dictionary/american/robust

Robust. (n.d.-b). In *Merriam-Webster online dictionary* (11th ed.). Retrieved from https://www.merriam-webster.com/dictionary/robust

Rothenberger, S. (2014, January 13). How important is having an effective manager? *Advisory Board Company Expert Insight.* Retrieved from https://www.advisory.com/talent-development/employee-engagement-initiative/members/expert-insights/2011/how-important-is-having-an-effective-manager

Schwartz Center for Compassionate Healthcare. (n.d.). Schwartz Rounds™. Retrieved from http://www.theschwartzcenter.org/supporting-caregivers/schwartz-center-rounds

Sermeus, W., Aiken, L.H., Van den Heede, K., Rafferty, A.M., Griffiths, P., Moreno-Casbas, M.T., … RN4CAST Consortium. (2011). Nurse forecasting in Europe (RN4CAST): Rationale, design and methodology. *BMC Nursing, 10,* 6. doi:10.1186/1472-6955-10-6

Shirey, M.R. (2006). Stress and coping in nurse managers: Two decades of research. *Nursing Economics, 24,* 193–203, 211.

Sikka, R., Morath, J.M., & Leape, L. (2015). The Quadruple Aim: Care, health, cost and meaning in work [Editorial]. *BMJ Quality and Safety, 24,* 608–610. doi:10.1136/bmjqs-2015-004160

Strumwasser, S., & Virkstis, K. (2015). Meaningfully incorporating staff input to enhance frontline engagement. *Journal of Nursing Administration, 45,* 179–182. doi:10.1097/NNA.0000000000000179

Thompson, A. (2013). How Schwartz rounds can be used to combat compassion fatigue. *Nursing Management, 20*(4), 16–20. doi:10.7748/nm2013.07.20.4.16.e1102

Vonderhaar, K., & Simmons, M. (2016). *The data-driven prescription for leader engagement: Best practices for engaging managers and directors.* Retrieved from https://www.advisory.com/research/hr-advancement-center/studies/2016/the-data-driven-prescription-for-leader-engagement

Warshawsky, N.E., & Havens, D.S. (2011). Global use of the Practice Environment Scale of the Nursing Work Index. *Nursing Research, 60,* 17–31. doi:10.1097/NNR.0b013e3181ffa79c

Warshawsky, N.E., Rayens, M., Lake, S.W., & Havens, D.S. (2013). The nurse manager practice environment scale: Development and psychometric testing. *Journal of Nursing Administration, 43,* 250–257. doi:10.1097/NNA.0b013e3182898e4e

Yarbrough, S., Martin, P., Alfred, D., & McNeill, C. (2017). Professional values, job satisfaction, career development, and intent to stay. *Nursing Ethics, 24,* 675–685. doi:10.1177/0969733015623098

Yu, D., Harter, J., & Agrawal, S. (2013, April 26). U.S. managers boast best work engagement. *Gallup Economy.* Retrieved from http://www.gallup.com/poll/162062/managers-boast-best-work-engagement.aspx

CHAPTER 8

Communication Strategies in the Multigenerational Workforce

Connie Carson, PhD, and Brittany Lively, BS, PA-C

Allow me to introduce a man named Ptah-hotep, who lived about 4,500 years ago in Egypt. There were no pyramids built in his honor; he was just a bureaucrat, an adviser to a pharaoh. But he left behind an inestimable treasure. He wrote the world's oldest book.

You might expect his hieroglyphics to chronicle heroic deeds in battle, or burial rites or tax collection, things we know were important in antiquity. But Ptah-hotep set forth something else entirely. . . . He had a lot to say about showing respect for authority. . . . But he also urges us to honor the people around us by being "bright-faced," generous, and humble, and by helping them feel comfortable and appreciated. Ptah-hotep's purpose is social harmony.

Things were pretty much falling apart in the twenty-fifth century BC, in his view. Kids weren't obeying their parents . . . . Leaders were prone to absolutism. So our ancestral author, composing what would become the urtext of human civilization, made an exhaustive effort to set things right with a plea for understanding, composure, and care.

"Kindness is a man's memorial," he wrote. . . . Also: "If thou be powerful, make thyself to be honoured for knowledge and for gentleness."

. . . He calls on leaders to be patient with subordinates and to allow them to vent without interruption: "Be gracious when thou hearkenest unto the speech of a suppliant." He directs those in power to leave behind a legacy of compassion.

—Sarah L. Kaufman (2016, pp. xxi–xxii)

Introduction

The authors of this chapter transcend four generations: maturer, baby boomer, generation X, and millennial. In addressing dynamics unique to different generations, it is relevant to acknowledge that some strategies are timeless. The teachings of Ptah-hotep are poignant and applicable to the past, present, and future.

While acknowledging limitations to the characteristics used to describe the five generations currently in the workforce, this chapter will define these generations and include communication strategies for leaders. Excellent leadership and management strategies will be identified with recommendations to enhance performance in the multigenerational workforce. This chapter will also explore the dynamics of the spoken word, word perceptions, active listening, nonverbal communication, written language, and electronic interactions.

The workforce in America has been categorized into five generations: veterans or maturers (in some sources also referred to as "traditionalists"), baby boomers, generation Xers, millennials, and the iGeneration, or iGens. A wide variety of research exists on the topic of multigenerational communication styles (e.g., Bendix & Evans, 2009; Carver & Candela, 2008; Sherman, 2008; Stockburger, 2008; Weingarten, 2009). The concept of generations was first addressed in the 1920s by German sociologist Karl Mannheim in his essay "The Problem of Generations" (Mannheim, 1970).

Carver and Candela (2008) conducted an extensive review of the literature regarding organizational commitment and generational differences in employees. They summarized that leaders of healthcare organizations must understand what makes their work environment desirable to nurses of all ages who are seeking employment. By understanding these needs, employers can improve recruitment, retention, and organizational commitment of their nursing workforce.

In exploring the literature, it is difficult to determine the legitimacy and origin of these generational categories. Carson and Lasker-Hertz (2011) cautioned that the categories should not be interpreted definitively. Individuals cannot be placed in a given category solely by chronologic age. Some people fall in between groups because they are on the cusp of a generation span or they have a different life perspective. Just because an individual is a specific chronologic age does not mean he or she will automatically fit a given category.

Many agree that the categories "make sense"; however, because these were written decades ago, it warrants questioning as to the validity of each category. Who authored the original categories? Were minorities included in these categories? What geographic areas were assessed? Whom did the populations comprise? Urbanites? Students? Rural communities? Lesbian, gay, bisexual, and transgender individuals? People from other cultures and countries? What limitations should be considered? Finding answers to these questions is nigh to impossible.

Consider the following description of a generation: *A desire to choose their own way; question authority; distance themselves from the older segments of society; value honesty and joy; not concerned with job security; use cannabis, considering it pleasurable and benign; loyalty to one another; not interested in monogamy.* While it may describe the youth of today, it also describes maturers, when they were part of the hippie generation. Perhaps life scenarios have changed and technology has accelerated, but some basic characteristics apply to many of us, at different stages of life. Will millennials and iGens develop characteristics of the baby boomers and maturers, as they mature? Do millennials and iGens see the characteristics that have been written about their generation as legitimate?

To investigate this point, Lively (2016) conducted an online, unpublished focus group involving 14 medical professionals born between 1980 and 1991. The mean age of the group was 28. The survey did not allow the exploration of additional demographic diversity. All participants were asked to discuss both their perceived values and motivations as a generation. Common values described included work–life balance, loyalty, integrity, and respect. The far majority, 11 of 14 respondents, listed work–life balance as a top value of their generation. When asked to compare their own values to those of baby boomers, most felt that the baby boomer generation put more value on success, stability, and dedication. Additionally, the group was asked what motivates their generation. Responses varied but included answers such as "words of affirmation and appreciation," "monetary gain," "life outside of work," and "happiness." Participants also were asked to describe how they think members of their generation work best. Twelve of the 14 respondents stated that a group or team-based approach was ideal; however, five respondents mentioned that individual opportunity was key for success within their generation as well. Lastly, the group was asked to address the weaknesses of the next generation, the iGeneration, when compared to their own generation. Common answers included "taking too many shortcuts," "lack of thoroughness," "a sense of entitlement," and "lack of commitment." Eight participants felt that the iGeneration lacks interpersonal communication skills, with five of these participants directly linking this to the impact of technology and social media.

As a leader, view all staff as individuals, with unique values and beliefs. Get to know them and build relationships. Discover their likes and dislikes, their goals and aspirations; seek to meet them where they are. No one likes to be stereotyped, especially based on categories that are not truly evidence based.

Historical Background

An article in the *Harvard Business Review* encouraged managers to not dwell on the differences of "the Boomer mystified by Facebook; the Millennial who wears flip-flops in the office; the Traditionalist . . . who seemingly won't ever retire; the cynical Gen Xer who's only out for himself; and the Gen 2020er . . . who appears surgically attached to her smartphone" (Knight, 2014). "There is no evidence that 35-year-old managers today are any different from 35-year-old managers a generation ago," according to author and professor Peter Cappelli (Knight, 2014). Move beyond labels; get to know each person individually.

Bell (2013) suggested that gen Xers, "who grew up with Sesame Street and keeping themselves occupied, do not have the attention spans required for learning from traditional lectures. Many prefer role play, visual stimulation, and immediate feedback" (p. 208). Werth and Werth (2011) suggested that lectures should last no more than 15 minutes followed by group discussion. If that were the case, how have millennials gotten to the position where they currently function today, considering many are in their thirties? How did they obtain their nursing degrees? Advanced degrees? Become home owners and parents? As early as 2001, Weston provided coaching suggestions for different age groups. While that may appear ideal, one must use caution to avoid age discrimination or preferential treatment given to one age group to the exclusion of another. Chapter 16 explores teaching and learning strategies for multigenerational students in academia.

Stanley (2010) suggested that differences may actually be myths and that a degree of caution is required before people are labeled and boxed by their generational group. Within each generation, there are a multitude of individuals with their own unique personalities and cultural imprints.

Deal (2007) suggested that generation gaps do not exist, suggesting instead that each person is different. If an organization is healthy, it will be so for all employees regardless of their generational group. From this, the key principle is to treat everyone in the team equally and show respect for all (Stanley, 2010). Although it is relevant to quote Oliver Wendell Holmes Sr. (1809–

1894), "No generalization is worth a damn, including this one," it still is prudent and beneficial to define the categories proposed in the literature, with the supposition that they are not exclusively definitive.

Defining the Five Generations in the Workforce

Actual dates of generational demarcations are generally based on chronologic age and vary greatly across various published accounts. Most agree that maturers or veterans were born prior to 1946. Baby boomers were born roughly during the years 1946–1964. Generation X typically covers people born between the mid-1960s and the early 1980s. Millennials, or generation Y, were born between the 1980s and 2000. Generation Z, or the iGeneration (also referred to as nexters), includes children born after 2000 (Waterworth, 2013).

Maturers entered their careers during the time that research on the scientific and humanistic perspectives of management and communication theories was emerging. While a small number remain employed in the hospital setting, many are found in volunteer services and in our hospital beds—our Medicare patients (Cahill & Sedrak, 2012). If they are women, they feel pride in being the first generation of women to join the workforce. Throughout their careers, they averaged 5–10 years at each position. They respect honor, dedication, sacrifice, and duty. They take pleasure in their commitment to the company and the field of nursing. Solid and reliable nurses, they value consistency and are no-nonsense performers for which change does not occur easily (Hahn, 2011). Their bosses in the past primarily have been male, and they often have a hierarchical respect for physicians. Awed by technology, they previously were reluctant computer users. Although they are now computer literate, it may have been difficult for them to become so. They are not going quietly into old age. They may appear angry that their investments did not accumulate as anticipated, that unforeseen expenses occurred, or that their retirement funds are not lasting as long as predicted. Thus, they are working more years than previously envisioned. They respond best to clearly defined, measurable work goals with established deadlines.

Certainly, not all **baby boomers** participated in the sexual revolution nor boycotted the Vietnam War; however, a passion for causes typifies this generation. Today, they want to feel as though they make a significant contribution to the world. Their loyalty is to the people they work with and the hands-on experience they gain from their patients. They are motivated by money and have a strong work ethic. Many boomers are working today because they want to, because they enjoy the challenge, and they seek a position that is personally fulfilling. They are motivated by mentoring, flexible schedules, and rewarding work. Nelsey and Brownie (2012) stated that boomers accept decisions based on what is best for the organization, possess a high tolerance for being told what to do by management, and seek to facilitate rapport building and social cohesion in teams. They see technology as an important vehicle and are challenged by the computer savvy of generation Xers, millennials, and iGens. In contrast to what they envisioned in their youth during the 1960s and 1970s, they tend to be workaholics, service oriented, and optimistic (Kramer, 2010). Work is a major part of their identity, often prioritized before family.

Generation Xers have been particularly impacted by the dot-com boom and bust. They have seen huge opportunities for personal advancement shattered by corporate infrastructure. Bell (2013) stated they distrust companies, as they watched their parents lose jobs to downsizing. They are highly motivated by the now, see a satisfying position as one that makes them happy, and place their personal needs over the needs of the organization. Nursing is not necessarily a lifelong calling; it is something they are doing for the present. Hahn (2011) found that gen Xers want action rather than talk and promises. They want to lead as well as to follow. When placed on a team, they are interested in knowing how they will benefit from the experience. They want to be formulators of the plan and involved in decision-making strategies. A team for Xers may look different from anything previously seen. As they are directing their own course, expect innovative solutions. Give them some latitude and involve them in decision making. They show a reluctance to accept an authority figure merely because of the position held in the company. They have an ease and comfort with technology that boomers and maturers envy. They may question the work ethic of baby boomers because they want more individual freedom than they see in the lives of the boomers or maturers. Often, a good job for them is one in which they are happy. Working weekends and holidays does not make them happy.

Millennials are optimistic but do not have an employment history to substantiate their dreams. They are interested in their future, their goals, and their personal options. Reportedly, their heroes are themselves (Carson, 2011). Before the last recession, they were changing jobs and searching for new challenges. Often referred to as generation Y, many were computer literate in grade school. They have a comfort with technologic advancements that even generation Xers will not be able to experience. They are tolerant of other races, nationalities, and sexual orientations. Older generations have criticized the parents of millennials for being too involved in the lives of their children. Haim Ginott, in his 1969 textbook *Parents and Teenagers*, first coined the term "helicopter parents" as they hovered overhead, overseeing their child's experiences, particularly at educational institutions.

Teams for the millennial generation will take different forms, including virtual teams—team members they may never personally meet. They have high expectations but lack the blueprint for getting from where they are today to where they would like to go in the future. More than one in three American workers today are millennials (Fry, 2015). They are ambitious but need direction and the ability to make their own mistakes and choose their own courses. Hills, Ryan, Warren-Forward, and Smith (2013) offered practical suggestions for optimizing the potential of this generation. They suggested that all staff require feedback, praise, and the need to feel valued. A team approach may help to prevent ageism, promote intergenerational working, and ensure that the wisdom of older generations is passed to generation Y, as they are the successors and the next leaders for 21st-century health care.

Born after 1995, the **iGeneration** currently comprises 23 million individuals and is rapidly growing (Schroer, n.d.). As most are younger than 20 years old, they are new to enter the workforce. Many are in the healthcare setting as interns, volunteers, nursing students, or new graduates. They are commonly referred to as iGen because they have never known a world without the Internet, computers, or cell phones. They are also called generation Z because they follow generations X and Y. As they span the birth years from the mid to late 1990s to the present, the oldest of this generation are just now entering the workforce. Already, experts are predicting key traits by understanding the challenges these children will face: technology, terrorism, and climate change. To reach iGens, Schneider (2015) urged leaders to be transparent, personal, and overly social. Marketers must change the way they communicate with this generation of digital natives, or iGens will move on to brands that do.

They may never buy a house or wear a watch. They may not be able to write in cursive. Most of their communication takes place on the Internet or by cell phone. They are used to instant messaging, texting, and friending and unfriending, seemingly on a whim. They communicate through Facebook, Instagram, and Twitter, as well as programs unknown to many older generations, such as Reddit, Snapchat, and Tumblr, with new programs continually emerging. They may be very close friends with people they have never met. Their parents may have experienced financial difficulties or are unemployed. It has been suggested they may be less indulged and entitled than millennials ("Generation Z Characteristics," n.d.).

It is natural to hope that the newest group of people to enter the workforce will be the "brightest and the best," able to learn from the mistakes and accomplishments of the maturers, boomers, generation Xers, and millennials. Effective managers recognize generational and cultural differences, challenge their staff appropriately, and establish a work environment that tolerates and welcomes the needs and expectations of multigenerational employees.

Established Tools for Determining Individual Differences

Personal inventory tools can bring objectivity to communicating with staff members. These instruments can be beneficial for personal growth and team building, assist in embracing personality and behavioral diversity in the workforce, and result in improved hiring decisions. In addition, they can help to define job requirements, attract the best candidates, plan for future growth, improve productivity, retain potential leaders, and assist with succession planning. Some even adhere to the guidelines of the Equal Employment Opportunity Commission, as well as professional standards established by the American Psychological Association and the Society for Industrial and Organizational Psychology.

They transcend age, place, race, creed, employment, and gender. Numerous inventories are available to assess personal characteristics that affect job performance and workplace behavior. Although many inventory tools have been researched and developed, classics include the Predictive Index®, the Myers-Briggs Type Indicator®, the DiSC® personality assessment tool, the Leadership Practices Inventory®, and the Riso-Hudson Enneagram Type Indicator. Validating the specific characteristics that each employee brings to the workplace may help define strengths, address weaknesses, and provide insight into mentoring the skills of future managers and leaders.

Management and Leadership

Just because someone is an excellent manager, by job title, does not mean that same person is an effective leader. Likewise, leaders are not necessarily excellent managers. The go2 Tourism HR Society (n.d.) suggested that a manager is a position on an organizational chart and is defined by specific expectations and roles. Managers have people work for them; leaders have people follow them. Managers ensure that the day-to-day details are transpiring as they should. Leaders encourage people to follow a common vision and work toward its accomplishment. President Eisenhower has been quoted as saying, "Leadership is the art of getting someone else to do something you want done because he wants to do it." Characteristics that are applicable to both excellent managers and excellent leaders include the following:

• Foster collaboration within the hospital and also in their virtual network
• Handle difficult times with honesty, thoughtfulness, and sensitivity
• Learn from their mistakes and are not afraid to admit when they are wrong
• Empower their staff and are not hesitant to give important jobs to others, along with the authority to accomplish these tasks
• Know the importance of levity; laugh often, especially at oneself; and make room for fun
• Manage and embrace continuous change
• Recognize that patient care is difficult and personally exhausting, understand the emotional demands placed upon their staff, and acknowledge the value of their efforts
• Listen to and respect the opinions of others

- Establish positive relationships at all levels
- Offer genuine praise for a job well done, as immediately as possible and publicly when appropriate
  In dealing with the multigenerational workforce, excellent managers and leaders:
- Do not allow the chronologic ages of employees to influence their decision making
- Avoid pigeonholing employees based on non–evidence-based behavioral categories
- Offer fair initiatives and reinforcements regardless of age, ethnicity, or lifestyle
- Understand that all employees, regardless of their generational category, bring to the work environment different priorities, demands, expectations, and aspirations
- Encourage the transfer of knowledge from one generation to another and facilitate intergenerational cross-mentoring
- Hold each employee to the same employment expectations, organizational goals, and policies and procedures, while recognizing individual differences (Sherman, 2006)
- Meet with top employees within each generation to identify means in which employees can advance within the organization, facilitate work–life balance, offer better or more competitive remuneration and benefits, develop ways of providing respect and recognition for efforts, and offer educational opportunities for learning and development

Excellent managers and leaders also implement excellent communication skills—but what does that mean?

The Spoken Word, Word Perceptions, Active Listening, and Nonverbal, Written, and Electronic Communication Across Generations

According to the *Online Etymology Dictionary*, the term *communication* dates back to the late 14th century, from the Latin *communicationem*, meaning "to share, divide out; impart, inform; join, unite, participate in" ("Communication," n.d.). Everything one does involves communication—not just some things, but everything. An organization staffed by effective communicators benefits patients, patients' family members, the hospital or clinical care setting, managers, the physicians, nursing staff, allied healthcare providers, the human resource department, administration, the community, and the financial bottom line.

Whether one is in the employment setting, at home, or with friends, communication is dynamic—coming apart, expanding, deepening, or distancing. People working together may become friends, relationships may deepen, or tensions may occur. The workload may intensify and time previously available for more personal interactions may be limited.

Communication styles that were effective generations ago may not be relevant to younger employees. Patterns of interaction that were effective last year may be outdated today because of changes in technology, patient preferences, or the nature of health care. Healthcare workers today must possess a global awareness of pandemics and epidemics, fears that were only ethereal to previous generations. Nanotechnology, robotics, gene therapies, electronic health records, and biometrics have become a reality. Expert decision-making skills are essential. Politics invades all aspects of health care. The nurse leader must clearly understand and intervene in the ever-changing politics of health care.

Communication includes the spoken word, the written word, perceptions, listening, nonverbal communication, and electronic interactions. Words count for only 30% of interpersonal communication (Scott, 2009). Communication requires a two-way flow of information. It cannot be done in a vacuum. When one speaks, there is the implication that someone may hear, even if one speaks to oneself. Whereas one person in isolation can dispense language, communication requires reciprocity.

The tone of one's voice, the emphasis or inflections given to certain words, the pauses inserted in a sentence, and nonverbal behaviors contribute special meanings to the spoken word. Depending on the tone, inflection, and emphasis, a simple "yes" can convey anger, resentment, acknowledgment, happiness, or fated resolution. Vocal inflections and pitch can communicate alarm, annoyance, and fear; a slow tempo often signals uncertainty. Vocal quality can imply a message of caring or being too busy to listen to the needs of others. Some words do not translate from one generation to another. Language has many facets among different cultures and generations. For example, for iGeners, *bad* can mean "good," and "it's been a minute" means it has been a long time.

It takes more effort to be an active listener than to be an effective speaker. Active listeners are reticent to interrupt, wait for responses, and are comfortable with silence. When they listen well, they use empathy, suspend judgment, and ask questions appropriately. They try to listen long enough to hear what the person means. C.S. Lewis, the author of the *Chronicles of Narnia* series, wrote that to be truly heard "is the whole art and joy of words" (Lewis, 1956, pp. 293–294). Management theorist Peter Drucker, as quoted by Edersheim (2007), stated that the most important thing in communication is to hear what is not being said. Silence often conveys more than words. Oliver Wendell Holmes Sr. has been quoted as saying, "It is the province of knowledge to speak, and it is the privilege of wisdom to listen."

Nonverbal communication includes but is not limited to body language and physical movements. It also now includes the etiquette of electronic communication such as emails and texting. What we wear and how we sound also are considered nonverbal communication. We have become subtle in our verbal relationships with others, but we still rarely know how to lie nonverbally. Our tone of voice, eye contact, facial expressions, gestures, and posture convey our true intent. The nonverbal trumps the verbal in accuracy. Some of the most influential responses are genuine smiles, touch, affirmative head nods, and eye contact.

Times will arise when the only means of communicating to staff is in writing. Written communication is ideal when imparting a perception of formality and authority, leaving a permanent record, or ensuring that a large number of people have access to the same exact information. However, the written word possesses definite disadvantages. It limits immediate feedback when staff members need to ask questions or seek clarification. It often takes more time to put information into writing than it does to leave a voice mail message or contact an individual personally.

The ability of the astute healthcare provider to seamlessly integrate information, connect with patients, and communicate with staff is highly dependent on the use of technology. It is time to tweet about the Facebook page, which links to the blog that hosts a YouTube video of the podcast written on the recruitment of staff through LinkedIn, which cited journal articles found on PubMed. Electronic health records have emerged as a routine option for patients to take control of their medical data and become active participants in the push toward widespread digitized health care. Nurse leaders must look at the Internet not as a peripheral tool but rather as central to the clinical process. Porter-O'Grady and Malloch (2008) stressed that computerized documentation systems, electronic prescription systems, computerized physician order entry, caregiver smartphones or tablets, computers on wheels, and staff-to-staff wireless communication systems must be considered essential venues for patient care. Breakdowns in electronic communication can be just as devastating as breakdowns in face-to-face interactions. While traditional sources such as the National Library of Medicine (www.nlm.nih.gov), PubMed (www.ncbi.nlm.nih.gov/pubmed), and evidence-based medical resources are generally accurate, the quality of information on blogs and social networking sites is debatable. The great value of the Internet is its availability, but the potential always exists for misinformation and unauthorized secondary use.

Like the spoken word, electronic communication presents the opportunity for inappropriate or misconstrued emails. For example, attachments to a document may be incomplete, use of all capital letters or bolding the entire email and extra-large font may send an unintended message, or multiple email threads may include individuals to whom the information should not have been sent. An email may be written in haste and not reviewed appropriately before the "send" button is clicked. When this occurs, it is important for the person to acknowledge it, confess if necessary, explain when appropriate, and attempt to not repeat the error in the future. Always proof attachments. Think before you click "send," and attempt to repair relationships when they are damaged.

The Future

Grooming staff for leadership positions ensures that as aging employees retire, strong leaders will be ready to take their place. The jobs must be rewarding if they are to attract the workers of the future. Flexibility in schedules and work hours will be critical. Successful healthcare providers will be those who are accessible; build positive relationships; listen to the needs, concerns, and frustrations of each member of the workforce; praise job accomplishments; and demonstrate compassion for personal setbacks in the lives of each employee. Young staff require structured training in personnel management, financial planning, vision development, and long-term management of resources to develop the characteristics of leadership (Stockburger, 2008).

Summary

For millions of years, mankind lived just like the animals. Then something happened which unleashed the power of our imagination. We learned to talk and we learned to listen. Speech has allowed the communication of ideas, enabling human beings to work together to build the impossible. Mankind's greatest achievements have come about by talking, and its greatest failures by not talking. It doesn't have to be like this. Our greatest hopes could become reality in the future. With the technology at our disposal, the possibilities are unbounded. All we need to do is make sure we keep talking.

—Stephen Hawking

Throughout history, the ability of a society to survive has been predicated on its willingness to adapt to change. In addition, cultural changes between generations and a generation's effectiveness in passing knowledge and expertise to the next is important (Stockburger, 2008). A wide variety of research has been conducted on multigenerational communicational styles (Bell, 2013; Cahill & Sedrak, 2012; LaBan, 2013).

Future researchers are encouraged to apply evidence-based theory in validating the accuracy of the multigenerational categories. Decades of writings has substantiated the acceptable generational differences since Mannheim in the early 1920s. Being able to communicate across generations with staff is at the heart of leader success now and in the future.

References

Bell, J.A. (2013). Five generations in the nursing workforce: Implications for nursing professional development. *Journal for Nurses in Professional Development, 29,* 205–210. doi:10.1097/NND.0b013e31829aedd4

Bendix, J., & Evans, L. (2009). Bridging the generation gap: Generational differences can be a source of conflict, but they can also result in better medicine. *Medical Economics, 86*(5), 30–34.

Cahill, T.F., &, Sedrak, M. (2012). Leading a multigenerational workforce: Strategies for attracting and retaining millennials. *Frontiers of Health Services Management, 29*(1), 3–15.

Carson, C.J. (2011). Dynamics of communication. In M.M. Gullatte (Ed.), *Nursing management: Principles and practice* (2nd ed., pp. 77–95). Pittsburgh, PA: Oncology Nursing Society.

Carson, C.J., & Lasker-Hertz, S. (2011). Transforming management theory into practice. In M.M. Gullatte (Ed.), *Nursing management: Principles and practice* (2nd ed., pp. 45–62). Pittsburgh, PA: Oncology Nursing Society.

Carver, L., & Candela, L. (2008). Attaining organizational commitment across different generations of nurses. *Journal of Nursing Management, 16,* 984–991. doi:10.1111/j.1365-2834.2008.00911.x

Communication. (n.d.). In *Online etymology dictionary.* Retrieved from http://www.etymonline.com/index.php?term=communication

Deal, J.J. (2007). *Retiring the generation gap: How employees young and old can find common ground.* San Francisco, CA: Jossey-Bass.

Edersheim, E.H. (2007). *The definitive Drucker.* New York, NY: McGraw-Hill.

Fry, R. (2015). Millennials surpass Gen Xers as the largest generation in U.S. labor force. Pew Research Center. Retrieved from http://www.pewresearch.org/fact-tank/2015/05/11/millennials-surpass-gen-xers-as-the-largest-generation-in-u-s-labor-force

Generation Z characteristics. (n.d.). Retrieved from http://www.rocketswag.com/retirement/baby-boomer/generation-z

Ginott, H.G. (1969). *Between parent and teenager.* New York, NY: Macmillan.

go2 Tourism HR Society. (n.d.). Understanding the differences: Leadership vs. management. Retrieved from https://www.go2hr.ca/articles/understanding-differences-leadership-vs-management

Hahn, J.A. (2011). Managing multiple generations: Scenarios from the workplace. *Nursing Forum, 46,* 119–127. doi:10.1111/j.1744-6198.2011.00223.x

Hills, C., Ryan, S., Warren-Forward, H., & Smith, D.R. (2013). Managing 'Generation Y' occupational therapists: Optimising their potential. *Australian Occupational Therapy Journal, 60,* 267–275. doi:10.1111/1440-1630.12043

Kaufman, S.L. (2016). *The art of grace: On moving well through life.* New York, NY: W.W. Norton & Company.

Knight, R. (2014, September 25). Managing people from 5 generations. *Harvard Business Review.* https://hbr.org/2014/09/managing-people-from-5-generations

Kramer, L.W. (2010). Generational diversity. *Dimensions of Critical Care Nursing, 29,* 125–128. doi:10.1097/DCC.0b013e3181d24ba9

LaBan, M.M. (2013). A late Y2K phenomenon: Responding to the learning preferences of Generation Y—Bridging the digital divide by improving generational dialogue. *PM&R, 5,* 596–601. doi:10.1016/j.pmrj.2013.04.010

Lewis, C.S. (1956). *Till we have faces: A myth retold.* New York, NY: HarperCollins.

Lively, B. (2016). [Reflecting on a generation: A millennial focus group]. Unpublished raw data.

Mannheim, K. (1970). The problem of generations. *Psychoanalytic Review, 57,* 378–404.

Nelsey, L., & Brownie, S. (2012). Effective leadership, teamwork and mentoring—Essential elements in promoting generational cohesion in the nursing workforce and retaining nurses. *Collegian, 19,* 197–202.

Porter-O'Grady, T., & Malloch, K. (2008). Beyond myth and magic: The future of evidence-based leadership. *Nursing Administration Quarterly, 32,* 176–187. doi:10.1097/01.NAQ.0000325174.30923.b6

Schneider, J. (2015). How to market to the iGeneration. *Harvard Business Review.* Retrieved from https://hbr.org/2015/05/how-to-market-to-the-igeneration

Schroer, W.J. (n.d.). Generations X, Y, Z, and the others. Retrieved from http://socialmarketing.org/archives/generations-xy-z-and-the-others

Scott, G. (2009). Leading in hard times: Successful strategies to ensure employee commitment and loyalty in times of change. *Healthcare Executive, 24*(3), 60, 62–63.

Sherman, R.O. (2006). Leading a multigenerational nursing workforce: Issues, challenges and strategies. *Online Journal of Issues in Nursing, 11*(2), 2. Retrieved from http://www.nursingworld.org/MainMenuCategories/ANAMarketplace/ANAPeriodicals/OJIN/TableofContents/Volume112006/No2May06/tpc30_216074.html

Sherman, R.O. (2008). One size doesn't fit all: Motivating a multigenerational staff. *Nursing Management, 39*(9), 8, 10. doi:10.1097/01.NUMA.0000335251.85671.eb

Stanley, D. (2010). Multigenerational workforce issues and their implications for leadership in nursing. *Journal of Nursing Management, 18,* 846–852. doi:10.1111/j.1365-2834.2010.01158.x

Stockburger, W.T. (2008). Leadership challenges of a multigenerational workforce. *Radiology Management, 30*(1), 43–49.

Waterworth, N. (April 9, 2013). Generation X, Generation Y, Generation Z, and the Baby Boomers. *Talented Heads.* Retrieved from http://www.talentedheads.com/2013/04/09/generation-confused/

Weingarten, R.M. (2009). Four generations, one workplace: A Gen X-Y staff nurse's view of team building in the emergency department. *Journal of Emergency Nursing, 35,* 27–30. doi:10.1016/j.jen.2008.02.017

Werth, E.P., & Werth, L. (2011). Effective training for millennial students. *Adult Learning, 22*(3), 31–39. doi:10.1177/104515951102200302

Weston, M. (2001). Coaching generations in the workplace. *Nursing Administration Quarterly, 25*(2), 11–21. doi:10.1097/00006216-200101000-00005

CHAPTER 9

Compassionate Care Begins With Self-Care

LeAnn Thieman, LPN, CSP, CPAE

Every human being has the same potential for compassion; the only question is whether we really take any care of that potential, and develop and implement it in our daily life.

—Dalai Lama

Introduction

This chapter is purposefully written in a personal voice to give readers a sense of reconnecting with their innermost thoughts and feelings and reflecting on their own need for self-care as a professional caring for others. The author is one of the world-renowned authors of *Chicken Soup for the Nurse's Soul* (Canfield, Hansen, Mitchell-Autio, & Thieman, 2012).

Much has been written in the literature related to care of the caregiver and publications on recognizing and understanding compassion fatigue (Cocker & Joss, 2016; Najjar, Davis, Beck-Coon, & Doebbeling, 2009). Compassion fatigue as defined by Cocker and Joss (2016) reflects a convergence of secondary traumatic stress and cumulative burnout resulting in a state of physical and mental exhaustion caused by a depleted ability to cope with one's everyday environment. Self-care is critical to one's ability to deliver compassionate care to others. This definition parallels with that of *burnout*, which results from chronic work-related stressors (Leiter & Maslach, 2009).

In this chapter, I will take a more personable approach to enlightening the reader about self-care to minimize or eliminate compassion fatigue. Drawing from my decades of work with nurses and nurse leaders, I will take you on a journey to restorative self-care.

In these challenging times, healthcare leaders are called upon once again to do more with less. Organizational demands, patient care requirements, and personal economic challenges often leave nurses working longer hours and more days a week, sacrificing self, family, and sleep. Torn between the needs of administration and those of their patients and staff, nurse leaders and families are likewise experiencing stress, burnout, and health issues at rates equal to those of the people they manage. Expectations of staff to deliver comprehensive, compassionate patient care to improve care outcomes, satisfaction and engagement scores, and reimbursements continue to escalate. Yet, wise nurse leaders know that staff caregivers cannot meet those expectations if they are physically, emotionally, mentally, or spiritually exhausted. As leaders work tirelessly to meet the needs of their caregivers, they too frequently neglect their own. Yet, the best way to care for the patients and their caregivers is to care for their leaders. A review of the symptoms of stress and compassion fatigue can be very enlightening (see Figure 9-1).

Being a strong, effective, compassionate leader is not easy. It takes a lot of energy and resilience. To be fortified to manage in this way, we must nurture our own bodies, minds, and spirits every day. We can't just wait for weekends to catch up—sleep in late, eat a big breakfast, and go to church! This chapter will share recommendations for balance of body, mind, and spirit in the context of self-care.

Figure 9-1. Symptoms of Stress and Compassion Fatigue

Physical	Mental	Spiritual
• Appetite changes	• Forgetfulness	• Emptiness
• Headaches	• Poor concentration	• Loss of meaning
• Fatigue	• Dull senses	• Doubt
• Poor sleeping	• Lethargy	• Martyrdom
• Frequent illnesses	• Boredom	• Loss of direction
• Digestive problems	• Low productivity	• Cynicism
• Pounding heart	• Negative attitude	• Apathy
• Teeth grinding	• Anxiety	• Abandonment
• Rash	• The "blues"	• Worry
• Restlessness	• Mood swings	• Isolation
• Foot tapping	• Anger	• Distrust
• Finger drumming	• Bad dreams	• "No one cares"
• Nail biting	• Irritability	
• Smoking	• Crying spells	
• Increased alcohol intake	• Nervous laughter	
	• Loss of loving feeling	

Note. Copyright by LeAnn Thieman, SelfCare for HealthCare™, 2012. Used with permission.

Physical Balance

It is important to find balance of mind, body, and spirit. What happens when your heart stops singing and you lose the joy and passion for the work you have chosen as a nurse? Marcotte (2016) cited the value of a self-care toolkit for well-being. Some tools in the kit include psychological support, spiritual care, exercise, and family connection.

This section will share some of the key aspects and tips to finding that physical balance by paying attention to diet, sleep, and exercise.

Diet

We would never deprive someone we love of food and drink, yet often we do this to ourselves. We treat ourselves in ways we would never treat someone we cared for. Can you imagine saying to a patient, "You can't have anything to eat today; you ate too much yesterday"? Yet how often in our busy lives do we deprive ourselves of food and drink? We know about the four basic food groups, eating according to the MyPlate recommendations, and how to divide our plates into proper food proportions. We teach it, but do we do it? Most of us think we are eating better than we actually are. Keeping a dietary log for a week is most revealing and very helpful.

We also forget to drink—water, that is. We've all read about the importance of drinking five to six glasses of water a day. How simple is that? Yet how often do you remember to do it? Seventy-five percent of Americans are chronically dehydrated, causing daytime fatigue, memory impairment, difficulty focusing, headaches, nausea, and poor metabolism (New York Hospital–Cornell Medical Center, 1998). Epidemiologic evidence links recurrent dehydration associated with periodic water intake with chronic kidney disease (Hilliard et al., 2016).

To get the recommended amount of water daily, try filling a container or water bottle to consume throughout the day. Or drink a glass of water each time you go to the bathroom. (Yes, nurses do go to the bathroom!) Nurture your body with the quantity and quality of food and drink you know it needs and deserves.

Sleep

Research is proving the lifesaving importance of sleep. According to the National Sleep Foundation's (2014) Sleep Health Index™, 45% of Americans reported that poor or insufficient sleep affected their daily activities. While the science of how much sleep is needed is inconclusive, it is understood that the need is individualized and changes over time and age. The National Sleep Foundation published recommendations about the appropriate sleep duration. Their recommendation is that young adults and adults should get 9–11 hours of sleep, while older adults should strive for 7–8 hours of sleep (Hirshkowitz et al., 2015).

In their sample of 153 female nurses aged 20 years and older, Kunzweiler et al. (2016) found that 33% of the participants reported poor quality of sleep. Factors strongly associated with poor sleep quality in the study were lower quality of life, tachycardia, and unequal distribution of workload.

When sleep is inadequate, health deteriorates, resulting in lowered glucose tolerance, impaired thyroid function, fatigue, increased heart rate, decreased strength, higher blood pressure, stomach and bowel problems, pain, decreased ability to fight disease, lowered concentration, increased use of alcohol or aids to stay awake, increased fatty deposits, and decreased work performance, resulting in medical errors (Caruso & Hitchcock, 2010; Hersch et al., 2016; Nea, Kearney, Livingstone, Pourshahidi, & Corish, 2015; Sonati et al., 2015). In addition to these ill health effects on nurses' well-being, stress is a major contributor to attrition and shortages in the nursing profession (Hersch et al., 2016). I believe I have your attention!

Sleep problems contribute to obesity, and obesity contributes to sleep problems (National Sleep Foundation, n.d.-a; Nea et al., 2015). During sleep, the hormone leptin, which controls our appetites, rises in our systems (National Sleep Foundation, n.d.-b). The higher our leptin levels, the less hungry we are. Poor sleep interrupts leptin's rise, so those who do not get enough sleep tend to be hungrier. Have you noticed that when you are overtired, that you feel even hungrier? I still remember getting off 11 pm to 7 am shifts feeling starved until I was able to fall asleep.

Television watching and Internet use can be impediments to adequate sleep. Technology affects our sleep by cognitive stimulation. As our brains rev up, the electrical activity increases and neurons start to race—the exact opposite of what should be happening before sleep. Responding to an unpleasant email can make our bodies tense, resulting in increased levels of the stress hormone cortisol, creating a situation hardly conducive to sleep. More than one female healthcare leader has admitted to me that when she gets up to go to the bathroom at 2 am, she checks her email! *Turn off technology. Turn off electricity. Go to sleep.*

Exercise

In our overscheduled chaotic lives, it often is hard to set aside time for exercise. Yet, research is showing that we do not necessarily have to work out in a gym or have a personal trainer. A recent study of 334,161 European men and women showed that as little as 20 minutes of brisk walking a day could prevent us from dying prematurely (Ekelund et al., 2015). This Cambridge University study found that people who engaged in moderate levels of daily exercise, equivalent to taking an energetic 20-minute walk, were 16%–30% less likely to die prematurely than those classified as inactive. Adults should aim to do at least 150 minutes of moderate-intensity activity a week, which is about 20 minutes a day. We are running out of excuses, because 10-minute sessions are acceptable—the results are cumulative.

As busy as we are, it makes sense to incorporate exercise into our everyday activities. But this is where my grandma must be laughing down from heaven because for all generations before us, men and women got their exercise *from* their everyday activities. But now many Americans pay people to clean our houses, shovel our snow, rake our leaves, and mow our lawns . . . so that we have time to go to a health club and work out! And when we get there, we drive around and around looking for a parking place next to the door so we do not have to walk so far to get our exercise! Be creative in finding ways to incorporate exercise into your daily activities. Park in the farthest corner of the parking lot. Take the time to walk the stairs. Have walking meetings. Take advantage of all the exercise opportunities your employer provides.

A great life balance tool is to incorporate exercise into the priorities of our lives. If your partner is a priority, participate in sports and outdoor activities together or go dancing, a great form of exercise—and you get to hold each other, too! If community service is a priority, lift boxes at the food distribution center or paint a house for Habitat for Humanity. If a priority is caring for family, get exercise with your sweetheart or kids by biking, walking, hiking, swimming, or simply playing ball in the backyard. You are sure to feel young again after some energizing and rigorous exercise. Exercise not only lowers your risk of heart attacks, diabetes, bone cancer, osteoporosis, arthritis, backaches, high blood pressure, depression, and stress (University of Maryland Medical Center, 2012), but it can also increase your family's health and happiness, too.

It is time to care for yourself as consciously as you do others—time to give your body the nutrition, sleep, and exercise it needs. You deserve it.

Mental Balance

Mental balance and well-being are major factors in achieving self-care. This section will outline key aspects of mental balance, and starting with something as simple and basic to life as breathing and followed by equally important actions.

Breathing

Deep relaxation breathing is one of the best and most effective tools for mental rest, relaxation, and focus; however, it is so simple that most people discount it. Relaxation breathing relieves stress and tension and releases endorphins.

As a childbirth educator for 13 years, I taught moms to breathe slowly, deeply, and easily to reduce stress and pain in labor. The same principles apply as we "labor" through life.

When laboring women get too stressed, they experience increased adrenaline, which shuts down the release of oxytocin and delays the delivery. Too much adrenaline from too much stress makes for a longer, harder labor for mom . . . and for us. Breathing and relaxing decrease adrenaline output and allow our organs and body parts to work at their best.

So, several times a day, for three minutes, during stressful times or otherwise, breathe slowly in through your nose to the count of four, then out through your mouth to the count of four. "In, two, three, four; out, two, three, four. I am, two, three, four; relaxed, two, three, four."

In *The Strange Case of Dr. Jekyll and Mr. Hyde*, Robert Louis Stevenson wrote, "Quiet minds cannot be perplexed or frightened, but go on in fortune or misfortune at their own private pace, like a clock during a thunderstorm." *Breathe. Relax.*

Relaxation

We schedule many activities into our day, but we should also schedule relaxation. Ideally, we should allocate at least 15 minutes a day for deep breathing and relaxation, which can also be combined with meditation or prayer. When we do, it becomes a habit, and we can tap into those feelings at any time (see Figure 9-2).

Figure 9-2. Relaxation Exercise

Sag back in your chair. Start relaxing every muscle, beginning with your toes. Stretch out your legs, flex your ankles, try to push your toes right off your feet, then let everything go limp. Let your head fall back. Roll it around so your neck muscles loosen up. Let each hand fall on your knees and rest there as limp as a wet leaf on a log. Open your eyes wide, then pretend invisible weights are attached to your eyelids, slowly pulling them shut. Imagine a soft gentle hand lightly touching your face, smoothing the tension lines away. Picture the tensions draining out of your body, leaving it calm and peaceful and relaxed.

Now see yourself alone in your favorite forest on a perfect summer's day. You are sitting with your back against a tree; you can feel the rough bark through your shirt. All around you is a forest of fir, spruce, and evergreen. The air is scented with balsam. You can hear the gentle sighing in the tree-tops as birds and crickets chirp. The breeze brushes against your face and cools it. In the far distance, green hills are outlined against a tranquil blue heaven. The sky is mirrored in the gleaming mountain stream gently rolling beside you, babbling along smooth, glistening rocks. The warm sun falls on your face like a benediction.

Now visualize that sun warming your body, ever so slowly from your toes toward your head. The warmth is slowly moving from your legs, over your hips, past your stomach. The warm feeling of relaxation is now entering your chest. As it does, concentrate on your breathing. Breathing in ever so slowly, and breathing out. As you breathe in, you are breathing in rays of energy and comfort. Feel the warmth of these rays as they enter your lungs and radiate warmth throughout your body and relax you. As you breathe in, think slowly to yourself "I am," and as you breathe out, think "relaxed." I am relaxed, I am relaxed.

Feel that relaxation spread from your chest to your shoulders and down your arms toward your fingertips. You may feel some tingling sensations in your hands, feet, or down your spine. That's okay; it's just the discharge of nervous energy as you become more and more relaxed.

Now that total relaxation has been achieved, visualize that bright, energizing sun above your head. Feel the warmth from the rays covering and immersing your body in a blanket of warmth. The sun's rays are drawing from you all of your tensions and thoughts. The day's hassles, problems, and worries are leaving you now and your mind is clear and at peace. Everything about you, everything around you feels good. Your whole body from your head to your toes is now engulfed in these magical, golden rays of sun. You feel warm, soothed, and relaxed. Totally at peace and comfortable. Your breathing is slow and deep. Your face is calm and expressionless. You are relaxed. You are calm. You feel wonderful.

Look around at the sights and hear the sounds of your relaxation place. Get to know it well, for once you have created your visualization, the trip back will not be as time consuming and may become instantaneous. Take time now, to feel the sun, hear the soothing songs of the birds—the rippling stream—as you relax.

Note. Copyright by LeAnn Thieman, SelfCare for HealthCare™, 2012. Used with permission.

Relaxation can be enhanced by adding music. Many people find that music with the 4/4 beat makes their hearts beat to that time and will eventually slow to 60 beats per minute, the same as the music. Listening to the same music repeatedly often makes relaxation instantaneous. Keeping our bodies relaxed keeps our emotions under control. We are only as relaxed as our hands and our face. We need to uncurl our fists, decrease our stress, breathe deeply, and relax.

Laughter

As healthcare leaders, we often forget to laugh. Certainly, we would never laugh *at* someone, but we need to laugh often and freely at situations and, mostly, ourselves. Laughter is good for our minds, bodies, and spirits. Children innately know this; they laugh 400 times a day. Adults laugh only 15 times a day (Smith, 2002). You probably know adults who can't meet that quota.

According to the Association for Applied and Therapeutic Humor (n.d.), an organization of doctors and other healthcare professionals, laughter has so many health benefits that they think it should become part of patients' written prescriptions. If a drug had great physiologic, psychological, and immunologic effects, the U.S. Food and Drug Administration would be on it like crazy, regulating it and running trials on it.

Laughter is a form of physical exercise. It is like jogging on the inside. It lowers blood pressure and heart rate, improves lung capacity, massages internal organs, increases memory and alertness, reduces pain, improves digestion, and lowers stress hormones. It is good for the muscles involved in laughter, the chest and abdomen, and it exercises those muscles not involved (Mayo Clinic Staff, 2016).

Loma Linda University proved that laughter decreases the stress hormones epinephrine, norepinephrine, and cortisol. This mechanism explains the connection between laughter and immune function, and from there to improved health outcomes (Berk, Felten, Tan, Bittman, & Westengard, 2001). Laughter has also been proved to reduce pain (Mahony, Burroughs, & Hieatt, 2001).

Laughter offers psychological benefits in addition to physical benefits. It teaches us to be out of control, brings us into the moment, helps us transcend our problems, brings us closer to people, and helps us think more clearly.

Even smiling has physical and mental benefits. Smiling releases endorphins, natural pain killers, and serotonin. Together, these make us feel good. When we smile, immune function improves, and blood pressure lowers (Stibich, 2016).

My mama often advised, "When you see someone without a smile, give them one of yours." Wouldn't our workplaces and the world be better, happier places if we all followed that old proverb? Find ways to create laughter in your everyday life (see Figure 9-3).

Things that make us smile and laugh are all around us; we just need to be more receptive to finding them. Let's reclaim the laughter of our youth. It is a gift to ourselves, those around us, and our world.

Positive Thinking

There is tremendous power in positive thinking. Norman Vincent Peale (1987) wrote a book, *The Amazing Results of Positive Thinking*, detailing the premise that we get what we expect in life. We get what we think about and visualize. We become our most dominant thought. We see this in our workplaces every day. Negative thinkers have negative behaviors, resulting in negative outcomes.

It is said that the average person has 60,000 thoughts per day, of which 80% are negative (Cleveland Clinic Wellness, n.d.). Every time we have a negative thought, our brain releases

---

Figure 9-3. Creating Laughter in Your Life

- Make a list of things that make you laugh and add them to your everyday life.
- Record, replay, and rent funny movies, shows, cartoons, and bloopers and watch them often.
- Listen often to the comedian who makes you laugh until you wet your pants.
- Plan a regularly scheduled comedy night.
- Tough times at work and home? Each day, put a piece of tape on your sleeve, indicating where you've had it up to.
- Throw a party funded by money put into the laughter pot every time someone is caught being grumpy.
- Write "FUN" on the top of every meeting's agenda and start with something funny.
- Surround yourself with funny pictures of friends, family, and yourself.
- Create a laughter bulletin board at work and home where everyone can contribute cartoons, baby pictures, and so forth.
- Challenge others to have a best joke contest.
- Buy funny greeting cards. Stop while you shop and read a few.
- Listen to kids laugh. It's contagious.

Note. Copyright by LeAnn Thieman, SelfCare for HealthCare™, 2012. Used with permission.

---

chemicals that make our bodies feel bad. Think about the last time you were upset. How did your body feel? Did your heart rate increase, your jaw clench, your breathing quicken? Now, imagine one of your happiest times. When you do so, your brain releases chemicals that make your body feel good. You will notice a slower heartbeat; deeper, easier breathing; and relaxed muscles.

When we combine positive visualization with positive thinking, even more remarkable changes occur. Peale (1987) had his patients who suffered from depression picture these letters on a neon sign: D.E.P.R.E.S.S.I.O.N. Then he had them mentally extinguish the first two and the eighth letters. Instead of depression, they visualized P.R.E.S.S. O.N.

Positive imagery is also effective in controlling anger. When we have a "short fuse," we can see it igniting. Then we must calmly visualize extinguishing it in our minds. Anger is one letter away from danger, and that is how it damages our health.

Amazingly, our bodies and minds do not distinguish the difference between visualization and experience. They react as if both are real. Have you ever awoken from a nightmare, sweating, and your heart racing? Although the scary event did not happen to you physically, your body responded as though it had. This phenomenon can work to our benefit, too. Recall your most successful moment and live it out again, visualizing it with all five senses. You can reclaim the same feelings again as your body releases the same chemicals as when you experienced it.

Create your own list of positive affirmations and read and repeat them often (see Figure 9-4). At first, some of these affirmations are simply lies. "I don't feel the least bit centered," you say. But when you repeat phrases over and over, your brain begins to believe them and starts to respond to them and cues your body to do the same. Your brain can literally be "rewired" with positive thinking. Some neurologic connections are strengthened while others are replaced. New thoughts and images stimulate new pathways in the brain and, when constantly repeated, have a great impact on behavior.

Positive thinking and imaging are powerful and mysterious forces in human nature, capable of bringing about dramatic improvement in our lives. Einstein said, "Imagination is more important than knowledge" (Viereck, 1929, p. 117). It's a kind of mental engineering. Your mind is a computer; you have sovereign control over the input.

In his 1926 book *Sand and Foam*, Kahlil Gibran (2007) wrote, "We choose our joys and our sorrows long before we experience them." *Choose joy.*

Figure 9-4. Positive Affirmations

- I am relaxed and centered.
- I love life.
- I love me.
- I am living my priorities every day.
- I am happy and blissful just being alive.
- I am vibrantly healthy and radiantly beautiful.
- I love doing my work, and I'm richly rewarded, creatively and financially.
- The light of God within me is producing perfect results.
- I always communicate truthfully, clearly, effectively, and lovingly.
- I bring joy and laughter to all I do.
- I invest my time wisely on what's really important.
- My relationship with _____ is growing happier and more fulfilling every day.
- I have enough time, energy, wisdom, and money to accomplish my desires.

Note. Copyright by LeAnn Thieman, SelfCare for HealthCare™, 2012. Used with permission.

Forgiveness

An oft-forgotten and underappreciated mental balance tool is forgiveness, yet it is possibly the most important. We waste a lot of our energy, our health, and even our lives when we fail to forgive.

First, we must forgive ourselves. For any past mistakes, indiscretions, or regretted decisions, we forgive ourselves. What we did then was based on who we were and what we knew then. It has nothing to do with who we choose to be today.

Next, we must forgive somebody else, no matter how horrific the offense (see Figure 9-5). When we refuse to forgive someone, it doesn't hurt them; it hurts only us. Why would we give someone who wounded us so deeply the power to continue to harm us with sleepless nights, upset stomachs, and headaches? We must forgive them, whether we think they deserve it or not; we do.

Failing to forgive affects health and well-being. People who will not forgive have more illnesses, lower immune system function, and increased heart disease (Worthington & Scherer, 2004). Those suffering from chronic low back pain found that anger, affective pain, and sensory pain were all lower after forgiving (Carson et al., 2005).

Forgiveness is an empowering choice. Sometimes forgiving other people is the greatest gift we can give ourselves. It is freeing. It is healing. So, starting today, besides yourself, who are you going to forgive?

Figure 9-5. Steps to Forgiveness

- First, realize you have been unjustly treated and have a right to be angry.
- Second, decide that forgiveness is an option of choice. A positive decision. Forgiving does not equal forgetting, and sometimes there is no reconciliation. A widely accepted definition of forgiveness is to pardon, to release from further punishment.
- Third, reframe the offender. Acknowledging how they were raised and treated helps reveal how they were probably victims of similar treatment, while not condoning or excusing it.
- The fourth stage occurs when you begin to develop feelings of empathy or even compassion for the offender. Not because of what they did, but in spite of it. Finally, you can forgive, often breaking the cycle and putting to rest feelings of revenge, anger, and guilt.

Note. Copyright by LeAnn Thieman, SelfCare for HealthCare™, 2012. Used with permission.

Spiritual Balance

Creating a spiritual balance is as crucial as mental and physical balance, for we cannot cope and be whole without it. It is not about religion. Most profess to have a spiritual connection to our universe.

Polls estimate that more than 92% of Americans believe in God (Newport, 2011). If you are among that majority, I encourage you to be in touch with the deity you believe in every single day. We can't just wait for weekends.

Even if it is just for 15 minutes, take time for prayer, meditation, or reflection. Studies describing the association between prayer, faith, spirituality, and medicine are increasing (Gullatte, Brawley, Kinney, Powe, & Mooney, 2010; Jantos & Kiat, 2007; Maclin, 2012; Ventres & Dharamsi, 2013). I know in our frenetic lives that we barely have time to eat, sleep, and exercise, so it is a real challenge to carve out time to nurture ourselves spiritually. Yet it is critical to our survival. Lubinska-Welch, Pearson, Comer, and Metcalfe (2016) conducted a descriptive study exploring the self-care practices of nurses in a rural hospital setting. In their findings, the most prevalent self-care practices by nurses were humor, laughter, music, spirituality, prayer, healthy nutrition, walking, and healthy sleep habits (Lubinska-Welch et al., 2016).

As I was grappling with this lack of discipline in my life, I happened to talk to a friend who was telling me, in idle conversation, about his busy week. He had worked over sixty hours, driven fifty miles to a neighboring city several times, harvested his garden, and even visited a friend's brother in jail. Then he casually mentioned something that came to him during his hour of prayer that morning. I interrupted. "Bob, I can barely find time for 15 minutes; how do you do an hour?"

Then he said the words that still echo in my head every day: "If I didn't start my day that way, I would never have time for the rest." I wanted that level of productivity, that focus, and that inner peace and sense of well-being.

That's when I bought a little daily reading book. But having a task-oriented, productive nurse personality, I didn't have time to sit down and read it, so I read it while drying my hair every morning. A few weeks later it occurred to me: I was supposed to sit down, shut up, and listen.

Listen. To that deep inner voice. You can call it intuition, the Holy Spirit, gut feeling—whatever fits your spiritual beliefs. Few of us see burning bushes or hear the actual voice of God, but we all have the inner voice, which is the divine guidance for our lives, and we cannot hear it in chaos. The relevance of spirituality in nursing practice is inclusive of care providers as well as patients. In a study by Giske and Cone (2015), the authors summarized that leaders must pay close attention to how they can foster openness to spiritual matters that are pathways to personal and professional maturity. The focus of this section is about balance of the spirit, which is one dimension of delivering compassionate care.

I soon learned that 15 minutes was a great investment. Within a few weeks, I noticed I was happier, more centered, more productive—a better person.

One night on the evening news, I saw Dan Rather interviewing Mother Teresa. He asked, "What do you say when you pray?" She said, "Nothing. I just listen." Dan queried, "What does God say?" She answered, "Nothing. He just listens." In that listening-silence is the wisdom, the guidance, the direction we can only "hear" in peace and quiet.

Modern medicine is finally learning that we are not just physical beings, but spiritual beings, too. The spirit has a great effect on healing. The American Medical Association requires medical schools to teach students to inquire about a patient's religion. Ninety percent of medical schools address spirituality in their curricula because of the impact on patients' health. Ninety-nine percent of doctors believe there is an important relationship between the spirit and the flesh (Koenig, Hooten, Lindsay-Calkins, & Meador, 2010). So often we choose a way of life that best suits our bodies. Let's create one that also nurtures our souls.

The Mind, Body, and Spirit Connection

Science is proving more and more the critical connection between body, mind, and spirit. It has been irrevocably proved that anxiety, stress, alienation, and hopelessness are not just mental states. Neither are love, serenity, and optimism. All are physiologic states that affect our health, just as clearly as obesity or physical fitness. Crane and Ward (2016) acknowledged that emotional and spiritual health are interrelated with mental and physical aspects of one's life. The challenge is to nurture each system to sustain and heal the others.

As we try to balance our lives physically, mentally, and spiritually, it often helps to combine the three aspects. Some people enjoy prayer-walking to care for their body and spirit at the same time. Some listen to spiritual recordings as they walk. Some sing hymns or simply yammer on and on to their Creator (who is always listening).

Many people listen to motivational recordings while driving or exercising. Some listen to comedians to exercise their mind and body with laughter. Others listen to religious music or spiritual recordings while they work out.

You, too, can combine the physical, mental, and spiritual in simple creative ways. Take a walk or hike to a peaceful setting, then relax there. Walk or bike to your next appointment, enjoying the sights, nurturing your five senses, clearing your mind. Sleep in late on a Saturday morning, then awaken and read an inspirational book. Massages, manicures, and herbal baths also are lovely ways to nourish the mind, body, and spirit.

Summary

When a toddler figures out what he needs, he asks for it until he gets it. "I want juice. I want juice. I want juice. I want juice. I want juice!"—until someone gets the kid some juice. Take time—quiet time—to evaluate your life. Is your physical, mental, or spiritual self a little out of balance? What is lacking? What do you need more of? How can others support you in acquiring it? Give this careful thought; make a list. Then be more like the toddler and ask for what you need to get your life in better balance again. Ask for your "juice" lovingly, not blamefully, from yourself, your family, your superiors, your coworkers. Schedule the time and support you need to nurture your body, mind, and spirit.

As a leader, you seek to positively transform, engage, enlighten, and inspire others to go beyond their current mental, physical, and sometimes spiritual situations. You recognize that although you need to provide tools, resources, and models that show strategic pathways to guide and develop teams, you also must tap into the reservoir of strengths—the hearts and minds of those you lead.

To develop teams that deliver compassionate care, we must be compassionate leaders. To be compassionate leaders, we must be of strong mind, body, and spirit. We are always role modeling. Let's transform patient care by developing compassionate caregivers and by being one.

References

Association for Applied and Therapeutic Humor. (n.d.). Home. Retrieved from http://www.aath.org

Berk, L.S., Felten, D.S., Tan, S.A., Bittman, B.B., & Westengard, J. (2001). Modulation of neuroimmune parameters during the eustress of humor-associated mirthful laughter. *Alternative Therapies in Health and Medicine, 7*(2), 62–78.

Canfield, J., Hansen, M.V., Mitchell-Autio, N., & Thieman, L. (2012). *Chicken soup for the nurse's soul: Stories to celebrate, honor, and inspire the nursing profession.* Cos Cob, CT: Backlist.

Carson, J.W., Keefe, F.J., Goli, V., Fras, A.M., Lynch, T.R., Thorp, S.R., & Buechler, J.L. (2005). Forgiveness and chronic low back pain: A preliminary study examining the relationship of forgiveness to pain, anger, and psychological distress. *Journal of Pain, 6,* 84–91. doi:10.1016/j.jpain.2004.10.012

Caruso, C.C., & Hitchcock, E.M. (2010). Strategies for nurses to prevent sleep-related injuries and errors. *Rehabilitation Nursing, 35,* 192–197. doi:10.1002/j.2048-7940.2010.tb00047.x

Cleveland Clinic Wellness. (n.d.). Lesson 3, Topic 2: Don't believe everything you think. *Stress Free Now.* Retrieved from http://www.clevelandclinicwellness.com/pages/SFN.htm

Cocker, F., & Joss, N. (2016). Compassion fatigue among healthcare, emergency and community service workers: A systematic review. *International Journal of Environmental Research and Public Health, 13,* 618. doi:10.3390/ijerph13060618

Crane, P.J., & Ward, S.F. (2016). Self-healing and self-care for nurses. *AORN Journal, 104,* 386–400. doi:10.1016/j.aorn.2016.09.007

Ekelund, U., Ward, H.A., Norat, T., Luan, J., May, A.M., Weiderpass, E., … Riboli, E. (2015). Physical activity and all-cause mortality across levels of overall and abdominal adiposity in European men and women: The European Prospective Investigation into Cancer and Nutrition Study (EPIC). *American Journal of Clinical Nutrition, 101,* 613–621. doi:10.3945/ajcn.114.100065

Gibran, K. (2007). *Kahil Gibran, the collected works.* New York, NY: Random House.

Giske, T., & Cone, P.H. (2015). Discerning the healing path—How nurses assist patient spirituality in diverse health care settings. *Journal of Clinical Nursing, 24,* 2926–2935. doi:10.1111/jocn.12907

Gullatte, M., Brawley, O., Kinney, A., Powe, B., & Mooney, K. (2010). Religiosity, spirituality, and cancer fatalism beliefs on delay in breast cancer diagnosis in African American women. *Journal of Religion and Health, 49,* 62–72. doi:10.1007/s10943-008-9232-8

Hersch, R.K., Cook, R.F., Deitz, D.K., Kaplan, S., Hughes, D., Friesen, M.A., & Vezina, M. (2016). Reducing nurses' stress: A randomized controlled trial of a web-based stress management program for nurses. *Applied Nursing Research, 32,* 18–25. doi:10.1016/j.apnr.2016.04.003

Hilliard, L.M., Colafella, K.M.M., Bulmer, L.L., Puelles, V.G., Singh, R.R., Ow, C.P.C., … Denton, K.M. (2016). Chronic recurrent dehydration associated with periodic water intake exacerbates hypertension and promotes renal damage in male spontaneously hypertensive rats. *Scientific Reports, 6,* 33855. doi:10.1038/srep33855

Hirshkowitz, M., Whiton, K., Albert, S.M., Alessi, C., Bruni, O., DonCarlos, L., … Hillard, P.J.A. (2015). National Sleep Foundation's sleep time duration recommendations: Methodology and results summary. *Sleep Health, 1,* 40–43. doi:10.1016/j.sleh.2014.12.010

Jantos, M., & Kiat, H. (2007). Prayer as medicine: How much have we learned? *Medical Journal of Australia, 186*(Suppl. 10), S51–S53.

Koenig, H.G., Hooten, E.G., Lindsay-Calkins, E., & Meador, K.G. (2010). Spirituality in medical school curricula: Findings from a national survey. *International Journal of Psychiatry in Medicine, 40,* 391–398. doi:10.2190/PM.40.4.c

Kunzweiler, K., Voigt, K., Kugler, J., Hirsch, K., Bergmann, A., & Riemenschneider, H. (2016). Factors influencing sleep quality among nursing staff: Results of a cross sectional study. *Applied Nursing Research, 32,* 241–244. doi:10.1016/j.apnr.2016.08.007

Leiter, M.P., & Maslach, C. (2009). Nurse turnover: The mediating role of burnout. *Journal of Nursing Management, 17,* 331–339. doi:10.1111/j.1365-2834.2009.01004.x

Lubinska-Welch, I., Pearson, T., Comer, L., & Metcalfe, S.E. (2016). Nurses as instruments of healing: Self-care practices of nurses in a rural hospital setting. *Journal of Holistic Nursing, 34,* 221–228. doi:10.1177/0898010115602994

Maclin, S.D., Jr. (2012). Explorations into the synergy between faith, health, and health-care among Black Baptists. *Journal of the Interdenominational Theological Center, 38*(1–2), 53–90.

Mahony, D.L., Burroughs, W.J., & Hieatt, A.C. (2001). The effects of laughter on discomfort thresholds: Does expectation become reality? *Journal of General Psychology, 128,* 217–226. doi:10.1080/00221300109598909

Marcotte, C.D. (2016). When your heart doesn't sing anymore: Recovering from burnout. *AHNA Beginnings, 36*(4), 10–12.

Mayo Clinic Staff. (2016). Stress relief from laughter? It's no joke. Retrieved from http://www.mayoclinic.org/healthy-lifestyle/stress-management/in-depth/stress-relief/art-20044456

Najjar, N., Davis, L.W., Beck-Coon, K., & Doebbeling, C.C. (2009). Compassion fatigue: A review of the research to date and relevance to cancer-care providers. *Journal of Health Psychology, 14,* 267–277. doi:10.1177/1359105308100211

National Sleep Foundation. (n.d.-a). How losing sleep affects your body and mind. Retrieved from https://sleep.org/articles/how-losing-sleep-affects-your-body-mind

National Sleep Foundation. (n.d.-b). Obesity and sleep. Retrieved from https://sleepfoundation.org/sleep-topics/obesity -and-sleep/page/0/1

National Sleep Foundation. (2014, December). *Lack of sleep is affecting Americans, finds the National Sleep Foundation* [Press release]. Retrieved from https://sleepfoundation.org/media-center/press-release/lack-sleep-affecting -americans-finds-the-national-sleep-foundation

Nea, F.M., Kearney, J., Livingstone, M.B.E., Pourshahidi, L.K., & Corish, C.A. (2015). Dietary and lifestyle habits and the associated health risks in shift workers. *Nutrition Research Reviews, 28,* 143–166. doi:10.1017 /S095442241500013X

Newport, F. (2011). More than 9 in 10 Americans continue to believe in God. Retrieved from http://www.gallup.com /poll/147887/americans-continue-believe-god.aspx

New York Hospital–Cornell Medical Center. (1998, April 14). [Survey of 3003 Americans conducted by Yankelovich Partners for the Nutrition Information Center at The New York Hospital–Cornell Medical Center and the International Bottled Water Association]. New York, NY: Author.

Peale, N.V. (1987). *The amazing results of positive thinking.* Englewood Cliffs, NJ: Prentice-Hall.

Smith, C.M. (2002, March). Laugh yourself fit. *IDEA Health and Fitness Source, 2003*(3). Retrieved from http://www .ideafit.com/fitness-library/laugh-yourself-fit

Sonati, J., De Martino, M., Vilarta, R., Maciel, E., Moreira, E., Sanchez, F., … Sonati, R. (2015). Quality of life, health, and sleep of air traffic controllers with different shift systems. *Aerospace Medicine and Human Performance, 86,* 895–900. doi:10.3357/AMHP.4325.2015

Stibich, M. (2016, December 19). Top 10 reasons you should smile every day. Retrieved from https://www.verywell .com/top-reasons-to-smile-every-day-2223755

University of Maryland Medical Center. (2012, May 26). Exercise. Retrieved from http://umm.edu/health/medical /reports/articles/exercise

Ventres, W., & Dharamsi, S. (2013). Beyond religion and spirituality: Faith in the study and practice of medicine. *Perspectives in Biology and Medicine, 56,* 352–361. doi:10.1353/pbm.2013.0023

Viereck, G.S. (1929, October 26). What life means to Einstein: An interview by George Sylvester Viereck. *Saturday Evening Post,* pp. 17, 110, 113, 114, 117. Retrieved from http://www.saturdayeveningpost.com/wp-content/uploads /satevepost/what_life_means_to_einstein.pdf

Worthington, E.L., Jr., & Scherer, M. (2004). Forgiveness is an emotion-focused coping strategy that can reduce health risks and promote health resilience: Theory, review, and hypotheses. *Psychology and Health, 19,* 385–405. doi:10.1080/0887044042000196674

CHAPTER 10

Interprofessional Team Collaborations in Improving Patient Outcomes and Value-Based Care

Tracy Gosselin, PhD, RN, AOCN®, NEA-BC, and
Christina Cone, DNP, APRN, ANP-BC, AOCNP®

It is amazing what can be accomplished when nobody cares about who gets the credit.

—Robert Yates

Introduction

The need for interprofessional teams has never been more critical than it is today. Like all industries, health care is going through a rapid evolution. These changes are grounded in meeting a Triple Aim that focuses on three dimensions (Berwick, Nolan, & Whittington, 2008): (a) improving the patient experience of care (includes quality and satisfaction), (b) improving the health of populations, and (c) reducing the per capita cost of health care (see Chapter 7 for further details).

The Patient Protection and Affordable Care Act, passed in 2010, incorporated the dimensions of the Triple Aim while shifting the lens onto healthcare financing and value-based care. The Affordable Care Act opened opportunities for healthcare providers to work together in teams to improve our models of care, patient outcomes, and value. Value takes into account quality, cost, appropriate care, and how processes of care, patient satisfaction, and mortality affect the value proposition and outcomes. Payment reform and the need to incentivize high-value, patient-centered care are now urgent priorities for oncology providers and policy makers (American Society of Clinical Oncology, 2015). A 2015 systematic review of the literature on cancer care team effectiveness found 16 articles that met the inclusion criteria, and although some noted improvement in screening and treatment planning, many did not address how the team members worked together to achieve this (Taplin et al., 2015). To improve results, we first must understand how we work together. Nurse leaders play a pivotal role on interprofessional teams. The challenges faced today need innovative thinking, visionary leadership, and the ability to provide a voice for those issues and populations that often go unaddressed. The 2011 Institute of Medicine (now called the Health and Medicine Division of the National Academies of Sciences, Engineering, and Medicine) report *The Future of Nursing: Leading Change, Advancing Health* had two specific recommendations relevant to this chapter:

- Recommendation 2: Expand opportunities for nurses to lead and diffuse collaborative improvement efforts.
- Recommendation 7: Prepare and enable nurses to lead change to advance health.

These recommendations, although broad in their intent, serve as a call to action for nursing leadership across our profession and in the communities we serve. This changing landscape is also revolutionizing leadership by creating new organizational cultures that are shifting from paternalistic command styles to one of collaboration leveraged by empowered interprofessional teams (Fontenot, 2012). Our individual and collective knowledge has the ability to shape future administrative, clinical, educational, and research endeavors that influence patient care, healthcare delivery systems, and the workforce of the future. The astute nurse leader can facilitate and support this cultural shift by implementing strategies that create the conditions for collaborative work redesign through interdisciplinary partnerships, continuous quality improvement, and governance structures.

Interprofessional Teams

Interprofessional teams comprise members who each represent the unique viewpoint of their discipline (Stokols, Hall, Taylor, & Moser, 2008) and regularly come together to solve problems or provide services (Reeves, Lewin, Espin, & Zwarenstein, 2010). Team members draw on their own unique professional knowledge, skills, and training (Brush et al., 2015), which provides diversity of thought when coming together. Healthcare providers are exposed to similar content in their training programs, yet much of this is done within educational silos (Jukkala & White, 2014) with little to no interdisciplinary exposure. For nurse leaders, it is important to think through the what, why, and how, but in the case of establishing an interprofessional team, thinking through the who and the composition of the team is critical. Individual values play a significant role in how individuals function within a team and are particularly relevant in cancer care (see Table 10-1).

Whether part of a task force, committee, or governing board, team leaders must ensure the team is successful in accomplishing their objectives. Chapter 20 captures an innovative look at two nurse chief executive officers and their journey from the bedside to the C-suite. Determining the process and outcomes measures early will help ensure success. Sustainability of a team is critical from both a leader and contributor standpoint (see Figure 10-1). Leaders need to be thoughtful in their approach, show openness to transparent dialogue, and foster collaboration among team members. These leadership skills assist nurses in leading from bedside to conference room to boardroom. In 2011, a group of nursing organizations founded the Nurses on Boards Coalition to increase the presence of nurses on boards (American Nurses Association, 2014). Governing boards represent a unique opportunity for nurses to contribute to the conversation and to share not only their clinical expertise but also their knowledge about finance, operations, and partnerships (Everett, 2015; Richardson & Opollo, 2015).

Table 10-1. Five Personal Values That Characterize the Most Effective Team Members	
Value	**Description**
Honesty	Place high value on effective communication, including transparency about aims, decisions, uncertainty, and mistakes, which is critical to the team's continued improvement and for maintaining mutual trust.
Discipline	Carry out role and responsibilities even when inconvenient. Seek out and share new information, even when it may be uncomfortable.
Creativity	View the possibility of tackling new or emerging problems creatively. See errors and unanticipated bad outcomes as potential opportunities to learn and improve.
Humility	Recognize differences in training but do not believe that one type of training or perspective is uniformly superior. Team members can rely on each other to help recognize and avert failures, regardless of where they are in the hierarchy.
Curiosity	Demonstrate dedication to reflecting on lessons learned in the course of daily activities and using those insights for continuous improvement of their work and that of the team.

Note. Based on information from Mitchell et al., 2012.

Figure 10-1. Six Values of Team Sustainability
1. Self-aware leadership
2. Purposeful cultivation of the team
3. Unambiguous job descriptions and expectations
4. Support, coaching, and mentorship
5. Respectful recognition
6. Praise for achievements of individual and team milestones

Note. Based on information from Glenn Llopis Group, 2014.

Strategies to Build Partnerships

The dynamics of workplace relationships create myriad challenges for teams, and the increasingly complex healthcare environment is threatened by these obstacles. Nurse leaders must identify and correct the underlying barriers to foster collegial workplace relationships to improve care delivery and clinical outcomes (Alexanian, Kitto, Rak, & Reeves, 2015; Almost et al., 2015). Creating an environment of strong collaboration among care providers and nursing leadership helps hospitals maintain a competitive nursing workforce (Ma, Shang, & Bott, 2015). Effective nurse–physician collaboration is essential to quality care; however, the relationship between them is often described as tense and adversarial (Caricati et al., 2015). Although there are many key relationships to consider, the nurse–physician relationship is one of the most critical and will be discussed further in this chapter.

Nurses and physicians are often the closest coworkers in healthcare delivery. Historically, nurses have been viewed as having less power than physicians because of entrenched patterns of domination that have created barriers to true partnerships (Bajnok, Puddester, Macdonald, Archibald, & Kuhl, 2012; Eisler & Potter, 2014). Failure of interprofessional practice has been attributed to lack of clear role definitions among staff, lack of time for team building, and interprofessional conflicts based on threats to professional identity (Bajnok et al., 2012). Professional identities emerge from healthcare professionals' socialization; professionals have been educated separately with different established ideologies and practice frameworks (McNeil, Mitchell, & Parker, 2013). Bridging this gap and illuminating the interdependencies among roles is critical to partnership development.

The culture in health care must shift to not only support and promote but also to expect collaboration among all healthcare professionals. This requires a partnership perspective rather than a domination perspective with vertical hierarchies (Eisler & Potter, 2014). Purposeful cultivation of teams is essential to building effective collaborative partnerships. Several evidence-based approaches to team cultivation exist. One example is the Team Strategies and Tools to Enhance Performance and Patient Safety (TeamSTEPPS®), which is a set of teamwork tools aimed at optimizing patient outcomes by improving communication and teamwork skills among healthcare professionals (Agency for Healthcare Research and Quality, 2016).

Leadership should use the principles of team-based health care and the core competencies for interprofessional collaborative practice to (a) develop a clear articulation of the team's shared mission, vision, and goals, (b) identify and delineate team member function, responsibilities, and accountabilities, and (c) outline communication strategies that facilitate discussions, interactions, conflict resolution, and specific process improvement strategies that will increase the effectiveness of interprofessional teamwork (Interprofessional Education Collaborative Expert Panel, 2011; Mitchell et al., 2012; Porter-O'Grady, 2009). Leaders could use the Interdisciplinary Management Tool (IMT) to guide the process.

The IMT is an evidence-based change tool designed to facilitate reflective practice to improve interdisciplinary teamwork (Nancarrow, Smith, Ariss, & Enderby, 2015). The IMT's Team Action Learning approach was specifically developed to help interdisciplinary teams develop their collective teamwork and maintenance skills. It includes a series of structured exercises that teams participate in to review and reflect on current team working and service delivery challenges (Smith et al., 2012). The structured facilitation guide helps teams develop a shared mental model and team identity based on domains relevant to interdisciplinary teamwork (Interprofessional Education Collaborative Expert Panel, 2011; Nancarrow et al., 2015). A shared mental model provides a common understanding of situations and the roles and tasks of team members and has been identified as one of the critical underpinnings for effective teamwork (Agency for Healthcare Research and Quality, 2016; Weller, Boyd, & Cumin, 2014). Purposeful cultivation of teams will create the necessary environment for successful quality improvement, care redesign, and development of new models of care.

Quality Improvement

Quality is linked to an organization's service delivery. Quality improvement involves systematic and continuous actions that lead to measurable improvement in healthcare services or in the health status of a targeted population. At its core, quality improvement is a team process, and leadership must create the infrastructure that organizes and supports the work of finding the ways to provide better patient care (Health Resources and Services Administration, 2011). At the macro level, quality improvement occurs through care redesign and the development of new models of care. At the micro level, quality improvement occurs at the hospital unit or ambulatory clinic point of care. Establishing a shared governance model through continuous quality improvement councils at the point of care is one strategy to assist organizations in achieving their quality improvement goals (Burkoski & Yoon, 2013).

Recently, the National Cancer Institute and the American Society of Clinical Oncology launched an initiative focused on teams in cancer care (Kosty, Bruinooge, & Cox, 2015). This initiative brings together clinicians, patient advocates, and researchers to serve on writing teams to address a specific clinical case and apply principles of team-based care. For more information on evidence-based practice implementation and nurse-led research, see Chapter 19.

Professional Governance

A common expression in leadership circles is that organizational culture undermines strategy every time (Newman, 2011). Organizational cultures where nurses' locus of control is so narrow that they prefer to perform only routine and functional nursing tasks, are comfortable with the status quo, and expect all decisions to be made at the management level must change (Newman, 2011). Correcting operational failures and decreasing healthcare costs while improving the quality of value-based care is the responsibility of both executive nursing leadership and frontline nurses. However, frontline nurses often are not prepared to share the leadership and accountability required for transformation (Dearmon, Riley, Mestas, & Buckner, 2015). Education on hospital-acquired conditions and Patient Safety Indicators 90 (see Figure 10-2) is fundamental to nursing care and a central piece of the value proposition. Nurse executives and managers are in a position to empower and mentor frontline nurses through shared governance structures. Shared governance empowers nursing professionals through decision-making control over individual clinical practice and leads to decentralized management and collective accountability (Meyers & Costanzo, 2015). Shared governance and likewise the evolutionary terminology of professional governance share the principles of partnership, equity, accountability, and ownership (Burkoski & Yoon, 2013; Clavelle, O'Grady, Weston, & Verran 2016; Porter-O'Grady, 2009). A system-level intervention to improve quality of care and patient safety is to enhance the nurse work environment (Ma et al., 2015). Chapter 3 provides a more in-depth review of professional governance.

Ma et al. (2015) conducted a study to identify the effects of unit collaboration and nursing leadership on quality of care and nursing outcomes. They were able to demonstrate that improved collaboration between nurses and nurse practitioners not only improved the quality of patient care but also led to positive nursing outcomes. The study also suggested that nurse-to-nurse collaboration cannot be underestimated because the quality of teamwork among nurses affects outcomes as well (Ma et al., 2015). The findings confirm the importance of investing in training courses on interprofessional collaboration, teamwork, and communication. Quality improvement also occurs through care redesign using structured, evidence-based methods.

Care Redesign

Healthcare organizations are facing immense pressures to continually improve healthcare operations through care redesign that emphasizes care integration across the continuum (Korda

---

Figure 10-2. A Sampling of Hospital-Acquired Conditions and Patient Safety Index Measures

- **Hospital-acquired conditions:** Air embolism, falls and trauma, stage III and IV pressure ulcers, foreign object retained after surgery, catheter-associated infections (blood and urine)
- **Patient Safety Indicators 90 (PSI 90):** Pressure ulcer rate, iatrogenic pneumothorax, central venous catheter–associated bloodstream infection, postoperative respiratory failure, postoperative sepsis, accidental puncture or laceration

Note. Based on information from Agency for Healthcare Research and Quality, 2013; Centers for Medicare and Medicaid Services, 2015b.

& Eldridge, 2011; Rudisill, Callis, Hardin, Dienemann, & Samuelson, 2014) and care coordination, which is a strength of the nursing profession (Dailey & Dawson, 2014). Priorities in redesign include reducing waste, eliminating duplication of unnecessary care, streamlining care delivery, focusing on activities that improve population health, improving access across the spectrum of providers, and controlling healthcare costs (Korda & Eldridge, 2011; Rudisill et al., 2014). Understanding the workflow of each team member and their interdependencies with other team members is critical in redesign endeavors. Organizations should take advantage of several evidence-based quality improvement techniques to intentionally improve multiple systems through collaborative interprofessional partnerships.

The Lean Transformation Process is a methodology created by the Toyota Production System that focuses on examining work processes, improving quality, and maximizing efficiency (Belter et al., 2012; Lin, Gavney, Ishman, & Cady-Reh, 2013) (see Chapter 6 for more details). Six Sigma is an organized method for process improvement. The Lean and Six Sigma methods have been successfully modified and applied to the healthcare industry for quality improvement and care redesign initiatives (Belter et al., 2012; Duska, Mueller, Lothamer, Pelkofski, & Novicoff, 2015; Lin et al., 2013; Rudisill et al., 2014). Combining the two approaches into Lean Sigma focuses on how efficiently resources are being used and questions what value is being added for the patient in every process (Lawal et al., 2014). Many healthcare organizations are actively engaging in care redesign by creating new models of care, and these tools may help teams move their work forward.

New Models of Care

Service delivery is at the center of healthcare reform, and the most prominent delivery models currently include accountable care organizations and patient-centered medical homes. Accountable care organizations are networks of physicians, hospitals, and other healthcare providers that offer integrated service delivery and have collective responsibility for the healthcare quality and costs of a population (Korda & Eldridge, 2011). Patient-centered medical homes are focused on accessible, holistic, comprehensive, coordinated care that is delivered by an interprofessional team. Both models offer complementary approaches to reformed care delivery (Edwards et al., 2014; Korda & Eldridge, 2011). These models can thrive or collapse based on the healthcare team's ability to effectively collaborate, coordinate, and communicate.

The pressure for health systems to engage in population health initiatives is high, and creating the infrastructure for team-based care models is a top priority for leaders. Oncology care teams provide care across the cancer continuum, including medical assessment, diagnosis, treatment planning, supportive care, survivorship care, palliative care, and hospice care. Oncology could be categorized as a population-based focus rather than just a specialty, and oncology nurses are ideal to participate in the development of oncology patient–centered medical homes. The Oncology Care Model has been proposed as one such model (Centers for Medicare and Medicaid Services, 2015a). Oncology nurse leaders can assist with the development of standardized processes for care delivery and coordination, measure guideline adherence and outcomes, and track rates of emergency department utilization and hospitalization (Eagle & Sprandio, 2011). Oncology nurses are in a unique position to facilitate care delivery redesign that focuses on payment models that create greater healthcare provider accountability for the Triple Aim outcomes of better health, improved patient experiences, and lower cost to the oncology patient population. Close attention to stakeholder engagement from the beginning of the redesign, a flatter management structure to promote collaboration and shared decision making, and the ability to tailor to specific needs will create an environment where all team members are empowered to participate as full partners in care delivery (Korda & Eldridge, 2011; Watts et al., 2016).

Systemwide Impacts

The value in organizations depends on the relationships of all roles and functions in the system from the point of service to administrative leadership (Porter-O'Grady, 2009). Major shifts to value-based care and improved performance expectations require measurable and sustainable improvement through increased levels of engagement, shared accountability, and purposeful collaboration at all levels within the healthcare organization (D'Alfonso, Zuniga, Weberg, & Orders, 2016). A matrixed governance model offers the opportunity to bring various perspectives to the table to develop effective practical improvements (Phillips et al., 2015). Projects are evaluated by a diverse group of stakeholders based on understanding and fit to the system. Decisions are made by consensus and reflect the organization's priorities and goals (Porter-O'Grady, 2009).

Gathering Input and Feedback

Nurse leaders must develop robust systems of transparent communication with consistent methods to provide information and gain input from staff. Several effective communication strategies are well documented in the literature. Leaders must make a conscious effort to help employees understand the why, and the first step is to facilitate understanding of the external environment and its effect on the internal environment (Studer, 2009). This can be accomplished through several avenues, including employee forums, communication boards, newsletters, and rounding.

Employee forums are one venue that offers the opportunity for transparent communication between senior leaders and those providing care. Transparency creates accountability and increases motivation (Porter-O'Grady, 2009; Studer, 2009). Communication boards are another strategy to provide information regarding the external environment and its impact on the internal environment. Specific data to share may include service (data from the Agency for Healthcare Research and Quality's Consumer Assessment of Healthcare Providers and Systems surveys), quality (specific quality indicators [central line–associated bloodstream infections, falls, medication reconciliation, pressure ulcers, etc.]), finance (cost, revenue, etc.), people (new hires, turnover, recognition, and reorganization), growth, and community. Newsletters, whether electronic or in print, present another communication strategy, and leaders must be aware of what is in the newsletters and how often they are distributed. Newsletters can offer talking points for leaders to engage staff on rounds (Studer, 2009).

Leadership rounding is a tactic to communicate with frontline/clinical staff as well as to gather input and feedback. Rounding is a useful technique to engage with staff members who are usually not that verbose. Interactions during rounding offer the opportunity to obtain feedback from those who may prefer lower profiles or who are not comfortable speaking up in meetings. Rounding should be purposeful, and leaders should be prepared to answer questions directly, honestly, and compassionately (Saver, 2015). Capturing and analyzing feedback obtained during rounding creates accountability for taking necessary actions for improvement. The lack of follow-up after rounding may lead to disengagement and possibly resentment (Saver, 2015; Studer, 2009). As the shift to value-based care continues, the work of nonclinical colleagues will be equally critical to the successful mission of our care delivery systems. Fostering these partnerships will be essential. One strategy is to include nonclinical colleagues in clinical rounds to enhance their understanding of the organization's clinical missions and appreciation of caregiver roles (Greenwald, Nowacki, & Stoller, 2015). In addition to building teams, developing partnerships, redesigning care, strengthening relationships, and participating in continuous quality improvement initiatives, 21st-century leaders must also be able to successfully navigate the generational matrix of an organization.

Multigenerational and Diverse Engagement

Twenty-first century leaders must value diversity, whether it is by gender, age, culture, thought, or occupation. A diverse workforce will improve performance and the quality of decisions by leveraging different perspectives (Fontenot, 2012). This is an exceptional time in history in that five distinct generational cohorts are represented in the workforce. This presents unique challenges for nurse leaders. Understanding the generational differences is the first step to bridging the multigenerational gap in the workplace (Hahn, 2011; Outten, 2012).

Familiarization with characteristics and reported core values of each generation (see Table 10-2) facilitates understanding and improves teamwork (Hahn, 2011). Although much of the work highlighted is related to nursing, these same attributes apply to other segments of the workforce. Chapter 8 outlines more in-depth communication strategies for leading a multigenerational workforce. This section will provide a snapshot of the generations and share some tips on how to successfully partner, collaborate, and address the needs and concerns of a multigenerational workforce.

Veterans, born between 1925 and 1945, are senior nurses. They are solid, reliable nurses with a no-nonsense approach to work and find change difficult (Coulter & Faulkner, 2014; Hahn, 2011; Harding, 2011; Outten, 2012). Baby boomers, born between 1946 and 1964, are loyal employees with a strong sense of duty. They grew up during a time of economic prosperity and are a large cohort of nurses nearing the age of retirement (Coulter & Faulkner, 2014; Hahn, 2011; Harding, 2011; Outten, 2012). Members of generation X were born between 1965 and 1980 and are independent, self-directed, and prefer working alone as opposed to working on a team. For this cohort, quality of life and work–life balance are important (Coulter & Faulkner, 2014; Hahn, 2011; Harding, 2011; Outten, 2012). People in the youngest generation in the workforce now, the millennials or generation Y, were born after 1980. For millennials, technology and instant communication have always been a part of their lives. They, like the generation before them, want flexible working schedules to maintain a work–life balance (Coulter & Faulkner, 2014; Hahn, 2011; Harding, 2011; Outten, 2012). This generation, more than any other, may have been exposed to interprofessional classroom and clinical learning. There are variations in the literature on definitions and attributes ascribed to the generations. For more reading on communicating with the multigenerational workforce, see Chapter 8.

Nurse leaders can use several strategies to support a generationally comfortable work environment where employees focus energy on the institutional mission rather than individual differences and conflict. First, leaders must perform a self-assessment of their own management style and generational cohort to identify and understand any personal biases they may possess (Hahn, 2011). Next, the nurse leader can use the ACORN Imperatives, a valuable tool to deal with multigenerational conflict, to help their team effectively diffuse conflict in a setting of respectful, meaningful dialogue (Hahn, 2011). ACORN is an acronym for five principles: Accommodate employee differences; Create workplace choices; Operate from a sophisticated management style; Respect competence, initiative, and assume the best; and Nourish retention (Hahn, 2011). Commonalities exist among all generations and disciplines, and research has demonstrated that the greatest needs of any generation include the prospect to advance in the organization, work–life balance, improved benefits or more compensation, and access to educational learning and development (Outten, 2012).

Table 10-2. Multigenerational Workforce			
Generation	**Core Values**	**Generational Style**	**Generational Major Events**
Veterans Traditionalists Builders Maturers 1925–1945	Company loyalty Respect hierarchy Resistant to change Uncomfortable with conflict Dedicated	Stable Reliable Practical Loyal Prefer structure Face-to-face meetings	Great Depression New Deal World War II Pearl Harbor Korean War

Baby
boomers
1946–1964
	Loyalty
	Strong sense of duty
	Personal gratification
	Team player
	Uncomfortable with
	  conflict
	Work centric
		Workaholics
		Challenge the status quo
		Goal directed
		Career focused
		Competitive
		Face-to-face communi-
		  cation
			Civil Rights Movement
			Assassinations of Pres-
			  ident Kennedy, Robert
			  Kennedy, and Martin
			  Luther King Jr.
			Vietnam War
			Woodstock
			Moon landing

Generation X
1965–1980
	Self-sufficient
	Independent
	Adaptable to change
	Work–life balance
	Diversity
	Action rather than words
	Individual positive feed-
	  back
		Technologically savvy
		Shared governance
		Career advancement
		Autonomy
		Independence
		Communicate via text,
		  instant messaging, and
		  email as long as out-
		  come is clear
			Resignation of President
			  Nixon
			Watergate
			AIDS epidemic
			Challenger disaster
			Fall of the Berlin Wall
			Three Mile Island disas-
			  ter
			Desert Storm

Millennials
Generation Y/
iGeneration/
Nexters
1980–2000
	Ambitious
	Optimistic
	Sociable
	Value change
	Work–life balance
	Teamwork
	Confident
		Technologically savvy
		Determined
		Outcome driven
		Multitasking
		Open to change
		Real-time, asynchronous
		  communication
			Oklahoma City bombing
			Internet
			Violence in schools—
			  Columbine shooting
			Global war on terrorism
			Iraq War

Note. Based on information from Coulter & Faulkner, 2014; Hahn, 2011; Harding, 2011; Outten, 2012.

Summary

   As nurse leaders, our charge is clear—we must know when to advocate, contribute, and lead when we are called upon and to also look for opportunities where nursing is missing. Our ability to transform care and create value can be tied to the Triple Aim. We must be aware of the values that create and sustain high-functioning teams, as well as the differences that exist among healthcare professionals, including generational bias. Leadership is critical as we seek new ways to improve health and minimize suffering. Collaboration, communication, and coordination are critical elements that will enable us to serve on and lead interprofessional teams that will advance the art and science of health care. Partnerships that focus on breaking down real and perceived institutional and professional boundaries have the ability to transform our care delivery, governance, and educational systems. Innovative research that addresses how teams meet the Triple Aim can assist in forming the evidence base that can be tied to improved value in health care.

References

Agency for Healthcare Research and Quality. (2013, May). Patient safety for selected indicators: Patient Safety Indicators #90, technical specifications (AHRQ QI™ version 4.5). Retrieved from http://www.qualityindicators.ahrq.gov /Downloads/Modules/PSI/V45/TechSpecs/PSI%2090%20Patient%20Safety%20for%20Selected%20Indicators.pdf

Agency for Healthcare Research and Quality. (2016, September). TeamSTEPPS® 2.0. Retrieved from http://www.ahrq .gov/professionals/education/curriculum-tools/teamstepps/instructor/index.html

Alexanian, J.A., Kitto, S., Rak, K.J., & Reeves, S. (2015). Beyond the team: Understanding interprofessional work in two North American ICUs. *Critical Care Medicine, 43,* 1880–1886. doi:10.1097/CCM.0000000000001136

Almost, J., Wolff, A., Mildon, B., Price, S., Godfrey, C., Robinson, S., … Mercado-Mallari, S. (2015). Positive and negative behaviours in workplace relationships: A scoping review protocol. *BMJ Open, 5.* doi:10.1136/bmjopen-2015 -007685

American Nurses Association. (2014, November). *National coalition launches effort to place 10,000 nurses on governing boards by 2020* [Press release]. Retrieved from http://www.nursingworld.org/FunctionalMenuCategories /MediaResources/PressReleases/2014-PR/Effort-to-Place-Nurses-on-Governing-Boards.html

American Society of Clinical Oncology. (2015). *The state of cancer care in America 2015.* Retrieved from http://www .asco.org/sites/www.asco.org/files/2015ascostateofcancercare.pdf

Bajnok, I., Puddester, D., Macdonald, C., Archibald, D., & Kuhl, D. (2012). Building positive relationships in healthcare: Evaluation of the teams of interprofessional staff interprofessional education program. *Contemporary Nurse, 42,* 76–89. doi:10.5172/conu.2012.42.1.76

Belter, D., Halsey, J., Severtson, H., Fix, A., Michelfelder, L., Michalak, K., … De Ianni, A. (2012). Evaluation of outpatient oncology services using Lean methodology. *Oncology Nursing Forum, 39,* 136–140. doi:10.1188/12.ONF .136-140

Berwick, D.M., Nolan, T.W., & Whittington, J. (2008). The Triple Aim: Care, health, and cost. *Health Affairs, 27,* 759–769. doi:10.1377/hlthaff.27.3.759

Brush, J.E., Jr., Handberg, E.M., Biga, C., Birtcher, K.K., Bove, A.A., Casale, P.N., … Wyman, J.F. (2015). 2015 ACC health policy statement on cardiovascular team-based care and the role of advanced practice providers. *Journal of the American College of Cardiology, 65,* 2118–2136. doi:10.1016/j.jacc.2015.03.550

Burkoski, V., & Yoon, J. (2013). Continuous quality improvement: A shared governance model that maximizes agent-specific knowledge. *Nursing Leadership, 26*(Special Issue), 7–16. doi:10.12927/cjnl.2013.23363

Caricati, L., Guberti, M., Borgognoni, P., Prandi, C., Spaggiari, I., Vezzani, E., & Iemmi, M. (2015). The role of professional and team commitment in nurse–physician collaboration: A dual identity model perspective. *Journal of Interprofessional Care, 29,* 464–468. doi:10.3109/13561820.2015.1016603

Centers for Medicare and Medicaid Services. (2015a, February). *Oncology care model* [Fact sheet]. Retrieved from https://www.cms.gov/Newsroom/MediaReleaseDatabase/Fact-sheets/2015-Fact-sheets-items/2015-02-12.html

Centers for Medicare and Medicaid Services. (2015b). Hospital-acquired conditions. Retrieved from https://www.cms .gov/medicare/medicare-fee-for-service-payment/hospitalacqcond/hospital-acquired_conditions.html

Clavelle, J., O'Grady, T.P., Weston, M.J., & Verran, J.A. (2016). Evolution of structural empowerment: Moving from shared to professional governance. *Journal of Nursing Administration, 46,* 308–312. doi:10.1097/NNA .0000000000000350

Coulter, J.S., & Faulkner, D.C. (2014). The multigenerational workforce. *Professional Case Management, 19,* 46–51. doi:10.1097/NCM.0000000000000008

Dailey, M., & Dawson, J.M. (2014). Health, safety, and wellness: Improving care through high-performing interprofessional teams. *American Nurse Today, 9*(9), 36.

D'Alfonso, J., Zuniga, A., Weberg, D., & Orders, A.E. (2016). Leading the future we envision: Nurturing a culture of innovation across the continuum of care. *Nursing Administration Quarterly, 40,* 68–75. doi:10.1097/NAQ .0000000000000141

Dearmon, V.A., Riley, B.H., Mestas, L.G., & Buckner, E.B. (2015). Bridge to shared governance: Developing leadership of frontline nurses. *Nursing Administration Quarterly, 39,* 69–77. doi:10.1097/NAQ.0000000000000082

Duska, L.R., Mueller, J., Lothamer, H., Pelkofski, E.B., & Novicoff, W.M. (2015). Lean methodology improves efficiency in outpatient academic gynecologic oncology clinics. *Gynecologic Oncology, 138,* 707–711. doi:10.1016 /j.ygyno.2015.07.001

Eagle, D., & Sprandio, J. (2011, June 13). A care model for the future: The oncology medical home. *Oncology.* Retrieved from http://www.cancernetwork.com/practice-policy/care-model-future-oncology-medical-home

Edwards, S.T., Abrams, M.K., Baron, R.J., Berenson, R.A., Rich, E.C., Rosenthal, G.E., ... Landon, B.E. (2014). Structuring payment to medical homes after the Affordable Care Act. *Journal of General Internal Medicine, 29,* 1410–1413. doi:10.1007/s11606-014-2848-3

Eisler, R.T., & Potter, T.M. (2014). *Transforming interprofessional partnerships: A new framework for nursing and part-nership-based health care.* Indianapolis, IN: Sigma Theta Tau International.

Everett, L.Q. (2015). Communicating the value of nursing to governing boards: Three best practice strategies. *Voice of Nursing Leadership, 13*(5), 4–5.

Fontenot, T. (2012). Leading ladies: Women in healthcare leadership. *Frontiers of Health Services Management, 28*(4), 11–21.

Glenn Llopis Group. (2014, November). 6 ways successful teams are built to last. Retrieved from http://www.glennllopis.com/communications/6_ways_successful_teams_are_built_to_last

Greenwald, L.R., Nowacki, A.S., & Stoller, J.K. (2015). First time rounding experiences for nonclinicians: The Cleveland Clinic experience. *American Journal of Medical Quality, 30,* 167–171. doi:10.1177/1062860614521657

Hahn, J.A. (2011). Managing multiple generations: Scenarios from the workplace. *Nursing Forum, 46,* 119–127. doi:10.1111/j.1744-6198.2011.00223.x

Harding, A.D. (2011). Multigenerational workforce: Are we using the literature effectively? *Journal of Emergency Nursing, 37,* 75–76. doi:10.1016/j.jen.2010.05.007

Health Resources and Services Administration. (2011). Quality improvement: Part 3: QI programs—The improvement journey. Retrieved from http://www.hrsa.gov/quality/toolbox/methodology/qualityimprovement/part3.html

Institute of Medicine. (2011). *The future of nursing: Leading change, advancing health.* Washington, DC: National Academies Press.

Interprofessional Education Collaborative Expert Panel. (2011). *Core competencies for interprofessional collaborative practice.* Retrieved from http://www.aacn.nche.edu/education-resources/ipecreport.pdf

Jukkala, A.J., & White, M.L. (2014). The continued need for interprofessional collaboration and research. *Applied Nursing Research, 27,* 95–96. doi:10.1016/j.apnr.2014.02.005

Korda, H., & Eldridge, G.N. (2011). ACOs, PCMHs, and health care reform: Nursing's next frontier? *Policy, Politics, and Nursing Practice, 12,* 100–103. doi:10.1177/1527154411416370

Kosty, M.P., Bruinooge, S.S., & Cox, J.V. (2015). Intentional approach to team-based oncology care: Evidence-based teamwork to improve collaboration and patient engagement. *Journal of Oncology Practice, 11,* 247–248. doi:10.1200/JOP.2015.005058

Lawal, A.K., Rotter, T., Kinsman, L., Sari, N., Harrison, L., Jeffery, C., ... Flynn, R. (2014). Lean management in health care: Definition, concepts, methodology and effects reported (systematic review protocol). *Systematic Reviews, 3,* 103. doi:10.1186/2046-4053-3-103

Lin, S.Y., Gavney, D., Ishman, S.L., & Cady-Reh, J. (2013). Use of lean sigma principles in a tertiary care otolaryngology clinic to improve efficiency. *Laryngoscope, 123,* 2643–2648. doi:10.1002/lary.24110

Ma, C., Shang, J., & Bott, M.J. (2015). Linking unit collaboration and nursing leadership to nurse outcomes and quality of care. *Journal of Nursing Administration, 45,* 435–442. doi:10.1097/NNA.0000000000000229

McNeil, K.A., Mitchell, R.J., & Parker, V. (2013). Interprofessional practice and professional identity threat. *Health Sociology Review, 22,* 291–307. doi:10.5172/hesr.2013.22.3.291

Meyers, M.M., & Costanzo, C. (2015). Shared governance in a clinic system. *Nursing Administration Quarterly, 39,* 51–57. doi:10.1097/NAQ.0000000000000068

Mitchell, P., Wynia, M., Golden, R., McNellis, B., Okun, S., Webb, C.E., ... Von Kohorn, I. (2012). *Core principles and values of effective team-based health care.* Retrieved from https://www.nationalahec.org/pdfs/VSRT-Team-Based-Care-Principles-Values.pdf

Nancarrow, S.A., Smith, T., Ariss, S., & Enderby, P.M. (2015). Qualitative evaluation of the implementation of the Interdisciplinary Management Tool: A reflective tool to enhance interdisciplinary teamwork using structured, facilitated action research for implementation. *Health and Social Care in the Community, 23,* 437–448. doi:10.1111/hsc.12173

Newman, K.P. (2011). Transforming organizational culture through nursing shared governance. *Nursing Clinics of North America, 46,* 45–58. doi:10.1016/j.cnur.2010.10.002

Outten, M.K. (2012). From veterans to nexters: Managing a multigenerational nursing workforce. *Nurse Manager, 43*(4), 42–47. doi:10.1097/01.NUMA.0000413096.84832.a4

Phillips, R.A., Cyr, J., Keaney, J.F., Jr., Messina, L.M., Meyer, T.E., Tam, S.K., ... Challapalli, S. (2015). Creating and maintaining a successful service line in an academic medical center at the dawn of value-based care: Lessons learned from the heart and vascular service line at UMass Memorial Health Care. *Academic Medicine, 90,* 1340–1346. doi:10.1097/ACM.0000000000000839

Porter-O'Grady, T. (2009). *Interdisciplinary shared governance: Integrating practice, transforming health care* (2nd ed.). Burlington, MA: Jones & Bartlett Learning.

Reeves, S., Lewin, S., Espin, S., & Zwarenstein, M. (2010). *Interprofessional teamwork for health and social care.* doi:10.1002/9781444325027

Richardson, D., & Opollo, J. (2015). Nursing leadership in the boardroom: A full circle experience. *Voice of Nursing Leadership, 13*(5), 6, 8, 14.

Rudisill, P.T., Callis, C., Hardin, S.R., Dienemann, J., & Samuelson, M. (2014). Care redesign: A higher-quality, lower-cost model for acute care. *Journal of Nursing Administration, 44,* 388–394. doi:10.1097/NNA.0000000000000088

Saver, C. (2015). The three R's of staff engagement: Relationships, rounding, and recognition. *OR Manager, 31*(1), 1, 11–13.

Smith, T., Cross, E., Booth, A., Ariss, S., Nancarrow, S., Enderby, P., & Blinston, A. (2012). *Interdisciplinary Management Tool—Workbook* (2nd ed.). Retrieved from http://www.nets.nihr.ac.uk/__data/assets/pdf_file/0020/81551/A2-08-1819-214.pdf

Stokols, D., Hall, K.L., Taylor, B.K., & Moser, R.P. (2008). The science of team science: Overview of the field and introduction to the supplement. *American Journal of Preventive Medicine, 35*(Suppl. 2), S77–S89. doi:10.1016/j.amepre.2008.05.002

Studer, Q. (2009). *Straight A leadership: Alignment, action, accountability.* Gulf Breeze, FL: Fire Starter Publishing.

Taplin, S.H., Weaver, S., Salas, E., Chollette, V., Edwards, H.M., Bruinooge, S.S., & Kosty, M.P. (2015). Reviewing cancer care team effectiveness. *Journal of Oncology Practice, 11,* 239–246. doi:10.1200/JOP.2014.003350

Watts, B., Lawrence, R.H., Drawz, P., Carter, C., Shumaker, A.H., & Kern, E.F. (2016). Development and implementation of team-based panel management tools: Filling the gap between patient and population information systems. *Population Health Management, 19,* 232–239. doi:10.1089/pop.2015.0093

Weller, J., Boyd, M., & Cumin, D. (2014). Teams, tribes, and patient safety: Overcoming barriers to effective teamwork in healthcare. *Postgraduate Medical Journal, 90,* 149–154. doi:10.1136/postgradmedj-2012-131168

CHAPTER 11

Balancing Multiple and Competing Priorities

Mary Magee Gullatte, PhD, RN, ANP-BC, AOCN®, FAAN

> *The key is not to prioritize what's on your schedule, but to schedule your priorities.*
>
> —Stephen R. Covey, *The 7 Habits of Highly Effective People*

Introduction

In the *Merriam-Webster Online Dictionary*, *priority* is defined as the condition of being more important than something or someone else and therefore coming or being dealt with first ("Priority," n.d.). The challenge in today's health care is that the ranking of "first" means that a decision needs to be made when faced with multiple priorities. As multiple changes and transitions occur in health care, organizations and providers try to balance cost with quality outcomes necessary to remain viable and competitive in the marketplace, and nurse leaders are often faced with decisions of prioritizing the priorities.

One strategy to manage multiple priorities is to employ multitasking. In some cases, being able to multitask is seen as the mark of a good leader. However, some reports have questioned the belief that one can do multiple tasks with efficiency. Although studies on multitasking in health care are limited, recent reports reveal that multitasking reduces efficiency and performance because the brain can only focus on one thing at a time (Bradberry, 2014) and has been associated with medication errors in observation studies of nurses (Raban et al., 2015).

Healthcare leaders, regardless of area or practice setting, face multiple and competing priorities on a daily basis for which they often have to make immediate decisions as to what comes first in the grand scheme of the organization and business needs. Their focus has expanded beyond the process of how care is delivered to measurable outcomes of care (Thompson, 2008). Within the current context of healthcare success are competing demands that have an impact on the system, structure, people, processes, policies, and procedures.

Nurse leaders are and will continue to be faced with narrowing the cost and quality gap in leading the organization through a plethora of healthcare reform challenges and balancing budgets. Within the context of these challenges are opportunities to better the work environment, care delivery systems, and processes to improve efficiency, effectiveness, and outcomes of care for patients.

This chapter provides an overview of organizational theory related to managing multiple and competing priorities, discusses the challenges unique to the work of nurse leaders within the context of multiple priorities, and introduces an emerging related phenomenon known as complexity compression. Personal strategies for managing multiple and competing priorities are discussed along with specific approaches and tools for nurse leaders to successfully navigate current and future performance and outcome expectations.

Scheduling Priorities

Stephen R. Covey (1989) wrote that the key to success in scheduling your priorities is not in spending a lot of time prioritizing what is on your schedule. Leaders are continually challenged with deciding what or who will be the priority of the day or the moment (Covey, Merrill, & Merrill, 1997). The emerging culture of reducing healthcare costs and maintaining patient quality and safety while creating and sustaining a nurturing and healthy work environment has nurse leaders constantly striving for balance in priority management (Shirey, 2011).

The emerging healthcare environment and work demands of nurse leaders often exceed the resources available to meet demands. Nurse leaders must address existing competing priorities while successfully fulfilling their diverse role requirements across varying practice settings. One goal of the leader is to put supportive organizational strategies in place to help address competing leader priorities. Barasa, Molyneux, English, and Cleary (2015) proposed a framework to evaluate priorities in healthcare practice that involve both consequential and procedural conditional requirements. *Consequential* is based on taking into consideration the rules and guidelines for managing resources, whereas *procedural* requirements ascribe to the principle of achieving procedural fairness.

Using Shared Decision Making as a Strategy in Priority Management

Elements of shared decision making are inherent in meeting and balancing workforce challenges. Decisions are seldom made unilaterally but are the result of building relationships and working with and through others to accomplish the desired outcomes. In health care, a hierarchy of priorities exists, with employee and patient safety at the top tier. Involving others in decision making and priority setting is a good idea. Such involvement can lead to gaining an understanding of others' perspectives and can place emphasis on deliberation and democracy (Barasa et al., 2015). In a new age of team-based care, hierarchical-based decisions are being replaced by more shared decision making, not only among the interprofessional team but inclusive of the patient and family as integral to the team as well.

Theory Related to Managerial Priorities and Organizational Life

Managerial Priorities

The concept of managerial priorities is documented as far back as 1911 (Taylor). Yet, leaders are still struggling with how to strike a balance with workload and getting the work done. The problem of managing priorities is not new to the organizational literature, either. Both qualitative and quantitative research exists to explain how leaders acknowledge, weigh, and actually use information to sort among priorities for problem solving and decision making (Saaty, 2013; Smith, Mitchell, & Summer, 1985). A synthesis of this research indicates that when dealing with managerial priorities, the criteria for effectiveness include a three-category typology: (a) technical efficiency, (b) organizational coordination, and (c) political support. The three categories represent means to obtaining different outcomes that may be beneficial or effective for both individuals and organizations. Focusing on differing priorities requires critical thinking and assumes priority selection consistent with varying organizational dynamics and situations.

Technical efficiency, the first category within the effectiveness typology for managerial priorities, seeks short-term quantifiable criteria to evaluate decisions and achieve high levels of accomplishment. The technical efficiency category incorporates a "quick and dirty" as well as a "do it right the first time" (avoid do-overs) approach to managing priorities. *Organizational coordination* priority, the second category, incorporates concern for long-term organizational integration. The organizational coordination priority not only addresses the immediate issues at hand but also delves into building organizational synergies and requires more than a quick-fix approach to priority setting. The *political support* priority incorporates individual power and subordinate commitment. This priority asserts that managerial priority setting incorporates fairness and concern for subordinate attitudes and suggestions. Ideally, consideration should be given to all elements within the managerial priority and effectiveness typology. Effectiveness in sorting managerial priorities encompasses knowledge, skills, and abilities to achieve technical efficiency, broad perspective and systems thinking to accomplish organizational coordination, and communication and collaboration talent to facilitate political support (Smith et al., 1985).

Nurse Leader Priorities and Organizational Life

One of the pitfalls of organizations is generating strategic plans not based on goals but on multiple priorities. The use of the word *priority* often is misleading and leaves the organizational leaders in a quandary of what is really the most urgent or critical strategy for the organization to focus on. Leaders are then faced with trying to balance multiple and competing priorities. Within an organization, four key measures of importance exist: (a) quality outcomes, particularly related to patient safety metrics, (b) people: employees, patients and families, physicians, and other customers, (c) organizational growth in service lines and care offerings and sites, and (d) financial growth through cost reduction and new and existing programs.

Parallels exist between the work of a nurse leader and other leaders in the organization responsible for outcomes. The literature draws most of its focus on the work of executives and nurse managers. Studies over time have suggested a relationship between managerial priorities and organizational context (Ghoshal & Bartlett, 1994; Shirey, 2009, 2011; Smith et al., 1985). That is, nurse leaders set priorities and make decisions within the context of organizational life, which includes organizational values, culture, dynamics, and, of course, organizational strategic priorities. Hence, leaders may often change their priorities based on the organizational life cycle and take into account what is happening in the organization at the time, what key external drivers are leading change, and where the organization is in its evolution. For example, if in the life of an organization, the immediate priority initiative has to do with patient safety, priorities will shift around what is supported and rewarded within the organization at that particular time. External drivers include reimbursement (Centers for Medicare and Medicaid Services, third-party insurers, and private payers), journey to excellence via American Nurses Credentialing Center Magnet® recognition or the Malcolm Baldrige National Quality Award, or other organizational strategic goals. Regardless of position title or level of authority, priorities often are set based on past experiences and real or perceived future needs.

Once the leader develops a priority-setting approach that has proved successful, the likelihood of deviating from this approach diminishes. The more entrenched the leader becomes in one way of priority setting, the more difficult it becomes to modify the approach to priorities, even though organizational circumstances may have changed. To be effective, one must not lose sight of changing requirements and thus should adapt priority setting to acknowledge multiple data points. This suggestion illuminates that priority setting takes a broad perspective and includes selecting to do the right thing, at the right time, and for the right reasons.

Frequent Competing Priorities Facing Nurse Leaders

Evidence suggests that nurse managers practice in complex work environments and face competing priorities every day (Shirey, Ebright, & McDaniel, 2008; Shirey, McDaniel, Ebright, Fisher, & Doebbeling, 2010; Thompson, 2008). How nurse leaders deal with competing priorities may vary along a continuum that ranges from not handling immediate situations effectively to seamlessly juggling multiple scenarios and lack of effective delegation. Research suggests that nurses new to manager positions have greater difficulty handling the role's complexity, whereas more experienced nurse leaders, especially those in co-manager arrangements, demonstrate more aptitude in deciphering among competing priorities (Shirey et al., 2010).

More experienced nurse leaders often rely on learning from past experiences with similar difficult situations and competing priorities. They also possess a more developed decision-making skill set and expanded coping abilities. Although experience may be helpful, if inflexible thinking is present, it may detract from effectively managing competing priorities. Through trial and error, education, mentoring, and open-mindedness, novice nurse leaders can potentially acquire a broader coping skills repertoire and develop more sophisticated decision-making patterns needed for role success.

One pattern seen in experienced nurse managers' cognitive decision-making behavior is their ability to handle competing priorities through *stacking*. When faced with multiple competing priorities, experienced nurse managers mentally sort through possible alternative courses, adeptly reprioritize and handle the pressing priorities, and then "stack" the remaining priorities to address later. The stacking phenomenon has been reported in both experienced staff nurses (Ebright, 2009) and nurse managers (Shirey et al., 2008). The phenomenon may either be reported or inferred based on nurse manager narrative or observations of multiple files piled on top of the nurse manager's desk, credenza, office floor, or filing cabinets (Shirey et al., 2008). Although the stacking process may provide immediate disposition for a crucial priority, stacking equates to an inability to control workflow and may contribute to long-term work inefficiencies and personal stress. Nurse managers "equated stacking with feelings of getting further behind; the stacks were visible reminders of an inability to control their work or 'in boxes'" (Shirey et al., 2008, p. 127).

Effects of Complexity Compression

Complexity compression is a phenomenon that "nurses experience when expected to assume additional, unplanned responsibilities while simultaneously conducting their multiple responsibilities in a condensed time frame" (Krichbaum et al., 2007, p. 88). In the case of complexity compression, the workday may begin as a seemingly regular one but be altered as a result of "rapid fire" events that would challenge even the most experienced of nurse leaders.

Throughout the course of a day, multiple challenges arise that may include handling patient complaints, attending required meetings, mediating nurse–physician conflict, ensuring appropriate staffing, justifying budgetary variances, delivering performance evaluations, answering questions regarding a new policy, or completing an unexpected report for the nurse executive.

In the midst of this onslaught, the leader must prioritize what jobs need to be completed, when (or if) tasks are addressed, and who actually has the follow-through responsibility to finish the required assignment. Developing mental models for dealing with competing priorities before they happen thus represents an effective initial approach to this major manager work–life challenge. Recent literature has introduced the concept of social influence in decision making. One study reported that individuals often ignore their own opinions in favor of the opinions of others in decision making (Schöbel, Rieskamp, & Huber, 2016). Historically, this phenomenon has been referred to as *conformity behavior* (Asch, 1951). In these situations, studies have found that people will likely follow the behavior of others even when they provide inaccurate information. The role of leaders is to have the strength of their own convictions when making decisions about priorities. Strategies are available to effectively and efficiently manage competing priorities.

Managing Competing Priorities When Everything Is Important

Unraveling the Priorities

Management of competing priorities has generally fallen within the broader category of time management strategies, decision making, and priority theory (Hill, 2014; Saaty, 2013). This section examines three different methods, mapped out in Figures 11-1, 11-2, 11-3, and 11-4, that can be considered as a framework in helping to unravel the conundrum of competing and multiple priorities.

According to Covey et al. (1997), once goals are identified, priorities set, and an approach finalized, people should focus on those tasks that are urgent and important. Placing these elements in a four-quadrant grid, individuals may potentially classify activities using prioritizing nomenclature that labels activities as categories 1 through 4 based on their urgency (horizontal axis in grid) and importance (vertical axis in grid).

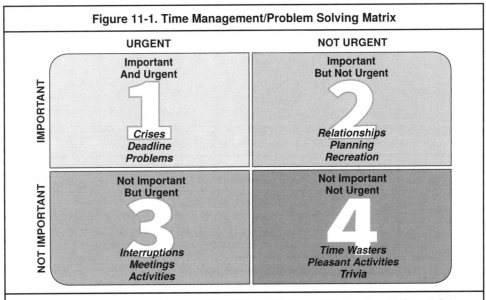

Figure 11-1. Time Management/Problem Solving Matrix

URGENT — NOT URGENT

IMPORTANT

1 — Important And Urgent: *Crises, Deadline, Problems*

2 — Important But Not Urgent: *Relationships, Planning, Recreation*

NOT IMPORTANT

3 — Not Important But Urgent: *Interruptions, Meetings, Activities*

4 — Not Important Not Urgent: *Time Wasters, Pleasant Activities, Trivia*

Note. From *The 7 Habits of Highly Effective People* (p. 151), by S.R. Covey, 1989, New York, NY: Simon & Schuster. Copyright 1989 by Stephen R. Covey. Adapted with permission.

The adaptation of the Eisenhower model of problem solving in Figure 11-1 offers some framework for decision making in determining the level of the priority (Covey, 1989; McKay & McKay, 2013; Melin-Rogovin, 2012). Category 1 tasks in the upper left quadrant are first-priority activities, as they are both urgent and important. These tasks need to be addressed now. Category 1 tasks for a nurse leader might include the need to find a replacement to fill an RN shift shortage today that was created as a result of a last-minute nurse absence. This staffing decision is a category 1 task because filling the staffing deficiency is important for providing safe patient care, and it must be addressed within an urgent time frame (today). Basically, in health care, the ultimate category 1 priorities would be about issues that involve patient or employee safety. Conversely, category 4 tasks in the lower right quadrant are the lowest priority because they are neither urgent nor important. For the nurse leader, a category 4 task might involve making time to sort and review spam e-mail to clean out his or her inbox. Category 3 tasks in the lower left quadrant are generally considered second-priority activities because they are not important to the individual but they are urgent to someone. These tasks are urgent but do not require immediate action. This category, in a word, seems like an oxymoron. This is one of the category priorities that should be completely off the priority list that could free up time. Category 3 tasks for a nurse leader might include an email that was marked urgent by someone yet in actuality does not require immediate action by the leader. The category 3 priorities are tasks that the leader should delegate to someone else. Category 2 tasks are not urgent but are important. An example of a category 2, or third-priority, task (upper right quadrant) that a leader might face would be responding to a memorandum that has a time deadline, but responding to it does not contribute toward immediate strategic goal achievement.

Strategic Rules for Prioritizing

Having a focused strategy to manage time and help set priorities is key to nurse leader success. This section will share two tools to assist when setting those competing priorities: the Rule of Three and the Rule of Four Ds. This section will also address procrastination, using a to-do list, and saying no. In addition, it is of utmost importance to get organized. It is necessary that the nurse leader have a built-in personal accountability factor by developing a productivity system. Such a system is recommended by Henry (2012), which he refers to as the trinity: cost, scope, and time. Even within this trinity, there must be balance as one sets priorities.

The Rule of Three is based on the premise of organizing tasks in three ways: simplify, eliminate, and delegate (Pritchard, 2015). Think about this Rule of Three as a way to reduce one's priority list and free up time for other things (see Figure 11-2).

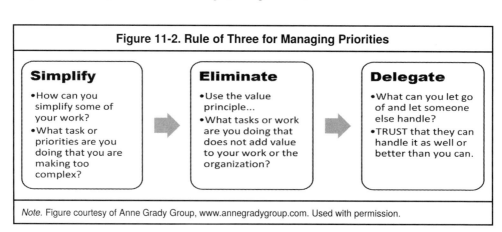

Figure 11-2. Rule of Three for Managing Priorities

Simplify
- How can you simplify some of your work?
- What task or priorities are you doing that you are making too complex?

Eliminate
- Use the value principle...
- What tasks or work are you doing that does not add value to your work or the organization?

Delegate
- What can you let go of and let someone else handle?
- TRUST that they can handle it as well or better than you can.

Note. Figure courtesy of Anne Grady Group, www.annegradygroup.com. Used with permission.

The concept of making a list is not new. Use of lists provides people more control over their time and life. Do not spend time on low-value tasks (Tracy & Stein, 2015). Tracy's philosophy is that every 1 minute of planning saves 10 minutes of execution. According to Tracy (2014), working from a list increases productivity by 25% per day. Some of his inspiring and instructional videos can be found at www.focalpointcoaching.com.

Some of his videos are also available on YouTube, including the short video Tips to Structure Your Day. The payoff for being able to manage multiple and competing priorities is about taking back control. Time management allows one to maximize productivity, performance, and output (Tracy, 2014). Tracy's model for how to structure a day is outlined in Figure 11-3. Another strategy is *single handling*, which refers to setting one single top priority item and working it to completion by the end of the day (Tracy, 2014). No perfect model for time management exists. Leaders should find one that fits well with their individual philosophy and stick to it.

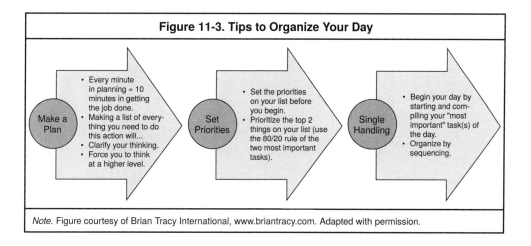

Figure 11-3. Tips to Organize Your Day

Make a Plan
- Every minute in planning = 10 minutes in getting the job done.
- Making a list of everything you need to do this action will...
- Clarify your thinking.
- Force you to think at a higher level.

Set Priorities
- Set the priorities on your list before you begin.
- Prioritize the top 2 things on your list (use the 80/20 rule of the two most important tasks).

Single Handling
- Begin your day by starting and compiling your "most important" task(s) of the day.
- Organize by sequencing.

Note. Figure courtesy of Brian Tracy International, www.briantracy.com. Adapted with permission.

Allen (2015) recommended the Rule of Four Ds to enhance productivity. The rule states that when determining tasks to be done, an individual will *do* (tasks that can be completed in two minutes or less), *delegate* (tasks that require more than two minutes to complete), *defer* (tasks requiring more than two minutes that cannot be delegated or dropped but are not urgent), or *drop* (tasks that are not important in achieving your goals) the task. This is a simplistic and easy way to manage tasks.

Allen (2015) identified the *two-minute rule* as an efficiency factor and suggested that incorporating it dramatically improves individual productivity. This approach involves critical thinking, as careful scrutiny should dictate which tasks get discarded from the to-do pile. If a task will take longer than two minutes, the best approach would be to delegate it, if at all possible. Allen (2015) suggested following a systematic approach using his preferred sequence to maximize efficiencies. The first choice would be to send the delegation request via email. The second choice would involve writing a note or sending an email to the appropriate person who will assume responsibility for the delegated task. The third choice entails leaving a voicemail for the person who will be accepting the delegated responsibility. The fourth choice would require adding the delegation activity to a meeting agenda and addressing it at the next conversation with the appropriate person. The fifth choice involves talking directly to the person who will assume responsibility for the delegated task and doing so either by phone or face-to-face. The fifth choice likely involves interrupting another person's work, and the downside to this approach would be that a written record would not be created to track the handoff and ensure task completion (Allen, 2015).

Tasks that take longer than two minutes to complete and cannot be delegated remain in the individual's inbox and become projects. Although these tasks may have been deferred, they still need to be sorted and prioritized. One way of sorting and prioritizing projects includes adding these to a to-do list or making a file for each project. A Gantt chart (defined as a project management tool) as well as electronic reminders (a tickler system) may be used to monitor task completion. At a minimum, the Gantt chart and project progression should be reviewed at least every other day with careful attention paid to the electronic tickler system.

Lean Methodology

Lean is a work production philosophy that focuses on value-added activities. It emphasizes the orientation of people and systems to deliver a continuous value stream and eliminate waste and deficiencies (Sayer & Williams, 2012). Although Lean methodology has been used in business and industry (primarily manufacturing), the methodology also has efficiency applications based on workflow optimization. Because managing competing priorities may potentially interfere with decision-making quality and workflow, the methodology has transferable applications that may help personal efficiency and effectiveness.

According to Halliday (2007), Lean methodology derives from the Japanese concept of "housekeeping" for the workplace. The approach used in Lean includes what is referred to as the Five S's: sort, straighten, shine, standardize, and sustain. Halliday (2007) said that by stepping out of the literal definitions, the approach can help with managing work-related competing priorities.

Sort involves creating an inclusive list of everything an individual wants or needs to do. Within the sorting activity, Halliday (2007) suggested that tasks be classified using the terms *step*, *stretch*, or *leap*. A *step* activity refers to all the daily tasks that need to be done because they are part of daily responsibilities. *Stretch* activities describe ideas and actions that are needed to accomplish short-term personal or professional goals. *Leap* activities refer to items that will propel the individual to greater accomplishments. Integration of the step, stretch, and leap categories helps to manage competing priorities such that short-term, daily to-dos may be addressed without losing long-term strategic focus.

Straighten involves organizing the master to-do list and categorizing tasks using Allen's (2015) Rule of Four Ds nomenclature. The idea is to take tasks individually and ask what could be done with each: do it, delegate it, defer it, or drop it. Tasks that are important and urgent should rise to the top and be handled first. Everything else that remains on the list should be quickly sorted— eliminating the drop-it items, deferring some items, and delegating others.

Shine refers to cleaning up not only the to-do list but also the manager's workspace. Lean methodology assumes that a person working in a clean and organized area will likely be more positive and productive (Sayer & Williams, 2012). Shine should include allocating daily time to sorting and handling ongoing competing priorities and refining systems that help.

Standardize requires fine-tuning the sorting process that has been developed. Standardizing any activity requires consistently applying processes each time a task is sorted. To *sustain* these processes necessitates incorporating schedules and systems to ensure process consistency and, thus, workflow efficiency and effectiveness.

Regardless of the mode or methodology for setting priorities, they all have common frameworks and tactics. Managing competing and multiple priorities will require putting some thought into each category before making decisions. Figure 11-4 summarizes task prioritization.

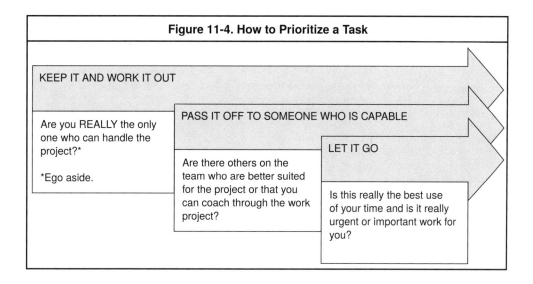

Figure 11-4. How to Prioritize a Task

Prioritizing Tasks

The "No" Strategy That Can Help to Decompress Your Life

Nurse leaders should not be afraid to occasionally say no to incoming demands. Done respectfully within a culture of safety and with renegotiated alternatives, using "no" as a selective strategy may help with managing competing priorities. Our days and nights can be filled with supervisors, friends, and family who count on our good will and tax our ability to keep priorities manageable and declutter our personal and professional lives.

There are times when it feels as if the word *no* is not in our vocabulary, particularly when it comes to the workplace. Yet, if it were used more, people would perhaps have fewer priorities to shift. Jacques (2015) described five ways to say no to professional obligations without regret (see Figure 11-5). Saying no to something you really do not have time for, or do not want to do, will free you up for those "yes" opportunities you are passionate about (Jacques, 2015).

Leaders have other alternatives to saying no when asked to take on another task. First, the nurse leader may say, "I cannot do this right now." This approach lends itself to the leader addressing the task later and working it in his or her schedule. Alternatively, the nurse leader may negotiate to complete the new task now in exchange for simultaneously giving up an old task. Second, the nurse leader who is uncomfortable saying no, especially to pushy people, can say, "Let me think about it and get back to you later." This delaying tactic can give the nurse leader time to review the possibility of taking on another task and decide the task's urgency and its importance relative to strategic goals and objectives. Third, if the nurse leader considers taking on this new demand but does not have the time to do so now, the nurse can say, "I am not at a place to take this on now, but I can do . . ." and agree to do something else in regard to specific tasks required to complete an assignment. This option allows the nurse leader to take advantage of partial involvement in a desired activity. One last strategy is to recommend a colleague who may be interested in and capable of fulfilling the request. Now, the nurse leader has managed-up a colleague and is no longer burdened with having to say yes when the answer really needed to be no.

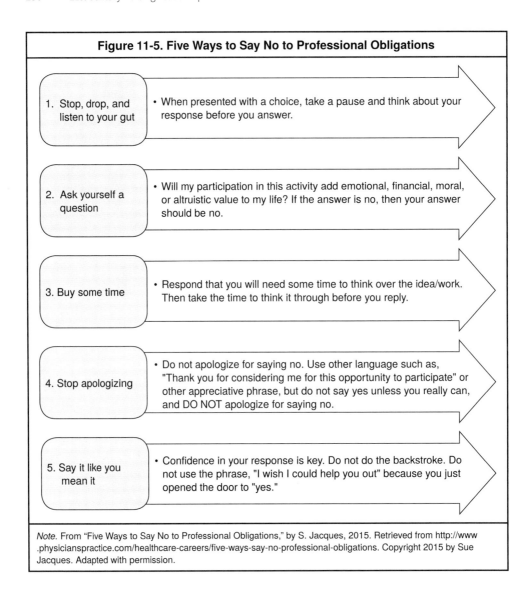

Figure 11-5. Five Ways to Say No to Professional Obligations

1. Stop, drop, and listen to your gut
- When presented with a choice, take a pause and think about your response before you answer.

2. Ask yourself a question
- Will my participation in this activity add emotional, financial, moral, or altruistic value to my life? If the answer is no, then your answer should be no.

3. Buy some time
- Respond that you will need some time to think over the idea/work. Then take the time to think it through before you reply.

4. Stop apologizing
- Do not apologize for saying no. Use other language such as, "Thank you for considering me for this opportunity to participate" or other appreciative phrase, but do not say yes unless you really can, and DO NOT apologize for saying no.

5. Say it like you mean it
- Confidence in your response is key. Do not do the backstroke. Do not use the phrase, "I wish I could help you out" because you just opened the door to "yes."

Note. From "Five Ways to Say No to Professional Obligations," by S. Jacques, 2015. Retrieved from http://www.physicianspractice.com/healthcare-careers/five-ways-say-no-professional-obligations. Copyright 2015 by Sue Jacques. Adapted with permission.

Goal Setting

One rule of goal setting is to overcome procrastination. Recognizing the value in setting goals as a means of giving focus to one's work is a major accomplishment. Do not put off tomorrow what you can do today . . . unless it can be eliminated, deferred, or delegated. Practice proactive goal setting. Base goals on the *SMART* principle (Locke & Latham, 2006). Over time, different terms have been associated with this acronym. For purposes of this chapter, the following terms will be ascribed to the acronym:

S = specific: Focus on the goal.

M = measurable: Include an element of how success will be gauged.

A = achievable: Do not set lofty goals that cannot be attained.

R = realistic: Be sure it is a goal that makes sense and can be done.

T = timed: Assign a timeline to the goal so there will be a measured time to achieve.

Developing goals with this principle in mind will lend structure and increase the likelihood of attaining those goals. The other key strategy is not to have too many goals so as not to become overwhelmed and lose focus.

In the business sector, management by objectives (known as MBO) is a systematic approach to aligning organizational goals and those of the employee (Mind Tools, n.d.). This is another methodology to use when working on setting priorities to align with those of the organization, managing priorities, and finding balance in one's work.

Planning Ahead With a Purpose

Some nurse leaders find it helpful to plan their day in advance as much as possible, which also means leaving room for the unexpected to occur. As mentioned earlier, Tracy (2014) found that working from a list reportedly increases productivity by as much as 25% in a given workday. Making a list does not mean checking it twice. The return on investment from planning ahead can yield big dividends for mental, physical, and emotional intelligence, especially when managing multiple priorities. Various methods to making a list exist. A list can be written on paper and posted to your home refrigerator or your computer monitor at work, where it is always visible. Or, lists can be developed on a smartphone or another electronic device and viewed at any time.

One can choose to make a master list of all the work to be done or make a weekly list that is used daily. Either way, it is a process that can be used to help one stay focused and provide a sense of accomplishment when an item is crossed off the list. The preplanning list can be developed at the end of each day in preparation for the next day or at the beginning of the workday, even before listening to voice mail or reading that first email. Part of preplanning can also include identifying time wasters, such as those massive reply-all email responses. Time wasters yield workflow inefficiencies that result in rote tasks that can cause frustration, waste time, and cost money. Apply the three-task rule or the four Ds to weed out the tasks that do not require immediate attention. Remember, there is always the *just say no* rule, as appropriate.

Summary

This chapter has focused on the complexities inherent in the work of nurse leaders and the ever-challenging task of managing and balancing multiple, often competing, priorities. Strategies have been addressed to assist leaders in achieving their goals of finding balance in the work. Emphasis has been given to setting priorities, using the Rule of Three and the Rule of Four Ds, incorporating Lean methodology, applying the Eisenhower priority categories, and, when appropriate, saying no to avoid adding more to one's already full workload.

Work life cannot ignore the complexity of the duality of individual and organizational synergy. Nurse leaders are on a continuous quest to find work–life balance. One might consider a different paradigm—the concept of *work–life choice* espoused by Jack Welch, former chief executive officer of General Motors. Work–life choice puts the power back in your circle of influence with the implication that you have some semblance of control over your work and life and how to set your own priorities. Avoiding procrastination, taking time to set goals, focused planning, making lists, and sorting and navigating through competing priorities should enhance individual and organizational efficiency, effectiveness, and sustainability.

One key statistic to remember is that every 1 minute of planning saves 10 minutes in execution (Tracy, 2014). Believe that choice is in your hands. Plan your time, and time your plan. Do not forget to prioritize some "me" time for yourself; otherwise, you will get lost in the time zone. You need time to rejuvenate, renew, and reenergize. Recalibrate your thinking that you have choices, and make that work for you. This level of thinking changes the dynamic and gives you back some control, which will result in a sense of accomplishment and reclamation of precious time.

Adapted from "Managing Competing Priorities" (pp. 865–872), by M.R. Shirey in M.M. Gullatte (Ed.), Nursing Management: Principles and Practice *(2nd ed.), 2011, Pittsburgh, PA: Oncology Nursing Society. Copyright 2011 by Oncology Nursing Society.*

References

Allen, D. (2015). *Getting things done: The art of stress-free productivity* (Rev. ed.). New York, NY: Penguin Books.

Asch, S.E. (1951). Studies of independence and conformity: I. A minority of one against a unanimous majority. *Psychological Monographs, 70*(9), 1–70. doi:10.1037/h0093718

Barasa, E.W., Molyneux, S., English, M., & Cleary, S. (2015). Setting healthcare priorities at the macro and meso levels: A framework for evaluation. *International Journal of Health Policy and Management, 4,* 719–732. doi:10.15171/ijhpm.2015.167

Bradberry, T. (2014, October 8). Multitasking damages your brain and career, new studies suggest. *Forbes.* Retrieved from http://www.forbes.com/sites/travisbradberry/2014/10/08/multitasking-damages-your-brain-and-career-new-studies-suggest/#541b41b42c16

Covey, S.R. (1989). *The 7 habits of highly effective people.* New York, NY: Simon & Schuster.

Covey, S.R., Merrill, A.R., & Merrill, R.R. (1997). *First things first every day.* New York, NY: Free Press.

Ebright, P.R. (2009, July). *Cognition and complexity in the work of nursing: Implications for safety and quality.* Paper presented at the 2nd Annual Plexus Institute Conference, Standish, ME.

Ghoshal, S., & Bartlett, C.A. (1994). Linking organizational context and managerial action: The dimensions of quality of management. *Strategic Management Journal, 15*(Suppl. 2), 91–112. doi:10.1002/smj.4250151007

Halliday, E. (2007, August 2). Managing competing priorities when everything is important. Retrieved from http://ezinearticles.com/?Managing-Competing-Priorities-When-Everything-Is-Important&id=668676

Henry, A. (2012). How to prioritize when everything is important. Retrieved from http://lifehacker.com/5877111/how-to-prioritize-when-everything-is-important

Hill, C.A. (2014). Self-management: Stress and time. In P.S. Yoder-Wise (Ed.), *Leading and managing in nursing* (5th ed., Rev. reprint ed., pp. 551–571). St. Louis, MO: Elsevier Mosby.

Jacques, S. (2015). Five ways to say no to professional obligations. Retrieved from http://www.artofmanliness.com/2013/10/23/eisenhower-decision-matrix

Krichbaum, K., Diemert, C., Jacox, L., Jones, A., Koenig, P., Mueller, C., & Disch, J. (2007). Complexity compression: Nurses under fire. *Nursing Forum, 42,* 86–94. doi:10.1111/j.1744-6198.2007.00071.x

Locke, E.A., & Latham, G.P. (2006). New directions in goal-setting theory. *Current Directions in Psychological Science, 15,* 265–268. doi:10.1111/j.1467-8721.2006.00449.x

McKay, B., & McKay, K. (2013). The Eisenhower decision matrix: How to distinguish between urgent and important tasks and make real progress in your life. *Art of Manliness.* Retrieved from http://www.artofmanliness.com/2013/10/23/eisenhower-decision-matrix

Melin-Rogovin, M. (2012). Managing multiple priorities: A how-to-guide for keeping your sanity. *Research Administration Nation.* Retrieved from http://researchadministrationnation.com/2012/08/12/managing-multiple-priorities-a-how-to-guide-for-keeping-your-sanity

Mind Tools. (n.d.). Management by objectives: Aligning objectives with organizational goals. Retrieved from https://www.mindtools.com/pages/article/newTMM_94.htm

Priority. (n.d.). In *Merriam-Webster online dictionary.* Retrieved from http://www.merriam-webster.com/dictionary/priority

Pritchard, A. (2015). Managing multiple priorities. Retrieved from http://www.strategicsolutionsgrp.com

Raban, M.Z., Walter, S.R., Douglas, H.E., Strumpman, D., Mackenzie, J., & Westbrook, J.I. (2015). Measuring the relationship between interruptions, multitasking and prescribing errors in an emergency department: A study protocol. *BMJ Open, 5*(10), e009076. doi:10.1136/bmjopen-2015-009076

Saaty, T.L. (2013). *Fundamentals of decision making and priority theory with the analytic hierarchy process* (2nd ed.). Pittsburgh, PA: RWS Publications.

Sayer, N.J., & Williams, B. (2012). *Lean for dummies.* Hoboken, NJ: Wiley.

Schöbel, M., Rieskamp, J., & Huber, R. (2016). Social influences in sequential decision making. *PLOS ONE, 11*(1), e0146536. doi:10.1371/journal.pone.0146536

Shirey, M.R. (2009). Authentic leadership, organizational culture, and healthy work environments. *Critical Care Nursing Quarterly, 32,* 189–198. doi:10.1097/CNQ.0b013e3181ab91db

Shirey, M.R. (2011). Managing competing priorities. In M.M. Gullatte (Ed.), *Nursing management: Principles and practice* (2nd ed., pp. 865–872). Pittsburgh, PA: Oncology Nursing Society.

Shirey, M.R., Ebright, P.R., & McDaniel, A.M. (2008). Sleepless in America: Nurse managers cope with stress and complexity. *Journal of Nursing Administration, 38,* 125–131. doi:10.1097/01.NNA.0000310722.35666.73

Shirey, M.R., McDaniel, A.M., Ebright, P.R., Fisher, M.L., & Doebbeling, B.N. (2010). Understanding nurse manager stress and work complexity: Factors that make a difference. *Journal of Nursing Administration, 40,* 82–91. doi:10.1097/NNA.0b013e3181cb9f88

Smith, K.G., Mitchell, T.R., & Summer, C.E. (1985). Top level management priorities in different stages of the organizational life cycle. *Academy of Management Journal, 28,* 799–820. doi:10.2307/256238

Taylor, F.W. (1911). *The principles of scientific management.* New York, NY: Harper & Brothers.

Thompson, P.A. (2008). Key challenges facing American nurse leaders. *Journal of Nursing Management, 16,* 912–914. doi:10.1111/j.1365-2834.2008.00951.x

Tracy, B. (2014). *Tips to structure your day* [Video file]. Retrieved from https://www.youtube.com/watch?v=4ysyybi4068

Tracy, B., & Stein, C. (2015). *Find your balance point: Clarify your priorities, simplify your life, and achieve more.* San Francisco, CA: Berrett-Koehler.

CHAPTER 12

Project Management and Business Planning for Nurse Leaders

Linda J. Shinn, MBA, RN, FASAE, CAE

In preparing for battle I have always found that plans are useless, but planning is indispensable.

—Dwight D. Eisenhower

Introduction

Today's healthcare environment is focused on outcomes, including outcomes that attest to the quality of health care; improve patient conditions; help institutions compete in a chaotic marketplace; ensure growth, payment for services, and income; or demonstrate a return on investment. Goals and plans are developed to achieve these outcomes. Yet, "organizations in the public and private sectors waste $109 million for every $1 billion invested in projects and programs—almost 11 cents on every dollar . . . . More than half of projects are over budget, a third fail to achieve business objectives, and 17% fail outright" (Langley, 2015).

Clearly, tools that help employees understand an organization's goals, strategies to implement the goals, timelines for accomplishment, resources required, and accountability measures are critical. Business planning and project management are tools that can help an organization achieve its goals or desired outcomes. In today's vernacular, the "GPS" for implementing strategic direction is business planning and project management. Business planning is how goals get accomplished. Project management is the portfolio of work that builds the "how." In some groups, a business plan lays out what is to be done, and the project plan follows, outlining the detail to get the job done. In some work settings, business planning may be bypassed and project planning used. In other situations, a combination of the two might be used; in settings in which no structure exists, "brute force management" occurs (Langley, 2015).

This chapter defines business planning and project management, explains their importance for nurse leaders, outlines the techniques of each, and identifies resources to assist nurse leaders in developing business and project management plans.

Importance for Nurse Leaders

The importance of business and project planning skills in the nurse leader's toolkit is increasingly being recognized. The Oncology Nursing Society (ONS, 2012) has identified leadership competencies that call for articulation of strategic direction as a competency important for the nurse leader. ONS defines the competency as "clear communication of the goals and strategies leading to desired outcomes and effective description of the steps needed to reach the imagined future" (ONS, 2012, p. 10).

The American Organization of Nurse Executives (AONE) has identified nurse executive competencies including business skills such as strategic management. For example, the executive should be able to "create the operational objectives, goals, and specific strategies required to achieve the strategic outcome" (AONE, 2015, p. 10).

In its 2011 report *The Future of Nursing: Leading Change, Advancing Health*, the Institute of Medicine (IOM, now called the Health and Medicine Division of the National Academies of Sciences, Engineering, and Medicine) set forth recommendations to transform the nursing profession. Recommendation 7 called for the profession to "prepare and enable nurses to lead change to advance health" (p. 14). A subset of the recommendation is that "nursing education programs should integrate leadership theory and business practices across the curriculum, including clinical practice" (IOM, 2011, p. 14). The IOM report also pointed out that nurse leaders need strategic and operational knowledge (i.e., strategic, business, and project management skills).

The business aspects of health care should not intimidate nurses. What nurses know is patient care and patients' needs. Bringing this information to business planning and project management tables is a valuable contribution. As the delivery of care becomes ever more complex, competitive, and costly, nurse leaders are increasingly being called on for help in managing costs, clinical improvement, personnel, and technology. All of this will require a focus on achieving prescribed results or outcomes. Skills in business planning and project management are paramount.

Business Planning

A business plan is about the future. It is a document that adds the "who, what, by when, and at what cost" to the organization's strategic plan. A well-crafted and fully used business plan serves four key functions: (a) a map for achieving goals, (b) a communication tool, (c) a financial resource, and (d) a performance evaluation instrument.

Map for Achieving Goals

A business plan is a map for achieving an organization's priorities. Business plans are essentially works of fiction—documents that talk about what is imagined, planned, and hoped to occur in the future, not what has already occurred (Power & Hill, n.d.). It is a plot to get from current circumstances to a desired future. Just like strategic planning, the thinking that goes into developing a business plan is as important as the document that results.

Synchronous with the strategic plan, the business plan is a tool to allocate human, fiscal, and technologic resources to implement the strategic plan. It is a document that can be used to track organizational progress, evaluate and celebrate that progress, and make midcourse corrections. A business plan can also help organizational leaders hold people accountable for how resources are managed and how work is done.

Communication Tool

As a communication tool, the business plan can be used in a variety of ways. It can be used to explain to a board of directors, employees, supervisors, members, investors, clients, suppliers, consultants, elected officials, media, the community, and others just what the organization is and does. It is an instrument to convey the rationale for a new business line, for example, a certification program or telephone hotline. It also is a document from which an organization can build its annual activity report or other report of accomplishments.

Often, two versions of the business plan will be created: an external version and an internal version. The external version must be consistent with the internal version but generally omits the "who" (e.g., specific employees, board of directors) and may be more selective in the financial information shared. The external plan usually is created for an audience, such as investors, consumers, or the media, outside of the organization. For investors, the version will be focused on what this audience wants (e.g., a description of the product or service for which funding is sought, the need for a product or service, competition, projected expenditures and revenue, anticipated return on investment). For consumers, it would focus on products and services, with a heavier emphasis on access. For the media, the content will be focused on promotion. An external version will be in lay terms and not use jargon or acronyms specific to a business or profession.

An internal rendition of a business plan will be more specific to those inside the organization, including employees or the board of directors. Technical terms or terms unique to the industry or profession (e.g., oncology) may be used. The organization's internal operations will be outlined in greater detail.

In addition, the business plan can serve as a reporting mechanism. It can be used to prepare an annual report or other report of accomplishments and to provide progress reports to investors, boards of directors, employees, members, and other stakeholders.

Financial Resource

A business plan often is used to persuade investors to finance a new venture. A group of oncology nurse managers might develop a business plan for the creation of a cancer center. A certification corporation might develop a business plan for a new line of business, for example, Magnet Recognition®. An existing business might use a business plan to secure money for a new product or service, such as pediatric hematology certification. A hospital might develop a business plan for a hospice facility in a nearby community.

A business plan is a key part of an organization's financial portfolio. It details how the group plans to acquire and spend its money and allocate other resources, provides a barometer of how things are going, and is a key to the likely success or failure of a new venture or the sustainability of current operations. A business plan can capture the value of intangible assets, such as customer loyalty or brand recognition, assets that can be very persuasive to investors and convey a business's competitive advantage (Campbell, 2008).

Performance Evaluation Instrument

Business plans are all about performance and can serve as an accountability tracking tool and evaluation mechanism. Leaders at every level of an organization may set performance goals based on the business plan and monitor progress according to the plan's requirements. Progress and performance can be measured against the plan. Midcourse corrections can be made. Nurse leaders can ask and answer the questions, "What led to achievement of our goals?" and "What did not?"

The pace at which the world moves requires constant attention to strategic and business planning. Plans are not static and require regular review to ensure that the organization is on course. Plans should be updated at least annually to reflect changes in the marketplace, resources, and timelines. Organization stakeholders, such as personnel, boards of directors, members, investors, funders, and creditors, should receive an annual report of progress, including accomplishments and information on any midcourse corrections.

Business plans come in a variety of sizes and shapes and are customized to fit the unique needs of an organization. Figure 12-1 outlines the business plan of the Washington State Nurses Association (WSNA). The business plan identifies the issues that WSNA will pursue to address the organization's mission and goals, the mechanisms to address the issues, and how members of the organization can be involved (WSNA, 2015). WSNA's business plan is dynamic in nature. The organization reviews its mission, goals, issues, and priorities periodically and allocates resources through its budgeting process.

Project Management

To achieve goals, implement business plans, or accomplish a body of work, activities or projects are undertaken. While the Project Management Institute (PMI) reports that "only eight percent of organizations are 'high performers' in managing projects" (Kogon, Blakemore, & Wood, 2015, p. 5), project management has become increasingly popular over the past 50 years. There is a distinct body of knowledge, standards, education programs, credentialing systems, and a professional association devoted to project management. It is becoming increasingly popular in all work settings, including health care (see interview later in chapter with Bridget Lynn, senior consultant at Capital Blue Cross).

Whether at home or work, almost everyone manages or is involved in a project. Personal projects might be the remodel of a bedroom or den, installation of a hot tub, or organization of family photos. Professional projects might include development of an online insurance claims program or articulation of a telephone triage protocol or a hospice admission protocol.

PMI defines a project as a "temporary endeavor undertaken to create a unique product, service, or result" (PMI, n.d.). Projects are designed to achieve a specific purpose and have a definitive beginning and end, a clear set of steps to get from start to finish, and people with clearly assigned tasks, tools, resources, and training to accomplish the undertaking. Projects can be big or small, simple or complex, cheap or expensive, short or long, and can succeed or fail.

To implement projects, organizations often create a project plan. A project plan is a blueprint for achieving a body of work. Execution of a project plan involves a team of people to do the work and a leader to oversee the undertaking. "Project management . . . is the application of knowledge, skills, tools, and techniques to project activities to meet the project requirements" (PMI, n.d.). A project and project plans are usually internal to an organization, although external resources (e.g., a consultant) might be used.

Figure 12-1. Washington State Nurses Association Issues and Priorities 2015–2017

Board of Directors

- Membership Campaign
- Financial Stability & Growth
- Enhance Engagement & Direct Communication with Members
- Association Operations Effectiveness
- Strengthen Districts and regionalization efforts
- Visibility/Nursing Image/Communications Campaign
- Increase collaboration with nursing and other labor partners
- Enhance Relationships with ANA, NFN, & AFT

Legislative & Health Policy Council

Issues
- Nursing Shortage
- Target Funding for Nursing Faculty & Education Programs
- ACA & Health Reform Implementation
- Funding/Revenue for Health Safety Net Programs
- Economic Value of Nurses
- Patient Safety & Quality Improvement in Health Care
- Public Health
- Health & Safety
- Safe Staffing
- Collective Bargaining, Free Speech Rights & Right to Work

Target for Member Involvement
- Political/Election Mobilization
- Nurse Legislative Day
- Legislative Advocacy Camp

Mechanisms to Address Issues
- Propose/Respond to Legislation & Regulation
- WSNA-PAC
- Coordinate Agenda with Other Specialty Orgs
- Educational Workshops
- Action Alerts
- WSNA Legislative/Regulatory Agenda

Professional Nursing & Health Care Council

Issues
- Nursing Workforce Issues
- Nursing Care Quality Assurance Commission
- Multistate Licensure/Interstate Compact
- Crossborder Practice
- Code of Ethics
- Evidence-based Practice
- Scope of Practice/Encroachment/New Roles
- Erosion of Public Health Nursing
- Patient Safety Culture/Medical Errors
- Workplace Health & Safety/Violence/Bullying
- Implementation of IOM Future of Nursing Recommendations
- Health Equality & Health Disparities
- Nursing Practice Issues in All Settings
- Environmental Health & Safety
- Changes to Health Care Payment & Reporting Requirements

Target for Member Involvement
- Build Relationships with Schools of Nursing, NSWS, and Other Groups of Nurses
- Professional Development/Continuing Education

Mechanisms to Address Issues
- Seek Direct Input from Membership, WSNA Org. Affiliates, WCN & Other Target Nursing Groups
- WSNF (Support Research & Education)
- Development of Position Papers, Toolkits & Other Resources

Cabinet on Economic & General Welfare

Issues
- Staffing Standards/Levels/Rules
- Mandatory Overtime/On-call/Rest Breaks
- Health & Safety (Violence/Fatigue/Safe Patient Handling)
- Wages/Working Conditions
- AFL-CIO Local Affiliations
- Protection of Nursing Practice
- Threats to Collective Bargaining/Anti-Union Efforts
- Ethical Work Environment/Just Culture

Target for Member Involvement
- Statewide Organizing
- Strengthen Local Units (Minimum of 75% in all Local Units)
- Leadership Development Conference
- Unity Activities

Mechanisms to Address Issues
- Contract Language
- Develop and Strengthen Local Unit Structure
- Local Unit Leadership Council and Regional Councils
- Develop Relationships with Labor Community
- Grievance/Arbitration/Litigation
- AFT Organizing Model

Note. From *WSNA Issues and Priorities 2015–2017*, by Washington State Nurses Association, 2015. Retrieved from https://cdn.wsna.org/assets/entry-assets/about/issues-and-priorities/Issues-Priorities-v15-12_1.pdf. Copyright 2015 by Washington State Nurses Association. Reprinted with permission.

PMI identifies the five steps in project management as (a) initiating, (b) planning, (c) executing, (d) monitoring and controlling, and (e) closing. Just as the nursing process is a mechanism to manage the care of a patient, project management is a blueprint for implementing the work of an organization. Both processes are focused on results.

Project management has many things in common with the nursing process. "The nursing process provides an ideal background for using project management techniques. The nursing process incorporates a systematic method of assessment, diagnosis, planning, implementation, and evaluation" (Overgaard, 2010, p. 53). Put another way, project management follows the same basic steps as the nursing process. Every project manager needs to define and initiate the project (assessment), develop possible solutions (diagnosis), plan the project (planning), execute the plan (implementation), and finally, monitor, control progress, and close out the project (evaluation) (InterOpNurse, 2011).

For purposes of illustration, commentary on these steps in the following sections arises from the work of the Grace Hospice, a fictional organization created for purposes of this chapter. One of the goals of the Grace Hospice is to engage in community partnerships. Another goal is to increase the interest of nursing students and RNs in hospice and palliative care. In an effort to achieve these goals, Grace Hospice decided to conduct a feasibility study related to partnering with a school of nursing to provide a clinical site for baccalaureate nursing students.

Initiating

Begin with the end in mind. This step sets the stage for the end result, or the work to be achieved by a specific project. It is important that deliverables be clearly described, quantified, and tied to the overall goals and business plans of the organization. To put it another way, what will success look like at the end of the project? PMI reports that "only forty-five percent of projects actually meet the goals they are supposed to meet" (Kogon et al., 2015, p. 5).

Stakeholders and decision makers should be on board with project expectations and desired outcomes. Those integral to the success of the project and to achieving the outcomes should "buy in" at the outset.

Grace Hospice has identified the outcome it wishes to achieve: the conduct of a feasibility study related to partnering with a school of nursing to serve as a clinical site. It will be important for Grace to convene a group of stakeholders integral to achieving the desired outcome to get buy-in, ideas, and commitment to the project. Potential stakeholders in this example might include the chief nurse executive and representatives of the nursing, chaplaincy, pharmacy, and social work departments.

Planning

The plan sets forth the tasks, steps, resources, and timelines required to achieve the outcome. The tasks are activities to be done. The steps are the sequence of work required to complete the activities. Resources contribute what it takes to get the tasks done and include people, tools, and money. The timelines identify who will do what and by when. The budget outlines project expenses. The plan also should include checkpoints so that midcourse corrections or go/no-go choices can be made. Overgaard (2010) noted, "Project plans should be both detailed and transparent" (p. 53).

An essential subset of the plan is a communication strategy. The old maxim "who needs to know, what do they need to know, and when do they need to know it" works here. Information about plan progress, bumps in the road, midcourse corrections, or changes should be shared with stakeholders on a regular basis.

It is also important to identify the risks or obstacles to achieving the desired outcomes. Then a risk management strategy can be put in place to work through the inevitable hurdles to getting a plan achieved. A critical path is an important adjunct to a plan and to managing the inevitable hurdles. "The critical path is the longest way to get from the beginning to the end of the project, and the earliest and latest that you can start and end each task without making the project longer" (Kogon et al., 2015, p. 109). Figure 12-2 is a partial plan for the Grace Hospice project.

Figure 12-2. Grace Hospice Feasibility Study				
Project: Conduct a feasibility study related to partnering with a school of nursing to serve as a clinical site. Project Lead: Chief Nursing Officer				
Task	**Steps**	**Resources**	**Timeline**	**Progress**
Create and charge a staff team to conduct a feasibility study.	Seek volunteers from nursing, social work, pharmacy, chaplaincy departments.	Chief nursing officer will call for volunteers and appoint staff team.	30 days	Appointed 7-member team
Identify and charge a project manager.	Appoint a project manager.	Chief nursing officer will appoint.	30 days	Appointed director of nursing professional development
Identify community partners to interview related to the study.	Project team will identify community partners to be considered. Interested community partners will be asked to appoint a representative to be interviewed by Project Team member.	Project team Roster of schools of nursing in community Letter to schools announcing project, seeking interest, and asking for representative to participate in interview	45 days	In process
Identify questions for interviews of community partners.	Project team will develop questions for interviews.	Project manager Consultant to help with question development and pilot testing	30 days	Consultant is being sought.
Interview partners.	Project members will interview partners.	Release time from work for interviewers Telephone time; time and resources to transcribe interviews Consultant to work with project team members to collate results	90 days	Consultant is being sought.
(Continued on next page)				

Figure 12-2. Grace Hospice Feasibility Study *(Continued)*				
Task	**Steps**	**Resources**	**Timeline**	**Progress**
Acquire and review HPNA Standards for Clinical Education of Hospice and Palliative Nurses.	Project manager acquires and reviews standards.	Web search Money for purchase and shipping	10 days	Retrieved
Acquire and review CNEA Standards of Accreditation.	Project manager acquires and reviews standards.	Web search Money for purchase and shipping	10 days	Retrieved
Acquire and review CCNE Standards for Accreditation of Baccalaureate and Graduate Nursing Programs.	Project manager acquires and reviews standards.	Web search Money for purchase and shipping	10 days	Retrieved
CCNE—Commission on Collegiate Nursing Education; CNEA—National League for Nursing Commission for Nursing Education Accreditation; HPNA—Hospice and Palliative Nurses Association				

Executing

Executing a plan is putting the plan to work. In most organizations, a project manager or leader is assigned the responsibility and accountability of project implementation. The leader oversees and manages the work, including the people, schedule, resources, risks, and communication.

People are the critical ingredient in plan execution. Project success is linked to people who know the outcome to be achieved; know what is expected of them and by when; have the tools, resources, and training to do the work; know to whom they are accountable; and know where to go when a problem arises. These principles apply to both project leaders and managers.

As noted in the Grace Hospice project plan, the chief nursing officer is the project lead. The final accountability falls to the chief nursing officer. In this example, a project manager is appointed as well. It will be important for the leader and manager to collaborate in getting the work done and to be clear about respective roles, responsibilities, and communication strategies.

In addition, project leaders and managers must be skilled in managing people. A person who listens, respects others, and is flexible, patient, transparent, willing to hold others accountable, committed to change management, and able to engage in problem solving will contribute immeasurably to the project's success. Project leaders and managers must not only bring the team together to do the work but also cross-check progress on a regular basis and communicate the status of work to relevant stakeholders.

Monitoring and Controlling

Keeping a project on time and on target is a big portion of monitoring and controlling. Continuous oversight is key to ensuring that the project stays focused on the work to be achieved, on schedule, and within budget. Keeping tabs on a project can alert the overseer to the need for midcourse corrections, clarification of expectations, modification of communication strategies, or adjustment of resources. Most importantly, the leader or manager can identify and address trouble spots before they become obstacles or roadblocks. Observations should be communicated regularly with team members and other stakeholders.

Monitoring and controlling also alerts those involved in a project to changes in the environment that might yield new information important to consider in the project trajectory. The two biggest dilemmas with projects are scope creep and timeline adherence.

Projects have a way of expanding beyond their original design, which is known as *scope creep*. Although scope creep is not always bad, catching it early gives project leaders an opportunity to contain it or direct it. Scope creep often involves expanding a project beyond its original intent.

In the case of the Grace Hospice project, scope creep could include expansion of the project to examine the feasibility of providing a clinical site for other student groups, such as chaplaincy or pharmacy. A change in scope might also result from a change of the environment within which the project operates, for example, a new set of accreditation standards or the departure of the chief nurse executive.

Many things can influence the timeline of a project, including change in scope, diminishing resources, or a drifting timeline. Identifying that a project is behind schedule, even a little bit, allows intervention before it becomes critical.

Monitoring and controlling a project requires thinking ahead, anticipating problems, observing progress, managing frustrations, and making midcourse corrections. "As one project manager said . . . 'good control reveals problems early—which means you'll have longer to worry about them'" (Kogon et al., 2015, p. 162). A written project plan is a good tool to monitor and control a project. Note that the Grace Hospice project plan has a column for reporting progress to date. This column can be used to report and monitor progress and might also be used for identifying and reporting on midcourse corrections. The progress column is also a handy reference to use when communicating about project status with stakeholders or other interested parties.

Closing

As noted earlier, projects have a definitive beginning and end. "There is no such thing as an ongoing project—that would be an oxymoron" (Kogon et al., 2015, p. 189). Closing a project signals the end of a body of work, usually accompanied by deliverables. Concluding a project should include a recording of the work for archival and historical purposes; recognizing the work of those involved; assessing what worked and what did not work, including ideas for process improvement; and a recounting of lessons learned.

When thinking about closing a project, ending a body of work with specific, measurable results is top of mind. In the Grace Hospice project, the following might be measured and reported:

• The number of partners willing to participate in the feasibility interviews
• The results of the feasibility interviews
• An account of the resources used
• Identification of what worked well and what did not work well

The creation and preservation of a written and electronic record of the experience is an important part of closing. Managers, team members, consultants, and community partners should be notified of the closing of the project and provided relevant materials or reports. Unused resources (e.g., money, tools) should be returned to originators as appropriate.

There are times when a project should be terminated. If the project is not meeting the goals of the project, the organization's mission has changed, a shift in the environment has occurred, a new public policy or regulation has been enacted, an alteration in resources or personnel has occurred, or leadership no longer supports the project, rethinking a project is a must. Cessation of a project may be the best option.

Resources

Numerous resources are available to help with business planning and project management. An Internet search on either topic reveals commercial websites offering tutorials and templates, some for a fee, and articles describing both for-profit and nonprofit business planning and project management. Colleges, business schools, and associations offer seminars. State and local governments and educational institutions offer small business incubators, a place where plans can be developed and nurtured. The Small Business Administration (www.sba.gov), an organization of the federal government, devotes a portion of its website to business planning and offers material on the subject, including a step-by-step online planning tool.

PMI (www.pmi.org) offers a wealth of resources for those involved in project management. It sets standards for project management and provides a variety of seminars and other tools. PMI also offers certifications for project management professionals.

The Institute for Healthcare Improvement (IHI, www.ihi.org) is focused on healthcare improvement. Part of IHI's work is concentrated on quality, cost, and values. IHI offers a variety of project planning tools, including a project planning form and project tracking tool (see Figure 12-3).

A number of project management resources are geared to nurses. The American Academy of Ambulatory Care Nursing has devised a Project Management Toolkit for members and others to use for short- and long-term projects. The toolkit can be accessed at www.aaacn.org.

The nursing literature is replete with books and articles on project management. For example, Springer Publishing Company has published a book titled *Project Management for the Advanced Practice Nurse* (Sipes, 2016).

Resources for business planning and project management also may be available in the workplace. The finance department or business office is a good place to start. Large healthcare systems may employ a full-time strategic planner or have a corporate planning office. The chief nurse executive and chief financial officer in most organizations are key players in business planning. These people can be tapped for help in developing business or project management plans or guidance in implementation, oversight, and management of roadblocks. Human resource departments also may provide guidance on planning, as they often are pivotal in the planning for and deployment of personnel.

Professional and trade associations, such as ONS, AONE, PMI, American Association of Critical-Care Nurses, Association of periOperative Registered Nurses, Emergency Nurses Association, National Small Business Association, and Healthcare Financial Management Association, among others, provide useful resources as well. These groups can serve as a resource for experts or consultants on business planning or project management.

Insights and Tips on Project Planning From an Interview With Bridget Lynn, MBA, RN, PCMH CCE

Bridget Lynn is a senior consultant at Capital Blue Cross and an advocate of project planning and management. Lynn has been involved in the design and management of quality/value-

Figure 12-3. Improvement Project Planning Form

Team:

Project:

Driver—list the drivers you'll be working on	Process Measure	90-Day Goal	Final Project Goal
1.			
2.			
3.			
4.			
5.			
6.			

Driver Number (from above)	Change to Test	Tasks to Prepare for Tests	Data Needed to Evaluate Test	Person Responsible	Timeline ("t" = test, "i" = implement, "s" = spread)
					Week
					1	2	3	4	5	6	7	8	9	10	11	12	13	14

Note. From "Project Planning Form," by Institute for Healthcare Improvement, 2016. Retrieved from http://www.ihi.org/resources/Pages/Tools/ProjectPlanningForm.aspx. Copyright 2016 by Institute for Healthcare Improvement. Reprinted with permission.

based care models. She has also been involved in numerous projects over the course of her career focused on value-based network design and cost-efficiency initiatives supportive of the Triple Aim. She is now working in the insurance arena and is focused on cost containment.

Lynn reports that an organization's business plan is a more global document and that a project plan is more granular or detailed, thus providing the building blocks for working toward successfully accomplishing a business plan. She notes that the project plan supports the intent of the business plan and contains specific and measurable objectives or outcomes.

Lynn notes that project planning has assumed greater importance in corporate America and that many organizations, including those focused on health care, have specific and structured corporate processes devoted to project planning and management.

Lynn comments that clinical nursing is algorithmic, with specific, evidence-based interventions being consistently applied to their associated disease processes. As nurses begin to assume greater leadership roles in project planning, it is critical to step outside of this algorithmic approach and embrace the iterative, dynamic nature of project planning. Although nurses may not be familiar with project planning or have training in basic business topics, they do have many of the skills required, including patience, agility, advocacy, and collaboration. Lynn observes, "Nurses are tireless advocates for their patients, and it is this same advocacy that will also facilitate the success of the projects they stand behind." Lynn suggests that it is a great time for RNs to get involved in project planning, as their guidance is increasingly being sought on strategies aimed at optimizing patient outcomes while minimizing financial inefficiencies.

Project planning can be time consuming; it can be challenging to engage nurses and other healthcare workers in planning efforts. Lynn suggests one of the best ways to motivate others to participate in project work is to have a clear understanding of what those involved in the project want to achieve or what value they feel successful completion of the project will bring to them.

Lynn offers the following tips for those involved in project planning:
- Articulate the value of the project and anticipated outcomes in clear, measurable terms; know what you want to accomplish.
- Identify how the project outcomes help support the mission and goals of the organization.
- Outline project milestones, including target dates for accomplishment.
- Acknowledge that barriers and obstacles are inevitable and be flexible enough to make mid-course corrections.
- Know that threats and opportunities in the environment can arise at any time and may necessitate changing plan milestones.
- Engage key stakeholders in project planning.
- Ensure senior leadership "buy-in," including those in the C-suite, prior to beginning the project.
- Understand that administrative support for projects may wax and wane over the course of the project, and leverage the value proposition to advocate for any additional resources needed as this support fluctuates.

Lynn cautioned that the following pitfalls might arise:
- Stakeholders fail to engage in continuous dialogue with each other.
- People become unwilling, or time constraints make it challenging, to pause and evaluate the effectiveness of attempted interventions.
- People are not held accountable for work to be done.
- Team members become reluctant to disengage from an approach that is not effective in accomplishing a specific milestone or project goal.

Lynn's go-to resource for planning is IHI. She cited IHI's PDSA (Plan, Do, Study, Act) cycle for quality improvement as a very useful approach. IHI has many tools for managing work and change, including the Improvement Project Planning Form (see Figure 12-3).

Summary

Organizational achievement is the watchword in health care today. Business planning and project management are critical tools in helping organizations attain desired outcomes. These tools are essential for nurse leaders to understand and use to be successful in helping employers and colleagues succeed and to realize their own goals. Prepare yourself by developing the leader skills you need for success.

Adapted from "Business Planning and Development" (pp. 861–848), by L.J. Shinn in M.M. Gullatte (Ed.), Nursing Management: Principles and Practice *(2nd ed.), 2011, Pittsburgh, PA: Oncology Nursing Society. Copyright 2011 by Oncology Nursing Society.*

References

American Organization of Nurse Executives. (2015). *AONE nurse executive competencies.* Retrieved from http://www.aone.org/resources/nec.pdf

Campbell, A. (2008). The latest in business plans—Interview with Tim Berry, CEO of Palo Alto Software. *Small Business Brief.* Retrieved from http://www.smallbusinessbrief.com/articles/planning/000468.html

Institute of Medicine. (2011). *The future of nursing: Leading change, advancing health.* Washington, DC: National Academies Press.

InterOpNurse. (2011, July 10). The nursing process and project management. Retrieved from http://interopnurse.com/2011/07/the-nursing-process-and-project-management

Kogon, K., Blakemore, S., & Wood, J. (2015). *Project management for the unofficial project manager* (Electronic version). Dallas, TX: BenBella Books.

Langley, M.A. (2015, August 6). 3 things CFOs should know about project management. Retrieved from http://ww2.cfo.com/business-planning/2015/08/3-things-CFOs-know-project-management

Oncology Nursing Society. (2012). *Oncology Nursing Society leadership competencies.* Retrieved from https://www.ons.org/sites/default/files/leadershipcomps.pdf

Overgaard, P.M. (2010). Get the keys to successful project management. *Nursing Management, 41*(6), 53–54. doi:10.1097/01.NUMA.0000381744.25529.e8

Power, D., & Hill, B. (n.d.). Ten tips to jump start your business plan. Retrieved from http://www.businessperform.com/articles/strategy-planning/business_plan_jump_start.html

Project Management Institute. (n.d.). What is project management? Retrieved from http://www.pmi.org/about/learn-about-pmi/what-is-project-management

Sipes, C. (2016). *Project management for the advanced practice nurse.* New York, NY: Springer.

Washington State Nurses Association. (2015). *WSNA issues and priorities, 2015–2017.* Seattle, WA: Author.

CHAPTER 13

Executive Leadership Acumen

Jane Englebright, PhD, RN, CENP, FAAN, and
Jane M. McCurley, DNP, MBA, RN, NEA-BC, CENP, FACHE

Introduction

The role of the executive nurse leader comprises two primary responsibilities: executive team member and chief nurse. As an executive team member, the executive nurse leader works with other executives to advance the vision of the organization. In this role, the executive nurse leader must build collaborative relationships while finding his or her voice on the executive team. As chief nurse, the executive nurse leader is responsible for establishing the vision for nursing services throughout the organization. In this role, the executive nurse leader must build a nursing leadership team that can carry forward the nursing agenda, define and execute strategies for change, create expectations for the work environment and individual behaviors, and drive toward results.

The executive nurse leader role is changing as the healthcare delivery system is changing. As the job title suggests, this role is a combination of executive leadership and nursing leadership. Executive leaders are responsible for overseeing organizational activities designed to fulfill the mission and goals of the organization, such as strategic planning, visioning, and overall decision making. The executive nurse leader is responsible for establishing the strategic agenda for nursing within the organization and guiding the execution of that strategy. This chapter will describe the two primary role responsibilities that distinguish the executive nurse leader role.

The Executive Nurse Leader as an Executive Team Member

One of the defining characteristics of the executive nurse leader role is membership in the executive team (American Nurses Association, 2016). For the executive nurse leader, typical titles are chief nurse executive (CNE) or chief nursing officer (CNO). The executive nurse leader serves with the executive team of the organization, often led by a chief executive officer (CEO) or president. Team members may have titles such as chief financial officer, chief operating officer, chief medical officer or executive, vice president of finance, or vice president of quality. Regardless of title or background, the common ground within the executive team is concern for the mission of the organization, concern for patients, and concern for employees.

The executive team is the primary workgroup for the executive nurse leader. This is the team with which the executive nurse leader will have the most interaction. This means the executive nurse leader spends most of his or her time working with non-nursing colleagues, assisting with guiding the overall direction of the organization. For nurse leaders, whose careers have previously been dominated by interactions with nurses and other clinicians, this can be a seismic shift in thinking and relationship building. The transition to executive nurse leader means entering a world that primarily comprises executive leaders from other, frequently nonclinical, components of the organization. The executive nurse leader is engaged as a full partner and collaborator with the executive team.

Case Study: Executive Team Interactions

Jeff is completing what he believes to be a successful interview to become the CNE of a large academic health center. After a full day of meeting people and touring the facilities, the CEO asks if Jeff would like to see his office. To Jeff's surprise, the CEO leads him out of the executive suite, down the hall several yards to a separate set of offices with the title "Nursing Administration" on the door. Jeff is shown a large, well-appointed corner office along with space for an administrative assistant, assistant CNO, and house supervisor offices.

As Jeff is leaving the facility, the CEO commits to getting back to Jeff the following week with the next steps. Jeff lets the CEO know how excited he is about joining this organization, leading the nursing team, and being a part of the executive team. He also expresses his concern that it will be difficult to be a full partner in the executive team if he is the only member of the team in a separate office suite. He respectfully requests that if he is selected for the position, some consideration be given to moving his office into the executive suite, even if that means a smaller office.

Building Executive Relationships

Effective relationships are critical to working within the executive team. These relationships start with respect for the unique knowledge and perspective that each member of the team contributes in guiding and directing the mission of the organization. The team members are accomplished subject matter experts in their field and lead an important segment of the organization. As a member of the executive team, the executive nurse leader is a peer of the executive leaders for finance, operations, medicine, and other functions identified by the organization. The structure and frequency of formal interaction among the executive team varies considerably based on the size and complexity of the organization and the executive leadership style. However, the collaborative nature of executive duties is not limited to formal meetings, and thus it is important for the executive nurse leader to have a good working relationship with each member of the executive team and be respected as an equal partner and decision maker.

The executive nurse leader may or may not be the only clinical voice at the table. Chief medical officers, chief quality officers, or other executives with clinical backgrounds are increasingly included in the executive team. While other members of the team may also have a nursing background, the executive nurse leader bears the primary responsibility for overseeing nursing services in the organization and bringing forward a nursing perspective in executive discussions. Consequently, the executive nurse leader is best positioned to ensure that nursing considerations are involved in the deliberations and decision making of the executive team. For example, a strategic discussion on transforming a low-census obstetrical program into a behavioral health unit may become focused on retrofitting the physical work setting. The executive nurse leader would be responsible for ensuring that the unique competencies of behavioral health nurses were understood and that an appropriate recruitment and education component was included in the transition plan.

Clinical performance is often a shared responsibility for the executive nurse leader and the executive physician leader. This provides an opportunity for modeling collaborative behaviors that are necessary to achieve peak clinical performance. Typically, the nurse leader will drive improvement efforts on nursing-sensitive performance indicators to drive patient safety and outcomes, such as pressure ulcers, patient falls, and urinary tract infections, supported by the physician leader. Conversely, the physician leader will typically drive improvement efforts on physician-sensitive performance indicators, such as sepsis and central line infections, supported by the nurse leader. The overall message to the organization is that quality of care is important and is a team effort. The nurse and physician leader relationship is critically important to the effectiveness of the role.

Case Study: Etiquette to Improve Collaboration

The executive team for a large community health center includes several clinicians, some of whom also provide patient care, and several individuals with doctoral degrees who are not physicians. The doctoral-prepared executive nurse leader has noted a power deference to individuals being addressed as "Doctor" or wearing white coats. The nurse leader decides to meet with other members of the executive team who are either clinicians or doctorally prepared and propose some etiquette guidelines for their teams with a goal of ensuring that every voice is heard and equally valued. After some frank discussion, the group proposes and agrees on the following guidelines:

- All doctorally prepared team members will have the following nameplates: Dr. <first name> <last name>.
- Meeting minutes will list names but not credentials of all attendees.
- All clinical executive team members will wear white lab coats in the clinical areas but will not wear them in administrative meetings.

The most important relationship for the executive nurse leader is with the CEO, who is the immediate supervisor for this role. The executive nurse leader must work with the CEO to achieve agreement about role responsibilities and expectations. Meeting these expectations requires understanding and appreciating differences in communication styles early in the relationship. A successful executive nurse leader will appreciate his or her supervisor's preferences for updates, including how often, in how much detail, and how to deliver bad news. By committing to these fundamentals early in the relationship, the executive nurse leader can build a solid foundation from which to grow.

At the executive level of the organization, feedback can be sparse unless actively sought. For continued growth, the executive nurse leader must ask for feedback from supervisors and peers on the executive team. It can be challenging to find constructive criticism, as subordinates and peers are often reluctant to provide negative feedback to a senior leader. Obtaining feedback from respected peers is a valuable way to continually hone executive skills and validate competencies.

Finding the Executive Voice

The executive nurse leader needs to learn to interpret, understand, and synthesize reports from other members of the executive team. In addition, the executive nurse leader must be comfortable with discussing and debating data and viewpoints on organizational and industry performance on financial, quality, medical, technologic, or other dimensions of the organization to be a contributing member of the executive team. The executive nurse leader brings nursing-specific data, information, and perspective to these deliberations. Translating and presenting the nursing perspective in a language that can be consumed by other members of the executive team is an important nurse executive competency.

Finding the right voice inside the executive team is important. The executive nurse leader is a nurse advocate, but not at the expense of the larger organization. The leader must always maintain a balance between the two roles of organizational executive and nurse leader. The executive nurse leader is challenged to look at issues from both perspectives. If an action is good for nurses, how will it affect other employees or the organization as a whole? If an action is good for the organization, how will it affect nurses? An effective strategy for balancing these roles and responsibilities is to find common values and principles that unify goals and perspectives, such as patient safety (Englebright & Perlin, 2008). The organization and all its employees, including nurses, are very concerned with patient safety. Reframing issues into a larger context and agreeing that patient safety will guide the final decision making often can help with finding common ground among the executive team.

Case Study: Finding the Executive Voice

When Mary joined St. Elsewhere, she noted that all executive team meetings started with each team member passing out a one-page statistical summary of how their respective components of the organization were performing on the key performance indicators in the strategic plan. The summary Mary had inherited from her predecessor was produced by the chief financial officer and contained productivity metrics and patient satisfaction scores for each nursing department.

Mary is frustrated that other important components of nursing performance are not being discussed or supported by the executive team. She realizes that she needs to create statistical representations of other elements of the strategic plan to get these areas introduced into the executive team deliberations. Mary works with the executive team members leading quality and human resources to add clinical quality metrics and RN turnover statistics to the nursing report. The expanded report provides Mary with a vehicle to routinely address clinical and workforce issues in the executive team meetings.

Executive Outreach

Finding the right voice outside the organization is also important. As a member of the executive team, the executive nurse leader is often assumed to be speaking on behalf of the organization. Indeed, representing the organization at meetings and events within the community is frequently an expectation of the role. However, comments and contributions made at those meetings should reflect the organization's views, not personal views. Understanding when a view or perspective first needs to be vetted by the senior executive team is a key attribute of the executive leader.

The executive nurse leader will want to review professional and personal memberships and commitments, as well as invitations to speak or publish, with those responsible for organizational integrity or image. In the executive role, the nurse leader needs to guard against the perception of impropriety or conflict of interest that could reflect negatively on the organization. When made by a member of the executive team, casual statements can be interpreted as policy. The nurse executive must work to ensure that responses to verbal, email, and written questions are based more on fact than opinion. When stating a personal opinion in a discussion, the executive nurse leader must be clear that it is not the perspective of the organization.

The Executive Nurse Leader as Chief Nurse

The executive nurse leader establishes the vision for nursing services within the organization. An effective executive nurse leader articulates this vision in a way that aligns nursing leadership teams, points efforts toward the future, and connects to the purpose of the broader organization. While honesty is the primary reason people follow leaders, the second most admired attribute is being forward thinking (Kouzes & Posner, 2012). The executive nurse leader must look for and recognize opportunities both within and outside of the organization.

This role has a strong outward-facing component, and the executive nurse leader must keep up with changing trends and remain sensitive to the external environment and its potential implications for the organization. Nurse executives not only observe and analyze a great deal of information about the direction of nursing care in general but also, more importantly, listen to colleagues, staff, and other leaders to understand priorities and desires. In this, the nurse executive becomes a source of inspiration for commitment to the purpose, helping to align the entire team to common values and the vision for the future (Kouzes & Posner, 2012).

Selling the vision to the organization is the responsibility of the executive nurse leader. While the work can be shared with other nurse leaders, it cannot be delegated away. The executive nurse leader must continuously keep the vision before the nursing organization and the executive team and inspire continuous efforts toward achieving that vision.

For many types of healthcare organizations, the responsibilities of the chief nurse are defined in the *Code of Federal Regulations* ("Condition of Participation: Nursing Services," 2011) and by accrediting bodies such as the Joint Commission (Schyve, 2009). Generally, these standards state that the chief nurse is responsible for the delivery of nursing care throughout the hospital or facility, including the organization, staffing, and delivery of nursing care. The executive nurse leader frequently has responsibility for nurses practicing in departments that report to other members of the executive team, such as imaging departments. The executive nurse leader also has responsibility for advanced practice nursing, even for members of the credentialed medical staff. These responsibilities can be accomplished in an infinite variety of ways, but they all start with building a nursing leadership team.

Case Study: Creating a New Nursing Delivery Model

The call center started three years ago as a marketing and customer-relationship management strategy. The nonclinical staff answering the phones provided basic information about the institutions within the healthcare system, such as directions and how to schedule an appointment or pay a bill. Over time, the center began providing services such as scheduling appointments or enrolling callers in classes. Last year, the center expanded to providing clinical services. The call center added RNs to provide health information and telephone triage. Now, the hospitals within the system are asking the center to begin performing post-discharge telephone calls for high-risk patients. The system's CNE has identified that the call center is providing nursing services. In a meeting with the director of the call center, the CNE discusses the need for a professional practice governance structure within the call center and asks that the nurse leader for the call center start attending the system nurse leader council. The CNE and the director of the call center outline a plan for how they will begin integrating the RNs in the call center into other nursing activities within the health system.

Building the Nursing Leadership Team

Having a seat at the executive table expands the reach of the executive nurse leader's voice, affecting strategic and operational decisions for the entire organization. However, this also means leaving behind the more direct and local influence of a nurse leader. Executive nurse leaders should be prepared to delegate much of the execution of the nursing vision and management of nursing services to a team of nurse leaders. They must also be prepared to support the decisions that these nurse leaders make. Building a leadership team by acquiring, developing, and retaining nursing leadership talent is a priority activity for the executive nurse leader (Loop, 2009).

A strong and capable leadership team that guides and directs nursing services enables the executive nurse leader to more fully participate in the executive leadership team. In addition, a strong nursing leadership team contributes to succession planning to ensure strategic continuity, operational effectiveness, and quality of care (Trepanier & Crenshaw, 2013). The executive nurse leader has a responsibility to assess current leadership talent, identify needs for the future, and develop strategies to meet those future needs. The nurse executive needs to engage in conversations with nurses at all levels to identify the talent and interest in development along the leadership pathway while also developing relationships with nurses in professional organizations and universities to provide a wide array of potential future leaders (Clipper, 2012).

The nursing leadership team should share the vision and values of the executive nurse leader. However, a diverse set of leadership skills, talents, and styles is desired for a balanced approach to leading complex nursing services. The executive nurse leader is charged with keeping challenging opportunities before the group to support individual growth and team development (MacPhee, Skelton-Green, Bouthillette, & Suryaprakash, 2012).

Defining and Executing Strategies

The executive nurse leader, with the leadership team, defines and executes the strategies that will realize the organization's vision. The strategies that support the vision always involve change. Gone are the days when a strategy was simply to maintain the current level of performance. In the rapidly evolving world of health care today, change is required. Today's healthcare organizations must continually reinvent themselves as the U.S. healthcare delivery system changes, technology advances, global health issues emerge, and diseases are eradicated and reemerge. Organizations that excel at change will survive and thrive.

Although other nurse leaders usually manage change initiatives, the executive nurse leader is critical to championing key initiatives, establishing priorities among competing initiatives, and ensuring that appropriate resources are available for success. There is no shortage of good ideas; however, finite resources are available to enact those ideas. The responsibility for ensuring the success of the initiatives that will be the most impactful to the vision and goals of the organization rests with the executive leaders. This often means delaying less impactful projects, moving resources from one area to another, and dealing with the consequences of those decisions. A key competency of the executive nurse leader is managing a broad portfolio of strategic initiatives and knowing when to change direction or stop a project to ensure that the most important projects are successful and organizational goals are met.

Inevitably, within this portfolio will be projects involving information technology (IT). Executive nurse leaders are increasingly being required to provide executive oversight to implementation and, more importantly, appropriate use of IT solutions. Competency in nursing informatics is an essential skill for executive nurse leaders (Simpson, 2013).

Case Study: Managing a Portfolio of Projects

This year, John is driving three major initiatives for nursing, along with five strategic projects for the organization. All eight are on schedule and within budget going into the third quarter of the year. Two of the projects involve IT: installing a new version of the electronic health record and upgrading the nurse call system. John is particularly excited about the upgrade to the nurse call system. He believes it will be appreciated by both patients and staff, as well as provide nurse leaders with important information for improving care processes. At the start of the third quarter, the IT department informs John that they will not be able to meet the timelines on these projects and deliver on the Centers for Medicare and Medicaid Services requirements for documentation in the rehabilitation unit that must be in place within six months. They are asking John for guidance on which of the three work activities they can postpone.

Driving for Results

Driving the nursing organization to achieve results is a combination of inspiration and execution. It certainly begins with clear communication of the objective and the reason for the change. Equally important is regular feedback on progress. The executive nurse leader is an important source of information and inspiration during this process. Clear, consistent, and frequent communication throughout the change is critical to success, whether the change is directly related to nursing services or involves the entire organization. When organizational change initiatives need the nursing workforce to embrace or even drive the change, the executive nurse leader becomes a motivating force. He or she must be able to inspire teams to achieve the organizational goals while maintaining consistently excellent patient care services.

A key to success in driving for results is keeping the focus on a small number of objectives. This is a significant challenge in health care today. The number of clinical, operational, and financial challenges facing healthcare organizations can tempt leaders into trying to execute on multiple fronts simultaneously. A realistic appraisal of how much the staff can assimilate into their workflow within a given time is important to pacing and sequencing to achieve sustainable improvements.

Case Study: Developing Strategies and Inspiring Achievement

Sally and Martha, the CNO and chief medical officer for a large hospital, are jointly leading a task force to reduce readmissions. They launched the initiative with an educational session for staff that outlined which types of patients were most likely to readmit to their hospital and why. Based on the data, they are implementing three new strategies this year around medication reconciliation and education, follow-up appointments, and homecare referrals. Direct care nurses are being asked to perform the medication reconciliation and education. Case managers are being assigned to all high-risk patients to be sure that follow-up appointments and homecare referrals are done. To provide feedback, the case managers are flagging charts when they identify that a patient is high risk, then following the nursing documentation to see when the education and reconciliation are complete. A report of the percentage of patients for whom this is completed is posted on each unit each day, along with the readmission rate for the hospital and the number of patients that had not been readmitted compared to last year. This report provided the nursing staff with insight into their individual performance, how it was contributing to the overall improvement for the organization, and how many patients had benefited. Sally and Martha referred to these results on rounds and in staff meetings throughout the year.

Creating the Work Environment

Together, the nursing leadership team creates the work environment in which nursing care happens for patients. The 2011 report *The Future of Nursing: Leading Change, Advancing Health* from the Institute of Medicine (now called the Health and Medicine Division of the National Academies of Sciences, Engineering, and Medicine) emphasized that the executive nurse leader bears the responsibility of helping to create the healthy and empowering work environment; this environment can be created by sharing power through equitable resource allocation, enhanced communication, and participative decision making (MacPhee et al., 2012).

To establish and sustain a healthy work environment, the executive nurse leader is called to consider six standards for principles of professional performance, as defined by the American Association of Critical-Care Nurses (2016) and in alignment with core competencies from the National Academy of Medicine (Greiner & Knebel, 2003), the Oncology Nursing Society (2012), and the American Nurses Association (2015): shared communication, true collaboration, effective decision making, appropriate staffing, meaningful recognition, and authentic leadership. Nursing recruitment and retention, patient safety, and nurse and patient outcomes are affected by the work environment (American Association of Critical-Care Nurses, 2016). The executive nurse leader accomplishes this by creating an environment that encourages and supports innovation and a frankness to explore new possibilities. The nurse leader challenges people to question the way things have been done before and then offers input and support to help them be successful with new ideas. For more detail on healthy work environments, see Chapter 6.

Having a healthy work environment, with nurses actively engaged in governance of practice, makes execution of strategy much easier for the leadership team. Similarly, behavioral expectations often flow naturally from a healthy work environment.

Setting Behavioral Expectations

Behavioral expectations begin with role modeling by the executive nurse leader and the entire leadership team. The professional deportment of these key leaders sets the tone for everyone in the organization. The organization may further codify behavioral expectations in a code of conduct or job description.

The guiding principle for developing behavioral expectations for all the complex relationships in a healthcare environment is respect. This begins with respectful professional relationships in the care environment, both with physicians and other members of the care team and within the nursing team. The nurse executive ensures collaboration is done in a positive and integrated pattern where behaviors are mutually supported (Porter-O'Grady & Malloch, 2016).

Case Study: Maintaining Behavioral Expectations

Jane, the CNO of a large academic medical center, observed Allison, a new advanced practice RN, giving handoff to Charles, an experienced advanced practice RN, in front of the team. Charles peppered Allison with questions during her report, frequently interrupting her. He would roll his eyes dramatically when she didn't know the answer to his question or had to go to the computer to pull up a result. At the end of report, Jane could see Allison was visibly shaken and several members of the team were uncomfortable. Charles walked off, shaking his head. Jane followed Charles down the hall for a private conversation. She asked him how his treatment of Allison in front of the team was helping to incorporate Allison into the team, build her confidence, and expand her knowledge. Was his approach in alignment with their commitment to respectful professional behavior? After some discussion, Charles agreed that he had fallen back into the pattern by which he had been taught rather than the new model they had agreed to use. He committed to apologize to Allison and to take a different approach at the next handoff.

Another important component of behavioral expectations is respect for patients and family members. The executive nurse leader needs to assure staff that there is a clear boundary of zero tolerance for violence against staff, while also providing training for staff on how to respond to and deescalate situations in which patients and family members are frustrated and angry.

Patients and family members often come into care settings when they are sick, tired, frustrated, and afraid. As such, they can be short-tempered and even rude. The executive nurse leader can set the expectation that staff, as caregivers, maintain an attitude of respect for what patients and family members are enduring and remember to act as a guide and mentor for their journey through this chapter in life. It is reasonable to expect staff to listen respectfully to the patient's frustrations and to take action to resolve issues or escalate the concerns to someone who can.

Reward and recognition programs are formal mechanisms for defining and communicating behavioral expectations. The executive nurse leader can reinforce desired behaviors and demonstrate the achievability of those behaviors through regular public recognition of individuals who meet or exceed behavioral expectations (Kubus, 2010).

Competencies for the Executive Nurse Leader

Nurses at all levels need leadership skills to influence the quality and safety of patient care (Institute of Medicine, 2011). But, like any other specialty, the executive nurse leader requires proficiency and competency in practices specific to the role (American Organization of Nurse Executives [AONE], 2015).

In *The Future of Nursing: Leading Change, Advancing Health*, the Institute of Medicine (2011) described two critical sets of competencies for nurse leaders. The first set are those competencies that are foundational for any leadership opportunity: knowledge of care delivery, working in teams, collaboration within and across disciplines, patient advocacy, ethical care, and foundations for quality and safety. The second is more tailored to a specific context and encompasses being a full partner in areas such as economics, regulatory frameworks, and financial policy.

AONE outlined five domains for nurse leader competencies: communication and relationship building, knowledge of the healthcare environment, leadership, professionalism, and business skills. Multiple competencies exist under each domain, and AONE (n.d.) has provided a self-assessment that can be used for identifying personal areas for growth, developing curriculum, or guiding the development of nurse leaders within an organization. The Oncology Nursing Society (2012) has also identified leadership competencies. Some specific applications of these competencies for the executive nurse leader include the following:

- Communication within the executive team, including learning to understand reports from other members of the team and participate in debate and dialogue, and learning to present nursing input in ways that are understandable to other members of the executive team
- Building a leadership team that shares a common vision but is diverse in skills and talents to execute and drive strategies and change initiatives
- Portfolio management, specifically prioritizing, sequencing, and managing competing agendas
- Development of nursing informatics competencies related to clinical systems use in patient care, system implementation, and optimal use of IT in the care environment
- Consistent application of respect for people in all relationships within the complex healthcare environment
- Mentorship of other nurse leaders and succession planning (see Chapters 3 and 22)

Summary

As healthcare organizations are undergoing significant change in the move to value-driven health care, nurse executive roles have become increasingly prominent in both traditional and novel healthcare organizations because of the significant role that nurses play in patient care. The executive nurse leader is particularly valuable in this transition because of the duality of this role as both an executive team member and chief nurse. As an executive team member, the executive nurse leader must be able to build and manage the relationships necessary to ensure that the nursing perspective is heard in executive decisions. As chief nurse, the executive nurse leader creates the team, environment, and motivation necessary to enact change in pursuit of the organizational mission. By existing at the intersection of these two areas, the nurse executive role demands a specific set of competencies but allows for the exploration of a wide range of activities that have the potential to effect tangible changes for nursing practice and patient care.

References

American Association of Critical-Care Nurses. (2016). *AACN standards for establishing and sustaining healthy work environments: A journey to excellence* (2nd ed.). Retrieved from http://www.aacn.org/wd/hwe/docs/hwestandards.pdf

American Nurses Association. (2015). *Code of ethics for nurses with interpretive statements.* Retrieved from http://www.nursingworld.org/codeofethics

American Nurses Association. (2016). *Nursing administration: Scope and standards of practice* (2nd ed.). Silver Spring, MD: Author.

American Organization of Nurse Executives. (n.d.). *AONE nurse executive competencies assessment.* Retrieved from http://www.aone.org/resources/executive-assessment.shtml

American Organization of Nurse Executives. (2015). *AONE nurse executive competencies.* Retrieved from http://www.aone.org/resources/nec.pdf

Clipper, B. (2012). *The nurse manager's guide to an intergenerational workforce.* Indianapolis, IN: Sigma Theta Tau International.

Condition of participation: Nursing services. 42 CFR § 482.23 (2011). Retrieved from https://www.gpo.gov/fdsys/granule/CFR-2011-title42-vol5/CFR-2011-title42-vol5-sec482-23

Englebright, J., & Perlin, J. (2008). The chief nurse executive role in large healthcare systems. *Nursing Administration Quarterly, 32,* 188–194. doi:10.1097/01.NAQ.0000325175.30923.ff

Greiner, A.C., & Knebel, E. (Eds.). (2003). *Health professions education: A bridge to quality.* Washington, DC: National Academies Press.

Institute of Medicine. (2011). *The future of nursing: Leading change, advancing health.* Washington, DC: National Academies Press.

Kouzes, J., & Posner, B. (2012). *The leadership challenge: How to make extraordinary things happen in organizations* (5th ed.). San Francisco, CA: Jossey-Bass.

Kubus, P. (2010). *Lead! Becoming an effective coach and mentor to your nursing staff.* Danvers, MA: HCPro.

Loop, F.D. (2009). *Leadership and medicine.* Gulf Breeze, FL: Fire Starter Publishing.

MacPhee, M., Skelton-Green, J., Bouthillette, F., & Suryaprakash, N. (2012). An empowerment framework for nursing leadership development: Supporting evidence. *Journal of Advanced Nursing, 68,* 159–169. doi:10.1111/j.1365-2648.2011.05746.x

Oncology Nursing Society. (2012). *Oncology Nursing Society leadership competencies.* Retrieved from https://www.ons.org/sites/default/files/leadershipcomps.pdf

Porter-O'Grady, T., & Malloch, K. (2016). *Leadership in nursing practice* (2nd ed.). Burlington, MA: Jones & Bartlett Learning.

Schyve, P.M. (2009). *Leadership in healthcare organizations: A guide to Joint Commission leadership standards.* Retrieved from http://www.jointcommission.org/assets/1/18/wp_leadership_standards.pdf

Simpson, R.L. (2013). Chief nurse executives need contemporary informatics competencies. *Nursing Economics, 31,* 277–287. https://www.nursingeconomics.net/ce/2015/article3106277287.pdf

Trepanier, S., & Crenshaw, J.T. (2013). Succession planning: A call to action for nurse executives. *Journal of Nursing Management, 21,* 980–985. doi:10.1111/jonm.12177

CHAPTER 14

Executive Competencies for a Disruptive Healthcare Future

Les Wallace, PhD

Introduction

While all centuries are different, the 21st century is proving itself quite turbulent across all business domains, particularly in health care. This environment demands greater environmental sensing, strategic thinking, transformation, innovation, partnering, and learning. If we think health care is special, we miss the core lesson of executive leadership: leadership is portable, and lessons from diverse domains can instruct leadership in health care. One healthcare pundit recently observed that movement of the healthcare industry toward value-based care has initiated a need for new competencies (Wagner, 2014).

Strategist, innovator, partner—meet the new executive nurse. The velocity of change is at an all-time high and shows no signs of slowing. A tumultuous environment increases organizational angst, and the complexity raises the currency value of transparent and voluminous communication. The nurse executive either can hold on to old-school leadership principles and competencies or step out onto the balcony (Heifetz & Laurie, 2001) with an enhanced, focused portfolio of capabilities necessary in a world of "volatility, uncertainty, complexity and ambiguity (VUCA)" (Bennett & Lemoine, 2014, p. 1). Donald Sull (2009) of the London Business School has written on the pressure and opportunity that uncertain markets bring to business and industry. Within this unrelenting and chaotic landscape, noted futurist Bob Johansen (2012) advised leaders to adopt their own VUCA skills around vision, understanding, clarity, and agility.

Executive Competencies

As centuries put new fingerprints on the leadership competencies for our enterprises, some basics still remain. A leader will struggle with success without interpersonal competencies and an ability to discern and focus on the vital few. Today's hectic environment puts a premium on both capabilities. Leaders will always be held to a higher standard of integrity, and the contemporary demands for transparency put an exclamation point on ethical behavior. Dealing with change has been a leadership challenge for the past two decades, but dealing with transformation and disruption raises the stakes on what being innovative and agile means today. Leading change is one thing; leading transformation is on a different scale. Leading disruption takes additional courage and the ability to assess risk yet not avoid it. Additionally, being able to change yourself—fast adaptive learning—is now considered crucial to leadership success. It is with these competencies as a backdrop that we look at leadership for executive nurses in a disruptive environment. (For a thorough treatment of contemporary "leadership competencies," see Dye & Garman, 2015; Zenger & Folkman, 2002.)

Googling "healthcare leadership competencies" uncovers more than one million citations. This is a popular topic with a wide variety of perspectives on what the healthcare field needs. It is a challenge to sort through one million sources to find the recognized core competencies that every nurse executive needs to assess, improve, and nurture. Surprisingly, the core competencies are common across most of the healthcare leadership literature, from nurses to physicians to healthcare executives.

Most of the healthcare leadership competency models try to apply broadly to the entire career of a nurse leader and cite personal characteristics that executive nurse leaders will have put in their toolbox years ago. Achievement orientation, initiative, accountability, team leadership, and negotiation have already been sorted out by the time one hits the executive suite. Project management, information technology, and human resource management are considered by most as mid-career competencies that are important but not central to executive suite success. What this means is that the nurse executive is expected to be an orchestrator of specialized organizational resources (human resources, lean process, information technology), not the expert. Think of this in another way: the nurse executive is not expected to be an "arborist" (a tree expert) but instead a "forest manager" overseeing all the components that make up a healthy forest. The nurse likely to be most successful in this volatile environment will have well-developed competency in these areas: learning, foresight, innovation, transformation, and partnering.

Leader as Learner

Leadership may be less about knowing and more about learning. Leaders are insatiable learners, and fast ones at that. They ask more questions, know what they don't know, and encourage experimentation. Globally recognized executive coach Marshall Goldsmith reminded those of us in leadership that "what got you here won't get you there" (Goldsmith, 2007, p. 10). In *The Truth About Leadership*, the authors make a cogent case that "the best leaders are the best learners" (Kouzes & Posner, 2010, p. xxiv). This widely accepted conclusion from the early 21st-century literature on leadership is the supporting competency for all the others. Authentic leaders can put ego and loss aside and garner lessons whether they are dealing with people, organizational systems, or the marketplace. The early work on "emotional intelligence" (Goleman, 2005) helped drive the learning commitment that leaders must make to be more authentic and aware, yet empathetic as a servant leader. More recently, Bill George, Peter Sims, and David Gergen framed the leader's need for authentic leadership as learning to move from "I" to "we" (George, 2007).

Today's leaders not only self-reflect on lessons learned, but also sponsor numerous after-action reviews of decisions and business moves they and others have made within the organization and the marketplace. As early as 2006, Senge's "learning organization" paradigm articulated the important role that leaders as learners play in helping organizations gain a competitive advantage by fast, constant learning (Senge, 2006). Read more in Chapter 2.

While leaders are learning, they are also ensuring that plenty of developmental learning exists throughout the organization. Put simply: executive leaders do not create followers; they create other leaders. Beyond mentoring, most executives also ensure a culture where leadership is well defined, encouraged, developed, and rewarded. The executive does not have to be the "technical expert" in creating a climate of leadership and leadership development, but they do have to be the voice and sponsor of the value proposition around a culture of leadership. This is where insistence on succession development, management and leadership learning investments, and career support is crucial to a learning environment. Leadership is learned, and in a disruptive environment, the nurse executive increases this investment as a central strategy for developing a sustainable culture of agile strategic thinking and acting. Despite the hectic life of an executive leader, many contemporary executives also find time to teach in the leadership curriculum so that other organizational leaders hear firsthand from their experience navigating complexity, risk, and transformation.

Foresight: Sensing and Strategic Thinking

Today's nurse executives help "future proof" their organization by teaching people to "think strategically," even disruptively, by challenging life cycles of processes and models and overall assumptions about how they do business (Wallace, 2016a). The days of taking months or years to reflect on the business environment and craft strategy are gone. In its place, executives create ongoing conversations about the future and a sense of urgency about strategic thinking and acting. Tracking progress and overseeing projects is tactical. Sensing early signals in the business environment, what James called "thinking in the future tense" (James, 1996), and deciding where and how to move is strategic. Frequent recalibrations and course corrections are now the leadership norm. Margaret Wheatley (2006), physicist turned leadership author, describes today's leadership dialogue as needing to speak more in terms of probabilities rather than predictions, and this impacts alert and lively execution because we are continually scanning developing scenarios. Scanning a compendium of recent articles on health care reveals themes such as how the end of reimbursement changes strategy and how strategy must be now based on value-based competition (Society for Healthcare Strategy and Market Development, 2015). This language, perspective, and advice of thought leadership in the field simply points to the types of strategic thinking conversations the nurse executive should be having.

Executives ensure that strategy conversations are no longer a once-a-year "retreat" of the board and executive team. The nurse executive spends time on the balcony scanning the business environment, looking for new signals, and is curious about disruptive moves rather than aghast or judgmental. Today's executives no longer "give vision"; rather, they create a constant rhythm of strategic discussions across the organization, helping people think in the future tense by applying foresight tools and creating dialogues contemplating possible scenarios (World Future Society, 2004). These conversations lead to a common energizing vision of the enterprise or initiative at hand.

Innovating, Inventing, and Entrepreneurship

Today's successful healthcare organizations realize that to thrive, they need to invest in innovation (Deloitte Center for Health Solutions, 2016). A culture of innovation begins with permission: permission for every employee to challenge processes and services, redefine market space, identify new partnerships, and offer ideas and radical suggestions for change beyond incremental improvements. Innovative organizations are regularly incubating and testing potential breakthroughs and ensuring there is a budget for these efforts. Executive leaders understand that not every idea will make it out of incubation and not every pilot test will succeed. However, they are astute enough to tap into the knowledge and expertise of nurse leaders at every level of the organization. As the old Texas adage goes, "You've got to drill a few dry holes to find a gusher." A tolerance for testing, failure, and a rapid learning cadence is crucial for the entire culture. "Rapid learning cycles" are core processes for research and development used by the most innovative companies worldwide and can be applied in health care as well (Radeka, 2014).

In today's healthcare environment, executives are acutely aware of the patient experience, how lean their processes must become, and that making patients and family partners drives high-quality care. Through all the strategic noise about these factors, the healthcare executive must choose when and where to disrupt and transform within the organization and the marketplace. Executives no longer manage change; they create and sponsor constant change in the way of innovative and original ideas and novel approaches to care delivery and community partnership. The nurse executive must have an intellectual curiosity that Helga Nowotny and Mitch Cohen envision as "insatiable" (Nowotny & Cohen, 2010). This reality must be lived daily in healthcare organizations as nurse executives are faced with the challenge of balancing quality and cost in providing care for patients.

Nurse executives realize that their leadership begins before anyone ever approaches a healthcare provider and continues long after a clinical engagement. Healthcare executives see their domain as a connected value chain that begins with helping people choose healthy living, deal with chronic conditions, and ultimately find compassionate end-of-life options. Each "healthcare touch" along the human life cycle—or the population life cycle—is an opportunity to create value consistent with the Triple Aim. Dust off the old "process diagram" used to assess discrete internal processes and apply it to the high-impact human touches within the healthcare system and discover obvious opportunities to positively disrupt the status quo and transform the wellness value chain.

As technology integrates into every part of contemporary life from banking to telehealth, "disruption" has become a commonplace expectation for advances in society and particularly in health care. Yet, disruption is taking place at the macro level with new partnerships, approaches to population health, outcome-based reimbursement, and report card transparency, and at the micro level with electronic records, app-driven care, telemedicine, home health, scrum teams, and new perspectives on both employee and patient engagement. The accelerating convergence of technology and biology portends major breakthroughs in diagnosis, treatment, and cures that will rock every healthcare entity. To be truly innovative and disruptive, entrepreneurial breakthrough thinking must be embedded in the organizational culture. Numerous huddles, tiger teams, and agile process teams must be expected to churn new ideas every day. Frequently, this requires the nurse to approach challenges and opportunities through nontraditional methods. Within this sea of white water, the executive must have both a bias for originality as well as a bias for action (Grant, 2016). Yesterday's committee is today's scrum team. Yesterday's incremental improvement must become today's 20% or more innovative breakthrough improvement (Wallace, 2016b).

Leading Transformation

"The status quo is slow death and transformational leaders help people let go of old models that worked in the past for new models that better fit the developing environment" (Wallace &

Trinka, 2007, p. 2). Today's executive nurse is driven to a higher investment in both sensing the changing business environment and finding positive ways to disrupt that environment. These investments, however, must be converted into transformational action. The nurse executive who has given the organization permission to challenge assumptions and processes must also make transformation a high-energy endeavor.

Transformation is a more challenging endeavor than simply managing change. Transformation calls on the enterprise to invest in significant refresh, redefinition, and redirection in the ways it has traditionally done everything, from patient intake to community partnering. While creating a culture of originality and innovation may be fun, and even easy at times, converting that into massive shifts in thinking about health care is a deep executive investment requiring motivation, coalition building, and constant influential communication about the rationale and the intended outcomes. This is where executives draw on their competencies in influencing, storytelling, dialogue, coalition building, political savvy, negotiation, and partnering. Creating this dynamic energy around "where we can go" rather than "where we are" is not done by broadcast communication but through dialogue (Ancona, Malone, Orlikowski, & Senge, 2007; Groysberg & Slind, 2012).

A single person cannot transform a complex organization. However, an energized and engaged organization empowered by involvement in the dialogue about the future and supported by executive leadership can accelerate radical transformation. Implementing shared decision making, forging collaborative partnerships, and engaging multiple and diverse stakeholders are key corporate strategies to accomplish goals. It takes a team!

Transformational leaders find strength in the facilitation of a common, energizing, long-term vision owned by architects organizationwide. High-impact transformational leadership is able to draw on the triple axes of top-down direction setting, bottom-up performance improvement, and core process redesign across the organization: "real transformations in performance come only when efforts along all three axes are coordinated and engaged" (Dichter, Gagnon, & Alexander, 1993, p. 4). It takes viewing leadership from a new lens and not one steeped in the traditional models of management and leadership. The future will require leader skills and competencies that are addressed throughout this book.

Partnering and Collaborating

The 20th century taught us that collaboration, alliances, and partnering among previously competitive elements is now the norm. Healthcare executives looking across the changing reform landscape must go beyond partnering with providers and also look to other healthcare systems, vendors, community organizations, and government agencies. Population health, for example, is not positively affected by a single organization's effort—it takes the coalescence and integration of numerous facilitated coalitions. In *The Innovator's Prescription: A Disruptive Solution for Health Care*, Christensen, Grossman, and Hwang (2009) stated: "Most disruptions have three enablers: a simplifying technology, a business model innovation, and a disruptive value network" (p. xlv). Nurse executives are finding that discerning and building those value networks has become a major portion of their leadership contribution (Christensen et al., 2009).

Partners must see common benefit and be willing to exchange intellectual and real capital in new relationships to succeed beyond their individual effort. This may be as simple as consolidating smaller players into larger systems or as complex as accountable care organizations sharing risk and responsibility to deliver the health impacts needed for today's population and reimbursement challenges. Partnering when you are down on your luck is a no-brainer. Partnering before urgency hits your enterprise is where the nurse executive creates new, flexible, higher-impact entities. Servant leaders look for this "common" interest across vast numbers of individuals and organizations and have the authentic interest and negotiating savvy to make partnerships work.

Summary

Not everyone will become chief nursing officer or chief executive officer. Yet, all nurses can lead from where they are. Leadership is scalable from the frontline supervisor to the C-suite executive. Competencies scale from micro to macro and from tactical to strategic as leaders move through the leadership hierarchy. If you are an aspiring nurse executive, you might get grounded by reflecting on the question, why should anyone be led by you? (Goffee & Jones, 2015, p. xi). If you haven't recently completed a comprehensive leadership self-assessment, you might benefit from one specifically designed for healthcare executives, such as the American College of Healthcare Executives' (2016) Healthcare Executives Competencies Assessment Tool. If you are currently a nurse executive, are you making time for regular leadership checkups and feedback? You might wish to reflect on "what to ask the person in the mirror" (Kaplan, 2011).

Understand that the processes of "disruption" are portable across business domains. If you want to disrupt your own thinking about leading in a VUCA environment, you'll go where the big thinking on innovation and disruption is happening, such as Fast Company Innovation Festivals, TED conferences, American Hospital Association leadership summits, or one of the many innovation programs delivered by some of the most prestigious graduate schools in the world.

References

American College of Healthcare Executives. (2016). *ACHE healthcare executive 2017 competencies assessment tool.* Retrieved from https://www.ache.org/pdf/nonsecure/careers/competencies_booklet.pdf

Ancona, D., Malone, T.W., Orlikowski, W.J., & Senge, P.M. (2007, February). In praise of the incomplete leader. *Harvard Business Review.* Retrieved from https://hbr.org/2007/02/in-praise-of-the-incomplete-leader

Bennett, N., & Lemoine, G.J. (2014, January). What VUCA really means for you. *Harvard Business Review.* Retrieved from https://hbr.org/2014/01/what-vuca-really-means-for-you

Christensen, C.M., Grossman, J.H., & Hwang, J. (2009). *The innovator's prescription: A disruptive solution for health care.* New York, NY: McGraw-Hill.

Deloitte Center for Health Solutions. (2016). *In pursuit of innovation: A CEO checklist.* Washington, DC: Author.

Dichter, S.F., Gagnon, C., & Alexander, A. (1993, February). Leading organizational transformations. *McKinsey Quarterly.* Retrieved from http://www.mckinsey.com/business-functions/organization/our-insights/leading-organizational-transformations

Dye, C.F., & Garman, A.N. (2015). *Exceptional leadership: 16 critical competencies for healthcare executives* (2nd ed.). Chicago, IL: Health Administration Press.

George, B. (with Sims, P., & Gergen, D.). (2007). *True north: Discover your authentic leadership.* San Francisco, CA: Jossey-Bass.

Goffee, R., & Jones, G. (2015). *Why should anyone be led by you? What it takes to be an authentic leader.* Boston, MA: Harvard Business Review Press.

Goldsmith, M. (2007). *What got you here won't get your there.* New York, NY: Hyperion.

Goleman, D. (2005). *Emotional intelligence: Why it can matter more than IQ* (10th anniversary ed.). New York, NY: Bantam Dell.

Grant, A.M. (2016, March). How to build a culture of originality. *Harvard Business Review.* Retrieved from https://hbr.org/2016/03/how-to-build-a-culture-of-originality

Groysberg, B., & Slind, M. (2012, June). Leadership is a conversation. *Harvard Business Review.* Retrieved from https://hbr.org/2012/06/leadership-is-a-conversation

Heifetz, R., & Laurie, D.L. (2001, December). The work of leadership. *Harvard Business Review*. Retrieved from https://hbr.org/2001/12/the-work-of-leadership

James, J. (1996). Thinking in the future tense: A workout for the mind. *Industrial and Commercial Training, 28*(7), 28–32. doi:10.1108/00197859610791584

Johansen, B. (2012). *Leaders make the future: Ten new leadership skills for an uncertain world* (2nd ed.). San Francisco, CA: Berrett-Koehler.

Kaplan, R.S. (2011). *What to ask the person in the mirror: Critical questions for becoming a more effective leader and reaching your potential.* Boston, MA: Harvard Business Review Press.

Kouzes, J.M., & Posner, B.Z. (2010). *The truth about leadership: The no-fads, heart-of-the-matter facts you need to know.* San Francisco, CA: Jossey-Bass.

Nowotny, H., & Cohen, M. (2010). *Insatiable curiosity: Innovation in a fragile future.* Cambridge, MA: Massachusetts Institute of Technology.

Radeka, K. (2014, September 16). *Why rapid learning cycles are the engine of innovation.* Retrieved from https://www.linkedin.com/pulse/20140916182925-5047395-why-rapid-learning-cycles-are-the-engine-of-innovation

Senge, P.M. (2006). *The fifth discipline: The art and practice of the learning organization* (Rev. ed.). New York, NY: Doubleday.

Society for Healthcare Strategy and Market Development. (2015). *Futurescan 2015: Healthcare trends and implications 2015–2020.* Chicago, IL: Health Administration Press.

Sull, D. (2009). *The upside of turbulence: Seizing opportunity in an uncertain world.* New York, NY: Harper Business.

Wagner, K. (2014). Core competencies for a changing healthcare environment. *Healthcare Financial Management.* Retrieved from http://www.hfma.org/corecompetencies

Wallace, L. (2016a). Future proof your board of directors. Retrieved from http://www.signatureresources.com/our-capabilities/future-proof-your-board-directors

Wallace, L. (2016b). Reclaiming creativity to achieve innovation. Retrieved from http://www.signatureresources.com/about-us/reclaiming-creativity-achieve-innovation

Wallace, L., & Trinka, J. (2007). *A legacy of 21st century leadership.* Lincoln, NE: iUniverse.

Wheatley, M.J. (2006). *Leadership and the new science: Discovering order in a chaotic world.* San Francisco, CA: Berrett-Koehler.

World Future Society. (2004). *The art of foresight: Preparing for a changing world.* Retrieved from https://www.aacc.edu/future/file/Art%20of%20Foresight.pdf

Zenger, J.H., & Folkman, J. (2002). *The extraordinary leader: Turning good managers into great leaders.* New York, NY: McGraw-Hill.

CHAPTER 15

Ethics and Nursing Leadership

Laurie Badzek, LLM, JD, MS, RN, FAAN, Lisa Hardman, DNP, RN, CDE, VHA-CM, and Patricia J. Maramba, DNP, RN

> *Nurses are leaders who actively participate in assuring the responsible and appropriate use of interventions in order to optimize the health and well-being of those in their care.*
>
> —American Nurses Association (2015, p. 2)

Introduction

One hallmark of a profession is having a code of ethics that espouses the core values of the group. Modern nursing in the United States did not have a formal code of ethics until 1950; however, the understanding that the profession of nursing is guided by moral values can be traced to the first meeting of a group of nurses in New York City in 1896 that would eventually become the American Nurses Association (ANA). In the past, many nurses believed erroneously that ANA's *Code of Ethics for Nurses* (2015) was a guide only for staff nurses at the bedside. The 2015 *Code of Ethics for Nurses* (also referred to as the Code) states in the preface that nursing practice encompasses all roles and all settings. Nurses, including managers, supervisors, administrators, and executives and other leaders, are held to the values and obligations within the Code.

ANA has taken responsibility for reviewing and updating the *Code of Ethics for Nurses* but has encouraged all nurses to participate in the evaluation and updating of the Code. ANA acknowledges that the Code is for all nurses, not just members of ANA. The current version of the code, which was published in 2015, is the most recent expression of values, duties, and commitments that nurses and nursing make to our society. More than 3,700 responses from individuals and groups, totaling over 9,000 comments, directed the work of two committees in the revisions of the current Code. This is the nonnegotiable standard for the profession and a succinct statement of obligations that every nurse is expected to uphold (ANA, 2015).

As part of the revision process for the *Code of Ethics for Nurses*, the number of references to managers, supervisors, administrators, and executive responsibilities has increased dramatically. More than two dozen specific references to nurse administrators, managers, supervisors, executives, and leaders appear in the text of the document. The responsibility of all nurses to be leaders, as well as the need for support, resources, and assurances from those with authority in higher-level nursing roles, is evident.

Ethical Principles

Numerous approaches exist for addressing ethical dilemmas that may arise in situations or practice. Ethical theories such as feminism, social ethics, ethical principles, or virtue-based ethics may all be helpful when the nurse is faced with an ethical dilemma. Key ethical principles include nonmaleficence; beneficence; respect for persons, including respect for autonomy; justice; and privacy/confidentiality. Nurses are required to exercise moral accountability, which means the nurse will make reasoned judgments about what is right and then act accordingly. Leaders have a special responsibility to collaborate with others to foster outcomes that support ethical and safe practice environments that promote evidence-informed nursing care and ensure that nursing's primary commitment to the patients is maintained.

ANA's (2016) *Nursing Administration: Scope and Standards of Practice* identifies a specific standard of professional performance in ethics: "The nurse administrator practices ethically" (p. 45). Key among the 18 competencies listed is the statement that the nurse leader "promotes systems to address and resolve ethical issues" (p. 46). The scope and standards also define that nurse leaders communicate authentically to address ethical issues in health care. The American Organization of Nurse Executives (AONE, 2015) identifies that nurse leaders, without regard to their level of leadership, title, or setting, be competent in (a) communication and relationship building, (b) knowledge of the healthcare environment, (c) leadership, (d) professionalism, and (e) business skills. According to AONE (2015), leaders' responsibilities for ethics fall under the professionalism competencies and include the ability to (a) convey ethical principles in day-to-day operations and standards, (b) integrate ethical standards and accountability into day-to-day practice and operations, and (c) create a culture where open discussion, resolution, and learning comes from ethical dilemmas. Although these key principles sound straightforward and easy to accomplish, they are oftentimes challenging for even the most experienced leaders. The complexity of healthcare systems, the diversity of settings in which nurses practice, and the evolving world of technology that leads us to face uncharted ethical issues are just a few factors that make ethical decision making difficult. One role of key leadership is to ensure that all levels of employees have a strong understanding of ethical standards, are provided with a framework to apply these standards to situations, and have organizational support enabling them to apply these principles.

Creating an Ethically Centered Organization

Strong ethical foundations in healthcare organizations have been shown to have a positive ripple effect leading to increased patient satisfaction (Bottrell, 2013) and less employee turnover (Bottrell, 2013; Simha & Cullen, 2012). Leaders are responsible for inclusion and reflection of ethical beliefs in the mission, vision, and values of the organization. These values should not only be evident in written form but displayed in the day-to-day functions of the organization. Policies, practices, and decisions should reflect ethical values and filter through employees of the organization, extending to vendors and external partners. Ethical organizations start with ethical leadership. Employees pay close attention to the actions of leaders and are conscious to what the organization rewards and what is not tolerated. In making ethical decisions, employees will look to leadership to identify what is right and how the right thing may be achieved. Organization leaders, in conjunction with employees, should frequently evaluate policies and practices to ensure they are meeting the changing needs of the organization and to incorporate practices of preventive ethics.

The introduction of ethics in the organization should begin early in the hiring process, be included in orientation, and be an integral part of employee education and competency assessment. Employers can be empowered to promote an ethical environment by providing education, developing trusting relationships, providing open forms of communication, removing barriers, and promoting autonomy. All nurses, whether employers or employees, must have sufficient knowledge to be ethically competent, which enables them the freedom to discuss ethical concerns and think critically through ethical situations. Providing information on ethical decision-making frameworks and processes, including case study and simulation activities, will provide employees with critical thinking and experience that will aid in effective action and potential resolution when ethical dilemmas are encountered. Ethical leaders are responsible for providing an organizational climate that encourages questions and the expression of concerns. Still further, ethical leaders should help employees to understand the role of the organizational leaders when a problem has grown to a level where additional assistance or an appropriate higher authority should be engaged in the process. Providing education regarding ethics alone may not fully empower employees; however, it should develop an awareness of ethical issues, provide the foundation needed to make informed decisions, describe the organization's ethical process, and identify the procedure for obtaining additional help if needed. Leaders should be cognizant that their actions, or lack of action, may have an impact on organization climate. Employees are more likely to displace ethical behavior when they observe leaders using values to make decisions and ensuring that organizational practices are in line with these values.

Ethical Challenges in an Era of Next-Generation Science, Technology, and Social Change

Ethical dilemmas can occur in any healthcare setting. An ethical dilemma exists when two or more values conflict and the appropriate or right choice is not clear. Advancements in evidence-based practice, easy access to personal health information, and the ever-evolving social and technologic advancements challenge healthcare organizations to face new, uncharted dilemmas.

The media are replete with stories of ethical dilemmas in health care. Healthcare providers at all levels of the organization struggle to determine what is right and just. In addition to more common ethical concerns faced by organizations, new challenges with healthcare technology, genomic testing, and nontraditional threats to privacy are becoming more common occurrences. The field of genomics includes opportunities to identify disease states early. This can allow individuals to take specific measures to prepare for the future. Each day, translation of genomic science to the bedside grows larger, often with dramatic health results. However, many areas of genomics pose ethical dilemmas. Ethical concerns have been raised about the utility of genetic testing, including the ethics of ordering tests that provide little or no probability of improved outcomes; lack of understanding of the impact of the information to the patient and extended family; the validity of testing; and the potential for increasing healthcare costs that may exhaust healthcare resources.

Nurses at all levels and practice settings should be prepared to address controversial issues and work through ethical dilemmas. In addition to contributing clinical knowledge, nurse leaders must be adept in articulating the key ethical question and the conflicts of values that are present. As health care continues to surge forward with technologic advancements through the delivery of telehealth, use of social media, access to large data sets, and connectivity of medical data with a variety of parties, including the patient, so do the risks of breaches in patient privacy and confidentiality. Nurse leaders must remain committed to ensure that nurses and patients are informed about, and understand, the Health Insurance Portability and Accountability Act and other legislation and policies that protect health information. Organizations are responsible to have established precautions in place to protect patient privacy and confidentiality without impeding the functioning of the organization.

Nurses in all roles and settings should be aware of organizational policies, have a strong understanding of organizational expectations for their behavior, identify how to report violations, and understand ramifications for violations (ANA, 2015). Nurses at every level must be knowledgeable of what encompasses ethical misconduct and uphold high ethical standards in all aspects of nursing practice. Unfortunately, ethical misconduct may still occur. Nurse leaders must be prepared to rapidly address issues of ethical misconduct. Employees should be encouraged to report unethical conduct without fear of retaliation.

Multiple companies now offer direct-to-consumer genetic testing, leaving the burden on the healthcare provider to explain the results and develop a plan of care, usually with limited empirical evidence to guide the process. The healthcare provider may face an ethical dilemma of either attempting to satisfy the requests of the patient or withholding testing that does not lead to improved health outcomes. Nurse leaders should provide guidance to providers about the importance of discussing the use of genetic testing in practice. Providers should openly discuss the probability of the genetic testing improving outcomes, the efficacy of the test, and what steps could be taken to improve the outcome if there is a genetic link and what the patient may be willing to undergo. Providers also need to offer resources about the potential cost of testing and attempts to prevent or delay the onset of the disease.

Additionally, results from genetic testing may indicate that an individual is at low risk for a certain condition, not clarifying that other factors, such as lifestyle, may increase a person's risk. This provides a false sense of security and could interfere with the patient's adoption of important health behaviors, potentially leading to harm for the individual. For example, patients with a low genetic risk for diabetes mellitus may have a false security that they will not get the disease and may decide against reducing modifiable risk factors. Other concerns to healthcare providers include the use of large data sets, often called big data. *Big data* refers to large collections of unrelated data that when analyzed may identify trends and relationships that could lead to benefits to organizations. Data used in this analysis may include personal health information without the knowledge and consent of the individual. In some cases, individuals may be informed that their data are going to be used, but if they do not agree, they will not be able to use the service. This puts individuals in a predicament to either share information against their will or to not benefit from use of the service. Data may be collected from sources such as telephone applications, health devices, and social media. Leadership should evaluate privacy policies and license agreements and thoroughly understand the risks to patients and the organization. Policies should include transparency for patients about how their data will be used and allow them to opt out of participating.

In response to the ever-growing use of social media, many organizations have policies regulating the use of social media platforms to protect the rights of patients and to protect employees and the organization. Special attention should be taken to adhere to National Labor Relations Board and other regulatory guidelines in the development of these policies. Prohibiting the use of taking photos with private smartphones and without appropriate consent, disclosure of private information on social media, and use of devices during work time have become topics of discussion. Telehealth similarly has increased access to remote patients, as well as allowing close management of certain disease states and even access to emergency services. In light of these technologic advances, some ethical concerns have been noted regarding the transmission of personal health information that may be prone to hackers, exposing the patient. Distrust and fear of breaches may prevent patients and healthcare providers from considering the use of telehealth. Organizations should use a code of conduct to clearly inform employees of expectations, reporting requirements, and consequences of violations. The code of conduct should identify that the safeguards are established to protect patients, employees, coworkers, and the organization.

Ethics and the Law

All that is legal is not necessarily ethical, and vice versa. Generally, the law follows the ethical thinking of the majority; however, reliance on the majority can lead to unethical behavior. Consider slavery, segregation, and discrimination. At one time or another, all these actions were legal, but they were never ethical. The law speaks to what we must do. Failure to act in a legal manner can lead to consequences such as fines or imprisonment. Ethics is about what we should or ought to do. Ethics is about good or right action and behavior. The individual nurse leader or manager is expected to be responsible and accountable for making "right" decisions. Moral accountability does not mean agreement with others but rather making determinations that are defensible and justifiable on moral grounds.

Ethical determinations are made using a model or framework of ethical decision making that reflects on the ethical question, considers all the parties involved, defines the conflicts and potential responses, and ultimately selects the solution to the dilemma that least infringes on the values of the people involved in the conflict. Laws generally are defined by the constitution, legislation, or judicial decisions.

Some ethical conflicts are not able to be resolved by individuals and healthcare organizations. These unresolved dilemmas have often resulted in legal case decisions or laws that mandate specific behavior in healthcare issues. For example, unresolved ethical dilemmas regarding continuing care when quality of life seemed unclear have directly resulted in laws that address patient autonomy and the validity of advance directives. Other areas that present ethical challenges in health care include the care of minors; treatment decisions, including informed consent and patient decision-making capacity; and patient privacy. Effective nurse leaders and managers continually scrutinize the facility and environment, as well as the literature, for ethical issues and legal decisions that may affect the organization. The accountability and responsibility of the nurse are both individual and role dependent. Obligations increase as the nurse becomes more experienced. Nurse leaders and managers are expected to be able to assist others whom they direct or for whom they are responsible. The *Code of Ethics for Nurses* (ANA, 2015) and *Guide to the Code of Ethics for Nurses With Interpretive Statements* (Fowler, 2015) contain further discussion and clarification of accountability and responsibility.

Ethics and Quality

The ethical principles of autonomy, beneficence, and nonmaleficence are the building blocks of strong quality care. Today's healthcare leaders struggle with meeting the needs of the organization while ensuring that appropriate resources are allocated to keep the organization financially stable. In trying to achieve this balance, ethical concerns may occur. Concerns may include determining appropriate utilization of resources, ensuring equitable access, and making sound decisions that do not pose the potential to cause harm.

Programs such as pay-for-performance that hold healthcare providers responsible for poor outcomes and errors may lead to ethical dilemmas. The healthcare team may be conflicted in their roles to improve outcomes in an era of patient-centered care where patients may refuse unwanted medical treatment. In addition, nurses may be faced with providing the same or more services in an environment of resource rationing.

More than ever, healthcare organizations need to ensure that quality improvement activities are in accordance with ethical principles. Streamlined processes for nurses to report areas of ethical concerns related to quality should be implemented, and the topic should be addressed frequently. Modeling a true internal moral compass is essential; however, it is only one of the ways that nurse leaders influence organizational culture. Ethical leadership sets the tone for the followership. Day-to-day conduct is an indicator of a leader's ethical character. The actions a leader disciplines and rewards and how a leader allocates resources and reacts to events are constantly visible to followers and essentially convey the minimum expectations to which followers adhere (Fox, 2010). Therefore, the extent of an organization's ethical health can be inferred from the degree to which an ethical environment exists.

Frequently, ethics is thought of as a way of discerning right from wrong, episodic in nature, and a method to manage dilemmas in the pursuit of providing quality care. In the nearly 20 years since the release of *To Err Is Human* (Kohn, Corrigan, & Donaldson, 2000) from the Institute of Medicine (now called the Health and Medicine Division of the National Academies of Sciences, Engineering, and Medicine), quality and safety have firmly been established as fundamental principles in healthcare organizations. Quality measures abound and exist not only as an outward measurement of an organization's commitment to outcome achievement but, now, to avoid financial penalty. In an effort to increase quality, healthcare reform has tied quality metrics to reimbursement, thereby placing the fiscal viability of an organization at stake. For organizations to provide high-quality care, they must make a commitment to recognize the threats and weave this commitment throughout the organization.

Organizations continually work toward creating processes that minimize risk. While standards are set and policies are implemented, the strength of the process is inextricably linked to knowing where failures occur. The creation of a just culture is critical in identifying these shortcomings; an environment free from the fear of retribution must exist (Dauterive & Schubert, 2013). Providing an environment where blame is eschewed and fairness and openness are embraced involves striking the balance of enforcing the rules through discipline when standards are breached while still imparting the values espoused by an organization (Fox, 2010). Errors in care are never construed as "quality" and can signal a departure from ethical standards.

One key strategy nurse leaders can use to foster an environment of just culture is involvement of employees in strategic initiatives to define mission and vision models that state commitments to creation of healthy, safe, ethical work environments. Nurse leaders are instrumental in educating employees and engaging them in the process of designing the strategic initiatives and healthcare delivery model. When leaders focus on employee engagement in a culture of change rather than blame, negative outcomes are reduced or eliminated and employees are more vested and likely to report errors in an effort to influence better care (ANA, 2016).

Ethics in Research With Human Subjects

History provides a tainted record of research practices both domestically and internationally, including injustices such as medical experimentation on prisoners and soldiers. Today, federal laws and regulations provide ethical guidelines on research involving human subjects, especially with regard to informed consent. Protection of human subjects is the responsibility of all healthcare providers. Although managers may not be directly involved in research studies, they must be aware of basic human subjects research guidelines and understand their role in ensuring that the organization is meeting its ethical obligations to protect patients. In addition, staff involved in research should receive formal training and have full understanding of their ethical responsibilities. Leaders can promote the respect of research participants by ensuring that research has been evaluated by the institutional review board. Assessment of research practices to ensure safety of research participants is an ongoing process. Privacy and confidentiality should be upheld for all participants at all times during the study. Participants should be informed of the risks and benefits of the study and have the opportunity to ask questions and discontinue the study at any time. Ethical principles should guide the entire research process from selection through withdrawal or conclusion of the study.

The *Code of Ethics for Nurses* (ANA, 2015) specifically addresses the protection of research participants in the third provision. The provision puts responsibility on the nurse to ensure patient protection as well as integrity in research. Every nurse has a duty to question and, if necessary, report and refuse to participate in research that is morally objectionable. The ethical responsibility for ensuring the protection of participants in research falls to all nurses. In addition to the ethical responsibility in provision 3, nurses also are ethically responsible for advancement of the profession, including knowledge development found in provision 7. Knowledge development, dissemination, and application are responsibilities of the profession; therefore, all nurses should engage at some level in development of scholarly inquiry. "All nurses must participate in the advancement of the profession through knowledge development, evaluation, dissemination, and application [of research and scholarly inquiry] to practice" (ANA, 2015, p. 27). Ongoing scholarly inquiry including research with human subjects is necessary for the profession to fulfill its obligations to promote optimal standards of nursing education and practice that promote the health and well-being of all persons. Nurse administrators lead by example as both investigators and users of knowledge. Through education of employees and facilitation of research, leaders demonstrate the importance of nursing inquiry and scholarship to improve patient outcomes and health policy development.

Organizations where genomic research is being conducted should clearly address whether participants will receive their results; whether specimens and samples will be stored; whether results will be provided to participants' relatives; and what will occur with participants' data in the event of their death. In any research study, it is important that participants are fully aware of how their data will be used and with whom data will be shared.

Protocols should identify the risks of not providing genetic information to participants or sharing with relatives. With genomic research, some participants may not understand intricate research findings for themselves or how knowledge of the results may prevent serious harm for relatives who may share the genetic link. Information regarding the implications to the participant, and if chosen, the relatives, should be thoroughly addressed in the research protocol and clearly stated in the consent form. Healthcare providers may find themselves in ethical dilemmas when participants decide not to share findings regarding genetic links that may lead to serious health conditions for relatives. Leaders should encourage providers to discuss with patients how they plan to use the information prior to the test being conducted. In addition, patients should be assessed about their emotional readiness in the event they are informed they are at risk for a life-altering illness. Patients should be well informed about how to share results so that families will be best able to use the information. In addition, patients should be informed about the potential for harm to family members if they decide not to disclose this information. Ethics consults should be sought as needed.

Ethical concerns with Internet-based research have become an ever-growing concern. Those conducting research via the Internet may not have ethical oversight, may not need to submit their protocol to institutional review boards, and may not meet the same ethical standards involving human subjects. Difficulties verifying patient identity, obtaining informed consent, and protecting vulnerable groups can be challenging when working with Internet-based research. Organizations should include guidance in these areas. A thorough assessment of all research studies prior to adoption should ensure that Internet-based studies meet standards upholding the rights of human subjects.

Summary

Nurse leaders at every level should have a strong and clear sense of what is in the profession's ethical code, the policy statements for nursing and health care, and the laws that govern health care. The responsibility and accountability of the nurse as leader are greater today than in the past. Knowledge of key documents, as well as individual responsibility and accountability for nursing practice, will assist the nurse leader in meeting the ethical and legal obligations to provide optimal patient care.

The nurse leader can employ many strategies to create an ethical environment. Use of healthcare ethics committees and other mechanisms to empower nurses will ensure an environment that supports acknowledgment of ethical dilemmas and strategies for resolving those dilemmas. Understanding and use of an ethical model or framework will result in not only decisions that nurse leaders feel are right or good, but also in actions that can be justified.

Adapted from "Nursing Ethics" (pp. 597–606), by L. Badzek, L. Hardman, and P.J. Maramba in M.M. Gullatte (Ed.), Nursing Management: Principles and Practice *(2nd ed.), 2011, Pittsburgh, PA: Oncology Nursing Society. Copyright 2011 by Oncology Nursing Society.*

References

American Nurses Association. (2015). *Code of ethics for nurses with interpretive statements.* Silver Spring, MD: Author.

American Nurses Association. (2016). *Nursing administration: Scope and standards of practice* (2nd ed.). Silver Spring, MD: Author.

American Organization of Nurse Executives. (2015). *AONE nurse executive competencies.* Retrieved from http://www.aone.org/resources/nec.pdf

Bottrell, M.M. (2013, Summer). Ethics quality helps build healthy organizations. *VHA Organizational Health, 19,* 4–5.

Dauterive, F.R., & Schubert, A. (2013). Ethics, quality, safety, and a just culture: The link is evident. *Ochsner Journal, 13,* 293–294.

Fowler, M.D.M. (2015). *Guide to the code of ethics for nurses with interpretive statements: Development, interpretation, and application* (2nd ed.). Silver Spring, MD: American Nurses Association.

Fox, E. (with Bottrell, M.M., Berkowitz, K.A., Chanko, B.L., Foglia, M.B., & Pearlman, R.A.). (2010). Integrated Ethics: An innovative program to improve ethics quality in health care. *Innovation Journal: The Public Sector Innovation Journal, 15*(2), Article 8. Retrieved from https://www.innovation.cc/scholarly-style/fox_integrated 8ethics_8_final.pdf

Kohn, L.T., Corrigan, J.M., & Donaldson, M.S. (Eds.). (2000). *To err is human: Building a safer health system.* Washington, DC: National Academies Press.

Simha, A., & Cullen, J.B. (2012). Ethical climates and their effects on organizational outcomes: Implications from the past and prophecies for the future. *Academy of Management Perspectives, 26*(4), 20–34. doi:10.5465/amp.2011.0156

CHAPTER 16

Leading Future Innovations in Nursing Education

Nancy P. Wingo, PhD, MA, and
Deborah Kirk Walker, DNP, FNP-BC, NP-C, AOCN®, FAANP

> *So, I never lose an opportunity of urging a practical beginning,*
> *however small, for it is wonderful how often in such matters the*
> *mustard-seed geminates and roots itself.*
>
> —Florence Nightingale

Introduction

Historically, nursing educators have been challenged to look at new pedagogies for classroom and clinical learning experiences. Initially, nurses were trained in hospitals using a practical training approach. It was not until 1873, when Bellevue School of Nursing in New York adopted a Nightingale ideology, that nursing education started to change. Bellevue was the first school that promoted nursing theory and practice outside the hospital (Dock, 1901), which established the foundation for how nursing is taught today.

Nursing education continued to gain momentum throughout the 1900s with several key documents, including the Goldmark Report in 1923, which recommended minimal education standards in nursing education, and the Burgess Report in 1928, which called for major changes in the profession in regard to education (Scheckel, 2009). The National League for Nursing Education (now the National League for Nursing) also published *Standard Curriculum for Schools of Nursing* in the early to mid-1900s, encouraging early nursing education programs to extend the amount of time for didactic and clinical experiences (Scheckel, 2009). Many more influential reports throughout nursing education history have been key to establishing a variety of pedagogic practices for instruction. From the first practical and diploma programs, to associate and baccalaureate degree programs, and on to postgraduate education, many nursing pioneers have influenced nursing education programs.

Nursing education continues to evolve. Today's teaching environment challenges educators to use active learning strategies to promote critical thinking. For example, educators are encouraged to use problem-based learning, cooperative learning, and service learning as ways to promote active learning for students (Crookes, Crookes, & Walsh, 2013; Hart, 2015; Murray, 2013). Nursing education has also become extremely complex, as health care rapidly advances and students become more diverse across generations, genders, and cultures. Instructors in nursing must be nimble and innovative in educational delivery methods to meet the needs of a variety of students. Ultimately, a change from traditional methods to more innovative and interactive methods will be required to keep students engaged and inspired and to meet expectations of the learning experience.

This chapter will discuss strategies for innovative teaching, whether as simple as a classroom or course activity or as complex as course design and delivery. Selected methods should use strategies to engage instructors and students in the teaching-learning environment. The chapter provides an overview of innovative strategies for nursing education and how to engage and cultivate future nursing instructors and discusses recommendations for teaching strategies in a multigenerational classroom in terms of characteristics and learning styles. Finally, the chapter briefly discusses approaches to lifelong learning for nursing professionals.

Innovative Teaching Strategies

The role of the instructor has traditionally been that of the "sage on the stage" (King, 1993, p. 30) who conveys information to students within a limited time frame in a face-to-face setting. However, this method often does not appeal to adult learners, who are self-directed, want to understand the relevance of all they are learning, and enjoy being in charge of their own learning processes (Knowles, 1980). Furthermore, with the proliferation of distance-accessible courses, emerging technologies, and digital-native students who expect to have knowledge at their fingertips, faculty can no longer afford to adopt this teacher-centered approach. As a result, nursing faculty must remain flexible and visionary in terms of teaching methods, implementing various kinds of strategies and tools in different learning environments with a goal of promoting lifelong learning.

This section outlines some innovative teaching strategies that nursing instructors are using to engage students. Each strategy is described in practice, noting benefits and challenges of each, and suggestions are made for what types of instructors might be most comfortable implementing these strategies in various learning environments.

Active Learning

In their identification of the seven principles of good practice in undergraduate education, Chickering and Gamson (1987) claimed that "learning is not a spectator sport" (p. 4). They noted that students must actively apply their learning to make it part of themselves. Instructors who implement active learning strategies find ways to ensure that students are not just passively listening during class; instead, students participate in activities that require them to use higher-order thinking skills (i.e., analysis, synthesis) as they discuss, debate, create, master skills, or solve problems (Bonwell & Eison, 1991). Instructors may choose to intersperse short lectures or presentations with these active learning experiences. Activities can be as simple as asking students to stop, turn to the student next to them, and share the most important point they learned in a "think-pair-share" exercise. Students can also write "one-minute papers" discussing the main idea or the "muddiest point," so that instructors can better gauge learning progression. Other active learning strategies might include semistructured discussions or debates, skits, role playing, or simulations. Students may use art or music to illustrate their understanding of concepts. The number of active learning techniques is truly boundless; it is limited only by the instructor's imagination and willingness to try new strategies.

Active learning strategies are not limited to the face-to-face classroom. Instructors in distance-accessible courses with mostly online interaction can still use strategies that engage students in active, self-directed learning. Instructors can ask students to engage with others asynchronously (e.g., discussion boards, modules) or synchronously (e.g., virtual classrooms, video chat, text messaging). For these activities to be successful, instructors must be willing to embrace new technologies and have the patience to master new ways of conveying course content.

The benefits of using active learning strategies have been documented in educational research showing that actively engaging students in their learning can promote better learning outcomes, attitudes toward learning, and long-term retention (Fata-Hartley, 2011; Prince, 2004; Ruhl, Hughes, & Schloss, 1987; Wankat, 2002). Although there are few empirical studies confirming the benefits of active learning in nursing education (Waltz, Jenkins, & Han, 2014), anecdotal reports from instructors are often positive, especially when instructors work with students who are highly engaged and enthusiastic about playing an active role in class discussion and interaction. Challenges in implementing active learning include the need for the instructor to give up some control of class activities, the need for extensive class preparation time, difficulty in implementing active learning in large classes, and occasionally, student resistance to new approaches. Instructors who implement active learning strategies must have a fundamental belief in students' ability to take control of their learning. They must also be flexible, willing to fail, inventive, and organized. A sense of humor and a tolerance for "organized chaos" will also benefit instructors who use active learning exercises.

Flipping the Classroom

In 2007, Jonathan Bergman and Aaron Sams began to use video PowerPoint presentations and lectures to deliver course content to high school students who had to miss class for various reasons (Bergmann & Sams, 2012). They soon realized that students who had listened to pre-recorded material used class time to apply what they had learned, and they interacted with the instructor in ways that had not happened before. Their continued success with students using this format led them to launch the flipped class movement.

In a flipped classroom approach, the instructor requires students to engage with new content prior to class, saving the time spent in class to apply knowledge students have learned. The classroom is essentially "flipped," because instead of exposing students to new content and then sending them off to apply it on their own, the instructor spends valuable time interacting with students, modeling various ways their new knowledge can be applied, and coaching them as they attempt to integrate their learning in practice. When using this approach, the instructor must plan carefully, choosing readings, videos, podcasts, or other learning materials that introduce concepts in clear and succinct ways. Activities chosen for class (e.g., team activities, games, simulations, experiments, debates) should be directly relevant to the material introduced to students ahead of time. When chosen carefully and implemented well, these activities should promote critical thinking and encourage active learning during class time.

Many instructors choose to give a short assessment of some kind on the assigned material when students first arrive to a flipped classroom. This way, students will quickly learn that they must be prepared to participate in class. It is also important for instructors to initially clarify concepts, allow students to ask questions, highlight the most important material, and give clear instructions about learning activities—not only telling students how activities will be done but why they are doing them, explaining their relevance to the new concepts the students have learned.

Flipping the classroom can also be implemented in distance-accessible courses by using virtual classroom applications. Instructors could assign material ahead of time and either assess students when they "arrive" in a virtual classroom or use a tool to test them prior to class. Various learning activities (e.g., group discussions, debates, case studies, problem solving) can also be accomplished in virtual classrooms.

Flipping the classroom has several benefits: (a) students take direct control of their learning instead of sitting passively in class, (b) time spent in class is more productive, as instructors can coach students and model specific behaviors and skills, and (c) students often are more engaged in active learning in class. It also has challenges: (a) the instructor must carefully and thoroughly plan preclass materials, assessments, and in-class activities, and (b) students must learn that they have to prepare ahead of time for the activities to be successful. Instructors who choose to implement a flipped classroom should be organized (for planning purposes), innovative (to develop engaging activities for the classroom), and flexible (to adjust if plans go awry or technology does not cooperate).

Gamification

Gamification is "the use of game design elements in non-game contexts" (Deterding, Dixon, Khaled, & Nacke, 2011, p. 9). The rising trend of using game design elements across broad disciplines has been linked to a need to increase engagement, enhance social interaction, stimulate intrinsic motivation, and encourage innovation (Hamari, Koivisto, & Sarsa, 2014). Most millennial students grew up playing games on various kinds of devices and thus are comfortable with the idea of extending game concepts into many aspects of their lives. However, students of all ages can find gaming to be a stimulating way to learn.

Implementing gamification into nursing courses could include using one or more games at various times throughout a semester, playing one game consistently throughout a course, or gamifying an entire course (a method many instructors find daunting) so that students have complete control over how they engage with material and complete assessments. Games can be used in face-to-face or online courses in various ways. Some instructors take classic games such as Simon Says or Heads Up and adapt the instructions to allow for questions/answers and player advancement. Others use online tools such as crossword puzzle generators or flashcard makers to allow students to apply or retain knowledge. Still others develop their own new games to customize questions, game rules, and competition based on the learning objectives for their courses. Instructors could even work with computer programmers to develop online learning games specifically for healthcare professionals. Indeed, adapting games for nursing education is limited only by the creativity of the instructor.

Using games in educational settings can be quite successful for a number of reasons. First, learners may be less intimidated by content if they perceive learning as "gaming." Second, players motivated by competition may persist more in learning, as they continue to play a game in an effort to win. Also, team-based games may motivate students to persist while engaging with their peers. Finally, many learners simply appreciate using alternative and fun methods for learning. On the other hand, students could get so caught up in competition or the game itself that they lose sight of the learning that is supposed to be taking place. Mediating disputes about game rules or player mistakes could take up precious time for an instructor. If a game is too complicated, it can cause more problems than anticipated. Careful planning and pilot testing of extensive games can help an instructor avoid these pitfalls and allow for a successful educational game experience in face-to-face and online learning environments.

Learning in Teams

In 2011, the Interprofessional Education Collaborative (IPEC), representing six healthcare professions, developed a set of core competencies for interprofessional collaborative practice. While allowing for differences among professions, these competencies emphasized the goal of "deliberately working together" (IPEC, 2011, p. 3) to deliver high-quality, safe patient care. To prepare nurses for this kind of interprofessional collaboration, it is essential that students learn how to work in teams.

Designing instructional strategies for team learning can be challenging. Students often resist the idea of working in teams based on the notion that their grades could be adversely affected. They may also view team collaboration as a burden because they perceive it as "busy work," or they resent having to adjust their schedules to those of their peers. To alleviate these concerns, instructors should clearly explain to students why it is essential that they learn to work in teams and how they can build their interprofessional collaborative skills through practice. Instructors should also carefully weight grading scales so that assignments completed in teams play a significant part in the overall course grade. This way, students will not perceive these tasks as busy work, and most students will attempt to complete them diligently. At the same time, instructors should weight team versus individual grades according to the learning objectives for a course.

Peer reviews can also be particularly helpful in adjusting team scores to reflect participation and effort on the part of individual students. One useful method of peer review includes allotting each team a certain number of points, then asking each student to divide those points among team members according to their contribution. No matter the scoring model, students should be given an opportunity to reflect on their team experiences and provide feedback to the instructor on how they worked together to accomplish a goal.

The idea of learning in teams should not be confused with the term *team-based learning* (TBL), which is a specific teaching strategy originally developed by Larry Michaelsen and others in the 1980s to facilitate active learning in large classes (Michaelsen, 1992). This strategy has been developed and tested extensively since its origination and has been proved to be successful in a variety of settings. Its features include a purposeful selection of heterogeneous groups, a combination of individual and team testing, a focus on small group activities, and a sequence of activities in six steps repeated throughout a course (Michaelsen, 1992). A literature review conducted by Sisk (2011) on using TBL in nursing courses found 17 original studies published between 2003 and 2011, most of which showed that student engagement was higher and learning outcomes greater in courses using this teaching method.

Learning in teams (including TBL strategies) can be accomplished online as well as in face-to-face settings by using group settings in learning management systems to offer various tools for engaging students from a distance. Instructors who implement team learning should plan extensively, think strategically, and attempt to place students of varying abilities and interests in the same group if possible. As with other innovative strategies, instructors who are organized, yet flexible, are more likely to embrace the idea of students learning in teams.

Other Innovative Teaching Strategies

Innovative teaching strategies may take place in various settings or scenarios. For instance, using simulation is a central teaching strategy that allows students a safe place to think critically, apply knowledge, learn to communicate with peers, and practice nursing skills. Instructors should strive not only to use simulation but also to create customized simulation scenarios that hone critical skills needed for students to master diverse learning objectives. With enough resources, instructors also may employ other innovative strategies (e.g., virtual reality tools, case studies, service learning) to enable students to solve clinical problems or engage in learning in new ways.

Cross-Generational Teaching Strategies

For the first time, instructors in the classroom, workplace, and community are challenged with teaching across four, sometimes five generations (Knight, 2014) (see Table 16-1). To be successful, instructors must understand learning theories, different learning styles and preferences, and the various generations that are represented. Finding the right mix of strategies without trying to appeal to all generations at the same time will continue to challenge the instructor. This section briefly describes the characteristics of the various generations and teaching strategies to engage learners.

Table 16-1. Generations Snapshot				
Generation	**Birth Years**	**Values and Characteristics**	**Communication**	**Teaching Strategies**
Traditionalists	1927–1945	Hard work Sacrifice Loyalty	Formal letter	Bullet points Outlines Emphasis on important topics
Baby boomers	1946–1964	Workaholics Personal fulfillment Competitive Team oriented	Telephone	Team projects Organized content Time to practice No role playing
Generation X	Early 1960s–early 1980s	Eliminate the task Want structure and direction Value time Life–work balance	Email and text message	Short lectures Bullet points Pictures or graphics Want feedback Do not like group work
Generation Y ("millennials")	Early 1980s–early 1990s	What's next Goal oriented Multitasking Team oriented and collaborative Work to live	Text message and social media	Activities Technology Creativity Give supplemental information Praise over feedback Fast-paced learning
Generation Z ("after the millennials")	After 1994	Connections Independence Self-directed	Handheld communication	Need process- and skills-based instruction Not team players Creative activities Like small amounts of information at a time

Note. Based on information from Johnson & Romanello, 2005; West Midland Family Center, n.d.

Traditionalists

The traditionalists (also referred to as veterans or maturers) are those born between the early 1900s and before 1945. Although most have retired or are nearing retirement, some are still in the workforce. The traditionalists are known for their hard work and sacrifice and usually are very loyal to employers and expect the same. They work well with others but enjoy schedules that are flexible so that they can work on their own. Teaching strategies for this group include bullet points and outlines. They appreciate emphasis on the important points (Johnson & Romanello, 2005; Nelsey & Brownie, 2012).

Baby Boomers

Baby boomers (1946–1964) grew up during the Civil Rights Movement. They are currently the largest group in the workforce and believe work ethic is based on hours worked. Teamwork and relationships are important in the work environment. This generation appreciates being given extra time for practicing new skills, organizing information, and working on team projects, and avoids role playing. (Johnson & Romanello, 2005; Nelsey & Brownie, 2012).

Generation X

Generation X (1960s–1980s) was the first generation to work and feel comfortable with technology. At work, they enjoy a friendly environment, transparency, and flexibility. Unlike baby boomers, they appreciate work–life balance. Their characteristics include independence, multitasking, and strong self-reliance. This generation appreciates attention in the classroom, as well as short lectures, bullet points, and pictures (Johnson & Romanello, 2005; Nelsey & Brownie, 2012).

Generation Y

This generation, also known as millennials (1981–1994), grew up with technology all around them, creating an open, constant communication mentality. They often are described as working to live, rather than living to work. This generation grew up in an environment where "everybody wins," and they want instant gratification. This is the second largest generation to be entering the workforce. Instruction of this group should include many creative activities that use technology and up-to-date information (Johnson & Romanello, 2005; Nelsey & Brownie, 2012).

Generation Z

Generation Z are those born after 1994 and are still being defined. Like generation Y, they like instant gratification, are "connected" through the Internet and social media, and thrive on "what's next" and their independence. This generation is predicted to be more self-directed and less of a team player. Instruction for generation Z students should focus on skills and use technologic learning activities (Johnson & Romanello, 2005).

Engaging Future Faculty

While shortages in the nursing workforce are a critical issue affecting health care, the nursing faculty shortage is a related problem. Many schools of nursing in the United States lack enough faculty to teach aspiring students because of factors such as retiring instructors, workload, and low faculty salaries (American Association of Colleges of Nursing [AACN], 2015; Chan, Tam, Lung, Wong, & Chau, 2013; Roehrs, 2011). In fact, AACN (2015) reported that more than 68,000 qualified nursing school applicants were rejected in 2014 because of a lack of faculty and other resources. Nursing schools must not only address this issue by retaining current faculty members, but they also should find ways to recruit future instructors who will build lasting careers in nursing education.

Leaders building nursing programs face the challenge of engaging future faculty who, after completing graduate coursework, will likely have a range of possible job offers that could bring more financial rewards than an academic career. Therefore, schools of nursing need to cultivate faculty in ways that offer other rewards, such as possibilities for professional development and opportunities to teach courses that they find rewarding. Leaders also should attempt to understand common challenges encountered by nursing instructors who are teaching in face-to-face courses, clinical rotations, and online classes so that they can build institutional infrastructures for strong mentoring, effective training, and instructional design support.

Potential nursing faculty could be inhibited by expectations that they must succeed in various roles of teaching, research, scholarship, clinical practice, and community service. Yet, faculty who believe they have some autonomy in choosing how to balance these roles might not find them daunting. One large national study found that faculty who felt they were experts in teaching had strong intentions to stay in the faculty role, and those who believed they still had a choice to pursue a professional career in nursing were more likely to stay as well (Candela, Gutierrez, & Keating, 2013). Another study of nursing faculty's intent to leave showed that faculty who were most satisfied found their work meaningful, felt safe in the workplace, had strong relationships with colleagues, and believed they had autonomy and independence in their faculty role (Roughton, 2013). These results suggest that building nursing faculty's self-efficacy in teaching and practice can promote their satisfaction in the faculty role.

Continuous Learning

Lifelong learning for both personal and professional development can occur along any point of the career path for any generation. Nurses beginning their career may seek to advance their nursing practice and knowledge through continuing education programs or by obtaining special certification (e.g., oncology, critical care, perioperative, medical-surgical). Other nurses may seek to advance their career and seek an advanced degree (e.g., licensed practical nurse to a registered nurse, master's to doctoral degree). Regardless of the learner's motive, academic, practice, and regulatory institutions should prepare themselves with a variety of approaches to meet the needs of the learners. Nurse leaders in these institutions can encourage lifelong learning by supporting collaborative learning activities, mentoring for leadership, and identifying significant career advancement and professional development opportunities for employees.

Many approaches to continuous learning exist for nursing professionals. As methods are modified to teach in a multigenerational classroom, instructors also must change the way they think about continuing education and lifelong learning. In 2010, the Association of American Medical Colleges (AAMC) and AACN produced a report titled *Lifelong Learning in Medicine and Nursing*, which discussed continuing education and lifelong learning for health professionals. The report had four main recommendations focusing on continuing education methods, interprofessional education, lifelong learning, and workplace learning. The recommendations were directed toward academic, practice, and regulatory institutions, challenging them to provide an environment where lifelong learning can occur (AAMC & AACN, 2010). The report recognized barriers, including lack of infrastructure and finances, but still suggested a supportive environment for learners. Specifically, educators should integrate lifelong learning skills to better equip learners in knowledge retrieval, review, and application (AAMC & AACN, 2010).

Summary

Nursing education has transformed from hospital-based practical training into a dynamic and innovative approach, with the Nightingale Era as foundational to nursing theory and practice. Figure 16-1 presents key points regarding this transformation. As nursing education evolves and becomes more complex because of recent healthcare advances and multigenerational classrooms, educators are encouraged to look for new pedagogies for classroom and clinical learning experiences. To keep up with the rapidly changing healthcare environment, instructors must also evolve and remain open to new ways of learning. Instructors who implement strategies such as active learning techniques, flipped classrooms, gamification, simulation, and other innovative learning activities that encourage critical thinking and collaborative skills can help students to become lifelong learners. Institutions also may engage and retain faculty by encouraging professional growth for innovative teaching to create enriching learning communities.

Figure 16-1. Key Points

- Innovation in nursing education may include one or more teaching techniques to engage students from different generations.
- Building future nursing programs will require instructors who are nimble, organized, and technologically savvy.
- Teaching across generations will require finding the right mix of strategies without trying to appeal to all generations at the same time.
- Lifelong learning can promote personal and professional development.

References

American Association of Colleges of Nursing. (2015, March 16). Nursing faculty shortage fact sheet. Retrieved from http://www.aacn.nche.edu/media-relations/FacultyShortageFS.pdf

Association of American Medical Colleges & American Association of Colleges of Nursing. (2010). *Lifelong learning in medicine and nursing.* Retrieved from http://www.aacn.nche.edu/education-resources/MacyReport.pdf

Bergmann, J., & Sams, A. (2012). *Flip your classroom: Reach every student in every class every day.* Eugene, OR: International Society for Technology in Education.

Bonwell, C.C., & Eison, J.A. (1991). *Active learning: Creating excitement in the classroom* (1991 ASHE-ERIC Higher Education Reports). Retrieved from http://files.eric.ed.gov/fulltext/ED336049.pdf

Candela, L., Gutierrez, A., & Keating, S. (2013). A national survey examining the professional work life of today's nursing faculty. *Nurse Education Today, 33,* 853–859. doi:10.1016/j.nedt.2012.10.004

Chan, Z.C., Tam, W.S., Lung, M., Wong, W.Y., & Chau, C.W. (2013). A systematic literature review of nurse shortage and the intention to leave. *Journal of Nursing Management, 21,* 605–613. doi:10.1111/j.1365-2834.2012.01437.x

Chickering, A.W., & Gamson, Z.F. (1987). Seven principles for good practice in undergraduate education. *AAHE Bulletin, 39*(7), 2–6. Retrieved from http://files.eric.ed.gov/fulltext/ED282491.pdf

Crookes, K., Crookes, P.A., & Walsh, K. (2013). Meaningful and engaging teaching techniques for student nurses: A literature review. *Nurse Education in Practice, 13,* 239–243. doi:10.1016/j.nepr.2013.04.008

Deterding, S., Dixon, D., Khaled, R., & Nacke, L. (2011, September). From game design elements to gamefulness: Defining "gamification." *Proceedings of the 15th International Academic MindTrek Conference: Envisioning Future Media Environments,* pp. 9–15.

Dock, L.L. (1901). History of the reform in nursing in Bellevue Hospital. *American Journal of Nursing, 2*(2), 89–98. doi:10.2307/3402052

Fata-Hartley, C. (2011). Resisting rote: The importance of active learning for all course learning objectives. *Journal of College Science Teaching, 40*(3), 36–39.

Hamari, J., Koivisto, J., & Sarsa, H. (2014). Does gamification work? A literature review of empirical studies on gamification. *Proceedings of the 47th Hawaii International Conference on System Sciences,* pp. 3025–3034. doi:10.1109 /HICSS.2014.377

Hart, S. (2015). Engaging the learner: The ABC's of service–learning. *Teaching and Learning in Nursing, 10,* 76–79. doi:10.1016/j.teln.2015.01.001

Interprofessional Education Collaborative. (2011). *Core competencies for interprofessional collaborative practice: Report of an expert panel.* Retrieved from http://www.aacn.nche.edu/education-resources/ipecreport.pdf

Johnson, S.A., & Romanello, M.L. (2005). Generational diversity: Teaching and learning approaches. *Nurse Educator, 30,* 212–216. doi:10.1097/00006223-200509000-00009

King, A. (1993). From sage on the stage to guide on the side. *College Teaching, 41,* 30–35. doi:10.1080/87567555.1993 .9926781

Knight, R. (2014, September 25). Managing people from 5 generations. *Harvard Business Review.* Retrieved from https://hbr.org/2014/09/managing-people-from-5-generations

Knowles, M.S. (1980). *The modern practice of adult education: From pedagogy to andragogy* (2nd ed.). New York, NY: Cambridge Books.

Michaelsen, L.K. (1992). Team learning: A comprehensive approach for harnessing the power of small groups in higher education. *To Improve the Academy, 11,* Paper 249. Retrieved from http://digitalcommons.unl.edu/cgi/viewcontent .cgi?article=1248&context=podimproveacad

Murray, T.A. (2013). Innovations in nursing education: The state of the art. *Journal of Nursing Regulation, 3*(4), 25–31. doi:10.1016/S2155-8256(15)30183-6

Nelsey, L., & Brownie, S. (2012). Effective leadership, teamwork and mentoring—Essential elements in promoting generational cohesion in the nursing workforce and retaining nurses. *Collegian, 19,* 197–202. doi:10.1016/ j.colegn.2012.03.002

Prince, M. (2004). Does active learning work? A review of the research. *Journal of Engineering Education, 93,* 223–231. doi:10.1002/j.2168-9830.2004.tb00809.x

Roehrs, C.J. (2011). Getting started: Needs and preferences of Colorado faculty for graduate education in nursing. *Nursing Education Perspectives, 32,* 84–88. doi:10.5480/1536-5026-32.2.84

Roughton, S.E. (2013). Nursing faculty characteristics and perceptions predicting intent to leave. *Nursing Education Perspectives, 34,* 217–225. doi:10.5480/1536-5026-34.4.217

Ruhl, K.L., Hughes, C.A., & Schloss, P.J. (1987). Using the pause procedure to enhance lecture recall. *Teacher Education and Special Education, 10,* 14–18. doi:10.1177/088840648701000103

Scheckel, M. (2009). Nursing education: Past, present, future. In G. Roux & J.A. Halstead (Eds.), *Issues and trends in nursing: Essential knowledge for today and tomorrow* (pp. 27–61). Retrieved from http://www.jblearning.com /samples/0763752258/52258_CH02_Roux.pdf

Sisk, R.J. (2011). Team-based learning: Systematic research review. *Journal of Nursing Education, 50,* 665–669. doi:10 .3928/01484834-20111017-01

Waltz, C.F., Jenkins, L.S., & Han, N. (2014). The use and effectiveness of active learning methods in nursing and health professions education: A literature review. *Nursing Education Perspectives, 35,* 392–400. doi:10.5480/13-1168

Wankat, P.C. (2002). *The effective, efficient professor: Teaching, scholarship, and service.* Boston, MA: Allyn and Bacon.

West Midland Family Center. (n.d.). Generational differences chart. Retrieved from http://www.wmfc.org/uploads /GenerationalDifferencesChart.pdf

CHAPTER 17

Leading the Global Transformation of Health Care

Jeannine M. Brant, PhD, APRN-CNS, AOCN®, FAAN, and Sultan Kav, PhD, RN

And wherever the need arises—on whatever distant shore—I ask no higher or greater privilege than to minister to it.

—Mary Seacole

May we hope that when we are all dead and gone, leaders will arise who have been personally experienced in the hard, practical work, the difficulties and the joys of organizing nursing reforms, and who will lead far beyond anything we have done.

—Florence Nightingale

Introduction

Nurses are strategically positioned to transform health care globally in the 21st century. As the world's largest healthcare professional workforce, providing more than 70%–80% of health care globally, nurses influence the care of patients, families, communities, and healthcare systems (World Health Organization [WHO], 2015). The roles of nurses are diverse, thereby enabling them to revolutionize health care in a variety of settings, whether it is at the bedside, in the board room within an organization, through the development of new knowledge, or through healthcare policy development. This chapter will address the leadership of nursing in transforming global health care. Definitions and rationales for global health, historical perspectives, unique and common challenges including workforce issues, and international exemplars will be highlighted.

Overview of Global Health

Global health is an evolving concept not only in nursing, but in health care around the world. It can be defined as an area of study, research, and practice that places priority on improving health and achieving equity in health for all people worldwide (Koplan et al., 2009). The focus is not only on cross-border issues but also on domestic disparities within each country. As international borders become blurrier with migration of healthcare workers and people around the world, diversity is more often a community norm rather than the exception. So why should nurses lead the transformation of global health? Nurses hold social responsibility for the improvement of health for patients, families, and communities. The spread of nurses throughout the world, in diverse settings from large urban cities to small rural villages, provides an ideal opportunity for nurses to lead and influence global health (Opollo, Bond, Gray, & Lail-Davis, 2012).

Historical Perspectives

Historical nurse leaders paved the way for today's nursing practice and nursing leadership toward healthcare transformation in the 21st century. Challenges in early times were abundant and included the suffrage of women, racial discrimination, and hierarchies in medicine, some of which continue to exist today (Bleich, 2015). Early nurse leaders were able to overcome these challenges, but often not without difficulty. Their leadership and persistence to promote quality patient care, change healthcare environments, facilitate social change, and establish policies and laws that promoted health around the globe are foundational principles for nurse leaders today.

While Florence Nightingale is the quintessential nurse leader, others deserve recognition for exemplary contributions to nursing. Some of the most influential early global nurse leaders and their contributions to nursing care are listed chronologically in Table 17-1.

Several recurring themes central to these nurse leaders exist. Many overcame adversity and perceptions during their time about the role of women, race, and role-related hierarchies. All of these leaders were able to accomplish goals that had not previously been recognized or even considered. Many of them were instrumental in forwarding significant health-related topics, including sanitation reform, collaborative interprofessional relationships, evidence-based practice and research, policy development, and public health advocacy. Nursing continues to face many challenges similar to those that faced our historical leaders. Learning to effectively overcome some of the global challenges in nursing is the first step in achieving progress. Today's nursing force can use these early leaders' examples to move health care forward and advance quality and care in ways that have not previously been recognized.

Global Nursing Challenges

Healthcare challenges are abundant around the globe and vary depending on a region's development. No matter where one lives, personal well-being depends on how health issues are managed around the world. In developing countries, basic access to health care, child mortality, the aging population, and chronic illness are growing concerns (Gantz et al., 2012).

Table 17-1. Early Nurse Leaders and Their Contributions to Nursing		
Nurse Leader	**Background**	**Contributions to Nursing**
Dorothea Lynde Dix (1802–1887)	Worked during the Civil War Taught Sunday school at a women's prison, which motivated her movement to improve conditions and care for the mentally ill	Created the first mental health system in the United States Served as superintendent of the Union Army Nurses during the Civil War Showed compassion for soldiers, regardless of being Confederate
Mary Seacole (1805–1881)	Jamaican Black Learned patient care from her mother, who was a healer Provided direct patient care around the world, including Jamaica, United Kingdom, Crimea, and Panama	Developed expertise in the care of patients with yellow fever, cholera, dysentery, and other tropical diseases; developed a medication to effectively treat cholera Promoted public health and sanitation Overcame racial discrimination and became a symbol for minority nurses and feminists who spoke against a restrictive nursing system Noted as an advanced practice nurse in her time—roles included diagnosis of disease, preparation and prescribing of herbals and pharmaceutical medicine, minor surgery, and performing a postmortem
Florence Nightingale (1820–1910)	British Privileged background Provided direct patient care during the Crimean War	Promoted public health and sanitation Conducted research on patient outcomes Developed nursing education programs Fostered the development of nurse–physician relationships Overcame gender discrimination and role hierarchies Collaborated with citizens and policy makers Honored annually on her birthday in May through Nurses Week celebrations around the globe
Clara Barton (1821–1912)	Cared for her ill father early in life, which inspired her nursing career Worked during the Civil War	Cared for soldiers on the battlefield itself Received a directive from President Lincoln to find missing Union soldiers Established the American Red Cross in 1873 and served as its first president
Ellen Dougherty (1844–1919)	From New Zealand, which was the first country to initiate the Nurse Registration Act	Became the first registered nurse in the world

(Continued on next page)

Nurse Leader	Background	Contributions to Nursing
	Table 17-1. Early Nurse Leaders and Their Contributions to Nursing *(Continued)*	
Mary Eliza Mahoney (1845–1926)	African American woman Worked at the New England Hospital for Women and Children for 15 years before she was admitted into nursing school	Noted as the first African American graduate nurse Recognized the need to improve the status of African American nurses in the early 1900s Helped overcome racial discrimination and segregation Cofounded the National Association of Colored Graduate Nurses, which became part of the American Nurses Association Was instrumental in the women's suffrage campaign
Margaret Sanger (1879–1966)	One of 11 children born to a Catholic-Irish family Attended Massachusetts Institute of Technology	Pioneered the women's health movement Provided public education on birth control Authored topics on menstruation and sexuality Founded the American Birth Control League, which eventually became Planned Parenthood Initiated the first legal birth control clinic in the United States
Dame Cicely Saunders (1918–2005)	English Anglican nurse Also became a social worker and physician Work inspired by her love for a Polish-Jewish patient and refugee who escaped from a Warsaw ghetto and later died of cancer	Founded the modern hospice movement Introduced the idea of "total pain," which included physical, emotional, social, and spiritual distress Helped establish St. Christopher's Hospice, the first "hospice house" in the world Honored by Queen Elizabeth II for her work

Note. Based on information from Harper et al., 2014; Ridgway, 2016; Seaton, 2016.

Global issues in the 21st century can affect healthcare systems and immobilize existing nursing resources and progress (Ferguson, 2015a). Some of the shared global issues are included in Figure 17-1. Never has there been a more important time for interdependence among countries and the need to work together.

Aside from the global challenges that exist, nursing as a profession has its own challenges. According to an analysis of documents published by the six WHO regions between 2007 and 2012, four key issues at the global level are workforce issues and shortages, the need for nursing to affect health care, the need to clearly identify nursing professional status, and the need to consistently define education of nurses (Wong et al., 2015). Regarding the workforce, a tremendous need exists to recruit and attract young people to nursing, retain them in the profession, provide competitive remuneration, and attain a favorable work environment. Workforce needs are even more pressing in developing countries. Nurses who receive education in low- and middle-income countries often migrate to more developed countries for better pay and quality of life, thus widening workforce gaps in developing countries and threatening progress and health outcomes even more. Thus, despite educating and cultivating new nurses, the developing country remains short of nurses and is left with the same workforce shortage problems. WHO estimates the global nursing workforce to be 21.2 million individuals. Yet, a workforce shortage is looming and has already arrived in many parts of the world, resulting in critical gaps in care and

Figure 17-1. Worldwide Challenges Affecting Health Care
• Travel and migration • Inadequate public health infrastructure • Urbanization • Globalization of trade • Aging and chronic disease • Epic natural disasters • Infectious diseases • Climate change • Conflict and war

unmet healthcare needs, especially in low-resource countries (WHO, 2014). WHO estimates the healthcare worker shortage to be at least four million, and this number could increase as the population ages around the globe. Reasons for the shortage include faculty shortages, lack of incentives to enter the nursing profession, and inadequate investment in healthcare education. Less than 2% of total healthcare expenditure worldwide is spent on healthcare education and training (WHO, 2013).

The need for nurses to affect health care is tremendous, and organizations, including WHO, rely on nurses to fulfill this task. Nurses have opportunities to influence quality care; improve accessibility to care, especially through advanced practice nursing roles; and influence policy. Assuming leadership roles in healthcare organizations, volunteering for organizations that advance health care, and taking the initiative to apply for policy and healthcare decision-making boards are some of the opportunities that exist. Unfortunately, the nursing voice often is absent in policy discussions and continues to be overpowered by hierarchical traditions. Nurses should request to be present at these discussions and agree immediately when opportunity arises.

The professional status of nursing also is an issue to consider. Professionalism in nursing is reflective of the status of women within a culture and is influenced by low-level education and a lack of standardization of the profession. Nursing education varies greatly around the globe, leading to wide gaps in instruction. A consistent level of education should be the goal for nurses around the world, with defined curriculum requirements, clinical and theoretical requirements, and interprofessional content. Once nursing defines its basic academic requirements and competencies, then professional status can be recognized by other leading healthcare professionals, thereby increasing the nurse's voice and raising the power of nursing as a profession (Ferguson, 2015a, 2015b).

Current Global Initiatives Involving Nursing

Worldwide, the healthcare system and nursing have been undergoing rapid changes and face a number of challenges in providing quality, safe, and cost-effective care. These challenges include an aging population increasingly affected by chronic disease, rising healthcare costs, technologic change, and the need to improve the equity and accessibility of the healthcare system. Moving into the future, treatments will become increasingly specific because of new technologies and scientific discoveries that require skilled nurses to administer complex therapies, as well as to provide personalized care to the patients and their families. Nurses should be full partners with physicians and other health professionals in redesigning health care. Nurses need strong and effective leadership to ensure that health and nursing care is delivered with the highest standard. Additionally, healthcare professionals need to be better prepared to care for people with multiple chronic conditions in all settings.

How do nurses overcome the magnitude of barriers that exist? The 2011 hallmark report *The Future of Nursing: Leading Change, Advancing Health* from the Institute of Medicine (IOM, now called the Health and Medicine Division of the National Academies of Sciences, Engineering, and Medicine), aligns with WHO themes on global health. The IOM report challenges nurses to lead the way in improving health and redesigning health care. Although recommendations are focused on the U.S. healthcare system, a ripple effect can be realized globally as nurses shape the landscape of health care in individual communities around the world (Shaffer, Davis, To Dutka, & Richardson, 2014). Nurses around the world can dialogue and network to solve common problems. Often, one setting may have overcome a problem that another global community is currently facing (Gantz et al., 2012). Because of these types of exchanges, it is often a surprise that more similarities than differences exist between countries and cultures. The IOM report and other health initiatives suggest the need for increased education and leadership from nurses to address the healthcare needs of our nation and the world. To accomplish these changes, leadership is essential and serves as a common theme in all organizations in which initiatives have been placed. Some of these initiatives are described below.

International Council of Nurses

The International Council of Nurses (ICN) is a federation of national nursing associations that facilitates nurses to speak with one voice to influence health care and advance the profession of nursing (Benton, 2012; Benton & Ferguson, 2014). ICN has been responding for many years to needs identified by member associations to change and improve the way nurses are prepared for management and leadership. Over the years, ICN has initiated many projects to prepare nurses for leadership. Some of its leading initiatives are described in this chapter (ICN, 2014).

The Leadership For Change™ (LFC) program aims to prepare nurses and other health professionals for leadership roles in nursing and the broader health sector during these challenging times of health system change and reform. The program was launched in 1996 as a project to strengthen leadership skills among nurses and has been implemented in more than 60 countries. This program imparted new skills and knowledge to enable participants to manage and implement appropriate and proactive leadership strategies. The vision of the ICN LFC program is that 21st-century nurses and other health professionals will have the knowledge, strategies, and ability to lead and manage in complex and dynamic nursing and health service arenas so as to influence the development of the profession and the advancement of health and social policies toward healthier futures for all populations (Ferguson et al., 2016).

The Leadership in Negotiation project, another ICN initiative, has been implemented in several regions of the world. The project began in 1982 in Africa and has since been adapted to the needs of nurses in the Caribbean, Eastern Europe, Latin America, Southeast Asia, the Pacific Rim, and the South Pacific. The project has facilitated the training of nurse leaders worldwide in problem solving, negotiation, communication, human resource development, occupational health and safety, association management, and marketing. At the same time, the project sensitizes participants to the impact of labor issues and the work environment on the delivery of care. The focus of this active-learning project is the personal and professional development of nurses, resulting in an effective voice in health sector decision-making bodies, improved workplaces, and stronger professional organizations (Ferguson, 2015a).

The Global Nursing Leadership Institute (GNLI) represents the third arm of ICN's leadership development strategy. Established in 2009, GNLI has prepared nurse leaders for the global house. GNLI offers an advanced leadership program for nurses or midwives at senior and executive positions in member countries across the world. Leader participants are motivated to review and enhance their national and global leadership knowledge and skills within a collaborative and stimulating learning culture. GNLI is a six-day residential program that takes place in Geneva, Switzerland, during September of each year. The program also focuses on sustainable development, teaching nurses how to provide quality nursing care while planning human resources for health (HRH) to meet the care needs of future generations. Around the world, political agendas are focusing on the importance of HRH planning to achieve sustainable development goals and universal health coverage. Globally, nurse leaders are facing some of the greatest opportunities to build partnerships and alliances, to strengthen the health workforce, and to effectively influence policy (see www.icn.ch/what-we-do/leadership-development).

Sigma Theta Tau

Sigma Theta Tau is an international organization whose mission is to advance world health and celebrate nursing excellence in scholarship, leadership, and service. The Honor Society of Nursing, Sigma Theta Tau International (STTI) International Leadership Institute is one of several global initiatives and has offered many leadership training programs (see www.nursingsociety.org/learn-grow/leadership-new/international-leadership-institute). Some of the programs include the Maternal-Child Health Nurse Leadership Academy, the Gerontological Nursing Leadership Academy, and the Nurse Faculty Leadership Academy.

Nurses from around the world can be part of STTI and engage in leadership development in their specialty field or complete the general leadership or board training. STTI also sponsors mentoring and global think-tank events.

Oncology Nursing Organizations

Internationally, the contribution of cancer nurses must be valued at all levels of the healthcare and political systems. In 2015, the Asian Oncology Nursing Society, Canadian Association of Nurses in Oncology, Cancer Nurses Society of Australia, European Oncology Nursing Society, International Society of Nurses in Cancer Care, and Oncology Nursing Society developed a position statement titled "The Role of Cancer Nurses in the World."

It is anticipated that cancer may soon become the leading cause of death in the world. The growing demand for cancer care, from prevention to palliative care, along with rapidly changing healthcare systems provides opportunities for cancer nurses to play a pivotal and increasingly important role in delivering high-quality, safe, effective, and efficient health care to people affected by or at risk for cancer. As the largest group of healthcare providers globally, in most countries around the world nurses are the backbone of the healthcare delivery system (Sheldon, Brant, Hankle, Bialous, & Lubejko, 2016).

Prevention and Management of Noncommunicable Diseases

The prevalence rate of noncommunicable diseases (NCDs) is increasing throughout the world (WHO, n.d.). Nurses make an important contribution to tackling NCDs and, as the largest group of healthcare professionals, are the key providers of NCD prevention, treatment, and management. As the point of first contact, nurses are well positioned to detect, treat, and refer patients with NCDs, as well as to provide information, education, and counseling to the public on prevention of NCDs. With their holistic approach to care, nurses are well prepared to provide behavioral and lifestyle interventions that consider the social determinants of health while building on the strengths and resources of individuals and their communities. Using a person-centered approach to care, patients are encouraged to increase their health literacy—the ability to understand and act on health information—and are empowered to become active participants in their own care. Nurses can advocate for health policies that integrate NCD prevention into health planning, nursing curriculum, and workforce strengthening.

In different countries, similarities are observed in nurse-led community-based interventions involving promotion of physical activity, weight and salt intake reduction, lowering the frequency of tobacco use, and risk management. Nurse-led clinics are increasingly common. Services are being coordinated with physicians and other health professionals, thus emphasizing an interprofessional approach. Nursing roles also are strengthened by specialized trainings, which further empower practice as nurses are recognized for their specialty roles and responsibilities on the team. Through these services, family-based care is made possible and more accessible to the general population. In contrast to the local setting, public health nurses (PHNs) do not have explicit roles as described in protocols in NCD prevention programs in health centers. Usual tasks for PHNs include assisting with consultations, providing direct care, coordinating community resources, and performing clerical tasks. In some countries, specialized nurses serve at the primary contact rather than being employed in any agency. For example, similar to PHNs, ostomy nurses and diabetes nurses contract their services with the patients with referrals coming from physicians. This is a progressive model that could be spread globally to meet healthcare gaps.

Upcoming roles for nurses include nurse navigators and nurse coaches. Nurses have well-rounded skills for advocacy, problem identification, and the potential to focus on health and wellness in the individual, family, community, and environment. Nurse navigators and coaches also are equipped to implement evidence-based strategies and translate research findings into practice to influence the health and well-being of all people (Dossey & Hess, 2013).

Where Nursing Could Make an Impact

Nurses bring an important voice and point of view to management and policy discussions. A significant need exists to prepare more nurses to help lead improvements in healthcare quality, safety, access, and value. A 2011 survey of 1,000 hospitals in the United States by the American Hospital Association found that nurses account for only 6% of hospital board members. Physicians account for 20% of hospital board members, and other clinicians make up about 5%. No statistics are available worldwide, but globally, lower nursing participation is expected compared to the United States. Nurses need to see themselves as decision makers and able to influence health outcomes.

Recent authors explored the literature to identify the extent and ways in which nursing leadership, collaboration, and empowerment can have a demonstrable impact on patient safety (Richardson & Storr, 2010). Evidence supporting nursing's contribution to patient safety through empowerment, leadership, and teamwork is limited, and the task of quantifying the contribution of each by analyzing their direct impact on the safety of care is at an early stage of development. More importantly, nurses can promote a culture of patient safety and positive patient outcomes whether they are a direct care provider, a manager, or an organizational or health policy leader (DiCuccio, 2015). Creating that culture includes talking about safety and patient outcomes on an ongoing basis, implementing quality improvement initiatives on the nursing unit level or outpatient department, and acknowledging those who promote this positive culture.

Another global solution includes transformational leadership. Transformational leadership empowers nurses to have a voice while advocating for healthcare quality, care access, and expanded roles of nursing, similar to historical nurse leaders. Developing transformational leaders can only occur through mentoring, which is needed to stimulate leadership development and to pave the way for young nurse leaders. Rather than maintaining a narrow organizational focus, nurses and organizations need to think globally, to lend a hand, to learn from one another, and to foster international dialogues that promote global health care. Organizational exemplars can serve as examples for learning systems, gleaning themes that can be expanded globally and applied to individual cultures. The exchange of ideas and information should occur in practice and academic settings and in research and policy development. Models of care, patient care policies, leadership initiatives, and academic curricula can all be shared with recommendations given for development of optimal infrastructure (Buckner et al., 2014). These shared exchanges can facilitate global change and camaraderie among the world's nurses. Some of these shared exchanges are already happening through current global initiatives in nursing. Global healthcare recommendations for nurses, derived from all of the global initiatives and organizations, are listed in Table 17-2.

Table 17-2. Global Health Recommendations for Nurses	
Recommendation	**Comments**
Health System and Practice Recommendations	
Clearly understand how healthcare policy and economics affect health and its outcomes.	To effectively lead healthcare reform, nurses must be educated on how healthcare systems work around the world. Economics drive equitable care and healthcare access issues, and health care cannot move forward without consideration of the underlying economic issues that exist.
Contribute to healthcare policy development.	Healthcare policy is instrumental in shaping healthcare systems and improving the quality of health care. Policies can address disparities, such as opioid availability and access to care.
Develop healthcare systems and models of care to reach disparate populations.	Urbanization has caused a flux of healthcare workers in urban areas, leaving rural areas without care. Homecare and long-term care models should be developed that reach these disparate populations.
Promote global evidence-based practice (EBP).	EBP resources are now globally available, and nurses should implement EBP into daily practice to improve care quality.
Develop an international nursing research agenda that explores nursing workforce issues, models of care, nursing roles and leadership, and nursing-sensitive patient outcomes.	Nurses have the opportunity to conduct collaborative research to explore similar issues and generate new nursing knowledge. Nursing can collaborate internationally to examine and find solutions to some of the most daunting research questions.
Ensure practice environments where nurses practice to the fullest scope of their degree.	Nurses are charged to lead healthcare reform and can only do so by practicing at their fullest scope. Nurses should be given the privilege to use their skills and knowledge to the fullest ability, to serve on leadership boards, and to be recognized as an integral part of the leadership team.

(Continued on next page)

Table 17-2. Global Health Recommendations for Nurses *(Continued)*	
Recommendation	**Comments**
Nursing Education Recommendations	
Be culturally competent.	Global health relies on individual cultural awareness and ability to interact and relate to diverse people. Nurses should self-reflect on their cultural backgrounds and learn about the backgrounds of others. Embracing diversity is an essential foundational element of global healthcare transformation.
Incorporate global health courses into nursing curricula.	Blurred borders and diverse populations have led to an increase in shared global health needs. Global health education should be incorporated into basic nursing and continuing education courses so that all nurses can be more globally aware.
Standardize minimum competency requirements for nursing education.	Lack of standardized nursing education has led to disparities in nursing and leadership potential. Minimum competency requirements will allow nurses to have a voice and clearly articulate the value of nursing to stake-holders.
Develop nurse residency programs that facilitate the transition from basic education into practice.	Retention of nurses relies on a smooth transition from education into practice. Residency programs can help nurses develop critical thinking in a supportive environment and transition socially into the healthcare environment.
Educate nurses to prepare them for healthcare challenges and leadership positions that meet current global needs.	All nurses are leaders in some capacity. Leadership training should be a standard part of education to better prepare nurses for key leadership positions.
Ensure nurses engage in lifelong learning.	The healthcare environment, technology, and knowledge are evolving rapidly. Nurses must stay current with healthcare trends to improve the quality of patient care. Lifelong learning is an essential part of being a healthcare leader.
Foster interprofessional learning collaboratives.	Collaboratives with physicians and other colleagues helps to break down hierarchical chasms. Interprofessional teams can promote gender equality and empower women and, subsequently, empower nursing.
Improve education in gerontologic nursing, chronic disease management, and palliative care.	The aging population will require nurses who are specifically trained in these areas. Because a large portion of the world's population will eventually be diagnosed with cancer and chronic diseases, palliation of symptoms is essential to promote quality of life for patients and their families.

(Continued on next page)

Table 17-2. Global Health Recommendations for Nurses *(Continued)*	
Recommendation	**Comments**
Workforce Recommendations	
Attract and retain new talent to ensure workforce viability and strength.	Workforce shortages are significant. Attracting and retaining talented nurses will ensure the workforce's ability to lead healthcare reform.
Improve workforce conditions for nurses.	Migration of nurses is related to workforce conditions and widens care gaps. Healthcare systems should ensure nurses receive optimal salary and benefits and provide favorable work environments.
Develop an international database for workforce benchmarking.	The database will allow for benchmarking and national comparisons that can be used to improve workforce quality.

Note. Based on information from Bleich, 2015; Institute of Medicine, 2011; International Council of Nurses, 2014; McGilton et al., 2015; Opollo et al., 2012; Peluso et al., 2014; Shaffer et al., 2014; Wong et al., 2015; World Health Organization, n.d.

Summary

Nurses are well-positioned to be leaders and facilitators of global healthcare transformation. Exemplary nurse leaders paved the way for improvements in healthcare quality during the 19th and 20th centuries, and the opportunity exists for nurses to lead the way in the 21st century. Overcoming barriers and grasping global initiatives will be pivotal for nursing to move forward. Interprofessional collaboration, leadership training, and recruiting and retaining new talent into the nursing profession will be instrumental and beneficial for both nursing and health care globally. The contribution of nurses leading global health initiatives spans research, academia, and practice. Many nurses participate in global health mission work, such as those who have experienced the Ebola crisis or when natural disasters have struck those in their professional associations, faith-based ministries, and government agencies. Wherever in the world there is a healthcare need, a nurse will be found there.

References

American Hospital Association. (2011, September). *Hospitals and care systems of the future.* Retrieved from http://www.aha.org/content/11/hospitals-care-systems-of-future.pdf

Asian Oncology Nursing Society, Canadian Association of Nurses in Oncology, Cancer Nurses Society of Australia, European Oncology Nursing Society, International Society of Nurses in Cancer Care, & Oncology Nursing Society. (2015). Position statement: The role of cancer nurses in the world. Retrieved from https://c.ymcdn.com/sites/www.isncc.org/resource/resmgr/Position_Statements/The_Role_of_Cancer_Nurses_in.pdf

Benton, D. (2012). Advocating globally to shape policy and strengthen nursing's influence. *Online Journal of Issues in Nursing, 17*(1), Manuscript 5. Retrieved from http://nursingworld.org/MainMenuCategories/ANAMarketplace/ANAPeriodicals/OJIN/TableofContents/Vol-17-2012/No1-Jan-2012/Advocating-Globally-to-Shape-Policy.html

Benton, D.C., & Ferguson, S.L. (2014). How nurse leaders are connected internationally. *Nursing Standard, 29*(16), 42–48. doi:10.7748/ns.29.16.42.e9060

Bleich, M.R. (2015). International perspectives in leadership development: Part I. *Journal of Continuing Education in Nursing, 46,* 343–345. doi:10.3928/00220124-20150721-13

Buckner, E.B., Anderson, D.J., Garzon, N., Hafsteinsdóttir, T.B., Lai, C.K., & Roshan, R. (2014). Perspectives on global nursing leadership: International experiences from the field. *International Nursing Review, 61,* 463–471. doi:10.1111/inr.12139

DiCuccio, M.H. (2015). The relationship between patient safety culture and patient outcomes: A systematic review. *Journal of Patient Safety, 11,* 135–142. doi:10.1097/PTS.0000000000000058

Dossey, B.M., & Hess, D. (2013). Professional nurse coaching: Advances in national and global healthcare transformation. *Global Advances in Health and Medicine, 2*(4), 10–16. doi:10.7453/gahmj.2013.044

Ferguson, S.L. (2015a). Transformational nurse leaders key to strengthening health systems worldwide. *Journal of Nursing Administration, 45,* 351–353. doi:10.1097/NNA.0000000000000212

Ferguson, S.L. (2015b). The World Health Organization: Is it still relevant? *Nursing Economics, 33,* 113–116.

Ferguson, S.L., Al Rifai, F., Maay'a, M., Nguyen, L.B., Qureshi, K., Tse, A.M., … Jeadrik, G. (2016). The ICN Leadership For Change™ Program—20 years of growing influence. *International Nursing Review, 63,* 15–25. doi:10.1111/inr.12248

Gantz, N.R., Sherman, R., Jasper, M., Choo, C.G., Herrin-Griffith, D., & Harris, K. (2012). Global nurse leader perspectives on health systems and workforce challenges. *Journal of Nursing Management, 20,* 433–443. doi:10.1111/j.1365-2834.2012.01393.x

Harper, D.C., Davey, K.S., & Fordham, P.N. (2014). Leadership lessons in global nursing and health from the Nightingale Letter Collection at the University of Alabama at Birmingham. *Journal of Holistic Nursing, 32,* 44–53. doi:10.1177/0898010113497835

Institute of Medicine. (2011). *The future of nursing: Leading change, advancing health.* Washington, DC: National Academies Press.

International Council of Nurses. (2014). *ICN strategic plan 2014–2018.* Retrieved from www.icn.ch/images/stories/documents/about/ICN_Strategic_Plan.pdf

Koplan, J.P., Bond, T.C., Merson, M.H., Reddy, K.S., Rodriguez, M.H., Sewankambo, N.K., & Wasserheit, J.N. (2009). Towards a common definition of global health. *Lancet, 373,* 1993–1995. doi:10.1016/S0140-6736(09)60332-9

McGilton, K.S., Bowers, B.J., Heath, H., Shannon, K., Dellefield, M.E., Prentice, D., … Mueller, C.A. (2015). Recommendations from the International Consortium on Professional Nursing Practice in Long-Term Care Homes. *Journal of the American Medical Directors Association, 17,* 99–103. doi:10.1016/j.jamda.2015.11.001

Opollo, J.G., Bond, M.L., Gray, J., & Lail-Davis, V.J. (2012). Meeting tomorrow's health care needs through local and global involvement. *Journal of Continuing Education in Nursing, 43,* 75–80. doi:10.3928/00220124-20111101-05

Peluso, M.J., Hafler, J.P., Sipsma, H., & Cherlin, E. (2014). Global health education programming as a model for interinstitutional collaboration in interprofessional health education. *Journal of Interprofessional Care, 28,* 371–373. doi:10.3109/13561820.2014.881789

Richardson, A., & Storr, J. (2010). Patient safety: A literature review on the impact of nursing empowerment, leadership and collaboration. *International Nursing Review, 57,* 12–21. doi:10.1111/j.1466-7657.2009.00757.x

Ridgway, S. (2016). Mary Mahoney, the first African-American graduate nurse: Challenging race and gender roles. *Working Nurse.* Retrieved from http://www.workingnurse.com/articles/mary-mahoney-the-first-african-american-graduate-nurse

Seaton, H.J. (2016). Another Florence Nightingale? The rediscovery of Mary Seacole. *Victorian Web.* Retrieved from http://www.victorianweb.org/history/crimea/seacole.html

Shaffer, F.A., Davis, C.R., To Dutka, J., & Richardson, D.R. (2014). The future of nursing: Domestic agenda, global implications. *Journal of Transcultural Nursing, 25,* 388–394. doi:10.1177/1043659614523474

Sheldon, L.K., Brant, J.M., Hankle, K.S., Bialous, S., & Lubejko, B. (2016). Promoting cancer nursing education, training, and research in countries in transition. In M. Silbermann (Ed.), *Cancer care in countries and societies in transition* (pp. 473–493). doi:10.1007/978-3-319-22912-6_31

Wong, F.K., Liu, H., Wang, H., Anderson, D., Seib, C., & Molasiotis, A. (2015). Global nursing issues and development: Analysis of World Health Organization documents. *Journal of Nursing Scholarship, 47,* 574–583. doi:10.1111/jnu.12174

World Health Organization. (n.d.). Noncommunicable diseases and mental health. Retrieved from http://www.who.int/nmh/en

World Health Organization. (2013). *Transforming and scaling up health professionals' education and training: World Health Organization guidelines 2013.* Geneva, Switzerland: Author.

World Health Organization. (2014). WHO global health workforce statistics database: 2014 update. Retrieved from http://www.who.int/hrh/statistics/hwfstats/en

World Health Organization. (2015). *Options analysis report on strategic directions for nursing and midwifery (2016–2020).* Retrieved from http://www.who.int/hrh/nursing_midwifery/options_analysis_report.pdf

CHAPTER 18

Health Policy and Advocacy for Nurse Leaders

Katherine Bell, MSN, APRN, ACNS-BC, and Alec Stone, MA, MPA

It is not enough to know, we must also apply; it is not enough to will, we must also do.

—Johann Wolfgang von Goethe,
as translated by T.B. Saunders
in *Maxims and Reflections of Goethe*

Personal Journey in Health Policy Advocacy: One Nurse's Perspective

How many times have you heard the phrase, "Whoever thought this was a good idea has never worked in health care"? Each day at the hospital, nursing staff fervently discuss a topic that has electrified our emotions. Between underserved populations, lack of coverage, poorly funded cancer research, or nursing shortages, there is always a policy affecting our daily lives. There are so many health topics that I find important to the public, and at some point I had to stand up and have my voice heard. As a graduate student at the University of Texas and an inspiring oncology nurse, I embarked on an experience as an Archer graduate fellow in public policy that changed my life. I wasn't always a nurse; in fact, my first career was in radio advertising sales. My background in sales afforded me the ability to convince someone else to share in my passion about health care.

After joining the Oncology Nursing Society (ONS), I was welcomed with open arms, as the association staff and leaders were eager to assist me with fostering my education. As part of my fellowship, I had the opportunity to work in Washington, DC, for the summer of 2012 under the mentorship of the ONS health policy director.

It was hot and muggy, not unlike the Houston weather I grew up with, and I traded in my scrubs for a suit and heels. It was an exciting time in Washington with a presidential election on the cusp and the Patient Protection and Affordable Care Act, more commonly known as simply the Affordable Care Act, hot on the minds of both party lines. Washington is like a bubble, where people live and breathe the causes near and dear to their hearts, or sometimes their pocketbooks and personal agendas. It was hard for me to realize the extreme polarity of politics until I started working and living in our nation's capital.

Many nurses have felt the deviation from unity over the past few years, as controversial topics become more and more mainstreamed. However, when I walked into a Congress member's office, I was someone who both parties respected, an oncology nurse, and my topic was one we could all agree on—a subject that was nonpartisan, nonpolitical, and touched everyone: cancer. Our passions as oncology nurses come from such a special place because we want to see policy that will better the lives of our patients and shape the face of oncology care. That veracity is what drives us to embrace change, and as leaders in the nursing community, it is our privilege to advocate for our patients, our fellow nurses, and funding to further the fight against cancer.

—Katherine Bell, MSN, APRN, ACNS-BC

Introduction

It is often said that politicians campaign in poetry but govern in prose. The political system is forever in flux, and we can never know exactly how it will play out. From campaigning and nominations to elections and governing, American politics is a complicated and layered process. It is by design and definition dynamic, because it is based on people. As nurse leaders, it is your honor to reform policy because you are the stakeholder, the voice of your profession, and the voice of your patients. This chapter will outline public policy and provide you with knowledge to empower you with information that will inspire you to be a stronger healthcare advocate.

Defining Public Policy

The Constitution of the United States encourages active advocacy from its citizens. In fact, in the Bill of Rights, the First Amendment states,

> Congress shall make no law respecting an establishment of religion, or prohibiting the free exercise thereof; or abridging the freedom of speech, or of the press; or the right of the people peaceably to assemble, and to petition the Government for a redress of grievances. (U.S. Const. amend. I)

The U.S. government has three branches: executive, legislative, and judicial. It was created with a system of checks and balances so that no one branch can exclusively make decisions on behalf of the nation. The executive branch is led by the president and includes the cabinet and 15 executive agencies, one of which is the Department of Health and Human Services (HHS). The executive branch is responsible for "implementing and enforcing the law" (White House, n.d.-a), and the president serves as head of state and commander in chief of the U.S. armed forces. The legislative branch comprises the House of Representatives and the Senate and is charged, among other things, with enacting legislation, investigating legislative action, and confirming executive appointments. For a bill to become a law, both the House of Representatives and the Senate must agree on the language and pass the bill, which is then sent to the president for final approval (White House, n.d.-c). Last is the judicial branch, which is a nonpartisan system of federally appointed judges that interpret and determine the constitutionality of legislation (White

House, n.d.-b). The U.S. Supreme Court consists of nine federally appointed judges and only hears cases that are brought forth to them and in which harm has previously been established. These cases are almost always in the appeal phase.

Most scholars agree that the intent of the Founding Fathers was that the citizens of the United States should not be intimidated by their own government. Having the right to approach, without fear of reprisal, was a unique concept at the time. Until this was documented, few countries or leaders allowed their own people to ask for favors or address the ruling class. When the Constitution was being written, it was important to the authors that the people be the dominant party in the relationship. The First Amendment "petition clause" was written to formally state the rights of American citizens to reach out to their government on any issue.

Since that time, as is the case with all amendments, clauses, and phrases in the Constitution, these rights continue to be tested through public engagement. Many challenges are being decided in the U.S. court system. And although they are not all newsworthy, these cases shape the way Americans feel and think about public policy. Using precedent-setting cases, plaintiffs and defendants hold strong to their ideals. Citing previous arguments and historical events, the courts have defined parameters in which Americans can interpret the laws of the land. This happens at the federal, state, and even local jurisdictions. As with all things, much of these decisions come down to political philosophy.

Americans take their politics seriously. Sometimes referred to as a "blood sport," politics takes the heated, emotional discussion of public policy directly to the people for heightened forms of participatory democracy. The idea that the government works best with "maximum direct participation in governmental affairs and decision-making by individual citizens" (Ladd, 1985, p. 100) as the driving force behind it was new. This is a powerful concept and an even more powerful mechanism in governing.

Decision makers, opinion leaders, and politicians work to both enhance, and, sadly, too often, to decrease, involvement from the people. Manipulating elections, voter turnout or suppression, voting rights, and identification requirements effectively discourages and intimidates those unfamiliar and uninterested in politics and policy. It is easier for people to walk away from any civic obligation than to have to "fight City Hall" to have their voice heard.

However, taking a stand is the essence of public policy. Redressing the government is the only way to make a change. Whether conservative or liberal, to have any influence on the outcome, people must take the first step. The government, as an entity, is designed to have elected officials, appointed personnel, and volunteer leaders. These people help set the rules and create the agenda. Through these mechanisms, committees are formed, councils are convened, and assemblies are elected. Within these bodies, leaders arise to direct the course of the discussion.

Party politics or control by a single side is not uncommon. Factions, or a group of like-minded individuals who seek to have sway over the whole, have been a part of American politics since Thomas Jefferson and Alexander Hamilton fought in George Washington's first presidential cabinet (Freeman, n.d.). One cabinet member fought for states' rights while the other fought for federal supremacy. From there, the principles and ideals of individual rights were rooted in different paths.

Who Influences Policy?

This section will guide you through important federal agencies that influence policies related to health care. This overview will provide a bird's-eye view of when these agencies were established, as well as their overall mission and influence on health policy.

Department of Health and Human Services

HHS is one of 15 executive departments. The executive cabinet is made up of the leaders or secretaries of each department. HHS is tasked "to enhance and protect the health and well-being of all Americans" (U.S. DHHS, n.d.-a). Before the official establishment of HHS, the government used other agencies for health and welfare programs. In 1953, President Eisenhower established the Department of Health, Education, and Welfare, which would later become what we now know as HHS (Miles, 1974). The agency was officially established in 1980 and at that time consisted of the Office of Human Development Services, the Public Health Service, Health Care Financing Administration, and the Social Security Administration. The Social Security Administration became independent of HHS in 1995.

HHS incorporates 11 divisions instrumental in providing research, education, and services to assist the public, including the National Institutes of Health (NIH), Centers for Disease Control and Prevention (CDC), Centers for Medicare and Medicaid Services (CMS), the Food and Drug Administration (FDA), the Agency for Healthcare Research and Quality (AHRQ), and the Health Resources and Services Administration (HRSA) (U.S. DHHS, n.d.-b). Each division is overseen by the Office of the Secretary, which comprises the assistant and deputy secretaries, directors, counselors, and the Surgeon General.

National Institutes of Health

NIH is the health and medical research agency for the nation. NIH is the leader of researching chronic illnesses, disease prevention, and acute diseases. It also is responsible for training researchers and scientists to foster further developments in fighting disease. NIH consists of 27 specialized institutes, including the National Cancer Institute (NCI) and the National Institute of Nursing Research (NINR).

National Cancer Institute

NCI was established by the National Cancer Institute Act of 1937, which was the first time the government allocated funding toward research for a noncommunicable disease (NCI, 2015). The act not only empowered NCI to conduct research but also gave it the responsibility of expanding research to the rest of the nation through education, grants, and mentoring. Since its inception, NCI has become the leading resource for dissemination of cancer research.

National Institute of Nursing Research

Despite that nurses have always made up the largest portion of healthcare providers in the nation, NINR was not established until 1985 (NINR, n.d.). NINR focuses efforts toward nursing research, funding, and training for nursing science. It is committed to enhancing evidence for disease prevention, chronic diseases, palliative care, and clinical practice. It historically has received the lowest allocation of funds compared to the other NIH institutes.

Centers for Disease Control and Prevention

CDC is "the nation's health protection agency" and is tasked with preventing disease and promoting health (CDC, 2014). The agency was established in 1946 as the Communicable Disease Center during the malaria outbreak to control the spread in the United States. Soon after, CDC expanded its role in public health and purchased a facility from Emory University in Atlanta, Georgia, where it is still housed today (CDC, 2015). The agency is still charged with prevention of injury, but the role now also focuses on health preparedness in a disaster and against bioterrorism. Each year since 1998, CDC in conjunction with other agencies produces the *Annual Report to the Nation on the Status of Cancer.* This report is extremely valuable to monitor disease patterns and morbidity and mortality of the cancer epidemic, and it is used to modify public health efforts to reduce incidence in vulnerable populations.

Centers for Medicare and Medicaid Services

CMS was established in 1965 as the agency to regulate and monitor the nation's healthcare system in response to the passage of Medicare and Medicaid by President Johnson. Medicare and Medicaid combined account for the largest health insurance program in America, covering approximately 33% of all Americans. Medicare covers 47 million Americans, most of whom are aged 65 and older, on an annual budget of approximately $550 billion funded by income taxes (CMS, 2016). The Center for Medicaid and Children's Health Insurance Program Services (known as CMCS) is funded by national and state governments and was established to care for America's vulnerable populations, approximately 72 million, including impoverished adults, children, and pregnant women (CMS, 2016).

As part of the executive branch, CMS has several advisory councils to aid it in providing up-to-date and evidence-based coverage, including the Practicing Physicians Advisory Council, the Advisory Panel on Outpatient Hospital Payment, the Medicare Economic Index Technical Advisory Panel, the Advisory Panel on Outreach and Education, and the Medicare Evidence Development and Coverage Advisory Committee. Coverage for certain procedures, medications, and services is influenced by these advisory committees, made up of experts in science, economics, public health, medicine, healthcare data, and medical ethics. They meet publicly on a regular basis to hear testimony on topics of interest and review the current state of the science regarding items that are to be covered by CMS. In turn, they provide guidance to the policy makers at CMS. The agency has also increased its transparency to the public and encourages public comments on upcoming changes.

Food and Drug Administration

FDA was first established in 1906 with the enactment of the Pure Food and Drug Act. The agency is charged with protecting Americans by regulating pharmaceutical, food, and biologic products, as well as products that emit radiation (U.S. FDA, 2016). It is responsible for regulating tobacco in all forms. It works closely with NIH, NCI, and the Surgeon General to educate the public on the harms of tobacco. It is responsible for the changes in warnings on packaging, the prohibition of sales and marketing to minors, and the delivery of tobacco products. FDA also has a council of stakeholders, including physicians and psychiatrists, that provide feedback on research and new information regarding products containing tobacco. New drug development is also highly regulated by FDA through a rigorous process to determine the effectiveness and efficacy of the medication. Companies claiming usefulness of a drug for use outside of its approved indications also must complete a strict regulatory process.

Agency for Healthcare Research and Quality

AHRQ was established by the Omnibus Budget Reconciliation Act of 1989 (42 U.S.C.A. § 299 et seq.). Its mission is to "produce evidence to make health care safer, higher quality, more accessible, equitable, and affordable" (AHRQ, 2017). Originally called the Agency for

Health Care Policy and Research, it was expanded and renamed AHRQ in 1999. That same year, the Institute of Medicine (now called the Health and Medicine Division of the National Academies of Sciences, Engineering, and Medicine) published *To Err Is Human* (Kohn, Corrigan, & Donaldson, 2000), a report that significantly shaped the direction of quality research and further validated the need for such an agency. AHRQ also is responsible for Consumer Assessment of Healthcare Providers and Systems, which surveys health consumers about their healthcare experiences to improve patient interactions with health care. Evidence-based clinical effectiveness and quality health care is a standard in nursing practice, and AHRQ provides research, tools, education, and resources to help healthcare providers reduce waste and prevent harm.

Health Resources and Services Administration

HRSA is another important agency within HHS that is responsible for providing access to vulnerable populations and building the healthcare workforce through education and scholarships (HRSA, n.d.). HRSA also is responsible for the national organ and bone marrow transplant program, along with poison control.

National Academies of Sciences, Engineering, and Medicine

The National Academies of Sciences, Engineering, and Medicine was established as the National Scientific Academy by President Lincoln in 1863 as a neutral advisory resource to provide expert opinion based on research of scientific affairs (National Academy of Sciences, n.d.). The Health and Medicine Division, formerly known as the Institute of Medicine, focuses on health issues facing the nation and beyond. The Academies host forums that bring together experts and stakeholders to provide dialogue and an arena to share information pertinent to the topic at hand. The Institute of Medicine's (2011) report *The Future of Nursing: Leading Change, Advancing Health* has helped nurse advocates strengthen their platform for advanced nursing education, quality nursing care, and nursing autonomy.

Policy Institutes

Policy institutes, also known as think tanks, are independent research organizations that focus on scientific, social, and political issues. They can be a very useful resource for current events, special population research, and policy analysis. Most think tanks are nonprofit organizations; however, many are skewed by political affiliations with conservative or liberal interpretations of information. Policy institutes often are generated to investigate a specific topic of interest that is concerning to one party or group. The Kaiser Family Foundation is an example of a think tank that has been instrumental in providing information and education on healthcare reform.

Public Policy Process

Comedian and writer Woody Allen is generally given credit for saying, "80% of life is showing up." There is a great deal to this expression, particularly when it comes to public policy advocacy. The first step is being there. Just being part of the team, being able to have your organization's face in front of decision makers, is important.

The Aha! Moment

Not every organization has full representation in Washington, DC. Many groups were established far from the nation's capital without any inclination to leverage their membership's expertise with policy makers. Legislative and regulatory issues were far from the top of their agendas when contemplating their organizational missions.

Connecting With Elected Officials

Then, one day, something happens that directly affects their membership's ability to successfully complete their goals. Sitting around a boardroom, someone says, "Let's call our Congressman!", and the process begins. These days, reaching out to an elected official is relatively easy. They are ubiquitous. U.S. representatives give out their cell phone numbers, senators text, and these days presidential candidates tweet! Politicians are trying to break through the clutter and receive media coverage like any celebrity. Their offices strive to both be in the forefront of a potential voter's mind and to complete any mundane task—pothole or street lamp repair, passport clearance—that a constituent may request. All elected officials have official websites, and people can search the Internet for their office information. There are both Washington, DC, offices on Capitol Hill, and state and district offices close to the voters. These are fully staffed, and most representatives make a concerted effort to be local and approachable in their home districts.

Making an appointment to meet your elected officials, or their staff, is merely a telephone call away. Be prepared, but it is fine to have more questions than answers. Remember, not only do you have the right to ask for assistance, but also most offices are interested in how they can demonstrate expertise and ability to help cut through the clutter for a constituent.

You've made the appointment. You've arrived with your folder of information on the issue. You've researched your agenda and are ready to make the request. The best advice is this: make the actual request. Before leaving the office, actually make sure you propose a formal request of the elected official. Too many people leave, thinking the conversation went well, the staff was encouraging, and the information was well received. That is not the same thing as actually making the request, so be sure to ask. The follow-up after the meeting is where the work begins. Be prepared to have a one-page document to leave with your elected official that states your key talking points and contact information. Part of the ask is a specific date or timeline for follow-up.

Everyone Else Is Doing It

Once an organization enters the arena, there is a better understanding of the environment. Sometimes it is challenging to carve out a specific space; other times it appears a little easier when there is a vacuum. Learn from other organizations that have an established presence in the political arena. Many organizations are willing to partner with nursing because of our trustworthy reputation. Being involved is the first step.

Richard Nixon often quoted President Theodore Roosevelt when referring to activism. In a speech delivered at the Sorbonne in Paris, France, on April 23, 1910, Roosevelt said,

> It is not the critic who counts; not the man who points out how the strong man stumbles, or where the doer of deeds could have done them better. The credit belongs to the man who is actually in the arena, whose face is marred by dust and sweat and blood; who strives valiantly; who errs, who comes short again and again, because there is no effort without error and shortcoming; but who does actually strive to do the deeds; who knows great enthusiasms, the great devotions; who spends himself in a worthy cause; who at the best knows

in the end the triumph of high achievement, and who at the worst, if he fails, at least fails while daring greatly, so that his place shall never be with those cold and timid souls who neither know victory nor defeat. (Almanac of Theodore Roosevelt, n.d.)

Advocacy can often be like a boxing match. Throwing jabs, taking punches, bobbing and weaving to avoid getting hit and maneuvering to a potentially better position. That is part of the reference to being in the "arena"—actually being there is important. Those engaged in the discussion have a far better chance of changing the situation than those sitting on the sidelines waiting, hoping for others to take up their cause. Nurses are advocates by personality, as well as by profession. We are constantly interacting with the healthcare system on behalf of patients, peers, or some other entity to change the environment for the better. Many nurses do not think of themselves as advocates, but they certainly are in their daily activities. It comes with the job, but it stays with the person.

Marathon, Not a Sprint

From the American Nurses Association to the smallest of affinity groups, organizations attempt to motivate and mobilize their membership. Public policy is always a difficult department in which to garner support. People are put off by politics. They are enraged by what they perceive as either a fixed game or a no-win scenario. The process is also intimidating. There are a lot of rules and bureaucratic barriers to real change. The system is methodical, or worse, it appears arbitrary. The entire experience is daunting and exhausting. But it can be exhilarating, especially when you get a win.

Annually, the Nursing Organizations Alliance sponsors a program that exposes nurses to the public policy process in Washington, called the Nurse in Washington Internship. This unique experience provides onsite education that provides nurses with the tools to influence legislation. Objectives include identifying legislation, interacting with lawmakers, understanding the policy practice, and visiting with the legislators. This opportunity is open to any nurse at any career level.

At annual meetings or events held in Washington, DC, societies take the opportunity to arrange what are known as Capitol Hill Days. These education and advocacy training days teach members what to do when they visit their federal representatives. It is a wonderful experience but can be foreign and off-putting if the member is not prepared. The training sessions teach the organizational member how to act, what to say, and why the system works as it does. Members leave thrilled that they made an impact, and often they do. But a single meeting, even if it is an annual one, does not a convert make. Not for the advocate, and certainly not for those to whom the organization has advocated. That is why follow-up work after the meeting—thank-you notes, emails, phone calls, district meetings—are so important. Meeting in Washington with a congressional staff is not the end of the process, but the beginning.

Squeaky Wheel

Everyone knows that the squeaky wheel gets the oil. While that is not exactly true in politics, it does help to be announced. Elected officials are concerned with many issues, but those that are brought to their attention, allowing them to take the lead and receive credit, tend to move up the list of priorities.

Nurses continue to be the most trusted American professionals according to a national Gallup poll (Gallup, 2015). This intrinsic trust allows nurses to be regarded as unbiased providers of information—a powerful tool when acting as a resource to decision makers. Policy professionals, opinion leaders, and elected officials have agendas. They are trying to move those forward and make a difference in the process and the outcome. When specific constituencies come forward with aligned priorities and are willing to help advocate for similar goals, the process becomes more engaging.

There is an African adage that says, "If you want to go fast, go alone, but if you want to go far, go together." This adage fits well with public policy advocacy work.

Powerful voices can make a difference, but often they simply make noise. But like-minded groups working together to accomplish a similar goal, such as a piece of legislation or some federal regulatory reform, have a broader base from which to bring people together. Larger, louder voices have a greater chance at achieving the desired results.

Coalition work requires coordination, setting the agenda, convening the meetings or calls, and agreeing to speak as one voice. While it might seem simple, it often means acquiescing your organization's voice for the greater good. Nurses work in health care and advocate for broad healthcare reform. This can be for the patient rather than for any one healthcare provider. When this happens, different providers accept the principle that patient-centeredness is a better message to send to policy leaders than any single provider and possible alternatives to the system for that group. Too often, "special interests" are perceived as negative because they seem to have undue influence with decision makers. Nurses do not have that particular problem, as polling suggests that nurses are trusted. This is the greatest leverage any group can have in the public policy environment. Nurses need to learn to use their powerful positive reputation to achieve their agendas.

Gathering those voices to send a message about a single specific change or addition to public policy is challenging, but powerful. When an issue such as health care, nursing workforce investment, or biomedical research for better treatment and care is brought to the attention of elected officials by nurses, it resonates. There are nurses in every congressional district across the country. Nurses vote, nurses speak, nurses act. They are activists by personality, as well as by profession. Being engaged in the process is the first step, and continuing to reach out to congressional offices, senate aides, and candidates resonates. It is that regular reminder that allows nurses to be thought of as a resource.

Being a Respected Voice

Part of the nurse's reputation is that it comes from a place of caring. The nurse is the provider who is closest to the patient. One oncology nurse has said,

> Nursing is more than a job. It is a commitment of opportunity in which there is constant change and daily decision making, and where continued education is not an option but a must. I cannot think of a better career choice than nursing. If you are looking for a career that is absorbing, stimulating, and rewarding, nursing is a field that might interest you. Many times you are taking care of people who are at the lowest point in their lives. The chance to make a difference in that life is an awesome experience. There are days I come home physically and emotionally exhausted, but thinking about making a difference for someone else makes it all worthwhile. It's what keeps me in nursing. One of my nursing instructors once told me that the satisfaction and rewards that come from nursing must come from within. I couldn't agree more. I once thought nursing was a gift that I had given myself, but after 17 years of nursing, I believe that it was a gift given to me.

Although many nurses may not consider themselves leaders, they are. Some quietly, some more loudly. The image of nurses in popular culture is diverse, but the underlying idea is that the nurse is an activist and powerful voice for those in need. That makes them leaders, whether they think of themselves as such or not. Leadership has many roles but is defined by two points: first, "personify the shared values," and second, "teach others to model the values" (Kouzes & Posner, 2007, p. 76). Nurses do these very things.

In scrubs or with a white hat and a red cross, the nurse "personifies" patient care. These symbols are immediately recognizable and provide assurance and relief for all involved in patient care. From provider to patient, from family member to care coordinator, the nurse's role is understood and accepted.

Nurses also teach others to model their values in their care and education of the patient. Similar expertise can be provided in advocacy as well. Too often, nurses will say they are not comfortable in the policy environment. However, once they make that leap and advocate for a cause, it becomes instinctual for them. It is part of the way nurses think and the processes that guide them to define the issue, provide examples, and make recommendations based on evidence for real change. It is the personal story, the journey, and the lived experience that helps shape health policy advocacy for the nurse.

Advocacy as an Art, Practiced as a Science

Unlike chemistry, physics, or biology, public policy advocacy is not a one-to-one formula. An advocate can do all the right things and not achieve the desired results. Conversely, that same advocate can do many of the wrong things and ultimately be successful in changing policy. Good lobbying is about giving the right people the right information at the right time. There are many moving parts, and often the environment sets the agenda and is guided by external factors having nothing to do with the issue at hand whatsoever.

Too often, the many faces of politics play an overpowering role in advancing or thwarting policy. A budget should not be considered a financial document, but a political one. It is a list of priorities that the federal government chooses to fund and at different levels from year to year. How and where the president or Congress allocates funding is based on the political priorities of their respective political party or branch of government. Healthcare and biomedical research may be high on that list, mentioned in an annual State of the Union address one year, and completely absent the following year, as international affairs take precedent. Shifting environments create shifting budgetary priorities. Good advocates will understand this and will make policy recommendations with this in mind.

Connections to elected officials certainly help. But for the rest of us, working the system and being involved as trusted resources for information is important. Assisting or campaigning for candidates and elected officials does make a difference. It is how a person or issue is known. Last-minute requests for major shifts in public policy do not necessarily work. Washington, DC, does not work like an operating room. Change is more methodical; it takes time, but it can be done.

Tips, Steps, and Plans

All of this is easy to talk about in the abstract, but how does a nurse effect the kind of real change in policy through advocacy that positively affects what happens with an individual patient? Oddly, it is quite similar.

- *Identify the problem:* Probably the easiest steps are to assess a situation, determine that the current state of affairs is not working correctly, and identify what steps need to be taken to change the situation or problem. Federal reimbursement issues top this list. Almost all healthcare providers will agree that time and money are integral parts of the system that could be changed to better serve all parties. Some are currently covered by CMS and others are not. Take the issue to a member of Congress and convince them to champion the cause.

- *Connect with the right people:* Finding a member of Congress to take the lead on any issue may seem easier than it is. Politics can get in the way. Several determining factors should be analyzed (Whelan & Woody, 2012). Is your member of Congress the right person for this issue? Does he or she sit on the appropriate committee of jurisdiction, have a large constituency in the home district to demand support, have enough clout and seniority on Capitol Hill to move the potential legislation along? Will negotiations be necessary to advance the legislation, while still adhering to the original principles of the proposed change? For a national organization, finding a champion shouldn't be difficult, as members are in every district. Use the vast network already in place to accomplish support.

- *Mobilize supporters:* Within every national membership organization, better and more discrete files are being kept. Once a potential member of Congress is selected, gather support within that elected official's state or district and request a meeting to introduce the issue. There is power in numbers, and showing that the state or district has a large constituency of nurses interested in a single issue will get attention from the staff and the official.

- *Offer expert advice:* Nurses are already seen as positive resources with little negative baggage associated with their work. Take this strong reputation, starting at a very high level, and use it to influence decision makers. Provide facts and figures on the cost of patients in the current situation and in the proposed change. Use comparison statistics, numbers, charts, and graphs. Don't forget to bring in the personal elements of a story—the people, the disease, the treatment. All of these factors play a part in the influence process. Certainly, for requests of immediate action, providing information is important. But for a long-term level of influence, being a trusted resource is essential. That call may not come today or tomorrow, but in the future an elected official's office will reach out and ask for insight into an issue based on the meeting they had with you. As a nurse, you are an expert and are perceived that way. It is one of your most important tools in advocacy.

- *Redesign the program:* A nurse who was advocating on Capitol Hill once said that as a nurse, she sees a problem, fixes a problem, and then moves on to the next problem. That does not happen in public policy. It might take years to get to a point to be able to change a policy. During that time, coalitions form and disband, political parties rise and fall, presidential administrations turn over. An advocate must be prepared for these eventualities. If the environment shifts, change the plan. The occasion may call for you to adjust your ask, and alter your proposal. Sometimes it works to go broad; sometimes it works to be more specific. Whatever the case, don't be afraid to reevaluate the target internally. Don't violate your own principles and ultimate goals, but be aware that what might have worked yesterday will not necessarily work today, and vice versa.

- *Continue the treatment:* I am sure you have heard the adage "If it ain't broke, don't fix it." Being a trusted and unbiased adviser is a great resource for any profession, and nursing is one of the few that fall into that category. "Often a lobbyist's best technique is simply to provide accurate information, either directly to a legislator or at a subcommittee hearing. The credibility gained gives the lobbyist more influence in arguing his or her point of view" (Cohn, 1991, p. 137).

These tips may seem obvious, but working the plan is how to make a difference. Strategize, advance the issue, and reevaluate when necessary. Campaigns are often referred to as wars, but they can just as easily be seen as healthcare treatment, with triage, wait-and-watch, survival rates, and readmissions as the focal points. Making the issue relatable is the best practice for success.

Review of Healthcare Reform

Health care is arguably the most important domestic issue for the past decade and likely into the future and continues to be on the minds of the American people. The World Health Organization's (2017) Global Health Expenditure Database reported that the United States' percentage of gross domestic product spent on public and private health expenditures was at or near 17% for the years 1996–2015, which reflects the highest in the world.

As the economy undulates, concerns continue to loom about the rising costs of health care. As a broad category, health care encompasses a variety of worries about the future. The quality of care, the cost of coverage, and the extent to which an individual should receive care are elements destined to keep health care at the top of the national political debate.

The Patient Protection and Affordable Care Act, enacted into law March 23, 2010, by President Obama, was the most significant law designed to reform the U.S. healthcare system since the Medicare and Medicaid enactment by President Johnson in 1965. The act had three primary goals: (a) to increase the quality and affordability, (b) to reduce the rate of uninsured in the United States by expanding public and private insurance coverage, and (c) to reduce healthcare costs for individuals at the state and national levels (Kaiser Family Foundation, 2013). Since its enactment, the Affordable Care Act has generated mixed reviews by the American public. The political divides continue to rage. The passage of the law has, to date, withstood two Supreme Court rulings as to its constitutionality. The Affordable Care Act continues to be political and will likely be so in the future.

Historical Journey to Healthcare Reform in America: Yesterday, Today, Tomorrow

Some may think of mandatory healthcare coverage as a relatively new idea. Today, the goal is to cover as many people as possible to even out the potentially high costs of health care for all. Those with healthcare coverage are paying higher costs to make up for those who do not have coverage yet continue to use the healthcare system. Benjamin Franklin was quoted as saying, "There is nothing certain except death and taxes." A similar idiom can be said about the inevitability of health, illness, and death. Because people are not going to stop getting sick or dying, those without coverage will continue to use emergency departments and providers, using either self-pay for those costs or not paying at all. This is not an effective or sustainable system. Providing opportunities for full or partial healthcare coverage for all has been a political and policy discussion for more than 20 years. From President Clinton to President Obama's Affordable Care Act, variations on care have been and continue to be dominating campaign issues.

Going back a bit more, the first U.S. Congress in 1790 "enacted a law requiring owners of ships of more than 150 tons to buy medical insurance for their seamen" (Emanuel, 2014, p. 127). So, if this was mandatory more than 225 years ago, why is there still so much angst about coverage now?

In 1955, and each subsequent congressional session after that, U.S. Representative John Dingell, a Democrat from Michigan, introduced the National Health Insurance Act to provide universal health care. It was frequently introduced in the U.S. Senate by Ted Kennedy, but it never got very far. President Johnson signed Medicare and Medicaid into law in the 1960s, giving expanded coverage to millions of Americans. This piecemeal coverage was not universally endorsed but has become a way of life, and few Americans would suggest it be altered now. By most accounts, covering children, the poor, and senior citizens with minimal health care is now a right as much as it is a privilege. Expanding the pool continues to be a contentious issue.

By 1993, in his first year as president, Bill Clinton convened an ad hoc committee headed by his wife, Hillary Clinton, and a colleague, Ira Magaziner (Emanuel, 2014). After meeting for 18 months, they unveiled their plan with core elements including health alliances to combine and coordinate insurance coverage for businesses and individuals and the requirement for employers to provide health insurance to all their employees. It seemed to be moving in the right direction with support, but the insurance industry was not in favor of the new plan (Emanuel, 2014). In a series of ads dubbed "Harry and Louise," a middle-class couple sat in their living room and discussed the confusing options and the bureaucratic role in deciding their insurance coverage. No one would be interested in that, and along with a host of other political scandals by members of Congress, the healthcare bill struggled to gain any real traction.

Ultimately, because of several factors of bad political judgment and timing, the bill did not pass. However, with the help of Senator Ted Kennedy, the Clinton administration was able to pass legislation that created the Children's Health Insurance Plan (CHIP) in 1997. "The program is modeled on Medicaid: it is jointly funded by the federal government and states, administered by states, and the children receive Medicaid-like benefits. Today CHIP covers approximately 8 million children, but it is not universal coverage" (Emanuel, 2014, p. 155). It was an important first step though.

By the presidential election of 2008, the biggest issue was the sputtering economy. Most point to the effort to pass the American Recovery and Reinvestment Act (ARRA) as the catalyst to jump-start the economy again. ARRA's goal was to infuse the economy with much-needed cash and to spur investment to engage a more robust economic driver. Health care was still a dominant issue, but not the primary issue.

As the process began anew and health care was becoming a topic again, politics played a key role. A barrage of special interest groups made sure their narrow interests were included in what was to be known as the Affordable Care Act, or colloquially referred to as Obamacare. That is politics, and many were included. By late 2009 and early 2010, it looked like things were going to move a bit faster and the legislation would be considered.

However, "this may be the most important of all imperatives for legislation. Anytime a legislator demands that a bill be slowed down for more hearings or debate, you know they are trying to kill it" (Emanuel, 2014, p. 165). But, seeing an opening, the White House persisted and reiterated the phrase that "if you like your healthcare plan, you can keep it" to ensure that change was not going to be adverse to current coverage. Working in coalitions and with the health and medical community, something not previously done, President Obama was able to secure the American Medical Association's endorsement of a healthcare plan. Finally, in March 2010, President Obama signed the Affordable Care Act into law. It has withstood two Supreme Court challenges and efforts by a Republican-controlled Congress to overturn it. The Affordable Care Act is now the law of the land, but only because of a plethora of political maneuverings and the help of a great deal of outside forces pushing to keep it in place. The drive to repeal, replace, or repair the Affordable Care Act may continue to loom in politics for some time to come. The foundational principle is providing affordable healthcare for American citizens.

Summary

The future calls for nurse leaders to commit to advocating on any level, including within their institutions and local, state, and national government. The nursing voice, which ultimately represents the voice of the patients, often is missing in many conversations regarding health care. Nurse leaders should be the continuous voice of the underserved, marginalized, and vulnerable populations to bring forth important issues related to access and safety of patients who need health care. Some of the actions may include the other side of issues important to nurses, such as workforce shortages, an aging workforce, and gaps in nurse-led cancer research. The issues close to our hearts should be on the minds of those enacting legislation because so few of them have ever seen the challenges that nurses witness every day while providing care to patients.

The opening for more nurse leaders to seize the opportunity to move from silence to voice in healthcare advocacy is upon us. Nurses are proven leaders as elected officials in local, state, and national government. There is room for many more to step into elected positions to be the voice at the table for improved health care for all. One voice and one vote can make a difference. This is your time, as a nurse leader, to step up and let your vote count and your advocacy voice be heard. When you are at the table, you can make a difference.

When it comes to the things that are worth advocating about, the list can be summed up in the quote by Ruben Hinojosa (n.d.), former U.S. representative for Texas: "At their core, Americans all want the same basic things: a quality education for their children, a good job so they can provide for their families, healthcare and affordable prescription drugs, security during retirement, a strongly equipped military and national security."

References

Agency for Healthcare Research and Quality. (2017, April). About AHRQ. Retrieved from http://www.ahrq.gov/cpi/about/index.html

Almanac of Theodore Roosevelt. (n.d.). Roosevelt, T. (1910, April 23). The man in the arena. Excerpt from the speech "Citizenship in a Republic," delivered at the Sorbonne, in Paris, France on 23 April, 1910. Retrieved from http://www.theodore-roosevelt.com/trsorbonnespeech.html

Centers for Disease Control and Prevention. (2014). Mission, role and pledge. Retrieved from https://www.cdc.gov/about/organization/mission.htm

Centers for Disease Control and Prevention. (2015). Our history—Our story. Retrieved from https://www.cdc.gov/about/history/ourstory.htm

Centers for Medicare and Medicaid Services. (2016, March). About CMS. Retrieved from https://www.cms.gov/About-CMS/About-CMS.html

Cohn, M. (Ed.). (1991). *How Congress works* (2nd ed.). Washington, DC: Congressional Quarterly.

Emanuel, E.J. (2014). *Reinventing American health care: How the Affordable Care Act will improve our terribly complex, blatantly unjust, outrageously expensive, grossly inefficient, error prone system.* New York, NY: Public Affairs.

Freeman, J.B. (n.d.). Jefferson and Hamilton, political rivals in Washington's cabinet. Retrieved from http://www.mountvernon.org/george-washington/the-first-president/washingtons-presidential-cabinet/jefferson-and-hamilton-political-rivals

Gallup. (2015). Gallup Poll on most trusted professions, December 2–6, 2015. Retrieved from http://www.gallup.com/poll/1654/Honesty-Ethics-Professions.aspx

Health Resources and Services Administration. (n.d.). About HRSA. Retrieved from https://www.hrsa.gov/about

Hinojosa, R. (n.d.). Advocacy quote. Retrieved from http://www.searchquotes.com/quotation/At_their_core%2C_Americans_all_want_the_same_basic_things%3A_a_quality_education_for_their_children%2C_a_g/118616

Institute of Medicine. (2011). *The future of nursing: Leading change, advancing health.* Washington, DC: National Academies Press.

Kaiser Family Foundation. (2013, April 25). Summary of the Affordable Care Act. Retrieved from http://kff.org/health-reform/fact-sheet/summary-of-the-affordable-care-act

Kohn, L.T., Corrigan, J.M., & Donaldson, M.S. (Eds.). (2000). *To err is human: Building a safer health system.* Washington, DC: National Academies Press.

Kouzes, J.M., & Posner, B.Z. (2007). *The leadership challenge* (4th ed.). San Francisco, CA: Jossey-Bass.

Ladd, E.C. (1985). *The American polity: The people and their government.* New York, NY: W.W. Norton and Co.

Miles, R.E. (1974). *The Department of Health, Education, and Welfare.* New York, NY: Praeger.

National Academy of Sciences. (n.d.). About NAS: History. Retrieved from http://www.nasonline.org/about-nas/history

National Cancer Institute. (2015, March 18). History of the National Cancer Institute. Retrieved from https://www.cancer.gov/about-nci/overview/history

National Institute of Nursing Research. (n.d.). About NINR: History. Retrieved from https://www.ninr.nih.gov/aboutninr/history

U.S. Const. amend. I.

U.S. Department of Health and Human Services. (n.d.-a). About HHS. Retrieved from http://www.hhs.gov/about/index.html

U.S. Department of Health and Human Services. (n.d.-b). HHS agencies and offices. Retrieved from https://www.hhs.gov/about/agencies/hhs-agencies-and-offices/index.html

U.S. Food and Drug Administration. (2016, March). About FDA. Retrieved from http://www.fda.gov/AboutFDA/default.htm

Whelan, E.-M., & Woody, M.P. (2012). Lobbying policymakers: Individual and collective strategies. In D.J. Mason, J.K. Leavitt, & M.W. Chafee (Eds.), *Policy and politics in nursing and health care* (6th ed., pp. 59–526). St. Louis, MO: Elsevier Saunders.

White House. (n.d.-a). The executive branch. Retrieved from https://www.whitehouse.gov/1600/executive-branch

White House. (n.d.-b). The judicial branch. Retrieved from https://www.whitehouse.gov/1600/judicial-branch

White House. (n.d.-c). The legislative branch. Retrieved from https://www.whitehouse.gov/1600/legislative-branch

World Health Organization. (2017). Global Health Expenditure Database. Retrieved from http://apps.who.int/nha/database

CHAPTER 19

Leading Clinical Nurse Engagement in Research

Nancy M. Albert, PhD, CCNS, CHFN, CCRN, NE-BC, FAHA, FCCM, FHFSA, FAAN

Nothing has such power to broaden the mind as the ability to investigate systematically and truly all that comes under thy observation in life.

—Marcus Aurelius Antoninus

Research is formalized curiosity. It is poking and prying with a purpose.

—Zora Neale Hurston, *Dust Tracks on a Road*

Introduction

Clinical nurse engagement in clinical research is important to the foundation of nursing science and also to clients, who expect delivery of high-quality, safe nursing care. Improvements in prevention and control of medical and nursing problems and in delivery and evaluation of population health require implementation research experiences (synthesis and data translation of published research that leads to evidence-based decision making) and implementation of clinical nurse-led pragmatic and idealistic research. Although awareness and agreement has increased among nurse leaders that evidence-based nursing practices are an integral component of optimal clinical outcomes and enhanced nursing efficiencies, there is a great need to move beyond awareness toward actions that include using and translating research and conducting nurse-led research.

What Is Known About Clinical Nurse Engagement in Research?

As a nurse leader (regardless of whether your title and roles reflect a formal leadership position), it is important to understand the current state of nurse engagement in research based on published findings and then complete a well-rounded assessment of the current state in one's own setting. An objective understanding of personal and health system strengths, barriers/weaknesses, opportunities, and threats related to engagement in research will create the backdrop for developing realistic solutions that can position the nursing team for success.

Using and Translating Research Into Practice

The literature contains many papers that reported barriers to using research in nursing practices. Commonly cited barriers included lack of access to research, lack of knowledge and skills in how to find and interpret research, unfamiliarity with the research process, lack of mentorship, insufficient time (Brown, Wickline, Ecoff, & Glaser, 2009; Chan et al., 2011; Gifford, Davies, Edwards, Griffin, & Lybanon, 2007; Oh, 2008; Silka, Stombaugh, Horton, & Daniels, 2012), lack of support from supervisors and leaders, lack of resources, and lack of collaboration by other nurses (Cummings, Estabrooks, Midodzi, Wallin, & Hayduk, 2007; Kajermo et al., 2008). Moreover, when nurses encounter organizational, social, political, environmental, and subject knowledge barriers, it is likely that growth in using and translating research may become an even bigger challenge.

Rather than assessing barriers, some investigators have sought to learn strengths. In a systematic review and meta-analysis to learn what strategies were used for promoting evidence-based behaviors from quantitative and qualitative data knowledge, researchers found that the most common bundled intervention involved education and use of a mentor (Yost et al., 2015). Yet, authors of the meta-analysis found that education and mentorship interventions were not effective in leading to self-reported changes in evidence-based practice behaviors. Of the other interventions studied by Yost et al. (2015), most were highly variable, and many had very low to moderate effect sizes, making it impossible to determine their value. Thus, even with education and use of a mentor, nurses may not understand how to transfer research knowledge into practice.

In another report on diffusion of a research intervention into practice, sites that were more successful in performing the complexities of research practice had strong leadership, good managerial relations, higher readiness for change, and a culture of staff training and staff time (availability) to complete processes (McMullen, Griffiths, Leber, & Greenhalgh, 2015). Further, the frontline staff recognized the benefit of the intervention, were emotionally comfortable carrying out the steps of the procedure, felt they were skilled in performing steps of the procedure, and were able to adapt the procedure in a way that led to embedding it in local working practices. Once the team gained early experiences, they became even more committed to recruiting participants (McMullen et al., 2015).

Based on available literature, many lessons learned can be globally transferrable to nurse leaders. Leaders with strong communication networks and good relationships with local managers, and local managers with the right resources to implement research findings, will be more likely to find success. When a good fit exists between the individual components of research to be translated and the team who is responsible for carrying out the steps (readiness for translating research), performance may be higher. When caregivers truly understand the benefits of the process to be implemented, are able to make local customizations, and receive leadership support and team feedback, success will be higher. Most important to understand from the literature is that translating interventions into practice may be complex and, even when seemingly simple, may take multiple steps to successfully integrate into current practice. Ultimately, nurse leader communication, resources, and supportive actions are integral to successful translation of research into practice.

Conducting Nursing Research

Very few research studies have addressed nurses' knowledge, attitudes, and behaviors toward the conduct of nursing research. Instead, nearly all studies targeted barriers to using and translating existing research. In one survey research study, nurses identified three significant barriers to conducting research: lack of time, lack of funding or compensation, and not knowing how to get started or being overwhelmed with the process of research. Two other common barriers to conducting research were colleagues' resistance to change and lack of mentorship (Silka et al., 2012). In a study of clinical nurse specialists' perceptions about conducting research, the majority did not conduct research as part of their work. Prominent barriers were lack of access to resources and lack of knowledge of statistics and research processes (Albert et al., 2016). In another report of hospital-based clinical nurse specialists, having a framework to carry out the research role was the only structure-related factor of importance. In addition, study participants cited years in their role as a factor related to conducting research (Kilpatrick, Tchouaket, Carter, Bryant-Lukosius, & DiCenso, 2016). If clinical nurse specialists, who have training and skills in conducting and using research, cite structure and knowledge as principal barriers to conducting research, it is no wonder that clinical nurses require support in terms of people resources, structure resources, and system and process resources. To advance clinical nurse engagement in research, nurse leaders must be able to speak to the value of clinical nurse engagement in research. In addition, they must provide meaningful support of research utilization and ensure that processes, structures, and systems that promote the conduct of research are developed, maintained, and nurtured.

Value of Encouraging and Guiding Clinical Nurse Engagement in Research

Nurse leaders recognize that there is a need for clinical nurses to strive for excellence in client care activities and that high-quality, evidence-based practices are dependent on many interactive and complementary factors, including engagement in research. Nurse leaders need to facilitate clinical nurses' understanding of evidence that informs clinical practice decision-making processes. It is not good enough for leaders and clinicians to assume that current nursing practices are evidence based, as foundational knowledge that led to current clinical practices is constantly changing as new evidence becomes available.

Nurse leaders should strategize and develop practical actions to encourage and guide their teams toward valuing research data, appraising literature for current evidence, and engaging in research. First, nurse leaders must make programs available that help clinical nurses learn how to critically appraise research evidence as a precursor to translating it into practice. Librarians and doctorate-prepared research nurses can educate leaders so that they understand expectations for their teams, including the time involved in appraising research literature. Once clinical nurses learn that high-quality evidence is available in the literature but that findings are disconnected from current nursing policies and procedures, they need to be able to take steps to translate research evidence into local practice. Nurse leaders need to be able to guide their teams to understand that translation of research into practice generally involves three options: (a) conducting *translational research* (also known as *implementation science*)—research aimed at promoting optimal, high-quality care practices, (b) revising or adding and then implementing institutional policies and procedures to match best practice evidence, or (c) developing quality improvement or practice change initiatives that lead to implementation of best practice evidence.

When nurses find evidence on a clinical practice topic to be low in strength (for example, case reports, expert opinions, and descriptive research) and quality (for example, research with methodologic or analysis issues and multiple limitations and biases), nurse leader support for engagement in the conduct of *idealistic or pragmatic research* can lead to development of new evidence that advances current practices and promotes excellence related to safe, high-quality care, optimal patient outcomes, and efficiencies in care delivery. Nurse leaders must understand and value the sequential, three-step processes that lead to best practices: first, critically appraising the evidence to determine the need to translate evidence from the literature or conduct new research; second, carrying out the steps of translating or conducting research; and third, using new knowledge derived from the translation or conduct of research as a precursor to implementing best practices. Ultimately, the parallel paths of using and translating research findings in practice and conducting research intertwine and promote the clinical outcomes nurse leaders strive for.

Nurse leaders can show that they value and support translating and conducting research in many ways. Residency programs for newly hired new-graduate nurses may include an evidence-based practice project that involves searching for current evidence on an issue or theme of interest, evaluating the strength and quality of current evidence, and developing a practice change or a plan of action aimed at advancing or improving current practices. Presentation of findings to nurse leaders creates awareness of the current state of clinical practice and modifiable gaps and disparities. For new nurses, an introduction to evidence-based practices increases awareness of research resources available and sets a foundation for future translation or conduct of research. Once developed and refined, the principles adopted in the residency program can be replicated for all hospital nurses if research and evidence-based practice time is included in operating budgets in a similar way that quality and education initiatives are budgeted.

The following three examples of completed hospital-based, nurse-led research provide a global reflection of nurse leader roles and the value of research evidence to nurse leaders in decision making.

Example 1: Low Strength of Available Evidence

Clinical nurses were asked by quality and safety physician leaders and pharmacists to develop a double-checking policy and procedure for insulin administration to decrease insulin administration errors, which are one of the most pervasive acute care hospital-based medication safety issues (Trief, Cibula, Rodriguez, Akel, & Weinstock, 2016). In a search of the literature, clinical nurses and diabetic and medical clinical nurse specialists learned that the benefits of a double-checking insulin administration procedure had not been studied other than to survey nurses. No objective data were available. The team consulted with a nurse researcher leader, who encouraged them in their desire to conduct a randomized controlled study to learn the value of embarking on a double-checking insulin administration policy and procedure. Leadership support included availability of a nurse researcher who provided mentorship in proposal development, analysis interpretation, and dissemination of findings. Biostatistician support and poster creation costs were covered by leadership, and time used to orient clinical nurses to research processes and collect data was covered under unit operating budgets. In analysis, the research team learned that the double-checking group had fewer insulin errors than the usual care group. However, the most frequent error, wrong time, would not be solved by a double-checking procedure. Further, the second most prevalent error, omitting insulin when it should have been given, would also not be alleviated by a double-checking procedure. In multivariable analyses in which the actual nurses who administered insulin or should have administered insulin were controlled, the only insulin error that differed significantly by group assignment was insulin omission errors (Modic et al., 2016). Because omission errors were not solved with a double-checking procedure, and because initiating and maintaining this policy and procedure would create work for clinical nurses but not create value for patients, the principal investigator and research mentor wanted nurse leaders to understand the research findings. After a presentation to chief and associate chief nursing officers within the health system, an evidence-based decision was made by leaders not to initiate a double-checking procedure for insulin administration. In this example, findings from a well-designed research study brought clarity to the value of a double-checking procedure for insulin administration. Nurse leaders saved dollars related to the cost of the procedure, based on nursing time. Research findings shifted attention from double-checking insulin administration to other initiatives that might decrease insulin administration errors.

Example 2: Low Strength and Quality of Available Evidence

The need to reduce hospital-acquired infections is at an all-time high since the Centers for Medicare and Medicaid Services began penalizing hospitals for poor performance in 2014 (Calderwood et al., 2016). Many nursing departments developed bundled programs to reduce the presence of microorganisms in the hope of reducing infections. Some companies began marketing disposable electrocardiographic lead wires to reduce the presence of bacteria after a report was published about the amount and types of bacteria present on cleaned, ready-to-use lead wires (Albert et al., 2010). However, presence of bacteria on inanimate objects was not equivalent to having hospital-acquired infections. The nurse manager and nurse researcher stakeholders met with the nursing director of the Heart and Vascular Institute to discuss next steps, because all options (switching from reusable to disposable electrocardiographic lead wires, completing new research, or continuing with the status quo) involved costs to clients, the hospital, or both. Prior to the meeting, stakeholders initiated discussions with a company to obtain financial support, primarily to provide disposable electrocardiographic lead wires. After receiving the clinical director's full support to conduct a randomized controlled study to learn if disposable lead wires reduced the incidence of infection among adults receiving care in medical, surgical, neuroscience, and cardiothoracic surgery intensive care units (ICUs), the study team obtained support from other clinical directors and all nurse managers of units targeted as data collection sites. After learning there were no between-group differences in infection outcomes (Albert et al., 2014), the study team met with the nurse leader, and a team decision was made to maintain reusable electrocardiographic lead wires. Nurse leaders and clinical nurses placed new attention on developing alternative interventions to decrease the risk of bacteremia infections. Further, nurse leaders and the nurse representative to the product evaluation committee used research findings in discussions with corporate partners and representatives.

Example 3: No Evidence Available at the Time of the Literature Review

In critical care, early exercise and mobility are part of the ABCDEF (Assess pain, Breathing trials, Choice of analgesia and sedation, Delirium assessment, Early mobility, and Family engagement) bundle, an evidence-based strategy to minimize critical care complications (Balas et al., 2013). Most research on early ambulation was conducted in adults who were recovering in medical and surgical ICUs. However, there were no reports on early mobility among critically ill patients with neurologic conditions. Nurse leaders, clinical nurses, and physicians in a neuroscience ICU were unsure if early ambulation would cause excess trauma or safety issues to adults with neurologic problems and intracranial pressure devices or drains. The unit's clinical nurse specialist and clinical director were eager to learn if early mobility could improve clinical outcomes and sought support from a nurse researcher. A translational research study was implemented using a two-phase approach. Prior to implementing an early mobility algorithm and intervention, data were collected based on usual care procedures (Mulkey, Bena, & Albert, 2014). After a four-month implementation period, data were collected again and analyses were conducted that compared clinical outcomes between groups. The team learned that early mobility and ambulation were safe and that hospital and ICU length of stays were decreased, and more patients were eventually discharged home (Klein, Mulkey, Bena, & Albert, 2015). Because reducing length of stay reduced throughput issues, patient complications, and cost of care, translational research findings were of great interest to nurse (and physician) leaders. Local nurse leaders promoted more extensive implementation of early mobility in the neuroscience ICU. An advanced practice nurse was given time and authority to revise the research algorithm into a clinical practice algorithm. The chief nursing officer and clinical director used the research findings to support the purchase of overhead lifts to facilitate the process of early mobility, and a team of nurse leaders worked collaboratively with physical therapy to purchase equipment to aid patients when ambulating.

Nurse leaders at every level should be interested in promoting outcomes of clinically led research if methods are high quality (reflecting few biases) and findings are widely generalizable. Top-level nurse leaders must encourage presentation of high-quality completed nursing research findings to the entire nursing leadership team. Research presenters should be prepared to respond to questions about research methods and results and should participate in leader discussions about resource utilization, cost savings, clinical improvements, client quality and safety, and clinical or administrative outcomes. Additionally, nurse leaders should share high-quality research findings with the chief financial, operating, human resources, and executive officers as a way of demonstrating nursing's commitment to optimal patient outcomes and global advancement of nursing practice.

Building Organizational Research Capacity

Excellence in client care activities includes an understanding of the need for novel interventions that are supported by research evidence. Support for research evidence becomes more apparent to clinical nurses when nurse leaders build an organizational research capacity. Elements and examples of organizational or nursing department–specific research capacity are discussed in the next two sections, along with chapter tables that highlight specific considerations, activities, and resources related to building this capacity. When clinical nurses utilize research resources and services, nurse leaders can expect to see growth in research engagement activities that promote excellence in client care. Further, nurses will be more likely to question clinical practices and determine their origins. Ultimately, organizational research capacity promotes opportunities to become involved in research, and research involvement leads to sustainable, replicable, and patient-centered outcomes that advance the foundation of nursing science and influence national nursing policy.

Leading Clinical Nurse Engagement in Using and Translating Research Evidence

Translation of new knowledge, even when knowledge is supported by high-quality scientific papers, is not a simple matter of communication and assessment of results. Because the process of translating new knowledge is often slow and complex, conceptual models are available to assist with navigation. Models provide great insights into the multiple overlapping, interlinked steps and systems needed to translate research into practice. Titler (2010) and Greenhalgh, Robert, Macfarlane, Bate, and Kyriakidou (2004) created models of principles of diffusion of innovation that facilitate translation of research into practice. Each is unique and offers a global view of linkages, multiple interfacing contexts, and an overall glimpse of a stepped approach to promoting translation of research into practice.

Titler's (2010) framework consists of four consecutive steps that build on each other. First, nurses must understand characteristics of the innovative intervention to be translated. Second, thorough communication of the intervention to all users and leaders is necessary to enhance buy-in and garner support. Once all users have received communication, nurses facilitating translation must determine the practical steps of implementation, such as orienting end users, developing policies and procedures, and developing systems and processes to ensure that implementation start-up occurs and is maintained. For example, a performance improvement metric might be created to monitor translation and communicate outcomes to users. The final step is adherence to new evidence. This is ultimately measured as the overall adoption rate (Titler, 2010).

In Greenhalgh et al.'s (2004) model, multiple complexities must be considered. System antecedents for innovation involve structure, absorptive capacity for new knowledge, and the context for receptiveness for change. System readiness for innovation involves the fit of the innovation within the system, power balances, the tension for change, and practical elements, such as resources and time availability to devote to translation, ability to monitor and provide feedback of implementation, and assessment of the implications of implementation. In addition to system antecedents and readiness, other system factors are adoption/assimilation, implementation processes (for example, frontline teams are able to make decisions, they have dedicated resources, and internal communication is consistent with the translation plan), and consequences (feedback on progress) that feed back into system antecedents.

Whether nurse leaders develop an evidence translation model or select a published model to guide local translation of evidence into practice, each step needs to be enhanced with details that answer whom to contact, what is needed to get started, and when in the process the next step can begin (when steps can be competed in parallel with other steps). Ultimately, clinical nurses should be able to use the model as a map or checklist. Nurse leaders should be advocates during the implementation phase of the steps of translation. They can remind nurses to be patient when progress is stalled and can recognize nurse perseverance and forward progress toward the goal. To gain momentum in diffusing new knowledge into practice, authors have advocated for interaction between actions, experiential knowledge, and public knowledge (mass media and stories from the field) to synthesize knowledge into practice, and they reminded readers that merely communicating with end users via education is not enough (Young & Borland, 2011). In the translation process, nurse leaders often are called on to create deadlines, make connections between work groups, provide background information to other leaders who can facilitate translation, suggest use of resources that minimize unnecessary work or maximize outcomes, and recognize translation progress, completion, or outcomes.

Because collaboration and iterative feedback are key processes in translating research, intervention research may facilitate translation (Phillips, Alfano, Perna, & Glasglow, 2014), as shown in example 3 of the value of encouraging and guiding clinical nurse engagement in research. When considering translating research into practice by conducting new research, leaders must recognize that the process might take longer than just implementing a change in practice, but there are great trade-offs. For example, implementation of a previous research intervention through a new translational research project (after the original research ends) may promote intervention implementation consistency that produces new outcomes that match previous research outcomes. Table 19-1 provides considerations of when to conduct research as a form of translation and when to use current research to implement practice changes within healthcare settings.

Table 19-1. Considerations for Translating Research Into Practice Within a Healthcare Setting

	Method	
Factor	**Conducting New Research**	**Implementing Change Processes**
Strength of previous research of practice	Limited strength due to lack of randomized controlled and multicenter research studies	Moderate to high strength of current evidence (at least 1 large, randomized, controlled study)
Quality of previous research of practice	Mixed or limited quality due to methodologic, analysis, or other research limitations	Moderate to high quality research based on published evidence; high expertise of principal investigator
Cost of practice (time, resources, physical space, etc.)	High for 1 or more	Low to moderate for most to all
Intensity of practice	High	Low to moderate
Frequency of practice	Low	High
Duration of practice	Intermittent or low and/or involves multiple sites/settings	Ongoing or high and/or within 1 setting
Level of expertise of users of the practice	High; must train the trainer	Low to moderate
Scope of practice based on current evidence	Limited range; range of use is unknown or research evidence is mixed	Wide range; can be used among diverse populations and/or settings
Opportunities to internally collaborate when developing and initiating the practice	Singular expertise of one or few stakeholders or limited ability to internally collaborate	Multiple stakeholders with high knowledge/skills within setting
Need for continuous improvement of practice during implementation (intervention refinement)	If risk of unintended consequences is high	If risk of unintended consequences is low to moderate
Flexibility when implementing the program	Rigid; low flexibility	Flexible; can be tailored to meet user needs
Global organizational support	Low	Moderate to high
Nursing and other healthcare provider support	Not enough evidence to fully support	Evidence is strong (high strength and quality)
External stakeholder support (community leaders, local organizations/groups)	Low or unknown	Moderate to high
Public health or national guideline alignment	Low or not stated	Moderate to high

(Continued on next page)

Table 19-1. Considerations for Translating Research Into Practice Within a Healthcare Setting *(Continued)*		
	Method	
Factor	**Conducting New Research**	**Implementing Change Processes**
Specific situational needs (for example, must have specific patient criteria)	Highly or moderately prevalent	No or few needs that would limit implementation
Objective measurement	Requires self-reports or other tedious methods of determining outcomes	Readily available (for example, electronic medical record or billing database)
Perceived value of outcomes to stakeholders	Low or little value to stakeholders; value unknown	High value to multiple stakeholders
Perception of harm of practice or viewed negatively by people affected	Moderate to high	Low
Intervention is packaged or available through purchase	No, must be prototyped or developed and created on site	Yes, available
Can develop policies and procedures to guide practice	Too soon; too many unknowns; too much variability in practice	Yes, able to state steps of practice that can be followed by most to all healthcare providers involved

Leading Clinical Nurse Engagement in Conducting Research

All nurse leaders, no matter the setting, job title, or role, must understand that success in conducting nursing research requires their support on many levels (see Figure 19-1 and Table 19-2) and that the general leadership roles of creating a culture, shaping values of the team, being a mobilizer, building team relationships, being a coach and facilitator, designing change, managing emotions, and influencing outcomes apply to conducting research, just as they apply to other leadership expectations. Because most clinical nurses are research naïve, resources are an important component of creating engagement (Siedlecki, 2016) and involve personnel; funding; an intranet website; a database of research activities; supplies, facilities, and programs; and education services (see Table 19-3).

Based on cited barriers to conducting research, a research mentor is a critical asset to any hospital-based program. For hospitals without the capability of hiring a dedicated doctorate-prepared research nurse, an academic–clinical, clinical–clinical, or corporate–clinical affiliation or partnership can facilitate new nurse-led research and grant submission (Davies & Bennett, 2008; Gallin et al., 2013; Havermahl et al., 2015; Lacombe, Burock, & Meunier, 2013). Table 19-4 provides key points when considering external clinical research affiliations or partnerships.

Finally, when promoting clinician-led research, leaders should keep in mind that not all research questions can be easily answered in a clinical setting (or be answered easily in any setting). The level of nurse leader support needed will increase as the strength of the research design and methods increase. For example, a randomized, controlled, multicenter study with double-

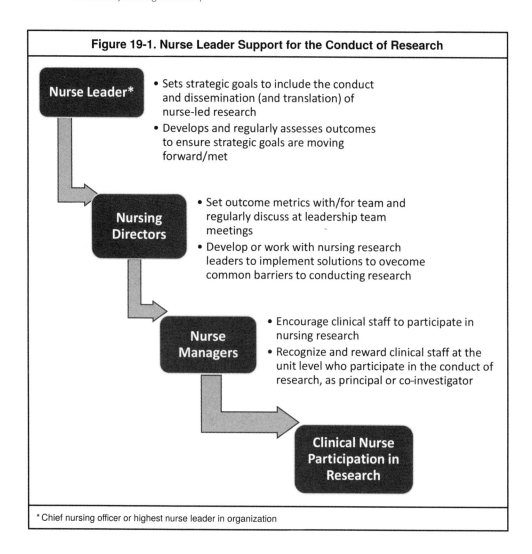

Figure 19-1. Nurse Leader Support for the Conduct of Research

Nurse Leader*
- Sets strategic goals to include the conduct and dissemination (and translation) of nurse-led research
- Develops and regularly assesses outcomes to ensure strategic goals are moving forward/met

Nursing Directors
- Set outcome metrics with/for team and regularly discuss at leadership team meetings
- Develop or work with nursing research leaders to implement solutions to ovecome common barriers to conducting research

Nurse Managers
- Encourage clinical staff to participate in nursing research
- Recognize and reward clinical staff at the unit level who participate in the conduct of research, as principal or co-investigator

Clinical Nurse Participation in Research

* Chief nursing officer or highest nurse leader in organization

blinded intervention and control arms will be a much harder research project to implement than a single-center, descriptive design that uses data from an electronic medical record, even if both studies have the same sample size. Often, a nurse leader may be asked to determine the best research question to move forward into a research project when multiple research questions are available. Nurse leaders may wish to use the following criteria, scoring each from 0 (not present) to 2 (fully present), to be objective in judging the merit of each research question:

- Is it important to clinical practice?
- Is the research an important area of interest for the research team?
- Does the research team have a high degree of expertise in the subject matter?
- Is there a large number of patients available/eligible?
- Are measurement tools available?
- Does data collection fit with practice routines?
- Is this project without political landmines?
- Is the project reasonable in scale and simple?
- Will the research project be fun to complete?

The research project or projects that score the highest should be initiated first.

Table 19-2. Specific Activities of Nurse Leader Support for the Conduct of Research

Leader Level	Leader Roles
Chief nursing officer (visionary)	Develop a strategic plan that includes the conduct of nursing research by clinical nurses Support the need for resources that will facilitate the conduct of research (see Table 19-3) If monetary support is not available at the level needed/desired, support need for nurse leaders to develop academic–clinical, industry–clinical, or organization–clinical partnerships that may involve sharing of resources (research, epidemiology, and biostatistician personnel, statistical analysis software [qualitative and quantitative], grant management programs, legal counsel, art department, library services) Demonstrate support for best practices through research knowledge in both verbal and nonverbal communication by asking for evidence of clinical, fiscal, efficiency, process, or structure outcomes when practices are introduced for support Discuss strength of totality of evidence Discuss quality of totality of evidence Support attendance at a local annual conference where clinical nurses can collaborate and network with each other, learn from nurse research experts, and present findings of their research Support attendance of clinical nurses and other nurse leaders at national organizational symposia that showcase nurse-led research findings Develop systematic methods of evaluating level of support of nurse-led research among direct reports (e.g., include in annual performance review) Lead change requests when needed (e.g., expect policies and procedures to include strength and quality of evidence; expect shared governance model to include actionable research initiatives)
Nursing director (facilitator)	Communicate and visibly foster research values led by visionary leader Empower direct reports (individually or as a team) to base clinical practices on highest strength and quality of evidence-based practices Develop systems, structures, and processes that enhance clinical nurse-led research (or facilitate methods already in place from visionary leader or nursing research personnel) Develop systematic methods of evaluating level of support of nurse-led research among direct reports (e.g., include in annual performance review for nurse managers, clinical nurse specialists, nurse practitioners, specialty nurses, others) Share team members' research results at team meetings Expect team to discuss nursing and medical evidence when supporting practice changes
Nurse manager (tactician)	Communicate and visibly foster research values led by visionary leader (e.g., post new evidence found in the literature on a current or emerging clinical practice) As guidelines are revised, share "sacred cows," discuss contemporary expectations, and develop plans for implementing practices that match best practices based on highest strength and quality of evidence Lead by example and/or share team members' research results at team meetings Refer clinical nurses to research mentor who can support their research questions/interest

(Continued on next page)

Table 19-2. Specific Activities of Nurse Leader Support for the Conduct of Research *(Continued)*

Leader Level	Leader Roles
All leaders	Build capacity Foster a spirit of inquiry Monitor and review current state against strategic goals Communicate clear expectations Energize nursing research programs: ask nurses conducting research to review current status and progress toward goals with you/team Lead by example Encourage participation in research (directly and indirectly) Empower clinical nurses to conduct research Listen to needs that will help research teams thrive Raise awareness of new and emerging practices and the evidence that led to changes Praise supportive behaviors Enhance commitment of direct reports for research activities Be a servant leader in nursing research activities, as needed, related to your boss, your subordinates, and your peers Lead yourself in research by learning how to assess the strength and quality of evidence so that you can coach and direct others

Table 19-3. Resources to Facilitate the Conduct of Nursing Research

Resource Theme	Specific Resources (in order of priority)
Personnel	Nurse researcher mentor/coach: full- or part-time nurse with a research doctorate (e.g., doctorate of philosophy or doctorate of nursing science) and experience in leading and conducting research as a principal investigator. History of the following will enhance productivity and outcomes: conducting research in a hospital setting, mentorship background in multiple research methods (multiple qualitative designs and analyses; observational/correlational, comparative, randomized, controlled trials; and "big data" designs and analyses), receiving grant support, and publishing in high-quality peer-reviewed journals Biostatistician to offer support in sample size determination, analysis plan development, analysis of data, and wording of stated themes when disseminating Analyst to pull data from electronic medical records and billing or other hospital databases Sponsored program grant officer/administrator or research accountant to support submission of grant applications for external funding and management of externally acquired research funding Legal support to develop confidentiality disclosure agreements, research contracts, limited data set agreements, and other legal paperwork with external research collaborators Librarian to complete literature reviews, retrieve papers, assist with website content on evidence-based practices, and participate on shared governance research councils Artist/graphic designer to create posters and figures/graphics as part of presentations and publications

(Continued on next page)

Table 19-3. Resources to Facilitate the Conduct of Nursing Research *(Continued)*	
Resource Theme	**Specific Resources (in order of priority)**
Programs that fund the conduct of research "time"	Internship/fellowship program in which nurses apply individually or as part of a group to participate in a 2-year (or longer) program that involves time for group education, 1:1 research mentorship, and research project development, start-up, completion, presentation, and dissemination in a peer-reviewed journal Internal research fund in which nurses apply individually or as part of a group to receive funding to offset time, supplies, and/or travel to present findings. Funding may be at a rate that includes 60–100 hours of time for 1 person to devote to nursing research activities over a set period of time.
Intranet site	Research website that includes many tabs, including the following: • Internal and external resources (internal: links to ethics review board and research education program offerings; external: links to sample size calculators, random number assignment and research toolkits, organizations and journals) • General information that includes research templates (e.g., proposal and budget template), checklists, research mentor contacts, and examples of the differences between quality and research • Conducting research that includes examples of valid, reliable tools; writing a research proposal; how to conduct a literature review; and internal funding mechanisms • Disseminating and translating research and evidence-based practices that include completed research posters, presentations, and research newsletters • Hospital research education requirements and research policies that include standards of research practice and research council activities, as well as dissemination
Research database	Database (e.g., Microsoft Excel, Access, or Sharepoint) that provides specific information about active, completed, and even abandoned nursing research projects. Information can assist with maintaining research statistics, determining research growth, and informing nurse leaders and clinicians of project information, including credentials of principal investigators, internal and external collaborators, funding, current project status, and, if completed, dissemination.
Supplies, facilities, groups	Ethics committee or review board that provides oversight of research proposal applications and responds to ethical dilemmas, adverse events, protocol deviations, and other best practices in conducting research Research analysis software for quantitative and qualitative research; can be individual purchase or web-based to allow multiple concurrent users Survey data collection program (e.g., Survey Monkey®) to facilitate electronic data collection of survey data Dedicated research computer with password protection and dedicated telephone in a private office or restricted location to meet confidentiality expectations when collecting or discussing individual subject data Locking file cabinets, binders, briefcase (if collecting data at multiple sites and transferring confidential paperwork) Research books to guide nurses who are new to research

(Continued on next page)

Table 19-3. Resources to Facilitate the Conduct of Nursing Research *(Continued)*	
Resource Theme	**Specific Resources (in order of priority)**
Education	Evidence-based practice education: generally offered as a 2-day course or self-study online or paper-based modules that include defining evidence-based practice, understanding the importance of using highest strength and quality of evidence, developing a research question using the PICO* format, searching for evidence via online search engines, reviewing literature (research and review papers) for strength of evidence and factors influencing quality of evidence, and synthesizing the literature
	Journal clubs to guide individuals and teams in reviewing published research and to review papers for strength and quality
	Research workshops: 1-hour (or longer) sessions of didactic and practice, group discussion, or other workshop formats, aimed at increasing clinical nurses' knowledge about multiple facets of developing, conducting, and disseminating research (oral or poster presentation and publication), grant writing tips, and grant funding tips
	Research presentations: 10-minute didactic presentations of completed research plus 5 minutes of questions and answers (4 presentations per hour) to disseminate new knowledge from colleagues
	Mandatory research education to meet ethics committee and research compliance requirements
	Research newsletter to share research news and also to feature research education, especially related to statistical analysis, research methods, benefits, and available resources
	"Sacred cows" handouts to acknowledge outdated clinical practices in a fun, easy-to-read format of 1 theme per handout
	Research terms handout
* PICO—population, intervention, comparison group, outcome	

Table 19-4. External Clinical Affiliations in Nursing Research			
Factors	**Academic**	**Clinical (Hospital)**	**Corporate**
Local or distance relationships possible	Yes, based on use of Internet links/services, telephone, email, and other systems and programs	Yes, based on use of Internet links/services, telephone, email, and other systems and programs	Research services may be centered in the corporate site, which may not be local.
Possibility of multiple scientists representing multiple fields	Yes, if collaborations span the entire college/school of nursing and there are multiple educators with research backgrounds	Yes, if collaborating site is a large hospital or hospital system with multiple nurse researchers with varying backgrounds	Possible, based on corporate headquarters and resources available. May have a team of epidemiologists focused on health economic outcomes research or clinical and basic research.
			(Continued on next page)

Table 19-4. External Clinical Affiliations in Nursing Research *(Continued)*			
Factors	**Academic**	**Clinical (Hospital)**	**Corporate**
Level of support	Negotiated; may require funding of academic nurse who spends time on hospital premises; often includes 1-hour paid-for consultation services customized to match the hospital clinical investigator's needs	Negotiated; may require funding of contracted services that include 1:1 and group education/support, discounts offered to attend annual conferences, and in-person visits	Negotiated; may vary and be limited based on the match of clinical nurse research theme and corporate research goals; corporation may have resources not available with academic or clinical affiliations
Benefits	Can create global or local affiliations Research partner(s) may have mutual interest because hospital can provide research participants that are not available at an academic site If research savvy, will have strong grant writing and research presentation/publication background May have statistical services May promote long-standing informal relationships between teams Brings new insights from collaborators who are not steeped in clinical hospital experiences May lead to use of graduate students who support hospital-based research as part of education May facilitate future career directions of clinical nurses Have administrative staff to assist with grant submission	Can create global or local affiliations Promotes multicenter, hospital-based clinical research Affiliated hospitals may have similar program goals that create ease in project selection if working on joint projects Because both affiliates involve hospital personnel, strong understanding of system capabilities may speed up the conduct of research May promote long-standing informal relationships between researchers Increased efficiencies of both hospitals in regard to training and costs of research Consultative nurse researchers serve as role models and are passionate about hospital-based nursing research and guiding investigators.	Research affiliates may not be nurses but may be very competent in using large data sets May be able to fund research if goals of hospital and corporation align May encourage innovative interventions May have in-house statistical services May foster global health initiatives Brings new insights from collaborators who are not steeped in clinical hospital experiences Enhances relationships between parties that could improve healthcare delivery and health outcomes

(Continued on next page)

Table 19-4. External Clinical Affiliations in Nursing Research *(Continued)*			
Factors	**Academic**	**Clinical (Hospital)**	**Corporate**
Weaknesses	Support may wane over time as workload of both academic and clinical site personnel vary or there is a change of goals; may be important to include clear, concise outcomes in the contract or consider an alternative to a fee-for-service contract. Faculty may not be committed to working across institutional boundaries over time because of demands of their own research programs. May need to negotiate principal investigator and first author status on papers Time and resource intensive regarding start-up and ongoing communications	As priorities change, support of 1 or both clinical sites may fluctuate unless clear, concise objective outcomes are included for payment or there is an alternative to a fee-for-service contract. Will need to negotiate principal investigator and first author status when disseminating findings Time and resource intensive regarding start-up and ongoing communications, especially if not in the same time zone	Corporate goals tend to shift from year to year; support could end abruptly if corporation changes directions. May be more difficult to share confidential data with corporation compared to academic or clinical affiliate if the corporation has personal interest in findings Internal and external threats to validity of research based on corporate interest (e.g., use of in-house statistical team)

Summary

To lead clinical nurse engagement in research, leaders must consider two parallel and often interwoven paths—using and translating research evidence in clinical practice and engaging clinical nursing in conducting research. Together, they promote the use of highest-quality evidence that promotes outcomes consistent with the healthcare setting's mission and goals. Ultimately, there is no point in engaging clinical nurses in conducting research if no structures, systems, or processes are in place to translate research into practice. Further, because translating evidence in the literature may involve the conduct of new research, both elements must be in place to truly lead clinical nurse engagement in research. Leaders benefit when both paths have equal prominence, as clinical nurses with inquisitive minds get excited about opportunities to seek answers to research questions and become involved in clinical solutions and improvements, both of which are necessary to create new value and transform health care.

References

Albert, N.M., Hancock, K., Murray, T., Karafa, M., Runner, J.C., Fowler, S.B., … Krajewski, S. (2010). Cleaned, ready-to-use, reusable electrocardiographic lead wires as a source of pathogenic microorganisms. *American Journal of Critical Care, 19,* e73–e80. doi:10.4037/ajcc2010304

Albert, N.M., Rice, K.L., Waldo, M.J., Bena, J.F., Mayo, A.M., Morrison, S.L., … Foster, J. (2016). Clinical nurse specialist roles in conducting research: Changes over 3 years. *Clinical Nurse Specialist, 30,* 292–301. doi:10.1097/NUR.0000000000000236

Albert, N.M., Slifcak, E., Roach, J.D., Bena, J.F., Horvath, G., Wilson, S., … Murray, T. (2014). Infection rates in intensive care units by electrocardiographic lead wire type: Disposable vs reusable. *American Journal of Critical Care, 23,* 460–468. doi:10.4037/ajcc2014362

Balas, M.C., Burke, W.J., Gannon, D., Cohen, M.Z., Colburn, L., Bevil, C., … Vasilevskis, E.E. (2013). Implementing the awakening and breathing coordination, delirium monitoring/management, and early exercise/mobility bundle into everyday care: Opportunities, challenges, and lessons learned for implementing the ICU pain, agitation, and delirium guidelines. *Critical Care Medicine, 41*(9, Suppl. 1), S116–S127. doi:10.1097/CCM.0b013e3182a17064

Brown, C.E., Wickline, M.A., Ecoff, L., & Glaser, D. (2009). Nursing practice, knowledge, attitudes and perceived barriers to evidence-based practice at an academic medical center. *Journal of Advanced Nursing, 65,* 371–381. doi:10 .1111/j.1365-2648.2008.04878.x

Calderwood, M.S., Vaz, L.E., Kawai, A.T., Jin, R., Rett, M.D., Grant, P.S., & Lee, G.M. (2016). Impact of hospital operating margin on central line–associated bloodstream infections following Medicare's hospital-acquired conditions payment policy. *Infection Control and Hospital Epidemiology, 37,* 100–103. doi:10.1017/ice.2015.250

Chan, G.K., Barnason, S., Dakin, C.L., Gillespie, G., Kamienski, M.C., Stapleton, S., … Li, S. (2011). Barriers and perceived needs for understanding and using research among emergency nurses. *Journal of Emergency Nursing, 37,* 24–31. doi:10.1016/j.jen.2009.11.016

Cummings, G.G., Estabrooks, C.A., Midodzi, W.K., Wallin, L., & Hayduk, L. (2007). Influence of organizational characteristics and context on research utilization. *Nursing Research, 56*(Suppl. 4), S24–S39. doi:10.1097/01.NNR .0000280629.63654.95

Davies, S.M., & Bennett, A. (2008). Understanding the economic and social effects of academic clinical partnerships. *Academic Medicine, 83,* 535–540. doi:10.1097/ACM.0b013e3181723033

Gallin, E.K., Bond, E., Califf, R.M., Crowley, W.F., Jr., Davis, P., Galbraith, R., & Reece, E.A. (2013). Forging stronger partnerships between academic health centers and patient-driven organizations. *Academic Medicine, 88,* 1220–1224. doi:10.1097/ACM.0b013e31829ed2a7

Gifford, W., Davies, B., Edwards, N., Griffin, P., & Lybanon, V. (2007). Managerial leadership for nurses' use of research evidence: An integrative review of the literature. *Worldviews on Evidence-Based Nursing, 4,* 126–145. doi:10.1111/j.1741-6787.2007.00095.x

Greenhalgh, T., Robert, G., Macfarlane, F., Bate, P., & Kyriakidou, O. (2004). Diffusion of innovations in service organizations: Systematic review and recommendations. *Milbank Quarterly, 82,* 581–629. doi:10.1111/j.0887 -378X.2004.00325.x

Havermahl, T., LaPensee, E., Williams, D., Clauw, D., Parker, R.A., Downey, B., … Myles, J. (2015). Model for a university-based clinical research development infrastructure. *Academic Medicine, 90,* 47–52. doi:10.1097/ACM .0000000000000535

Kajermo, K.N., Undén, M., Gardulf, A., Eriksson, L.E., Orton, M.-L., Arnetz, B.B., & Nordström, G. (2008). Predictors of nurses' perceptions of barriers to research utilization. *Journal of Nursing Management, 16,* 305–314. doi:10 .1111/j.1365-2834.2007.00770.x

Kilpatrick, K., Tchouaket, E., Carter, N., Bryant-Lukosius, D., & DiCenso, A. (2016). Structural and process factors that influence clinical nurse specialist role implementation. *Clinical Nurse Specialist, 30,* 89–100. doi:10.1097 /NUR.0000000000000182

Klein, K., Mulkey, M., Bena, J.F., & Albert, N.M. (2015). Clinical and psychological effects of early mobilization in patients treated in a neurologic ICU: A comparative study. *Critical Care Medicine, 43,* 865–873. doi:10.1097/CCM .0000000000000787

Lacombe, D., Burock, S., & Meunier, F. (2013). Academia–industry partnerships: Are we ready for new models of partnership? The point of view of the EORTC, an academic clinical cancer research organisation. *European Journal of Cancer, 49,* 1–7. doi:10.1016/j.ejca.2012.09.027

McMullen, H., Griffiths, C., Leber, W., & Greenhalgh, T. (2015). Explaining high and low performers in complex intervention trials: A new model based on diffusion of innovations theory. *Trials, 16,* 242. doi:10.1186/s13063 -015-0755-5

Modic, M.B., Albert, N.M., Sun, Z., Bena, J.F., Yager, C., Cary, T., … Kissinger, B. (2016). Does an insulin double-checking procedure improve patient safety? *Journal of Nursing Administration, 46,* 154–160. doi:10.1097/NNA .0000000000000314

Mulkey, M., Bena, J.F., & Albert, N.M. (2014). Clinical outcomes of patient mobility in a neuroscience intensive care unit. *Journal of Neuroscience Nursing, 46,* 153–161. doi:10.1097/JNN.0000000000000053

Oh, E.G. (2008). Research activities and perceptions of barriers to research utilization among critical care nurses in Korea. *Intensive and Critical Care Nursing, 24,* 314–322. doi:10.1016/j.iccn.2007.12.001

Phillips, S.M., Alfano, C.M., Perna, F.M., & Glasgow, R.E. (2014). Accelerating translation of physical activity and cancer survivorship research into practice: Recommendations for a more integrated and collaborative approach. *Cancer Epidemiology, Biomarkers and Prevention, 23,* 687–699. doi:10.1158/1055-9965.EPI-13-1355

Siedlecki, S.L. (2016). Building blocks for a strong nursing research program. In N.M. Albert (Ed.), *Building and sustaining a hospital-based nursing research program* (pp. 43–60). New York, NY: Springer.

Silka, C.R., Stombaugh, H.A., Horton, J., & Daniels, R. (2012). Nursing research in a nonacademic health setting: Measuring knowledge, attitudes, and behaviors. *Journal of Nursing Administration, 42,* 386–392. doi:10.1097/NNA.0b013e318261935d

Titler, M.G. (2010). Translation science and context. *Research and Theory for Nursing Practice, 24,* 35–55. doi:10.1891/1541-6577.24.1.35

Trief, P.M., Cibula, D., Rodriguez, E., Akel, B., & Weinstock, R.S. (2016). Incorrect insulin administration: A problem that warrants attention. *Clinical Diabetes, 34,* 25–33. doi:10.2337/diaclin.34.1.25

Yost, J., Ganann, R., Thompson, D., Aloweni, F., Newman, K., Hazzan, A., … Ciliska, D. (2015). The effectiveness of knowledge translation interventions for promoting evidence-informed decision-making among nurses in tertiary care: A systematic review and meta-analysis. *Implementation Science, 10,* 98. doi:10.1186/s13012-015-0286-1

Young, D., & Borland, R. (2011). Conceptual challenges in the translation of research into practice: It's not just a matter of "communication." *Translational Behavioral Medicine, 1,* 256–269. doi:10.1007/s13142-011-0035-1

Journey From Bedside to Boardroom

Nancy Howell Agee, MN, RN, and Ninfa M. Saunders, DHA, MBA, MSN, FACHE

A journey grounded with our passion to serve and to lead

—Ninfa M. Saunders and Nancy Howell Agee

Introduction

This chapter chronicles the personal inspirational journeys of two extraordinary nurse colleagues and leaders who are now chief executive officers (CEOs) of their respective health systems. The aim is to share their journeys toward excellence, learning, and servant leadership to enlighten you to the possibilities for your leadership career. You are limited only by your personal aspirations and goals.

Journey of Chief Executive Officer Nancy Howell Agee

It was 1980. I was a clinical nurse, having just returned with a newly minted graduate degree. I managed a National Institutes of Health–sponsored oncology grant. Some of you may remember; it was the era of big hair, shoulder pads, wide lapels, and polyester pantsuits. I had been invited to the administrative suite of the hospital to present to the CEO and the hospital board. I had prepared carefully that morning, practiced my talk, printed handouts, and dressed in a tomato red pantsuit. Arriving at the door to the boardroom, I took a deep breath and walked into a large, walnut-paneled room. Twelve dark-suited men were sitting around a massive table. As I walked in, 12 pairs of eyes stared at me. The room became eerily quiet until a gruff voice said, "What are *you* doing here? This is a *boardroom*; you must be in the wrong place." Heads nodded in agreement. No one smiled. My inclination was to turn and go back out the door I had entered as fast as possible. Somehow, I found my voice (albeit an octave higher than normal) and squeaked out, "I was invited by Mr. X" (the administrator who had invited me and who was conspicuously absent, seemingly having neglected to tell the CEO and the board chair that he had invited me). Summoning up my courage, I went on, "I am here for board education and would like to lead a board discussion about leadership." And I began distributing handouts.

Fast-forward more than 30 years to today. I found a seat at that table and changed the dress and gender code. I have been sitting at the board table for years. Now I sit at the head of that table as the CEO. The women and men around the table are engaged, truly interested in health care and healthcare delivery, quality, and patient safety. The dialogue is thoughtful, challenging, and considerate. The financial, operational, and strategic issues are complex. The board members understand the sometimes far-reaching consequences of decisions. Non–board members often are invited to provide clinical and operational updates and lead board discussions. I have vowed that their experience in the boardroom will be very different from my initial encounter. Board education is standard. I still carefully prepare for board meetings. And, sometimes, even wear a tomato red suit, sans shoulder pads!

In these scenarios are two real but differing experiences. Was the 1980 boardroom really that different from today's boardroom, or was my perception different? The answer isn't simple. It's both yes and no. A quarter of a century has changed my perspective. Likewise, the business climate and changes in health care have materially changed.

Principles of Organizational Leadership

Both boards (then and now) had considerable responsibilities for the environment of care for patients, for strategic plans for the future, and for relationships with the community. Both boards had to understand a balance sheet and the often-convoluted healthcare finance issues. Both boards were subject to nonprofit corporation law and had the legal duties of care, loyalty, and obedience. These duties are described as the following (BoardSource, 2010):

- Duty of care—This is the "care that an ordinary prudent person would exercise and in a like position and under similar circumstances"—that is, "the duty to exercise reasonable care when he or she makes a decision as a steward of the organization."
- Duty of loyalty—This is a standard of faithfulness; board members need to have "undivided allegiance when making decisions affecting the organization." In other words, the board member "must act in the best interests of the organization."
- Duty of obedience—Board members must be faithful to the organization mission. They may not act in a way inconsistent with the core goals of the organization.

Both boards had fidelity to confidentiality, ethics, and conflicts of interest; however, there are some differences. Healthcare financing, complicated as it was in 1980, is much more so today. The notion of fee for value rather than fee for service is rapidly evolving. Most payers have some form of value, or quality metrics, tied to reimbursement, including the Centers for Medicare and Medicaid Services. Thus, quality, patient safety, and the patient experience take center stage on both the CEO's agenda and in the boardroom.

Changes Affecting Health Care

The business climate has changed considerably too. The Sarbanes-Oxley Act of 2002 has radically changed the perspectives of boards and the role of the CEO. The act, often referred to as SOX, was in reaction to the major corporate and accounting scandals we followed in the media in the late 1990s at such well-known places as Enron, Tyco International, and Adelphia. The resulting public outcry led to Congress mandating increased board accountability and independence. The act also covered auditor independence, corporate governance, internal assessment, and enhanced financial disclosure (Sarbanes-Oxley Act of 2002, Pub. L. No. 107-204). While the act targeted for-profit companies, a number of nonprofit or tax-exempt companies such as hospitals and health systems have adopted elements of the act as good board practice.

Today's boards are engaged in strategic discussions and decision making. The board must ask challenging questions, share opinions, and expect detailed, thoughtful responses. The CEO has the dual responsibility to simultaneously lead and serve. The CEO is both a colleague and partner of the board and leads the health system according to the board's direction.

Why Aspire to Be a Chief Executive Officer?

I once had a colleague say the best answer to any question is usually a simple answer, but simple doesn't mean easy. So, why aspire to be a CEO? Simply put, it is the ability to effect change on a broader scale than can be done "at the bedside." The "why" is easy; the "how" is much, much harder.

If you are still reading this chapter, you must have some desire to become a CEO or perhaps lead as a board member, committee chair, or even a board chair. The journey from the bedside to the boardroom is often a long one, filled with twists and turns but also excitement and a sense of accomplishment and value. There are many reasons to take that journey, but the one most compelling, and most meaningful to nurses, is the opportunity to materially impact what is best for patients and staff.

Character Strengths of a Chief Executive Officer

I think an effective CEO in today's complicated healthcare environment is a maestro, a high-falutin word for conductor. The CEO isn't likely to have, and doesn't need to have, expertise in all aspects of healthcare delivery. He or she must be skilled at guiding a diverse and talented team in harmony. Perhaps that is why a nurse can be a very effective CEO. Nurses are educated and experienced in bringing together multiple members of the healthcare team. Nurses are skillful at developing, implementing, and evaluating a plan of action, and nurses are talented communicators, using varied skills to inform, teach, persuade, negotiate, collaborate, and direct.

Moreover, nurses are simultaneously compassionate and caring while possessing uncommon fortitude, backbone, and stamina. These traits may seem polar opposites; yet, these are skills that a CEO needs: an unyielding core coupled with flexibility and openness.

The term *steel magnolia*, popularized with the 1989 drama starring Julia Roberts, implies strength and kindness, an apt analogy to leadership and familiar to nurses. Effective leaders have both a strong core and sense of wonder. The strong core yields respect, discipline, and direction, while kind and caring communication lends openness for new ideas, fellowship, loyalty, and inspiration.

Chief Executive Officer Core Values and Attributes

There are core values every CEO should possess. One is uncompromising integrity. Honesty and ethical behaviors are the essence of leadership. Integrity is a sacred trust. The strong leader must have a consistent, unbendable fidelity to an honest, ethical core of values.

But what is also true of a strong leader is devotion to being open-minded and approachable, welcoming new ideas and diverse opinions, and seeking disparate information. The strong leader is energetic, engaged, and inspiring; skilled in relationship management; and treats others with respect and without favoritism. In short, the strong leader is curious and a good communicator. These softer values make the difference between a leader and a really good leader.

There are many attributes of good leaders in health care, but these are my top 10:
- Executive presence
- Energetic, engaged, inspiring
- Emotional intelligence
- Visionary
- Skillful communicator
- Approachable and open-minded
- Continuous learner
- Professional; setting a high standard
- Integrity
- Joyful

Evolution to Chief Executive Officer

Like many nurses, I moved into a management role as a way to effect changes on my unit and later across multiple units. I found the work challenging and interesting. Connecting the dots between the needs of patients and the expectations of staff wasn't always perfectly aligned but was worthwhile. A case in point: I was the evening supervisor and was called to the oncology unit. The nurse explained that a patient who had chemotherapy earlier in the day, and had been very nauseated, now wanted pizza. The nurse thought the patient should have "comfort foods," like Jell-O®, and as the nurse put it, "in any case, the kitchen is closed." After talking to the patient, I returned to the nurse and discussed with her why our teenaged patient might feel better eating something familiar like (a fairly bland) pizza. Together, we ordered the pizza to be delivered, shelled out a few dollars, and, at the end of the shift, ate pizza with our young patient. Whether it was tincture of time, the pizza, or the fellowship, the patient kept the food down, slept "like a baby," and the nurse and I went home knowing that we had given our patient excellent, personalized care.

I began to take on more management responsibilities, eventually applying for a vice president role. To my disappointment, I wasn't offered the position to which I had applied; rather, I was asked to accept a position as vice president of clinical and administrative support areas, like utilization management, social services, and continuing education. It turned out to be a great learning experience and superb groundwork for a CEO. Our disparate group of services found common ground around our mission, our complementary talents, and shared success.

As I became more entrenched in leadership, I found that my background in varied parts of the health system was enormously helpful. However, I needed more skills and experience. First, my background in financial management was limiting my career advancement. I asked a colleague in financial services to mentor me. He was a godsend! And we found our discussions about finance and clinical care mutually beneficial. Second, while I was "in my element" with clinicians, I was not as comfortable or confident in business settings. Reading books or perusing Internet discussions wasn't sufficient. I found that volunteering for a charity and later a local theater was a great way to meet many people from different businesses and backgrounds. Eventually, I served on several boards, honing business skills, making a difference, and having fun! Third, I have become a devotee of servant leadership. I found my natural style of leadership benefited from a deeper, disciplined understanding of the philosophy of servant leadership. Servant leadership, or "servant as leader," is the idea that leadership must be about service. Robert Greenleaf described it as the following:

> The servant-leader is servant first. It begins with the natural feeling that one wants to serve. Then conscious choice brings one to aspire to lead. The best test is: do those served grow as persons; do they, while being served, become

healthier, wiser, freer, more autonomous, more likely themselves to become servants? (Greenleaf, 1970, as cited in Spears, 1998, p. 1)

The premise of servant leadership resonates with a nurse's heart. As a nurse, we are never apart from the noble purpose of caring for others. Caring leaders are not comfortable or, ultimately, effective in a command and control environment. Servant leadership as a guiding framework encompasses the larger value of care with disciplinary stewardship and commitment.

My journey to CEO wasn't something to which I aspired. Rather, I've wished to make a difference and pursued or accepted roles that would improve health.

Yet, I did not just fall into new leadership roles. I had mentors, pursued new experiences, honed skills, and learned from feedback.

When invited to serve as CEO, I was thrilled, excited, and, yes, a little nervous. Could I do a good job? Was I competent to lead effectively, strategically, and with a caring heart? Would I be wise, thoughtful, and have foresight to lead when the road ahead wasn't clear?

Candidly, after some years as a CEO, I still wonder those same questions. I've learned most CEOs have similar trepidations. There is no magic formula. But I can tell you this: I wake up each morning delighted to have another day to serve! And being the CEO is a great job!

Recommended Readings

Aldo, P. (2014). *Understanding executive presence and how to make it work for you*. Norcross, GA: Gin Press.

Axelrod, A. (2000). *Elizabeth I, CEO: Strategic lessons from the leader who built an empire*. Paramus, NJ: Prentice Hall Press.

Bridgespan Group. (2010). What are the legal responsibilities of nonprofit boards? Retrieved from http://www .bridgespan.org/Home.aspx

Greenleaf, R.K. (1998). Have you a dream deferred? In L.C. Spears (Ed.), *The power of servant leadership* (pp. 93–110). San Francisco, CA: Berrett-Koehler.

Hock, D.W. (1999). Quite ordinary people. In *Birth of the chaordic age* (pp. 195–213). San Francisco, CA: Berrett-Koehler.

Hunter, J.C. (2004). *The world's most powerful leadership principle: How to become a servant leader*. New York, NY: Crown Business.

Monarth, H. (2010). *Executive presence: The art of commanding respect like a CEO*. New York, NY: McGraw-Hill.

Sarbanes-Oxley Act of 2002, Pub. L. No. 107-204. Retrieved from http://www.sec.gov/about/laws/soa2002.pdf

Sipe, J.W., & Frick, D.M. (2009). *Seven pillars of servant leadership: Practicing the wisdom of leading by serving*. New York, NY: Paulist Press.

Journey of Chief Executive Officer Ninfa M. Saunders

My childhood days were spent in a small, close-knit town in the Philippines, where church, family, education, and community were the focal points of our everyday life. I came from a family of eight children raised by inspirational parents, who were both academicians, and supported by a maternal grandmother, whose focus on education was a resolute agenda. For as long as I can remember, I have always wanted to be a nurse. Through the later part of my grammar school days and into high school, I would quietly admire a number of nurses who would walk past our house in their crisp uniforms with purposeful stride on their way to the local hospital. They exuded professional presence and were the epitome of grace. I specifically idolized one nurse, Merlita Gargullo, unknowingly my first of many mentors in nursing. On a few visits to the local hospital, I would see her minister to her patients with great care and compassion, an image that would stay with me as I mentally considered my dream, which turned into a plan, to become a nurse. This was an image that would stay with me through my nursing years and today. In my senior year of high school, I started my exploration of nursing schools. It was in that same year, 1966, that the world and I mourned the massacre of eight student nurses in Chicago, Illinois. One of those murdered was the nurse whom I idolized, Merlita Gargullo. This horrific event marked a turning point in my nursing pursuit.

After nursing school, I relocated to the United States, spending one year in Mississippi and eight years in New Jersey to pursue my desire to work in critical care, focused on cardiovascular nursing. Care of critically ill patients became my passion. Through my critical care experience, I learned the meaning and importance of teamwork, critical thinking, leadership, and professional commitment. It was an experience that would later inspire me to pursue and complete a Master's in Nursing at Rutgers University and become a clinical nurse specialist in adult critical care. From my practice as a clinical specialist, I became a clinical resource and expert, eventually becoming the curriculum developer and lead faculty for the organization's critical care course. My advanced practice and teaching experience taught me the value of effective knowledge transfer through concept simplification, teaching by modeling, and understanding the value of feedback.

The time I spent in clinical practice and teaching was cut short by an opportunity presented to me by the director and vice president for nursing—to be the assistant director of nursing, Administrative Services. This position was to be a dyad role with the assistant director of nursing, Clinical Services. I was convinced that the offer was a mistake and that she really meant to offer me the clinical leadership role. As she started to recite the functional description of the job, I quickly realized that she was intentional in her offer. I went from being perplexed to troubled and confused when I heard that I was to replace an authority figure whose role, influence, and power were way above my pay grade. I started to sweat bullets while trying my best to maintain my composure.

So at age 24, I entered the world of administrative work, wet behind the ears and scared of my own shadow. I was assigned a beautiful office with my name etched on the door and was introduced to my assistant and provided business cards.

While today all these seem so mundane to the world of an executive, I must tell you that I was so unnerved by it all. My office was next to the director of nursing, which meant I would see her almost every day. I was given an administrative assistant but had no idea what to do with one, until she sat me down one day to tell me that we were to be partners and that she would teach me how to best utilize her skills. What a relief! In my first true nurse administrative position, I was exposed to the art of negotiation as I was a member of the negotiating team for the nurses' union. I was exposed to the inner workings of administration and the global insight that it engendered, and I began to appreciate the leadership competencies at play. There was so much to learn and a push for speed to execution with not much room for error. This role helped to define the foundation of my role as a leader today. It stretched my capacity for learning. I became a sponge, soaking in all the nuggets of knowledge and wisdom I could amass. I learned the power of connectedness and engaging the people that you serve, both the patients and the staff. I learned the power of managing by walking around, the art of listening, and the beginning of what I know today as servant leadership. I learned lessons about partnership from my assistant. And thanks to the director of nursing, who saw in me something I did not see in myself, I appreciated the value of searching for talent, nurturing potential leaders, and the power of mentorship.

Less than four years into the role, my husband's job relocated us to Georgia. Georgia is the place I consider home. It would be in Georgia, at Emory University Hospital, Atlanta, that I would spend the longest period of my career as a healthcare executive. While my first time in New Jersey was spent in a teaching–quaternary organization, Emory University Hospital would be the first university-owned hospital I would work for. In 1980, I began my role at Emory as assistant director of nursing, Nursing Resources, a role that encompassed responsibilities for nursing recruitment and human resources, budget and financial matters, and the nursing float pool and registry. I had the opportunity to work with some of the industry's great leaders; most notable of all were Paul Hofmann, CEO, and Mary Woody, director of nursing.

At Emory, I would learn what is expected of a world-renowned organization whose mission, in part, is to train the best of the best and to be on the cutting edge of innovation and thought leadership.

From the CEO, I learned the intelligence and eloquence required of a CEO, the balancing of multiple number-one priorities, the effective way by which one scripts and messages the business agenda on hand, and the ability to effectively advance the teaching and care delivery agendas.

Mary Woody was an iconic figure in nursing. She was the nurse's nurse. While she understood the value of the business side of nursing, her focus first and foremost was the advancement of the practice of nursing and the training of nurses. It was from her that I learned the true concept of patient-centered care, way before it became a cliché. She invested heavily in preparing nurses to acquire advanced clinical competencies, and she positioned nursing clinical experts to lead and sustain innovative clinical programs. As interim dean of the Emory School of Nursing at the time, she appointed a number of us to associate professor positions, giving us dual appointments at the hospital and at the school.

As she was focused on her commitment to clinical excellence, she gladly entrusted to me the business operations of nursing, giving me the opportunity to master the trade. It was at this time in 1983 that I decided to pursue an Executive Master's in Business Administration at Emory University. The EMBA was an emerging concept in the United States at that time. The program was intended to target seasoned executives in other industries outside of health care. As this was primarily a weekend program designed for working executives, I was convinced that I could be a fit. My personal conviction was not enough to qualify me for admission. My nursing background and my mid-management experience were not convincing enough qualifiers to warrant immediate consideration. So, I decided that persistence and relentless pursuit would be my strategy. I met many times with the program director and the admission coordinator, presenting to them reasons and arguments, explaining to them my current role and how the program would make me better in it, and how I would add value to the class. Eventually, I was moved from the "no" list to the wait list. Four weeks prior to the semester's start date, I was officially accepted and was one of the first nurses to be accepted to and graduate from the program.

My experiences at Emory gave me the breadth and depth I needed to broaden my knowledge of the industry and expand my leadership horizon, as well as the opportunity to sharpen my skills in navigating the complicated landscape of running a healthcare delivery system. I learned from the best of the best and the most competitive of beings. I watched and appreciated with great interest the work of pioneers and the unquenchable thirst for excellence.

When I left Emory 13 years later, my heart was heavy, and I struggled with a question that plagued me for almost a year: Is there truly life after Emory? Paul Hofmann's and Mary Woody's words kept coming back to me, "Ninfa, Emory's role is to train the leaders of the future. You are meant to carry your knowledge, wisdom, and what you learned at Emory and disseminate it to the community and the world out there. That is how you will continue the legacy of Emory, so join those who have taken this step before you and make us proud. Emory will always be here and will always be your professional home." So, off I went, carrying to this day an armamentarium of skills and competencies that continue to serve me well. While I have traveled far and wide, Emory will forever be home.

In 1993, I left Emory and accepted the role of chief nursing officer at DeKalb Regional Health System (DRHS). This would be the first community hospital I would work for. Less than a year after my arrival, fate intervened and I was asked to take the position of chief operations officer at that same hospital. And so, I served. I learned as fast as I could and toiled day and night, along with many very capable leaders, to drive results. The volume and rate of my assimilation and immersion, the desire to make a critical difference in the organization, was rivaled only by the exceptional passion and engagement of the staff. My learning experience at DRHS broadened my horizon at a rate I have never experienced before. While I came with what I considered a lot of experience, that determination paled compared to the skill sets required for me to navigate the fast-changing landscape of health care at that time. Managed care and risk-based contracting were just beginning to manifest themselves. Independent community physicians were contemplating the formation of a physician hospital organization. Physician employment and practice acquisition was in vogue, and PROMINA, one of the nation's first joint operation organizations, was just formed and consisted of Atlanta's top eight hospitals, DRHS being one of them.

This was the beginning of a new era for health care. We found ourselves alternately and intermittently crossing the chasm between the traditional strategy of investing in bricks and mortar and the contemporary strategy of investing in infrastructure, new talent, and competencies. As we did both, we remained uncertain on what investment would give us the yield to secure our future.

Partnering with independent community physicians was an equally compelling challenge. We had a number of physicians who practiced in hospitals other than DRHS. Keeping them engaged and aligned with the organization was a continuous challenge.

The nursing shortage and the aging of the nursing staff has plagued the country, and we were not an exception. This dilemma propelled me to participate and engage in the state nursing association and the Department of Community Health as they considered a statewide manpower study and develop solutions on how to best abate a crisis in the making. My work in this field gave me insight on the importance of being part of the larger community and leading change by building a guided coalition and engaging other leaders.

While serving as president of the Georgia Organization of Nursing Executives and, one year later, as chair of the Nursing Executive Council for the Voluntary Hospitals of America, I had the wonderful opportunity to work with hospitals around the state, a new experience for me, as most of my work was limited to the Atlanta market. This experience opened my eyes to the challenges of vulnerable communities, the resource limitations that they face, and the impressive and creative talent they bring to the table. My overall experience at DRHS taught me lessons in vulnerability, creative thinking, and partnership with competitive entities, understanding the inner workings of governance and navigating the tortuous road of adversity.

After DRHS, I had a short stint working for then governor Roy Barnes through the Georgia Cancer Coalition. I found myself working with some of the brightest people in health policy development and formation. I clearly understood that I was in a world I knew nothing about and, although I took instructions well and implemented them to precision and learned a ton, I also quickly realized that this was not the type work I was destined to do. Through all of these opportunities, I fully embraced two strategies: (a) staying open to new opportunities, and (b) continuous learning (I observed; I listened; I studied; and I engaged).

In 2003, a year after leaving DRHS, my work brought me back to New Jersey when I accepted the role of executive vice president, Operations, for Virtua Health, the largest multihospital health system and largest employer in South Jersey. I would eventually move to the role of president for the system.

My work at Virtua was the covalent bond that integrated the many things I had experienced and learned thus far. In addition to learning and sensing from the people and the environment around me, I pulled from my repertoire of experiences, knowledge, wisdom, skill, competencies, and lessons learned and used all these to masterfully and successfully position Virtua as a high-performing organization in a highly competitive and aggressive market. While at Virtua, I had the opportunity to build the hospital of the future in a Greenfield site. I also guided the formation of a cohesive physician organization that became one of the largest and most successful in the market, and I led the financial turnaround of the system from a zero margin to a double-digit margin.

While working closely with the board and leadership, I helped set the stage for health system partnerships and potential mergers and acquisitions among key health systems in New Jersey and Philadelphia. I worked closely with the executive team to model a concept called "enterprise partnership" with other industries; preeminent among those relationships was our partnership with General Electric that focused on knowledge transfer. I was able to lead the simplification of our leadership system into three major focal areas: strategy, operations, and people, the most important of which was the people! Virtua was consistently awarded the best place to work in the South Jersey/Philadelphia area. Every year, our employee satisfaction and engagement score put us in the top decile of the comparison group in the nation. At Virtua, I became a holistic executive. I rejoiced in the power of the people and in their ability to drive an organization to an enviable place through cultural transformation. I fully comprehended the critical intersection among strategy, operations, and people and their power to catalyze execution.

In the midst of all that I was involved in, I finally acquiesced to my parents' request, especially my mom's, to pursue a doctoral degree. In 2006, I was conferred a Doctorate in Health Administration degree and graduated with highest honors at the Medical University of South Carolina. Two years later I was recognized with the Distinguished Alumni Award.

Life was good! My professional trajectory was more than I ever expected, my home life was phenomenal, and I marveled at the many professional and personal opportunities that came my way. Until that one horrid and dreadful night when my husband and I were faced with a tragedy that would be any parent's nightmare. My son, who had just arrived home for Christmas break, was in a very bad accident. He had multiple injuries and was in critical condition. Our lives were turned upside down and what mattered changed. The only one thing that really mattered was the life of our son. My priorities changed! Our family became the sole focus of our lives. His recovery was long, but the outlook was good. Our extended family from Georgia was at our side, ever ready to do what it took to support our son's recovery. It was during the many months of staying at our son's side that we decided to return home to Georgia.

Our desire to move back home and my job search brought me to where I am today. In 2012, I accepted the position of president and CEO of Central Georgia Health System, whose name would later change to Navicent Health. As the leader of a large health system, our flagship hospital being the second largest in the state, I focus my energy in strengthening Navicent Health in a number of key areas. We started with a four-year plan. The first year was all about laying the foundation for the organization; the second year focused on transformation; the third focused on becoming a high-performing organization; and the fourth and current year centered on systems integration.

Externally, I was sensitive to the many hospitals around us whose resources were limited and who served a wide geographic area in which access to care was a big challenge.

A little less than one year into my role, I decided to search for solutions on how to best help these vulnerable communities. So, in the early part of 2013, I collaborated with another CEO to form Stratus Healthcare, a non-equity collaborative of 30 hospitals in central and South Georgia. Stratus serves four major functions: first, assessment and meeting clinical gaps within our primary and secondary service areas; second, development of a clinical integrated platform; third, use of shared services beyond forming a group purchasing organization; and fourth, pursuit of strategic initiatives. Today, Stratus is a well-recognized model of alignment and partnership and is emulated by many across the United States.

While my work has honored me with a plethora of notable professional accolades and awards that I never expected nor sought, my resolve to serve has never faltered. My motivation and comfort do not lie in the recognition; instead, I find solace in my reflection of the mean-ingfulness of it all and all that I have been given in my life. When I think about the drivers, the factors and the reasons, my reflections bring me back to the following themes that I would like to impart to you:

- It is about **lifelong learning** and the insatiable desire to know, to understand, and to learn. My parents always told their children: "The more you know, the less you know."
- Finding that **authentic self**, which will at times elude you as you find your way and as your way gets confused with other people's values and ways.
- Finding the **courage** to render yourself **vulnerable**, as it is during these precious moments of vulnerability that humility becomes alive and the value of others manifests itself.
- The importance of **work–life blending**, for a perfect balance can never be achieved. When all is said and done and one's reign ends, the only constant is your **family**, as nothing should ever rival that priority.
- An adage derived from the teachings of Gandhi is to "be the change we wish to see in this world."
- We must take ownership of that which is entrusted to us, always remembering that we are but part of a bigger whole. Our work must clearly depict the message we want to send. This is what translation is all about, a much different concept from communication.
- A sense of **spirituality** that centers us, compelling us to possess discerning faculties, which guide and balance our ambition and our search for meaningful existence. After all, what good will it be for someone to gain the whole world, only to lose their soul? (Mark 8:35).
- Last, a sense of **gratitude** for a multitude of things. For me in particular, I am deeply grate-ful for parents who gave so much so I can be what I am today. I'm thankful for their inspira-tion and for imparting to me valuable life lessons that one will never find in a textbook. I'm grateful for a family who completes me and reminds me every day of what is truly important in life. I'm blessed to have staff, colleagues, mentors, and friends who have supported my con-tinuing journey to excellence.
- Simply said, it is indeed just the way my parents consistently and relentlessly instructed and compelled their children to think and do, and that is: **"You must always leave people and places better than when you found them."**

Recommended Readings

Barsade, S., & O'Neill, O.A. (2016). Manage your emotional culture. *Harvard Business Review, 94*(1/2), 58–66.

Benner, P.E. (1984). *From novice to expert: Excellence and power in clinical nursing practice.* Menlo Park, CA: Addison-Wesley, Nursing Division.

Bossidy, L., & Charan, R. (with Burck, C.). (2002). *Execution: The discipline of getting things done.* New York, NY: Crown Business.

Christenson, C., & Euchner, J. (2011, January 1). Managing disruption: An interview with Clayton Christensen. *Research-Technology Management, 54*(1), 11–17. doi:10.1080/08956308.2011.11657668

Cohen, W.A. (2010). *Heroic leadership: Leading with integrity and honor.* San Francisco, CA: Jossey-Bass.

Collins, J.C. (2001). *Good to great: Why some companies make the leap—and others don't.* New York, NY: HarperBusiness.

Colman, R., & Buckley, P. (2005). Blue ocean strategy. *CMA Management, 79,* 6.

Corporate strategy: A Harvard Business Review Reprint Series. (1979). Boston, MA: Harvard Business Review.

Covey, S.R. (1989). *The 7 habits of highly effective people: Restoring the character ethic.* New York, NY: Simon & Schuster.

Doohan, L. (2007). *Spiritual leadership: The quest for integrity.* New York, NY: Paulist Press.

Florida, R. (2013). The boom towns and ghost towns of the new economy. *Atlantic, 312*(3), 52–58. Retrieved from https://www.theatlantic.com/magazine/archive/2013/10/the-boom-towns-and-ghost-towns-of-the-new-economy/309460

Friedman, S.D. (2014). *Leading the life you want: Skills for integrating work and life.* Boston, MA: Harvard Business Review Press.

George, B. (with Sims, P.). (2007). *True north: Discover your authentic leadership.* San Francisco, CA: Jossey-Bass.

Gladwell, M. (2015). *David and Goliath: Underdogs, misfits, and the art of battling giants.* New York, NY: Little, Brown.

Goleman, D. (1995). *Emotional intelligence.* New York, NY: Bantam Books.

Greenleaf, R.K. (1977). *Servant leadership: A journey into the nature of legitimate power and greatness.* New York, NY: Paulist Press.

Kay, K., & Shipman, C. (2014). The confidence gap. *Atlantic, 313*(4), 56–66. Retrieved from https://www.theatlantic .com/magazine/archive/2014/05/the-confidence-gap/359815

Kolb, D.M. (2015). Be your own best advocate. *Harvard Business Review, 93*(11), 130–133. Retrieved from https://hbr .org/2015/11/be-your-own-best-advocate

Kotter, J.P. (2008). *A sense of urgency.* Boston, MA: Harvard Business Review Press.

Kotter, J.P. (2014). *Accelerate: Building strategic agility for a faster-moving world.* Boston, MA: Harvard Business Review Press.

Kotter, J.P., & Rathgeber, H. (2006). *Our iceberg is melting: Changing and succeeding under any conditions.* New York, NY: St. Martin's Press.

Lencioni, P. (2002). *The five dysfunctions of a team: A leadership fable.* San Francisco, CA: Jossey-Bass.

Looney, B. (2009). *Exceeding expectations: Reflections on leadership.* Montgomery, AL: Enso Books.

Lowney, C. (2003). *Heroic leadership: Best practices from a 450-year-old company that changed the world.* Chicago, IL: Loyola Press.

Malhotra, D. (2015). Control the negotiation before it begins. *Harvard Business Review, 93*(12), 66–74. Retrieved from https://hbr.org/2015/12/control-the-negotiation-before-it-begins

Marquet, L.D. (2012). *Turn the ship around! A true story of turning followers into leaders.* New York, NY: Portfolio.

Martin, R.L. (2014). The rise (and likely fall) of the talent economy. *Harvard Business Review, 92*(10), 41–47. Retrieved from https://hbr.org/2014/10/the-rise-and-likely-fall-of-the-talent-economy

Maxwell, J.C. (2009). *How successful people think: Change your thinking, change your life.* New York, NY: Center Street.

Neff, T.J., & Citrin, J.M. (2005). *You're in charge—now what? The 8-point plan.* New York, NY: Crown Business.

Patterson, K., Grenny, J., McMillan, R., & Switzler, A. (2012). *Crucial conversations: Tools for talking when stakes are high* (2nd ed.). New York, NY: McGraw-Hill.

Porter, M.E. (1980). Competitive strategy: Techniques for analyzing industries and competitors. New York, NY: Free Press.

Ramanna, K. (2015). Is the promotion worth the price? *Harvard Business Review, 93*(10), 123–125.

Rath, T., & Buckingham, M. (2007). StrengthsFinder 2.0. New York, NY: Gallup Press.

The results-driven manager: Getting people on board. (2005). Boston, MA: Harvard Business School Press.

Rice, C. (2010). *Condoleezza Rice: A memoir of my extraordinary, ordinary family and me.* New York, NY: Delacorte Press.

Sandberg, S. (with Scovell, N.). (2013). *Lean in: Women, work, and the will to lead.* New York, NY: Knopf.

Sharma, R.S. (2010). *The leader who had no title: A modern fable on real success in business and in life.* New York, NY: Free Press.

Sinek, S. (2009). *Start with why: How great leaders inspire everyone to take action.* New York, NY: Portfolio.

Trammell, J. (2014). *The CEO tightrope: How to master the balancing act of a successful CEO.* Austin, TX: Greenleaf Book Group Press.

Warren, R. (2002). *The purpose-driven life: What on earth am I here for?* Grand Rapids, MI: Zondervan.

Welch, J., & Welch, S. (2005). *Winning.* New York, NY: HarperBusiness.

Welch, J., & Welch, S. (2015). *The real-life MBA: Your no-BS guide to winning the game, building a team, and growing your career.* New York, NY: HarperBusiness.

Wright, W.C. (2005). *Don't step on the rope! Reflections on leadership, relationships, and teamwork.* Waynesboro, GA: Paternoster Press.

References

BoardSource. (2010). What are the legal responsibilities of nonprofit boards? Retrieved from https://www.bridgespan .org/insights/library/boards/legal-responsibilities-nonprofit-boards

Sarbanes-Oxley Act of 2002, Pub. L. No. 107-204. Retrieved from https://www.gpo.gov/fdsys/pkg/PLAW-107publ204 /pdf/PLAW-107publ204.pdf

Spears, L. (1998). Introduction. In L.C. Spears (Ed.), *The power of servant-leadership* (pp. 1–15). San Francisco, CA: Berrett-Koehler.

CHAPTER 21

Professional Nursing Association Membership and Board Leadership

Deidre Walton, JD, MSN, RN, Ronnie Ursin, DNP, MBA, RN, NEA-BC, FACHE, and Mary Magee Gullatte, PhD, RN, ANP-BC, AOCN®, FAAN

Every person has a longing to be significant; to make a contribution; to be a part of something noble and purposeful.

—John C. Maxwell

Introduction

The 2011 landmark report *The Future of Nursing: Leading Change, Advancing Health* has had a resounding effect on professional nursing from the bedside to the White House. The report, published by the Institute of Medicine (IOM, now called the Health and Medicine Division of the National Academies of Sciences, Engineering, and Medicine), set forth recommendations for an action-oriented blueprint for nursing's future. One of the key recommendations was to have more nurses represented on boards, on executive management teams, and in other key leadership positions as public, private, and government healthcare decision makers at every level. Serving on the board of a professional membership association is a valuable experience to prepare one for representation on corporate or health system boards.

Leadership is key to safe patient care and advancing the profession at every level. As we advance nursing practice and leadership, association membership and leadership become paramount to advancing healthcare and patient outcomes above and beyond our employer and employee relationship. Professional association leadership and membership are core to being a professional nurse. It is what makes one a knowledgeable and valuable healthcare employee or employer. One cannot truly be a professional today in the climate of care without membership in a professional association. Association membership also is essential to driving policy change, setting standards and scope of practice, and identifying competencies for nursing's future. From clinical nurses to advanced practice nurses, across practice settings, the role of nurses will continue to expand, and leadership is imperative.

Nurses represent the largest group of healthcare professionals (National Council of State Boards of Nursing, 2015). The latest data indicate that more than three million nurses are practicing in the United States (Health Resources and Services Administration, 2013). A delicate balance exists between the number of aging nurses leaving the workforce and the number of new nurses entering the profession. The aging of the nursing workforce continues to be top of mind for many organizations. In addition, the projected demand for nurses will exceed one million new nurses by 2022 (Elsevier, 2015), and there continues to be a need to attract diverse and multigenerational individuals into the nursing profession. Healthcare system executives are under continuing pressure to reduce the cost of delivering care, dealing with dynamic changes in federal and state health care, market dynamics, community needs, and trends aimed at improving quality (Wachtel, 2012).

Nursing has professional leadership opportunities spanning all aspects of the profession. Professional nursing associations provide an opportunity for nurses to connect with others and stay informed about professional practice standards, health policy, and advocacy and to create a stronger collective voice for the profession.

Although nurses have a work/practice home, they also need a professional home. That professional home is anchored in professional nursing association membership. A plethora of nursing associations exist, including those that focus on education, research, administration, and specialty practice (e.g., disease specific, ambulatory and acute care, legal nurse, informatics, minority nurse associations). Each member association needs nurse leaders to serve on executive boards and committees and in some cases to serve as chief executive officers.

An opportunity for association boards to change and transform is related to underrepresentation of certain groups in board leadership. This underrepresentation is multifaceted and inclusive of professional nurses, gender, age, and race. Research conducted by the American Hospital Association's Center for Healthcare Governance (Totten, 2010) found significant disparities in nurse participation on boards and that only 2% of nonprofit hospital governing board members are nurses. In 2015, McCambridge reported that 80% of nonprofit board members were White, compared with 92.7% of corporate board members. Less than half, 43%, of nonprofit board members were women. Likewise, McGregor and Schulte (2015) reported that only 19% of board seats in the United States are held by women. These data point to opportunities to close the gap related to underrepresentation of women and minorities serving on nonprofit boards. At some point soon, the age gap will need to be closed, infusing boards with members of the millennial generation. As leaders promote active membership of nurses in professional associations and ultimately participation of nurses on boards, it is imperative for nurses to understand their role and the competencies needed when preparing for board leadership. Nonprofit board leadership governance affords another opportunity for nurses to lead the profession. Serving on the board of a professional membership association is a valuable experience to prepare for representation on corporate or health systems boards.

This chapter will review the genesis, ethics, and governance of professional associations, as well as opportunities for a sustainable future through nurse leadership on boards, which begins with association membership. It also will expound on the 2011 IOM *Future of Nursing* report recommendation as it relates to the role of associations in supporting leadership development for nurses leading the transformation of health care. In addition, this chapter highlights the call from the Nurses on Boards Coalition to have 10,000 nurse leaders appointed to boards by 2020.

Genesis of Professional Nursing Associations

The origin of nursing associations dates back to as early as 1893 at the time of the World's Columbian Exposition in Chicago. A convention was held at the fair. The convention and exposition was a gathering of the International Congress of Charities, Correction, and Philanthropy (University of Pennsylvania School of Nursing, n.d.). It is reported that a group of nurses presented papers at the exposition on the status of nursing. The presentation reportedly prompted a call to action on three main issues: (a) the lack of formal education of nurses in the United States (only 10% were trained in hospital training schools, which at the time was the primary training of nurses), (b) the need for nurse licensure, and (c) the need for nurses to unite to advance the profession (University of Pennsylvania School of Nursing, n.d.).

In 1896, just three years after that historic meeting in Chicago, the Nurses' Associated Alumnae of the United States and Canada was formed. The organization was later renamed the American Nurses Association (ANA) (University of Pennsylvania School of Nursing, n.d.). History records show that expanded goals of the new association included the following: (a) promote licensure, (b) secure passage of a Nurse Practice Act, (c) establish a Code of Ethics, (d) promote the image of nursing, and (e) promote the financial interests of nurses (ANA & National League of Nursing Education, 1949). Today the goals of ANA include (a) advancing the nursing profession by promoting high practice standards, (b) supporting safe, ethical work environments, (c) strengthening nurses' health and wellness, (d) advocating on healthcare issues relevant to nurses and the public, and (e) improving health care overall (ANA, n.d.).

The first state nursing associations were formed in 1901 in New York, New Jersey, Illinois, and Virginia (Hostutler, Kennedy, Mason, & Schorr, 1999). In 1908, Martha Franklin founded the National Association of Colored Graduate Nurses (NACGN). The main goal of NACGN was to win the integration of Black RNs into schools of nursing, jobs, and nursing organizations (African American Registry [AAR], n.d.). NACGN successfully lobbied for an integrated U.S. Cadet Nurse Corps during World War II (AAR, n.d.).

In 1951, NACGN, having achieved its monumental goals, merged with the American Nurses Association (AAR, n.d.). The legacy that inspired the formation of nursing associations to support the advancement of the profession continues to be a core strategic goal of all nursing associations.

From the legacy beginnings of visionary and passionate nurse leaders more than 123 years ago, the profession of nursing has made and continues to make phenomenal gains in advancing the profession and preparing nurses for transformational leadership. This was one of the original association's goals in 1896. These goals, in modified form, continue to be relevant and explored today.

Professional nursing associations have grown from one core association to a plethora. They span across states, specialties and subspecialties, care settings, practice levels, practice domains, and ethnic groups. Specialty associations offer members connections with colleagues who have the same specialty practice and disease focus and the opportunity to learn and grow in a specific area of concentration different from general nursing associations.

Call to Action From the *Future of Nursing* Report

One recommendation from the *Future of Nursing* report detailed the need to prepare and enable nurses to lead change and advance health. Likewise, a call to action for nursing associations is to provide leadership development, mentoring programs, and opportunities to lead for all their members (IOM, 2011). Recommendation 2 from the report is

> to expand opportunities for nurses to lead and diffuse collaborative improvement efforts. Private and public funders, health care organizations, nursing education programs, and nursing associations should expand opportunities for nurses to lead and manage collaborative efforts with physicians and other members of the health care team to conduct research and to redesign and improve practice environments and health systems. (IOM, 2011, p. 11)

Recommendation 6 also has a call to action for nursing associations and accrediting bodies centered in lifelong learning for nurses (IOM, 2011).

The IOM charge to nursing associations is to prepare their members to lead the transformation of health care. One strategy for member associations is to identify action plans to achieve this goal for their members. Member associations are the professional home for nurses and should be a source for leadership development programs.

National Nurses on Boards Challenge

In 2014, nurse leaders from across the United States gathered with a coalition of nursing organizations to discuss the future of the nursing profession at the Future of Nursing: Campaign for Action Summit (Robert Wood Johnson Foundation, 2014). As several hundred nurse leaders and champions from around the country gathered, this powerful coalition of national nursing organizations launched an unprecedented effort to increase the presence of nurses on corporate and nonprofit health-related boards of directors.

The Nurses on Boards Coalition implemented a national strategy aimed at bringing the perspectives of nurses to governing boards and to national and state commissions that are working to improve health. The goal is to seat 10,000 nurses on boards by 2020 (Robert Wood Johnson Foundation, 2014). Nurse leaders at every level should consider being counted in this number.

Association Governance: Member Led and Staff Run

Most member associations are led by volunteer members who are elected or appointed to office and managed by paid staff, including the chief executive officer (CEO). The governance team champions the goals of the association to govern in the best interests of the members and the association at local, state, national, and international levels. The association staff, who may or may not be nurses, are charged with maintaining daily operations of the association and report to the CEO. The CEO is the one staff member hired by the board and reports to the board. Different specialty associations will have some variation in their governance structure regarding the work of the board, CEO, and staff. The goal is to have a genuine professional collaborative partnership between the board leadership and CEO to govern in the best interests of the association (Gullatte, Brown, Nevidjon, & Rieger, 2012).

Nurses are needed to provide vision to sustain and strengthen associations and boards for the future. This leadership requires gathering knowledge from a scan of the current environment and identifying historical trends to help inform future changes needed to sustain relevance. Being astute to these future directional road maps will help the nurse leader to make sound decisions to help set the strategic direction of the association.

The American Society of Association Executives (ASAE) has a number of publications for association executives to be aware of membership needs in sustaining a dynamic and relevant association. ASAE authors Sladek (2011) and Jacobs (2014) advised associations of the impending end of traditional membership and the must-haves for future sustainability and growth. These include four key areas: *niche*—representing the "go-to" resource for one target audience (avoid the urge to try to be all things to all people); *culture*—recognizing that the effectiveness of the association in recruiting and retaining diverse generational members lies with the culture of its executives and staff; *dues*—proving the value to members for the cost of membership; and *communication*—being able to relay the value and benefits of membership to current and prospective members. As association leaders and future leaders, it is important to maintain relevance (Jacobs, 2014; Sladek, 2011).

Likewise, Coerver and Byers (2011) advised associations of the need to evolve from the traditional model to being in tune with rapid changes in technology and the continual shifting of the environmental and healthcare landscape, not the least of which is recognizing the needs of a multigenerational professional nursing workforce. Leadership in a professional association is similar to that in clinical healthcare organizations, where basic leader competencies, strengths, and vision are required to advance the profession when serving on a nursing or other nonprofit board.

A strategic direction for all nursing associations is to identify tactics to engage a multigenerational nursing workforce in volunteer member association work. The needs of each generation of nurse leaders vary not only by race, gender, and age but by setting as well as specialty and subspecialty practices. This work should begin with a needs assessment of members, with the objective of offering a variety of services to meet the diversity of educational and developmental needs at varying practice points for each member.

Effective and transformational leaders in professional nursing associations are critical to growth, sustainability, and maintaining relevance. The requisite skills for organizational leadership come with the development of specific competencies. To successfully assume board positions, nurses must thoroughly understand the skills and competencies required to competently govern (Bradberry & Greaves, 2012; Hassmiller, 2012; MacKie, 2016; Rath & Conchie, 2008).

Essential Elements for Nonprofit Board Governance

A number of reference sources are available for information related to nonprofit board governance. Korngold (2012) provided critical perspectives on factors for effective governance of nonprofit boards, including achievement, accountability, ownership, and oversight. The four perspectives are explained in the following section.

Achievement

Achievement of the association's vision and mission is imperative to measuring success. Board members set the strategic direction of the organization. Alignment with the core ingredient of success, the mission, is imperative for a board member to succeed. The mission drives the direction in which each member of the board must work to achieve. Fiscal responsibility and other matters related to board participation help achieve the mission of the organization. Key responsibilities of the board include strategy, stewardship, governance, and management of the CEO, which includes hiring, performance review, and compensation.

As one example, the American Association of Critical-Care Nurses (AACN, n.d.) has a mission to contribute to consumer health and safety through comprehensive credentialing of nurses to ensure that their practice is consistent with established standards of excellence in caring for acutely and critically ill patients and their families. Thus, the board's focus, among other things, is on driving AACN's achievement of credentialing nurses based on standards of excellence in caring for patients at acute and critical levels of care.

Another example may be viewed through the American Organization of Nurse Executives (AONE). One of AONE's board responsibilities dictates, "Approve the strategic plan to meet the organization's vision, mission, and goals" (AONE, 2016, "Responsibilities"). The mission of AONE is "to shape health care through innovative and expert nursing leadership" (AONE, n.d., "Our Mission"). AONE focuses its activities on advancement of members through education, certification, research, and public policy. AONE integrates the duty of loyalty into practice to ensure board members understand that board leadership is a group responsibility and not a forum for individual achievement.

Likewise, the Oncology Nursing Society (ONS) has developed leadership competencies (see ONS, 2012). ONS continues to provide ongoing association leadership development opportunities for its members. For example, ONS holds an annual summer Leadership Weekend for current and emerging chapter and community leaders and other board leaders. In addition, ONS has an esteemed legacy of supporting the development of international oncology nursing associations in board governance and association leadership.

Accountability

A critical element to success for board leaders is to know and understand whether the association is achieving its established mission and vision. Board leaders are responsible for establishing ways to evaluate and answer a singular question: "How do we know that we, as an organization, are achieving what we set out to do?" Worrall (2013) viewed accountability as a core component of strength-based leadership that starts at the top.

Korngold (2012) stated that to help answer this question, collaboration with key stakeholders is important. Board members are expected to be prepared and engaged in regularly scheduled meetings and committees. Meetings are pivotal points where board members review association finances and programmatic initiatives. Data sharing in meetings allows board members to ask questions and discuss potential realignment of strategic direction based on outcomes. Attendance and engagement at meetings provide a forum for board members to discuss the factors, whether internal or external to the association, that may affect their ability to achieve success.

Ownership

The third essential element for effective governance is understanding by board members that the association's success is in the hands of the governing body. The association's CEO cannot achieve success without support of the member board. CEOs understand their significant role in capitalizing on the strength of the members of the association, rather than solely depending on the board to drive change in association culture to support the desired mission and vision.

Ingram (2009) identified 10 basic responsibilities of nonprofit boards (see Figure 21-1). Board governance encompasses the major scope of the board's work. The responsibilities are not to be taken lightly and require specific competencies for success.

ASAE is the membership organization for the association profession. It offers many member leader services and a home for association executives. One service offered is a certification program (ASAE, n.d.; Cox & Radwan, 2015). The certified association executive (CAE) is similar to other professional certifications in that it is designed to "elevate professional standards, enhance

---

Figure 21-1. Ten Basic Responsibilities of Nonprofit Boards

1. Determine mission and purpose. It is the board's responsibility to create and review a statement of mission and purpose that articulates the organization's goals, means, and primary constituents served.
2. Select the chief executive. Boards must reach consensus on the chief executive's responsibilities and undertake a careful search to find the most qualified individual for the position.
3. Support and evaluate the chief executive. The board should ensure that the chief executive has the moral and professional support he or she needs to further the goals of the organization.
4. Ensure effective planning. Boards must actively participate in an overall planning process and assist in implementing and monitoring the plan's goals.
5. Monitor and strengthen programs and services. The board's responsibility is to determine which programs are consistent with the organization's mission and monitor their effectiveness.
6. Ensure adequate financial resources. One of the board's foremost responsibilities is to secure adequate resources for the organization to fulfill its mission.
7. Protect assets and provide proper financial oversight. The board must assist in developing the annual budget and ensuring that proper financial controls are in place.
8. Build a competent board. All boards have a responsibility to articulate prerequisites for candidates, orient new members, and periodically and comprehensively evaluate their own performance.
9. Ensure legal and ethical integrity. The board is ultimately responsible for adherence to legal standards and ethical norms.
10. Enhance the organization's public standing. The board should clearly articulate the organization's mission, accomplishments, and goals to the public and garner support from the community.

Note. Copyright 2016 by BoardSource. Used with permission from www.boardsource.org. BoardSource is the premiere resource for practical information, tools, and training for board members and chief executives of nonprofit organizations worldwide. For more information about BoardSource, visit www.boardsource.org or call 800-883-6262. Content may not be reproduced or used for any purpose other than that which is specifically requested without written permission from BoardSource.

---

individual performance, and designate association professionals who demonstrate the knowledge essential to manage an association in today's challenging environment" (ASAE, n.d., para. 1).

Nurses with aspirations for association leadership should explore the websites of ASAE, American College of Healthcare Executives, AONE, and other organizations for more information about programs and services (see Figure 21-2). Specialty nursing associations are also good resources to explore, such as ONS, AACN, the Association of periOperative Registered Nurses, the Emergency Nurses Association, the Association of Women's Health, Obstetric and Neonatal Nurses, and the American Association of Nurse Practitioners, to name a few.

Di Frances (2005) stated that leaders must be visible. Board members should attempt to be visible to help support and resolve association strategic goals and tactics. Di Frances noted that visibility should be easily achieved through strategic and purposeful use of technology. Integrated use of social media will improve communication and help associations connect with multigenerational members.

Perkins (2010) suggested five key ways for board members to improve visibility and show ownership of the association. The first strategy is to get face time with the leadership team, specifically the CEO and, if appropriate, the executive team, especially when developing the strategic plan. The second strategy is to share success stories using the STAR method, which is a structured manner of responding to a behavioral-based interview question by discussing the specific situation, task, action, and result of the situation being described. The third tactic is to connect with staff in the organization when appropriate; one approach might be to have a process team leader present outcomes to the board about the progress made toward a particular strategic goal. The fourth suggestion is to train the team to capitalize on success and celebrate. This gives the staff a sense that the board is aware of the work they are doing and affords an opportunity for the

---

Figure 21-2. Select Healthcare Executive Associations

- **American Association of Colleges of Nursing (AACN):** AACN's mission statement is: "To be the collective voice for academic nursing, AACN serves as the catalyst for excellence and innovation in nursing education, research, and practice."
www.aacn.nche.edu
- **American College of Healthcare Executives (ACHE):** ACHE supports and leads a number of initiatives that advance healthcare management excellence and improves the delivery of healthcare. A primary activity for ACHE is education of healthcare executives about the public policy field and how to be effective in the public policy process.
www.ache.org
- **American Health Care Association (AHCA):** The American Health Care Association is a nonprofit federation of affiliate state health organizations, together representing more than 11,000 nonprofit and for-profit nursing facility, assisted living, and subacute care providers that care for approximately one million elderly and disabled individuals each day.
www.ahcancal.org
- **American Nurses Credentialing Center (ANCC):** ANCC offers certifications for nurse executives (NE-BC and NEA-BC). The mission of ANCC, a subsidiary of the American Nurses Association, is to promote excellence in nursing and health care globally through credentialing programs.
www.nursecredentialing.org
- **American Organization of Nurse Executives (AONE):** AONE has provided leadership, professional development, advocacy, and research to advance nursing practice and patient care, promote nursing leadership excellence, and shape public policy for health care nationwide.
www.aone.org/resources
- **American Society of Association Executives (ASAE):** ASAE is the essential organization for association management, representing both organizations and individual association professionals. Their mission is to help association professionals achieve higher levels of performance in diverse and inclusive leadership that brings a wide variety of perspectives and experiences to inform decision making.
www.asaecenter.org
- **BoardSource®:** BoardSource is a national organization working to strengthen nonprofit board leadership. Its mission is to inspire and support excellence in nonprofit governance and board and staff leadership.
www.boardsource.org/eweb
- **International Association of Health Care Professionals (IAHCP):** IAHCP is an exclusive community for healthcare professionals to interact, exchange ideas, educate, and empower each other. Members enjoy a wealth of resources, benefits, and services dedicated to enhancing their lives and promoting their careers.
www.iahcp.com
- **Nursing Organizations Alliance (NOA):** The Alliance™ is an association of nursing organizations united to create a strong voice for nurses that provides a forum for identification, education, and collaboration building on issues to advance the nursing profession.
http://nursing-alliance.org

---

board to acknowledge the team along with the CEO. The fifth strategy is to use social networking to assist with positioning the organization to reflect the human component of leadership. Understand that these may be new concepts for some association boards and is a step outside the traditional structure of "how it has always been done." However, this visibility should not interfere with the relationship and management of the staff by the CEO. Remember, the CEO is the only board employee, and the association staff report to the CEO.

Oversight

The goal of board oversight is to ensure that the executive officer or executive director manage in the best interests of individual stakeholders (Faleye, Hoitash, & Hoitash, 2013). Most nonprofit boards have three areas of responsibility regarding the executive position: design and implementation of executive compensation, removal of the executive, and declaration of executive compensation.

Faleye et al. (2013) found boards to be most effective when evaluating services and leader performance. Members of association boards are to be visible, strategic thinkers, advocates, and revenue generators who maintain national and international perspective on the future direction of health care. This board insight and connection with the larger environment will help inform the strategic direction of the association board. Connecting with the larger group can also be done through a sampling method called *crowdsourcing.* This strategy involves soliciting information and opinions from a representative sample of the association members. The information gathered helps to inform board decisions when member perspectives are solicited.

Board Governance Competencies

In his 2013 book *Principles of 21st Century Governance*, Les Wallace (author of Chapter 14) identified six competencies of executive board leadership: strategic thinking and planning, organizational transformation, policy leadership, leadership succession, guidance of a complex organizational enterprise, and governance (Wallace, 2013). These six competencies also complement the governance leadership competencies outlined by AACN in 2006.

The six AACN competencies were self-leadership; global thinking; visioning; consensus building; delivering effective messages; and knowledge and commitment to the mission, values, and work of the association (AACN, 2006). All of these competencies are necessary for strong association leadership governance of not only the executive team but the other leaders and staff as well.

Professional nursing organizations draw their strength and sustainability from maximizing the potential of its diverse membership. They must maintain a sustained growth strategy built on the collective knowledge and skills of its membership and its leadership. According to the Department of the Army (2006), "Leaders serve to provide purpose, direction, and motivation." An effective leader must demonstrate behavior that creates an inclusive environment and maximizes stakeholders' potential.

Leadership development seeks to engage in cultivating each member of the team to improve not only individuals but the team and the association. One of the core behaviors is an executive presence that produces synergy, enthusiasm, and courage to reach beyond the present. In addition, a focus should be on developing strength-based leadership through evidence-based executive leader coaching and development (MacKie, 2016; Rath & Conchie, 2008).

Impact of Ethics on Association Culture

Professional nursing associations and the elected leadership have a fiduciary responsibility to make ethical decisions and do what is right and in the best interest of the association and its members. According to Cooper (2012), ethics focuses on what is right, fair, just, and good. Chapter 15 presents an in-depth perspective of leadership ethics. Other responsibilities include setting practice standards in specialty practice, creating a research agenda to advance the science, and developing nurses for leadership (Lakey, 2010). These responsibilities are also in keeping with the 2011 IOM recommendations for the role of nursing associations. Generally, members of a professional association's board of directors have the same legal duties of those serving on other nonprofit and for-profit organizations. The National Council of Nonprofits (2016) suggested board membership holds individuals accountable to the duties of care, loyalty, and obedience.

A *duty of care* requires a board member to adhere to standards of reasonable care while performing in the capacity of a member of the board that could knowingly harm others. Professional association board memberships require nurses to ensure sagacious use of the organization's financial and capital assets and provide strategic forward thinking to advance programmatic and systematic sustainability.

A *duty of loyalty* appeals to a board member to act in the best interests of the organization. A member of a board must always be ascetic and not directed by self-interest. The duty of loyalty requires the member to act on behalf of the organization when making decisions; it is considered unreserved loyalty to the organization.

The *duty of obedience* is the duty to remain devoted to the goals of the organization (Moore, 2013). Duty of obedience requires each board member to follow governing documents of the organization, applicable laws, and restrictions imposed by contributors to ensure that the organization adheres to regulatory requirements. This duty also requires board members to ensure the association adheres to its purpose, mission, vision, values, and objectives.

Members of professional associations elect leaders to provide guidance and oversight according to the association's mission, vision, goals, and values. Decisions are made collaboratively, not unilaterally, after proper vetting with the member leadership and executive staff of the association. A strong organizational culture within an association is developed by having guiding principles, bylaws, and other governance structures such as policies and procedures that should be in place and agreed upon by the leadership before they are elected (Nguyen, 2011). A well-integrated corporate culture can have significant implications during a crisis (Kurtz, 2003). When the appropriate structure is in place and committed to by the leadership, it can help mitigate conflicts or at least provide a process for resolving conflicts, allowing the leadership to come to agreement or consensus on how to come to a decision.

Professional nursing associations must develop a strategic plan to facilitate the growth of its organization. Association leaders are responsible for constantly understanding the environmental scan to forecast strategic direction and to ensure continued relevance with the changing professional nursing demographics. They also need to stay in touch with the professional needs of a diverse, multigenerational membership, with different beliefs, needs, and ideals. For more on nurse ethics, see Chapter 15.

Steering Your Career Toward Association Board Leadership

One of the goals of associations is to develop members for leadership. This leadership can be either in a nursing association or on other healthcare organization boards. Influential nurse leaders have articulated essential competencies for nurse leaders to be effective board members. Hassmiller (2012) shared how nurses can take the first steps to serving on a board. Essential elements for board participation include stewardship, preparation, personal planning, collaboration, mentorship, and education. These elements coupled with core leader competencies can position the nurse for board leadership.

Board stewardship is the activity of protecting and being responsible for all aspects of the association. Effective board members place self-interests, such as career advancement, special interests, and personal agendas, well below what is in the best interests of the association. Instead of representing the interests of external groups, board members align with association values and base decisions on the needs of the communities served by the organization and its members.

Board preparation involves self-reflection of ability to function on a board. Understanding every facet of an organization and how all elements work in tandem is necessary for leader success. Nurses are encouraged to gain knowledge and leadership experience by seeking opportunities to increase responsibilities in work-related activities and volunteer roles within the community.

A professional road map or strategic plan outlines direction for board leaders. Association leaders must be able to articulate outcomes and detail necessary strategies and tactics to achieve said outcomes. Understanding achievement of outcomes is not accomplished by an individual but rather by using resources of personal networks. Hassmiller (2012) suggested that nurses find out what boards look for in prospective members, contributions a nurse makes, and special skills needed for success. Three primary tactics for nurses to build leader competencies identified by Hassmiller include the following:

- Build connections: Begin to build connections outside the nursing profession and more broadly within the community. Again, volunteer with an organization and fully embrace its issues.
- Find a mentor: Ask a mentor for concrete advice. Begin to develop a network of relationships in the community, especially those outside of nursing (read more about mentoring in Chapter 22).
- Seek ongoing education: Invest in continuing education on leadership and board governance.

Member Association Board Opportunities for Nurse Leaders

General and healthcare associations have championed the development of members through education, training, supporting, and coaching (Center for Health Leadership and Practice, n.d.). Associations provide tools, skills, and diverse leadership opportunities and experiences to maximize the contributions to board service (Schyve, 2009). Figure 21-2 identifies some of the leading boards for general and healthcare association leader development.

In addition to the list in Figure 21-2, each state has a hospital association, most with a subsidiary association of nurse leaders for the state. The American Hospital Association (www.aha .org) is the national organization that represents and serves all types of hospitals, healthcare networks, and their patients and communities. Likewise, a plethora of specialty healthcare associations exist with similar missions, for example:

- ONS (www.ons.org), which serves both national and international members and whose mission is to advance excellence in oncology nursing and quality cancer care
- Association of Community Cancer Centers (ACCC, www.accc-cancer.org), whose mission is to be the leading education and advocacy organization for the interprofessional cancer team (ACCC, n.d.)
- Association of Cancer Executives (ACE, www.cancerexecutives.org), which is a national organization committed to the leadership development of oncology executives through continuing education and professional networking designed to promote improvement in patient care delivery (ACE, n.d.)

As nurse leaders and healthcare executives, it is important to be aware of associations related to the nursing profession, specialties, and subspecialties. Figure 21-2 represents a few general associations that may be of interest. Once identified, leaders and executives may choose an organization to join as a member and aspire to serve on a board, especially given the call to action to increase the number of nurses on boards.

Summary

Professional nursing associations are critical to garner unity in the profession and to collectively respond to human rights issues, advocate for social and health policy, and set standards of practice. Professional nursing associations and the elected or appointed leadership have a fiduciary responsibility to make ethical decisions and do what is right and in the best interests of the association.

As a healthcare association leader, it is critical to concentrate on the needs of the members, as well as association relevance. An equally important role is developing policies and programs to benefit the membership and to focus on the mission, vision, and goals to transform care outcomes and advance the profession of nursing.

As healthcare associations respond to the call to action of the 2011 IOM landmark report *The Future of Nursing: Leading Change, Advancing Health*, as well as the challenge set forth by the Nurses on Boards Coalition, professional associations must continue to educate, develop, and prepare nurses to engage as advocates from the bedside to the White House. As the profession works to have more nurses represented on boards and serving on executive management teams and in other key leadership positions as public, private, and government healthcare decision makers at every level, nurses must focus on leader competencies and skills needed for success. Further, nurse leaders need to find their professional home and become actively engaged in professional associations to strengthen the voice and advancement of the profession.

References

African American Registry. (n.d.). National Association of Colored Graduate Nurses founded. Date: Tue, 1908-08-25. Retrieved from http://aaregistry.org/historic_events/view/national-association-colored-graduate-nurses-founded

American Association of Critical-Care Nurses. (n.d.). About AACN. Retrieved from https://www.aacn.org/about-aacn

American Association of Critical-Care Nurses. (2006). Framework for governance leadership positions. Retrieved from https://www.aacn.org/about-aacn/board/framework-for-governance-leadership-positions

American Nurses Association. (n.d.). About ANA. Retrieved from http://www.nursingworld.org/FunctionalMenu Categories/AboutANA

American Nurses Association & National League of Nursing Education. (1949). *Nursing practice acts and board rules: A digest.* New York, NY: Authors.

American Organization of Nurse Executives. (n.d.). About AONE. Retrieved from http://www.aone.org/about /overview.shtml

American Organization of Nurse Executives. (2016). 2016 AONE election fact sheet. Retrieved from http://www.aone .org/docs/About/election/2016%20Board%20Criteria%203%20yearcorrected.pdf

American Society of Association Executives. (n.d.). CAE certification. Retrieved from https://www.asaecenter.org /programs/cae-certification

Association of Cancer Executives. (n.d.). About Association of Cancer Executives. Retrieved from http://www .cancerexecutives.org

Association of Community Cancer Centers. (n.d.). About the Association of Community Cancer Centers. Retrieved from https://www.accc-cancer.org

Bradberry, T., & Greaves, J. (2012). *Leadership 2.0.* San Diego, CA: TalentSmart.

Center for Health Leadership and Practice. (n.d.). About us. Retrieved from http://www.healthleadership.org/about

Coerver, H., & Byers, M. (2011). *Race for relevance: 5 radical changes for associations.* Washington, DC: ASAE.

Cooper, T.L. (2012). *The responsible administrator: An approach to ethics for the administrative role* (6th ed.). San Francisco, CA: Jossey-Bass.

Cox, J.B., & Radwan, S.S. (2015). *ASAE handbook of professional practices in association management* (3rd ed.). San Francisco, CA: Jossey-Bass.

Department of the Army. (2006). *Army leadership: Competent, confident, and agile.* Retrieved from http://usacac.army .mil/cac2/Repository/Materials/fm6-22.pdf

Di Frances, J. (2005). *The six essential leadership attributes.* Retrieved from http://www.difrances.com/articles/six _essential_leadership_attributes.pdf

Elsevier. (2015, December 17). *3 nursing trends to expect for 2016.* Retrieved from http://www.confidenceconnected .com/blog/2015/12/17/3-nursing-trends-to-expect-for-2016

Faleye, O., Hoitash, R., & Hoitash, U. (2013, March 19). The trouble with too much board oversight. *MIT Sloan Management Review.* Retrieved from http://sloanreview.mit.edu/article/the-trouble-with-too-much-board-oversight

Gullatte, M., Brown, C., Nevidjon, B., & Rieger, P. (2012). Successful associations are volunteer led, staff run. *ONS Connect, 27*(6), 22.

Hassmiller, S.B. (2012). Professional development: Nurses on boards. *American Journal of Nursing, 112*(12), 61–66. doi:10.1097/01.NAJ.0000412641.93516.99

Health Resource and Services Administration. (2013). *The U.S. nursing workforce: Trends in supply and education.* Retrieved from https://bhw.hrsa.gov/sites/defalt/files/bhw/nchwa/projections/nursingworkforcetrnedsoct2013.pdf

Hostutler, J., Kennedy, M.S., Mason, D., & Schorr, T.M. (1999). Then and now: Nurses as leaders in health care. *American Journal of Nursing, 99*(12), 36–37. doi:10.1097/00000446-199912000-00038

Ingram, R.T. (2009). *Ten basic responsibilities of nonprofit boards* (2nd ed.). Washington, DC: BoardSource.

Institute of Medicine. (2011). *The future of nursing: Leading change, advancing health.* Washington, DC: National Academies Press.

Jacobs, S. (2014). *The art of membership: How to attract, retain and cement member loyalty.* San Francisco, CA: Jossey-Bass.

Korngold, A. (2012). The role of the nonprofit board: Four essential factors for effective governance. *Huffington Post.* Retrieved from http://www.huffingtonpost.com/alice-korngold/the-role-of-the-nonprofit_b_1867740 .html

Kurtz, R.S. (2003). Organizational culture, decision-making, and integrity: The National Park Service and the *Exxon Valdez. Public Integrity, 5,* 305–317. doi:10.1080/15580989.2003.11770956

Lakey, B.M. (2010). *Board fundamentals: Understanding roles in nonprofit governance* (2nd ed.). Washington, DC: BoardSource.

MacKie, D. (2016). *Strength-based leadership coaching in organizations: An evidence-based guide to positive leadership development.* Philadelphia, PA: Kogan Page.

McCambridge, R. (2015, January 27). BoardSource's Board Governance Index: Is your board "normal"? *Nonprofit Quarterly.* Retrieved from https://nonprofitquarterly.org/2015/01/27/nonprofit-board-governance-index-is-your -board-normal

McGregor, J., & Schulte, B. (2015, January 13). Women still hold only 19 percent of U.S. board seats. What could change that? *Washington Post.* Retrieved from https://www.washingtonpost.com/news/on-leadership/wp/2015/01 /13/women-still-hold-only-19-percent-of-u-s-corporate-board-seats-what-could-change-that

Moore, D.B. (2013, July 26). The fiduciary duty of obedience. *Moore Thoughts on Nonprofit Law.* Retrieved from http:// moorenonprofitlaw.com/the-fiduciary-duty-of-obedience

National Council of Nonprofits. (2016). Board roles and responsibilities. Retrieved from https://www.councilofnon profits.org/tools-resources/board-roles-and-responsibilities

National Council of State Boards of Nursing. (2015). Yearly NCSBN environmental scan released. *In Focus, 1*(4), 3. Retrieved from https://www.ncsbn.org/InFocus_Winter2015.pdf

Nguyen, S. (2011, February 14). Creating an ethical organizational culture. *Workplace Psychology.* Retrieved from https://workplacepsychology.net/2011/02/14/creating-an-ethical-organizational-culture

Oncology Nursing Society. (2012). *Oncology Nursing Society leadership competencies.* Retrieved from https://www.ons .org/sites/default/files/leadershipcomps.pdf

Perkins, P. (2010, July 6). 5 ways to improve your visibility as a leader: Good leadership requires teamwork. *Black Enterprise.* Retrieved from http://www.blackenterprise.com/career/5-ways-to-improve-your-visibility-as-a-leader

Rath, T., & Conchie, B. (2008). *Strengths based leadership.* New York, NY: Gallup Press.

Robert Wood Johnson Foundation. (2014, December 17). A goal and a challenge: Putting 10,000 nurses on governing boards by 2020. Retrieved from http://www.rwjf.org/en/library/articles-and-news/2014/12/a-goal-and -a-challenge--putting-10-000-nurses-on-governing-board.html

Schyve, P.M. (2009). *Leadership in healthcare organizations: A guide to Joint Commission leadership standards.* Retrieved from http://www.jointcommission.org/assets/1/18/WP_Leadership_Standards.pdf

Sladek, S.L. (2011). *The end of membership as we know it: Building the fortune-flipping, must-have association of the next century.* Washington, DC: ASAE.

Totten, M.K. (2010). Nurses on healthcare boards: A smart and logical move to make. *Healthcare Executive, 25*(3), 84–87.

University of Pennsylvania School of Nursing. (n.d.). Nursing, history and health care. Retrieved from http://www.nursing.upenn.edu/nhhc

Wachtel, A. (2012, August 1). Development strategies for a new era of health care. *Urban Land Magazine.* Retrieved from http://urbanland.uli.org/planning-design/development-strategies-for-a-new-era-of-health-care

Wallace, L. (2013). *Principles of 21st century governance: Journey to high performance boards.* Aurora, CO: Signature Resources.

Worrall, D. (2013). *Accountability leadership: How great leaders build a high performance culture of accountability and responsibility.* Carlton, New South Wales, Australia: Accountability Code

CHAPTER 22

Mentoring Current and Future Nurse Leaders

Angela Adjetey Appiah, MSN, MPH, MA, RN, FAACM, and
Mary Magee Gullatte, PhD, RN, ANP-BC, AOCN®, FAAN

Every great achiever is inspired by a great mentor.

—Lailah Gifty Akita

Mentoring is about influencing, inspiring, and empowering others to greatness beyond what they see in themselves.

—Mary Magee Gullatte

Introduction

Many healthcare organizations have embraced the concept of mentoring programs to onboard new employees at every level. The literature supports the findings that successful mentoring programs increase recruitment, retention, and job satisfaction (Colonghi, 2009; Douglas, Garrity, Shepherd, & Brown, 2016; Ellisen, 2011; Young, 2016). It is important that nurses engage in sharing knowledge with novice nurses at every level. Mentor–mentee relationships are forged in not only the clinical setting but academia and research as well. Mentoring is different from preceptorship, coaching, and role modeling. It is believed that mentoring assists both the mentor and mentee to be better than they would be individually prior to the experience (Grossman, 2012). Nurses at every level in their career could benefit from a wise and nurturing mentor. This chapter will focus on the role of mentorship in professional practice and succession planning.

Mentor, Mentee, and Mentorship Defined

In the context of professional nursing practice, the term *preceptor* denotes an individual who is experienced in practice and assigned to coach a novice nurse. Preceptors are usually assigned to a nurse who is new to the profession or practice specialty. In contrast, a *role model* is someone who another person admires and tries to be like ("Role Model," n.d.). Role models may or may not know that they are perceived as such a person by another professional. These two terms were in vogue in the early 1980s and through the early 2000s but have taken a back seat to the more popular concepts of mentor and coach. These roles will be discussed throughout the chapter.

Numerous definitions exist for the word *mentor*, a noun, which means a trusted and wise adviser ("Mentor," n.d.). Neither the word nor the concept is new. However, there is renewed interest in the concept, especially in health care, to support and develop mentees to transform themselves and their practice and achieve at a higher level. The most widely used application for healthcare organizations is in onboarding those new to practice as an RN. Regardless of the application, the return on investment of a mentor program for an organization is positive, with benefits including retention, job satisfaction, and recruitment.

Vance's (2011) definition of mentoring stresses the importance of empowering professional relationships. Vance defined mentoring as a developmental, affirming, and empowering relationship that contributes to personal empowerment, achievement, and professional excellence. The role of the mentor is a broad one, embodying elements of coaching, role modeling, teaching, precepting, and advising.

The mentor provides entrée to networks and professional contacts that may not be open to the mentee otherwise. The mentor possesses knowledge and skills that the mentee lacks, enabling the mentee to rise to a higher level within his or her environment (Maxwell, 2008; Vance, 2011). Research suggests that mentoring relationships are most valuable to mentees when structured with a broad sense of purpose or broad goals that are continually reexamined and change as the relationship evolves (Clutterbuck, 2008; Oberleitner, 2011).

Historically, most nurses have not been engaged in formal mentor–mentee relationships. This is in contrast to the experiences of professionals in other fields who are more likely to have been involved in one or more mentoring experiences. That paradigm is changing as more nurses see the value of the mentor relationship in advancing their practice and the profession.

Most executives of Fortune 500 companies view mentoring as an organizational best practice and a critical employee development tool. Recognizing the value and benefits of mentoring to the organization and individual employees, more than 70% of Fortune 500 companies sponsor formal mentoring programs for their employees (Wells, 2009).

The mentoring relationship is not left to chance. In some cases, incentives are awarded to mentors and mentees for their participation. In these formal relationships, mentors and mentees receive training to assist them in receiving the most benefit from the developmental relationship. For sustainability, companies view serving in the mentor role as a component of performance expectations and performance reviews. Organization leaders are encouraged to transition in and out of mentoring relationships as career goals change and as new professional needs arise. Evaluation of the effects of mentoring may be captured using surveys and examination of employee retention and turnover statistics.

The literature is silent on mentorship programs in health care beyond the C-suite. The opportunity exists for healthcare leaders to champion the corporate model of mentor programs to improve employee retention, satisfaction, and engagement at all levels of nursing and the organization (Douglas et al., 2016; Ellisen, 2011; Johnson & Ridley, 2009). Gray and Brown (2016) cited the importance of investing in a program to develop nurses to be mentors. Adding formalized structure will help to ensure success, value, and sustainability of the mentor program. How is the mentor role different from that of a preceptor, role model, or coach? Preceptors and coaches may be assigned; that is, nurses may not have a choice in who is selected to serve as their preceptor or coach. A role for preceptors and coaches continues to exist as the mentor role gains traction in health care. Coaching relationships most often address performance in some aspect of an individual's work or life, whereas mentoring relationships are more often associated with career development and progression (Adams, 2015; Clutterbuck, 2008). In the mentoring relationship, the mentee typically plays a more active role in the mentor selection process. In informal relationships, the mentee often reaches out to the prospective mentor and may initiate the mentoring relationship. Some healthcare organizations have formal leader development programs and may have a process of pairing mentors and mentees based on a set of behavioral criteria for best fit and benefit to both professionals.

Mentor Versus Coach

Vance (2011) defined a mentor as a person who provides various aspects of role modeling, precepting, and coaching but goes above and beyond. A mentor is a professional friend who is invested in the future development and success of the individual. Mentoring is a freely given gift of interest, time, and involvement. Coaching is guiding people toward their goals through the mutual sharing of experiences and opinions to achieve common outcomes and help individuals achieve their potential (Harvard Business School Press, 2006; Simpson, 2014).

Teaching is the focus of coaching. It occurs between an expert and a novice in the subject or area of the coaching opportunity. Yoder (2002) defined managerial coaching as a defined and focused relationship between a nurse manager and clinical nurse intended to improve skills and knowledge related to expected job performance.

A coach in this circumstance is coaching for future-focus. Mentors use a less formal process than a coach. They help the mentee gain leadership, political, or cultural information about a particular practice setting (e.g., unit, department, hospital) or field (e.g., nursing leadership). This enables the mentoring relationship to be focused on skill acquisition. However, it is not as explicit as the relationship between coach and learner. Leaders can coach others who are not part of their work teams if the agreement is mutual.

The mentor contributes wisdom, techniques, or information that will help the mentee advance in the subject or specialty area of his or her own choice. When the pupil is ready, the teacher will appear. Professional coaches can come from any background or profession and may be engaged by an organization for executive coaching in a specific area for the senior leader. Finding a good coach is a worthwhile investment of time.

Role of the Mentor

Mentees have described characteristics of the ideal mentor, citing individuals who communicate effectively, are highly skilled in interpersonal relationships, possess intelligence and knowledge in their field, and who are psychologically healthy (Johnson, 2003; Noe, Greenberger, & Wang, 2002). Effective and excellent mentors exhibit the following attributes (Grossman, 2012; Johnson & Ridley, 2009):
- Self-empowered
- Not interested in preserving the status quo and are intrigued by new challenges
- Politically astute in the workplace environment
- Able to balance work and personal responsibilities
- Respected by their peers and senior administrators
- Radiate warmth with friendliness, kindness, and approachability
- Good listener
- Willing to invest their time
- Nonjudgmental and are understanding with compassion
- Excellence without perfection

The best mentors typically have been mentored themselves and can recognize the value of the mentoring relationship in their own professional development. Good mentors volunteer to mentor others and have a positive track record (Grossman, 2012).

Zachary and Fischler (2012) and Deziel (2016) recommended several competencies that mentors should acquire to enable them to mentor most effectively:

- Listening
- Maintaining two-way communication
- Being specific and descriptive
- Delivering messages without anger or threats
- Asking for feedback
- Focusing on learning and behavioral change
- Soliciting from the mentee suggestions for best ways to provide ongoing support

The mentor should be committed to the time it takes to mentor someone. The mentor must also demonstrate good interpersonal skills, be supportive, encourage questions, instill confidence in the mentee, and possess the ability to set expectations.

Role of the Mentee

While it is important for mentors to understand their role, it is equally important that mentees understand their commitment to the relationship. Zachary (2009) developed a Mentee Skills Inventory that encompasses 10 key skills that contribute to the mentee's success. These include learning how to receive and give feedback, being self-directed, becoming an open communicator, taking initiative, valuing differences, being reflective, listening, following through, building relationships, and goal setting (Zachary, 2009). While it is important for mentees to understand their personal learning style, other competencies are important as well, such as building trust and accountability. Ellisen (2011) reported that the mentee's career path often is directly related to the mentoring relationship. The mentor and mentee should be evenly matched and have a good relationship based on mutual trust and respect. Zanchetta and Maheu (2015) mentioned the characteristics that mentors look for in mentees, including being a realistic individual who is motivated, self-determined, a flexible thinker, open-minded, inquisitive, intellectually humble, and able to endure uncertainty.

Mentors are excited when individuals with these characteristics present themselves. The mentee must be a willing participant. Deziel (2016) also mentioned the importance of the mentee being open to learning and proactively reaching out to the mentor. Mentees should have expectations, which can be in a form of skills, values, standards, behaviors, and tasks, to build their confidence to begin the socialization process of adapting to the relationship.

Mentoring improves overall performance, but it also provides other benefits for the mentee, including accelerated career mobility, improved professional identity, increased competence and career satisfaction, and increased likelihood to mentor others (Johnson & Ridley, 2009).

Mentor–Mentee Relationships

Mentoring is a two-way or reciprocal process in which, ideally, both partners derive benefit. Reciprocity plays a foundational role in mentoring relationships. It exists in the mentoring relationship when the mentor desires or receives some benefit from the relationship with the mentee. The goals of reciprocity in the mentoring relationship should be transparent, consensual, and beneficial to both partners. Reciprocity should not be coerced (Lee, Kitko, Biddle, & Riegel, 2015; Shore,

Toyokawa, & Anderson, 2008; Zachary, 2009). Benefits to the mentor include potential for rejuvenation of the mentor's career; increased professional stimulation, confidence, and personal fulfillment; and other benefits (Bryant-Lukosius, 2015; Ehrich, Hansford, & Tennent, 2004).

As with other close interpersonal relationships, mentoring relationships can range from highly functional to highly dysfunctional, with most falling somewhere in between (Gormley, 2008). Functional mentoring relationships result in positive outcomes for the mentor and the mentee, including facilitation of psychosocial development and enhancement of career progression (Gormley, 2008; Lee et al., 2015). Dysfunctional mentoring relationships can result in serious negative psychosocial consequences, such as increased stress and anxiety and feelings of inadequacy, and can have a negative impact on the professional role, resulting in job dissatisfaction, problems with job-related activities, and aversion to continuing in mentoring relationships (Lee et al., 2015).

Characteristics of dysfunctional mentors include ultra-aggressiveness, overconfidence, obvious insecurity, and self-centeredness. Poor choices for mentors include individuals with superficial skills and knowledge; negative attitudes about the organization, their work, and the mentee; and known personal problems. Potential mentors to avoid are those who have been mentored and assisted in their own career but take sole credit for their accomplishments and cannot or will not acknowledge that they received help. Other negative characteristics for a mentor include hostility, demeaning behavior, overt aggression, possessiveness, jealousy, credit-taking, deceitfulness, and psychologically or physically abusive behavior (Eby, Buits, Lockwood, & Simon, 2004; Grossman, 2012).

Boundaries in professional relationships provide the basic ground rules and structure for what is appropriate and acceptable in the relationship for both the mentor and the mentee (Barnett, 2008). A discussion of boundaries is particularly relevant in mentoring relationships in which a power differential exists. Boundaries that should be discussed prior to establishing a professional relationship include those related to touch, location, self-disclosure, time, personal space, and receipt of gifts or fees. In professional relationships, just as in personal relationships, boundaries can be rigidly enforced, crossed, or violated (Barnett, 2008).

Organizational policies, professional codes of ethics, and professional practice guidelines help mentors and mentees in determining appropriate situations and contexts within which professional boundaries may be crossed. Lee et al. (2015) reported the following insights on how to maintain a successful mentor–mentee relationship: (a) have common career goals and a shared vision, similar work ethic, and personality match, (b) have mutual commitment to the process, (c) demonstrate flexibility and alignment of needs with mentor's ability, (d) seek clarification when needed, and learn when to lead and when not to be involved, (e) ensure mutual support of career advancement, and (f) identify projects to work on together and celebrate the mentee's growth and success. Introducing the mentee to networking opportunities is also important. A successful mentoring relationship incorporates mutual respect from the mentor and mentee.

McBride (2011) emphasized the importance of mentoring. She stated that mentoring is important at all levels of career transitions. The gift the mentor provides by being available, appreciating individual differences, asking questions that clarify issues, facilitating development and networking, and celebrating achievements is a professional obligation, and institutional policies should support the development of mentoring structures.

The Heart of Mentoring

At the heart of mentoring are certain principles that are key to successful mentoring relationships. These include mutual respect, willingness to share knowledge, listening, compassion, and integrity (Stoddard, 2003).

Mentoring models can be either formal or informal. Mentoring does not always need to occur within the context of an organizational structure. Mentees might observe competencies and skills in another professional that they would like to learn more about. Perhaps they met that person at a conference, in their community, or other setting. In any case, mentees can approach potential mentors and let them know what they have admired in them and ask if they take on mentees. It is as simple as that.

Mentor–mentee relationships are not designed to be lifelong. These relationships exist to serve a mutual benefit. Once that benefit has been achieved, the relationship may not dissolve but could morph to another level—perhaps that of coach, colleague, or friend. Research in business and education settings has suggested that most mentoring relationships average about five years in length (Grossman, 2012; Johnson & Huwe, 2003; Pollock, 1995).

Formal mentoring programs differ in their structure and organization. Some mentoring programs train mentors, whereas others provide no formalized training for mentors. Some programs assign mentors to mentees, while in other programs mentees seek out their own mentors. Some organizations require specific processes that define when and where meetings between mentors and mentees take place, whereas others leave those decisions to the participants. Finally, some organizations systematically evaluate the outcomes of mentoring, whereas others have not integrated formalized evaluation mechanisms (Ehrich et al., 2004; Vance, 2011). Leaders need to evaluate their organizational culture and match the mentor program to the needs and culture of the organization. Leaders should weigh the benefits and fit for such a program before beginning. Leaders can be instrumental in engaging others in the value of initiating a mentorship program based on generating a shared vision of the benefits related to employee retention, engagement, and satisfaction.

Success of a program will require commitment from the senior executives to support financial investment in launching and sustaining a mentorship program. The budget development will involve work time for the key program leaders and the development team for education, planning, implementation, and establishment of a sustainability plan (Reitman & Benatti, 2014).

Mentor and mentee roles are evolving in several ways in contemporary workplace environments. For example, mentees are likely to be the same age or older than the mentor; mentees are likely to hold positions that are comparable to or at the same hierarchical organizational level as the mentor; and mentees are not likely to be as passive as in the past, especially when initiating a mentoring relationship. The traditional mentoring process is evolving into more of a collaborative relationship (Ortiz-Walters, 2009). Table 22-1 identifies emerging mentoring models.

Benefits of a Mentoring Relationship

Almost 50 years of research related to the mentoring process and the effects of participating in a mentoring relationship has revealed an array of advantages to mentees, mentors, and the organizations that sponsor mentoring relationships (see Figure 22-1).

While a body of research exists chronicling the benefits of mentoring relationships in other professions, there is an opportunity for conducting further research on the benefits and rewards of the mentoring relationship in nursing and across diverse healthcare practice settings. The available research for nursing reports positive outcomes similar to the results of studies conducted in other professions. For example, nurses who were mentored reported increased career satisfaction (Douglas et al., 2016; Ellisen, 2011) and reported valuing the impact of the mentoring experience in achieving their career goals (Colonghi, 2009). Several studies reported a significant decrease in the termination rates among nursing staff when a formalized mentoring

Table 22-1. Emerging Mentoring Models	
Term	**Definition**
Co-mentoring	Both individuals in the mentoring relationship assume a mentor and a mentee role on different aspects of career development.
Developmental mentoring	Focus of this relationship is on developing the quality of the mentee's thinking rather than on giving advice and facilitating entrée to networks or other professional connection; emphasis on mutuality of learning.
Group mentoring	This format may be used when few qualified individuals to serve as mentors are available.
International mentoring	Individuals are partnered with senior employees of a host country.
Mentoring circles	A form of the group mentoring model; one mentor works with a group of mentees, or a group of people mentor each other with the assistance of a facilitator.
Multiple mentoring	The mentor, the mentee, or both are involved in more than one mentoring relationship simultaneously.
Mutual mentoring	Also known as reciprocal mentoring; in this relationship, two individuals agree to mentor each other in areas of their expertise.
Peer mentoring	Individuals assume equal roles in the mentoring process; deemphasizes hierarchy and seniority.
Reverse mentoring	A more experienced individual seeks out a less experienced colleague who has acquired knowledge and skills in a unique or specific area of expertise; the mentee becomes the mentor.
Sponsorship mentoring	The mentor is powerful and influential and chooses to "sponsor" the mentee.
Virtual mentoring	Online access to mentors is provided, usually for a fee; can also include tele-mentoring and email mentoring.

Note. Based on information from Clutterbuck, 2008; Darwin & Palmer, 2009; Mayer et al., 2008; Ortiz-Walters, 2009; "Role Model," n.d.; Tourigny & Pulich, 2005.

From "Mentorship" (p. 851), by M.G. Oberleitner in M.M. Gullatte (Ed.), *Nursing Management: Principles and Practice* (2nd ed.), 2011, Pittsburgh, PA: Oncology Nursing Society. Copyright 2011 by Oncology Nursing Society. Adapted with permission.

program was initiated (Douglas et al., 2016; Gray & Brown, 2016; Greene & Puetzer, 2002). Focusing on the experiences of new graduates, Hayes and Scott (2007) described a new-graduate orientation program in which participants had one-on-one support from a faculty member or professional mentor from their school of nursing. Implementation of this initiative resulted in a 100% retention rate (full-time employment) of participants at one year and after two years of employment, representing a significant improvement in retention rates for new graduates at this facility (Hayes & Scott, 2007).

The long-term benefits of mentoring programs have not been widely reported in the literature. Grossman (2009) found that nurses in critical care valued peer collaboration (termed *peering*) as a complement to the mentoring process for nurses in their leadership/management rotation. Having a formal mentoring program in place has been credited with increased recruitment,

---

Figure 22-1. Advantages of Mentoring

Mentee	Mentor	Organization
• Quicker learning curve • Creation of allies for the future • Contributes to career success • Facilitates personal learning • Informational support • Increased productivity • Quicker advancement in the organization • Increased satisfaction with the job and the organization • Increased compensation • Information from mentor about the organization and specific role requirements • Career and psychosocial support • Better socialization and assimilation into the organization and professional networks	• Quicker learning curve • Creation of allies for the future • Contributes to career success • Facilitates personal learning • Informational support • Increased productivity • Quicker advancement in the organization • Increased satisfaction with the job and the organization • Increased compensation • Information from mentee regarding what is happening in the profession and at lower levels in the organization • Mentee can act as a catalyst of new ideas for the mentor. • Mentee can reinvigorate the mentor.	• Quicker learning curve for employees • Increased communication of corporate values • Reduced turnover • Increased employee loyalty to the organization • Enhanced one-on-one communication and team spirit within work groups • Increased employee productivity • Increased numbers of "promotable" employees • Increased employee satisfaction

Note. Based on information from Allen et al., 2004; Barnett, 2008; Greene & Puetzer, 2002; Grossman, 2012; Noe et al., 2002; Shore et al., 2008; Washburn & Crispo, 2006; Zachary & Fischler, 2012.

From "Mentorship" (p. 853), by M.G. Oberleitner in M.M. Gullatte (Ed.), *Nursing Management: Principles and Practice* (2nd ed.), 2011, Pittsburgh, PA: Oncology Nursing Society. Copyright 2011 by Oncology Nursing Society. Adapted with permission.

---

retention, and job satisfaction (Ellisen, 2011). As the mentoring model gains more prominence in developing leaders in health care, more nursing research will be needed in this area.

According to Barker (2009), mentorship research shows that individuals who have a mentor, compared to those who do not, demonstrate increases in job satisfaction, salary, self-esteem, confidence, opportunities for promotion and advancement, and role socialization and have a defined career path and plan. A mentor considers all of these when providing guidance to the mentee. Open, honest, discreet communication between a mentor and mentee uses real-life situations and experiences to enhance the relationship between the expertise of the mentor and that of the mentee.

Having a mentor within and outside the organization is beneficial. Barker (2009) stated that the benefits of having an internal mentor include that the mentor knows the organization and can observe behaviors and outcomes, receive feedback about the mentee's performance from others, and help the mentee make connections. Mentors external to the organization offer different insights and ways of approaching things and can provide the mentee with outside connections and perspectives.

Mentees can benefit from having more than one mentor, especially those from a different discipline or profession. Mentorship engagement can benefit individuals, and, for some, becoming a leader and mentor is a lifelong transformation process that grows from diverse experience and influential role modeling. Mentoring is proposed as a vehicle for nurturing personal, career, and intellectual growth and development, improving corporate knowledge, and making employees feel valued, as well as encouraging and challenging leadership potential and opportunities that prepare future nurse leaders. Mentoring is accepted as a core function of leaders (McCloughen, O'Brien, & Jackson, 2014).

Value of Mentorship in Nursing

Mentoring benefits are demonstrated by the positive outcomes of the mentor and mentee, including the benefit of belonging, professional growth, career optimism, competency, security, and leadership readiness. The practice of mentoring must include traits such as being welcoming, mapping the future, teaching the job, supporting the transition, providing protection, and equipping mentees for leadership (Jakubik, Eliades, & Weese, 2016). Mentoring is a central capacity of leadership and known as influencing the growth of nurse leaders. Many nurses may view it primarily as a mechanism that promotes career mobility. However, Grossman (2009, 2012) contended that nurses need to enlarge their conceptualization to include the role of mentoring in expanding nursing knowledge and science. Nurses who serve in mentoring roles expand the nursing science base in clinical and administrative practice by incorporating evidence-based strategies and best practices, which ultimately result in optimal patient care and organizational outcomes.

As described earlier, mentoring is an integral component of nurse residency programs. The primary goal is the retention of new graduates in practice settings by formalizing and extending transition-to-practice initiatives. As positive outcomes of residency programs focused on the retention of new nurses continue to be reported, leaders of professional nursing organizations are strongly recommending residency programs, with mentoring as an integral process, as an essential component in the successful transition into practice and retention of new-graduate nurses (Goode, Lynn, Krsek, & Bednash, 2009). Nurse leaders can influence the initiation of a mentor program in their organization by quantifying the benefits, including the cost benefit of decreased turnover when employee satisfaction and retention are high.

Outcomes of mentoring initiatives are increasingly being reported in the literature. For example, the California Nurse Mentor Project is focused on the retention of nurses with a special emphasis on the retention of multicultural, multilingual, and male nurses. The objective of this three-year project was to design and implement a formal mentoring program for new nurses, with particular emphasis on those nurses with "ethnic, generational, and gender differences from those in the traditional nursing population" (Mills & Mullins, 2008, p. 312).

A major objective of the California project was to create a program that other hospitals could replicate. Mills and Mullins (2008) reported that the project's effectiveness was assessed by external evaluators who validated several benefits. First, program participants demonstrated lower attrition rates. Second, mentees and mentors reported increased satisfaction and professional confidence. Third, nurses who served in the preceptor role and who were participants in the cultural competency aspect of the program reported positive changes in cultural competencies, such as increased cultural sensitivity and awareness lasting for at least one year after the conclusion of training. Fourth, evaluation of financial outcomes revealed that the program was cost-effective, with a net savings (after accounting for program costs) over three years of $1.4–$5.8 million. Initiatives such as the California Nurse Mentor Project underscore the importance of empirically quantifying and qualifying the value of mentoring to the retention and professional development of nurses, as well as cost-effectiveness.

Phases of the Mentoring Process

The length of mentoring relationships in health care varies. Anecdotally, some relationships continue to evolve over time and may last 10 years or longer, whereas others flourish in the short term. A successful mentorship program must have clear expectations and commitment from the senior leadership. The program must be "intentionally designed to build relationships that provide two-way inclusive interactions exchanging insights, knowledge, and expertise, which result in mutual learning benefits for both participants regardless of generational or workplace status" (Reitman & Benatti, 2014, p. 9).

The four major phases or stages associated with mentoring are initiation, cultivation, separation, and redefinition (Kram, 1983). During the *initiation phase*, which is the foundational phase of the relationship, mentors and mentees investigate and evaluate each other's qualities and determine the viability of an ongoing relationship. In this phase, the participants discuss ideas for establishing goals and parameters of the relationship. During the *cultivation phase*, the mentor and mentee more specifically define and finalize the form of the relationship. Specific goals and objectives for the relationship are proposed and formalized by mutual agreement. Schedules for meetings and activities are devised and put into motion. Although some mentorships end spontaneously, most successful relationships progress through the *separation phase*. In this phase, the mentor and mentee mutually agree to begin to limit their contact with each other, and the mentoring relationship gradually begins to terminate. During the separation phase, the mentee assumes greater independence from the mentor. The final phase of the process, the *redefinition phase*, results in both mentor and mentee feeling equally empowered. The relationship moves away from the mentor giving advice to the mentee to an environment where the mentor and mentee interact more as peers.

Creating a Mentorship Culture in the Workplace

Although little empirical evidence exists to support that organizational culture has an impact on mentoring, it is possible that the culture of an organization (norms, values, and rituals) influences mentoring initiatives (Bally, 2007; Oberleitner, 2011). Nursing leadership plays a critical role in designing and supporting an organizational culture in which mentoring is valued. Examples of aspects of nursing leadership that support mentoring outcomes include developing a mission statement and organizational philosophy that explicitly incorporate mentoring components and language, designing learning and evaluation activities focused on mentoring, establishing regular meeting times for all parties involved in mentoring relationships, providing financial incentives to support mentoring, promoting staffing and scheduling flexibility to participate in mentoring, and formally recognizing leadership in promoting mentoring (Bally, 2007).

Reitman and Benatti (2014) identified six elements for developing mentoring partnership accountability: holding regularly scheduled meetings; being prepared for meetings; addressing any concerns or miscommunication; validating learning goals; giving two-way feedback; and quickly resolving any conflicts that occur. In addition, a successful mentorship program and mentoring partnership require mutual commitment to the process and the goals.

Zachary and Fischler (2012) identified 10 indicators that a mentoring culture has been created in an organization. First, *accountability* for the program is taken seriously by all stakeholders. The second indicator is *alignment*—mentoring is aligned explicitly with organizational values, mission, and philosophy and is not an add-on. Third is *demand*: mentor and mentee pools are filled with individuals eager for the opportunity to participate in the program. The fourth consideration is *infrastructure*, which requires that meaningful resources, including financial resources, are allocated to the mentoring program. Fifth, a *common mentoring vocabulary* is evident among employees at all hierarchical and administrative levels of the organization. Next is that *multiple venues* are available to participate in mentoring activities. Another indicator is that *reward* systems for participation are evident in the organization. The eighth indicator is that *role modeling* of mentoring best practices is visible. Furthermore, a *safety net* is available to support all participants, and confidentiality is respected. Finally, *training and education*, particularly as related to skill building and renewal training, are offered and used.

Mentoring Across Culture, Race, Generation, and Gender

Although predominantly composed of Caucasian women, the RN workforce in the United States is becoming more diverse. As of the 2010 U.S. census, ethnic and racial minority groups accounted for 37% of the population (U.S. Census Bureau, 2012). However, this diversity is not currently reflected in the nursing profession in the United States.

In a 2013 survey, nurses who self-reported as a member of a minority group represented 19% of the RN workforce, while White/Caucasian nurses represented 83%. Black/African Americans and Asians represented 6% each, Hispanics/Latinos represented 3%, and American Indians/Alaskan Natives, Hawaiian/Pacific Islanders, and other represented only 1% each of the RN workforce (Budden, Zhong, Moulton, & Cimiotti, 2013). According to 2011 data, men in nursing represented 9.6% in the profession (U.S. Census Bureau, 2013).

Buerhaus, Auerbach, and Staiger (2009) contended that the underrepresentation of men and Hispanics in the RN workforce may be, at least in part, due to the lack of role models and mentors for men and Hispanics contemplating a career in nursing. The authors theorized that removing these and other barriers for those aspiring to enter the RN workforce could add enough new RNs into the workforce to avoid the projected deficit in the United States through 2025. The American Association of Colleges of Nursing (2015) reported that educating a more diverse workforce will increase the RN workforce as well as increase the ability to serve a more diverse patient population.

When the mentor and mentee share the same racial/ethnic background, it is termed *racial/ethnic concordance* (Oberleitner, 2011). Research indicates that racially/ethnically concordant mentors for minorities are important because the partners in the mentoring relationship share similar cultural experiences. Research also indicates that barriers to mentoring initiation may be particularly critical for members of minority groups in organizations that rely on informal mentoring relationships. In some cultures, because the expectation is for the teacher (mentor) to initiate contact, a mentee from a minority group may be especially hesitant to initiate a relationship with a prospective mentor. Being proactive in initiating a mentoring relationship may not be acceptable to members of minority groups (Hu, Thomas, & Lance, 2008).

Learning to be a culturally competent partner in a mentoring relationship includes a willingness to acquire knowledge of the practices of other cultures. In some cultures, for example, mentees are viewed as being in a position of weakness if they seek out a mentor. In other cultures, the mentor is viewed as holding the position of power, and the mentee must wait for the mentor to initiate a relationship.

Research seems to validate that cross-racial mentorships often can be more difficult to develop and sustain than racially concordant mentorships (Hu et al., 2008). In a recent study, male nurses looked more favorably on male mentors (Juliff, Russell, & Bulsara, 2015). Cross-racial mentorships may provide fewer mentoring functions than same-race mentorships, and most people, when queried for preference, prefer to be in same-race mentorships (Turban, Dougherty, & Lee, 2002). In general, research indicates that diversified mentoring is more complex and that race similarity has a positive effect on the outcomes of formal mentorships.

The effectiveness of cross-cultural or cross-racial mentoring seems to be linked to the following four elements (Zachary & Fischler, 2013):

- The cross-cultural or cross-racial competence of the mentor
- Willingness of the mentor to be flexible regarding the mentee's cultural practices and values
- Excellent communication skills
- Authentic desire to understand the impact of culture on individuals

As stated earlier, the lack of male nurse role models and mentors may play a role in the decision of some men not to pursue a career in nursing. Mentor and mentee training should include knowledge of professional boundaries and should provide both partners with the skills to clearly communicate to the mentoring partner when a boundary has been crossed.

Mentoring and Leader Succession Planning

Succession planning or *succession management* is defined as efforts or methods used to ensure the development, replacement, and strategic positioning of key people in an organization (Rothwell, 2016). Aligning the career aspirations of individuals with the current and future needs of the organization is a component of succession planning. Techniques and interventions such as coaching, mentoring, and job rotations to facilitate new skill acquisition are used as succession management strategies (Beatty, Schneier, & McEvoy, 1987). It is important that peer mentors be respected in the organization and volunteer to share their knowledge and expertise with colleagues to improve their colleagues' individual knowledge and skills in the desired realm.

Mentoring has been suggested as a solution for retention and succession planning. An example of a mentoring-centered model of succession management is the Strategic Collaboration Model, or SCM (Haynes & Ghosh, 2008). SCM incorporates mentoring as a key component in succession planning by using change methodology known as Appreciative Inquiry (Cooperrider & Whitney, 2005; Mohr & Watkins, 2002; Watkins, Mohr, & Kelly, 2011) to align employees' professional development needs with the organization's future leadership needs. Key components of SCM include the incorporation of strategic collaboration teams composed of senior managers who serve as mentors to junior managers desiring career development opportunities; interpersonal skills training in techniques such as active listening, conflict resolution, communication, and delivery of feedback; and strategic collaboration contracts, which define the team's goals and objectives and team members' responsibilities and commitment to attending scheduled meetings (Washburn & Crispo, 2006).

The Appreciative Inquiry model has five phases for positive change: define, discover, dream, design, and deliver (Cooperrider & Whitney, 2005). In the *define* phase, the core purpose and team are defined. In the *discovery* phase, individuals assess what unique contributions they make to organizational excellence. The *dream* phase is designed to elicit how identified strengths are aligned with the organization's preferred future. The *design* phase is intended to support the development and refinement of strengths identified in the dream phase. Finally, in the *delivery* phase, a career development action plan is devised (Cooperrider & Whitney, 2005; Washburn & Crispo, 2006).

Implementation of a mentoring-centered succession model such as SCM may prove helpful in succession planning efforts in health care and other organizations where many older nurses now occupy critical clinical and administrative leadership roles. What can an individual, association, or organization do to help the next generation learn to lead faster? Older, more experienced nurses not only possess acquired knowledge but also lifelong experiences. How then does the older generation mentor the next for succession? Providing a formalized mentor program is an option. An estimated 95 million individuals in the United States are 18–34 years old (Herbert, 2008). How many of these people are entering the healthcare field? What is an organization's vision and responsibility in pairing the younger generation with older, experienced veteran nurses, and what is the plan for leadership succession? In health care, this is an imperative part of focused succession planning.

Association and Organization Programs

Organizations receive proven tangible benefits from formal mentor programs. These include increased productivity and organizational commitment, as well as increased retention and a way to nurture and develop internal talent (Johnson & Ridley, 2009). The Institute of Medicine (now called the Health and Medicine Division of the National Academies of Sciences, Engineering, and Medicine) report *The Future of Nursing: Leading Change, Advancing Health* recommended that nursing associations provide mentoring programs, leadership development, and opportunities for their members (Institute of Medicine, 2011). Organizations benefit from planning formal, structured mentorship programs to assist employees who are new and those transitioning into a different role or setting within the organization. Some examples of professional nursing associations engaging in mentorship and leader development programs include the American Organization of Nurse Executives' Leader2Leader program (http://leaders.aone.org/home) and the American Nurses Association's online mentoring program (www.ananursespace.org /mentorprogram). The Oncology Nursing Society (ONS, www.ons.org) provides its members with ONS/Lilly Oncology Advancing Patient Care Project grants to implement mentorship programs within their chapters. The program trains leaders at the chapter level to lead mentorship programs. The goal of this program is to empower chapter members to participate in mentoring the next generation of leaders, as well as plan effective succession planning. Many professional nursing associations have such programs.

The National Mentoring Resource Center (www.nationalmentoringresourcecenter.org) is an organization dedicated to improving the quality and effectiveness of mentoring programs and relationships across the United States. It supports practitioners to deeply incorporate evidence-based practices into their work. The National Mentoring Resource Center (n.d.) lists six elements of effective practice for mentoring in any setting:

- Recruitment: Having the right participants makes a difference in the foundation for a successful mentoring program. Standards, benchmarks, and enhancements help mentoring programs of all types identify and recruit mentors and mentees who are appropriate for the program.
- Screening: Proper screening ensures that both the mentor and mentee have the characteristics and abilities to be successful in the program. It also helps with determining whether they have the time, commitment, and personal qualities to be effective.
- Training: Training provides participants with the skills and information they need to build strong, effective, and lasting mentoring relationships. The set of standards and benchmarks can help the program develop pre-match and ongoing training sessions that support program activities and goals, as well as provide participants with effective means of evaluating the program for enhancements such as the use of evidence-based training materials.
- Matching: A key to attaining the goals of the program is to make sure that program participants are matched appropriately with considerations and compatibility to build a strong, long-term mentoring relationship. This helps the program determine matching criteria and processes for an ongoing period.
- Monitoring and support: A system of monitoring and support can help the program develop an approach for checking in on participants who have been matched to ensure they are meeting program expectations and to provide support as needed. Celebration and recognition

should be part of the monitoring and support process. An example would be that each year, prior to match closure, the program thanks mentors and recognizes the contributions of their dedication and their relationship with the mentee.

- Closure: The mentorship should be brought to a smooth end in a way that supports the contributions of both the mentor and the mentee while providing an opportunity to assess the experience. An effective closure can help the program write policies and procedures for securing the best mentor–mentee match.

Programs that examine and apply these elements in their programs notice increased adherence in their members' participation and a clear standard to measure success.

Paying It Forward

Mentors make the commitment to be an integral part of the professional growth and development of another person or colleague. Mentoring is about willingly giving of oneself and sharing personal knowledge, gifts, and talent. The best mentor understands the value of building relationships with others. What one gives, one gets back in many ways. Maxwell (2008) wrote, "When you develop people, you are helping them improve as individuals and acquire personal qualities that will benefit them in many areas of their life" (p. 95). Development cannot occur unless the person is willing to accept the mentoring.

Mentors should choose mentees carefully and should not overextend by taking on too many mentees. Be an inquiring mentor and leader. Ask the right questions to challenge mentees to think about what they want out of the experience. *Question thinking* and *inquiring leadership* are what Adams (2015) referred to as characteristics of being self-aware, self-reflecting, and committed to continuous development for individuals, as well as those around them. These tenets incorporate asking the right questions and listening intently to empower others around them (Adams, 2015).

Mentors can connect with another person on a deeper level, which means taking the time to build the relationship. Mentoring allows someone the opportunity to pay it forward to the next generation of nurse leaders, while leaving a lifelong legacy for someone else to appreciate. Each mentor–mentee relationship builds a bond and a commitment to pay it forward.

Summary

Although research indicates that most professionals in other disciplines can participate in organization-sponsored formalized mentoring programs, most RNs have not had comparable professional development opportunities. Despite more than 60% of nurses (N = 468) in a national study recognizing the value of mentoring programs for recent nurse graduates, only 28% of the same nurses had observed the implementation of mentoring programs in their own institutions (Buerhaus, DesRoches, Donelan, & Hess, 2009).

With the increasing popularity of residency programs, additional opportunities should be available for new graduates to actively participate in some form of a mentoring program. Healthcare organizations also should recognize the value of mentoring programs for experienced nurses, for nurses entering the RN workforce from other countries, and for nurses contemplating transition to a different role. Nurse leaders can leverage the value of an organizational mentorship program by highlighting the benefits of professional development for leadership and succession planning, preserving positive organizational history, and passing on intellectual capital to the next generation, as well as demonstrating the organization's commitment to employees by fostering employee retention and engagement (Reitman & Benatti, 2014).

As a profession, nursing should be strategically positioned to transition the collective generational and professional wisdom, experience, and expertise of retiring nurses. Mentoring of inexperienced nurses by experienced nurses is a time- and research-proven technique to ensure nursing leadership and experiential succession. The continued development of professional nurses should be no less valued than the development of professionals in other disciplines. Given the need to develop nurses to lead the future of health care, this is more than a hope but an imperative to ensure a sustained strong and thriving nursing profession dedicated to mentorship, leadership, and continuous learning.

According to Jakubik et al. (2016), the goals of mentoring can be categorized as lifelong learning, professional advancement, employee engagement, and succession planning. The nursing profession continues to see positive changes in both clinical and leadership specialties. Nurse leaders must ensure that emerging leaders are in place and equipped with the skills needed to be successful. They should feel obligated to mentor and prepare the next generation of professional nurses. Engaging future and emerging nurse leaders at the system, organizational, national, and international levels will cultivate aspiring nurses to facilitate organizational goals, as well as gain the skills they need to be successful leaders. This can be done by involving aspiring leaders in unit initiatives, organizational and national task forces, work groups, and committees and councils. This involvement will allow emerging nurse leaders to understand how decisions and concerns are identified, as well as what goes into problem solving.

It is crucial that nurse executives and leaders allow emerging nurse leaders some opportunities to shadow current executive nurse leaders in the organization to increase their insight into leadership and become familiar with organizational structure and processes. Mentorship programs developed by organizations, academic institutions, and professional nursing associations can provide resources for emerging and future nurse leaders through sharing of knowledge, experience, and insight on matters that affect organizations and public policies that influence nursing and patient care. Mentoring can be an extremely rewarding experience for both mentors and mentees. Continued success of nursing and the nurse leader role challenges each nurse leader to engage in mentoring, succession planning, and the cultivation and growth of future nurse leaders.

Adapted from "Mentorship" (pp. 849–864), by M.G. Oberleitner in M.M. Gullatte (Ed.), Nursing Management: Principles and Practice *(2nd ed.), 2011, Pittsburgh, PA: Oncology Nursing Society. Copyright 2011 by Oncology Nursing Society.*

References

Adams, M. (2015). *Change your questions, change your life* (3rd ed.). San Francisco, CA: Berrett-Koehler.

Allen, T.D., Eby, L.T., Poteet, M.L., Lentz, E., & Lima, L. (2004). Career benefits associated with mentoring for protégés: A meta-analysis. *Journal of Applied Psychology, 89,* 127–136. doi:10.1037/0021-9010.89.1.127

American Association of Colleges of Nursing. (2015). Fact sheet: Enhancing diversity in the nursing workforce. Retrieved from http://www.aacn.nche.edu/media-relations/diversityFS.pdf

Bally, J.M.G. (2007). The role of nursing leadership in creating a mentoring culture in acute care environments. *Nursing Economics, 25,* 143–148.

Barker, A.M. (2009). Leadership development through mentorship and professional development planning. In A.M. Barker (Ed.), *Advanced practice nursing: Essential knowledge for the profession* (pp. 43–52). Burlington, MA: Jones & Bartlett Learning.

Barnett, J.E. (2008). Mentoring, boundaries, and multiple relationships: Opportunities and challenges. *Mentoring and Tutoring: Partnership in Learning, 16,* 3–16. doi:10.1080/13611260701800900

Beatty, R.W., Schneier, C.E., & McEvoy, G.M. (1987). Executive development and management succession. In K.M. Rowland & G.R. Ferris (Eds.), *Research in personnel and human resources management: A research annual* (Vol. 5, pp. 289–322). Greenwich, CT: JAI Press.

Bryant-Lukosius, D. (2015). E-mentorship: Navigation strategy for promoting oncology nurse engagement in research. *Canadian Oncology Nursing Journal, 25,* 472–473.

Budden, J.S., Zhong, E.H., Moulton, P., & Cimiotti, J.P. (2013). Highlights of the National Workforce Survey of Registered Nurses. *Journal of Nursing Regulation, 4*(2), 5–14. Retrieved from https://www.ncsbn.org/JNR0713_05-14.pdf

Buerhaus, P.I., Auerbach, D.I., & Staiger, D.O. (2009). The recent surge in nurse employment: Causes and implications. *Health Affairs, 28,* w657–w668. Retrieved from http://content.healthaffairs.org/content/28/4/w657.long

Buerhaus, P.I., DesRoches, C., Donelan, K., & Hess, R. (2009). Still making progress to improve the hospital workplace environment? Results from the 2008 National Survey of Registered Nurses. *Nursing Economics, 27,* 289–301.

Clutterbuck, D. (2008). What's happening in coaching and mentoring? And what is the difference between them? *Development and Learning in Organizations, 22*(4), 8–10. doi:10.1108/14777280810886364

Colonghi, P. (2009). Mentoring? Take the LEAD. *Nursing Management, 40*(3), 15–17. doi:10.1097/01.NUMA .0000347406.42707.9c

Cooperrider, D.L., & Whitney, D. (2005). *Appreciative inquiry: A positive revolution in change.* San Francisco, CA: Berrett-Koehler.

Darwin, A., & Palmer, E. (2009). Mentoring circles in higher education. *Higher Education Research and Development, 28,* 125–136. doi:10.1080/07294360902725017

Deziel, S.M. (2016). Successful mentoring equals a bright future. *Nephrology News and Issues, 30*(1), 31–32.

Douglas, V., Garrity, J., Shepherd, K., & Brown, L. (2016). Nurses' perceptions and experiences of mentoring. *Nursing Management, 23*(1), 34–37. doi:10.7748/nm.23.1.34.s29

Eby, L., Buits, M., Lockwood, A., & Simon, S.A. (2004). Protégés' negative mentoring experiences: Construct development and nomological validation. *Personnel Psychology, 57,* 411–447. doi:10.1111/j.1744-6570.2004.tb02496.x

Ehrich, L.C., Hansford, B., & Tennent, L. (2004). Formal mentoring in education and other professions: A review of the literature. *Educational Administration Quarterly, 40,* 518–540. doi:10.1177/0013161X04267118

Ellisen, K. (2011). Mentoring smart. *Nursing Management, 42*(8), 12–16. doi:10.1097/01.NUMA.0000399804.14328 .bc

Goode, C.J., Lynn, M.R., Krsek, C., & Bednash, G.D. (2009). Nurse residency programs: An essential requirement for nurses. *Nursing Economics, 27,* 142–159.

Gormley, B. (2008). An application of attachment theory: Mentoring relationship dynamics and ethical concerns. *Mentoring and Tutoring: Partnership in Learning, 16,* 45–62. doi:10.1080/13611260701800975

Gray, O., & Brown, D. (2016). Evaluating a nurse mentor preparation programme. *British Journal of Nursing, 25,* 212–217. doi:10.12968/bjon.2016.25.4.212

Greene, M.T., & Puetzer, M. (2002). The value of mentoring: A strategic approach to retention and recruitment. *Journal of Nursing Care Quality, 17,* 63–70. doi:10.1097/00001786-200210000-00008

Grossman, S. (2009). Peering: The essence of collaborative mentoring in critical care. *Dimensions of Critical Care Nursing, 28,* 72–75. doi:10.1097/DCC.0b013e318195d542

Grossman, S.C. (2012). *Mentoring in nursing: A dynamic and collaborative process* (2nd ed.). New York, NY: Springer.

Harvard Business School Press. (2006). *Coaching people: Expert solutions to everyday challenges.* Boston, MA: Author.

Hayes, J.M., & Scott, A.S. (2007). Mentoring partnerships as the wave of the future for new graduates. *Nursing Education Perspectives, 28,* 27–29. doi:10.1043/1536-5026

Haynes, R.K., & Ghosh, R. (2008). Mentoring and succession management: An evaluative approach to the strategic collaboration model. *Review of Business, 28*(2), 3–12.

Herbert, B. (2008, May 13). Here come the millennials. *New York Times.* Retrieved from http://www.nytimes.com /2008/05/13/opinion/13herbert.html

Hu, C., Thomas, K.M., & Lance, C.E. (2008). Intentions to initiate mentoring relationships: Understanding the impact of race, proactivity, feelings of deprivation, and relationship roles. *Journal of Social Psychology, 148,* 727–744. doi:10.3200/SOCP.148.6.727-744

Institute of Medicine. (2011). *The future of nursing: Leading change, advancing health.* Washington, DC: National Academies Press.

Jakubik, L.D., Eliades, A.B., & Weese, M.M. (2016). Leadership Series: 'How To' for Mentoring. Part 1: An overview of mentoring practices and mentoring benefits. *Pediatric Nursing, 42,* 37–38.

Johnson, W.B. (2003). A framework for conceptualizing competence to mentor. *Ethics and Behavior, 13,* 127–151. doi:10.1207/S15327019EB1302_02

Johnson, W.B., & Huwe, J. (2003). *Getting mentored in graduate school.* Washington, DC: American Psychological Association.

Johnson, W.B., & Ridley, C.R. (2009). *The elements of mentoring.* New York, NY: Palgrave.

Juliff, D., Russell, K., & Bulsara, C. (2015). The value of male faculty from the perspective of newly graduated male registered nurses. *Australian Nursing and Midwifery Journal, 23*(5), 25.

Kram, K.E. (1983). Phases of the mentor relationship. *Academy of Management Journal, 26,* 608–625. doi:10.2307/255910

Lee, C.S., Kitko, L., Biddle, M., & Riegel, B.J. (2015). Successful mentoring relationships: American Heart Association Council on Cardiovascular and Stroke Nursing. *Journal of Cardiovascular Nursing, 30,* 379–381. doi:10.1097/JCN.0000000000000275

Maxwell, J.C. (2008). *Mentoring 101: What every leader needs to know.* Nashville, TN: Thomas Nelson.

Mayer, A.P., Files, J.A., Ko, M.G., & Blair, J.E. (2008). Academic advancement of women in medicine: Do socialized gender differences have a role in mentoring? *Mayo Clinic Proceedings, 83,* 204–207. doi:10.4065/83.2.204

McBride, A.B. (2011). *The growth and development of nurse leaders.* New York, NY: Springer.

McCloughen, A., O'Brien, L., & Jackson, D. (2014). Journey to become a nurse leader mentor: Past, present and future influences. *Nursing Inquiry, 21,* 301–310. doi:10.1111/nin.12053

Mentor. (n.d.). In *Merriam-Webster online dictionary* (11th ed.). Retrieved from https://www.merriam-webster.com/dictionary/mentor

Mills, J.F., & Mullins, A.C. (2008). The California Nurse Mentor Project: Every nurse deserves a mentor. *Nursing Economics, 26,* 310–315.

Mohr, B.J., & Watkins, J.M. (2002). The *essentials of appreciative inquiry: A roadmap for creating positive futures.* Waltham, MA: Pegasus Communication.

National Mentoring Resource Center. (n.d.). Elements of effective practice for mentoring. Retrieved from http://www.nationalmentoringresourcecenter.org/index.php/what-works-in-mentoring/elements-of-effective-practice-for-mentoring.html

Noe, R.A., Greenberger, D.B., & Wang, S. (2002). Mentoring: What we know and where we might go. In G.R. Ferris & J.J. Martocchio (Eds.), *Research in personnel and human resources management* (Vol. 21, pp. 129–173). doi:10.1016/s0742-7301(02)21003-8

Oberleitner, M.G. (2011). Mentorship. In M.M. Gullatte (Ed.), *Nursing management: Principles and practice* (2nd ed., pp. 849–864). Pittsburgh, PA: Oncology Nursing Society.

Ortiz-Walters, R. (2009). Mentorship collaborations: A longitudinal examination of the association with job performance and gender. *Journal of Business and Economic Studies, 15*(1), 26–50.

Pollock, R. (1995). A test of conceptual models depicting the developmental course of informal mentor-protégé relationships in the work place. *Journal of Vocational Behavior, 46,* 144–162. doi:10.1006/jvbe.1995.1010

Reitman, A., & Benatti, S.R. (2014). *Creating a mentoring program: Mentoring partnerships across the generations.* Alexandria, VA: ASTD Press.

Role model. (n.d.). In *Merriam-Webster online dictionary* (11th ed.). Retrieved from https://www.merriam-webster.com/dictionary/role%20model

Rothwell, W.J. (2016). *Effective succession planning: Ensuring leadership continuity and building talent from within* (5th ed.). New York, NY: AMACOM.

Shore, W.J., Toyokawa, T., & Anderson, D.D. (2008). Context-specific effects on reciprocity in mentoring relationships: Ethical implications. *Mentoring and Tutoring: Partnership in Learning, 16,* 17–29. doi:10.1080/13611260701800926

Simpson, M.K. (2014). *Unlocking potential: 7 coaching skills that transform individuals, teams and organizations.* Grand Haven, MI: Grand Harbor Press.

Stoddard, D.A. (with Tamsay, R.J.). (2003). *The heart of mentoring: Ten proven principles for developing people to their fullest potential.* Colorado Springs, CO: NavPress.

Tourigny, L., & Pulich, M. (2005). A critical examination of formal and informal mentoring among nurses. *Health Care Manager, 24,* 68–76. doi:10.1097/00126450-200501000-00011

Turban, D.B., Dougherty, T.W., & Lee, F.K. (2002). Gender, race, and perceived similarity effects in developmental relationships: The moderating role of relationship duration. *Journal of Vocational Behavior, 61,* 240–262. doi:10.1006/jvbe.2001.1855

U.S. Census Bureau. (2012, December 12). *U.S. Census Bureau projections show a slower growing, older, more diverse nation a half century from now* [News release]. Retrieved from http://www.census.gov/newsroom/releases/archives/population/cb12-243.html

U.S. Census Bureau. (2013, February). *Men in nursing occupations: American community survey highlight report.* Retrieved from http://www.census.gov/people/io/files/Men_in_Nursing_Occupations.pdf

Vance, C. (2011). *Fast facts for career success in nursing: Making the most of mentoring in a nutshell.* New York, NY: Springer.

Washburn, M.H., & Crispo, A.W. (2006). Strategic collaboration: Developing a more effective mentoring model. *Review of Business, 27,* 18–25.

Watkins, J., Mohr, B., & Kelly, R. (2011). *Appreciative inquiry: Change at the speed of imagination* (2nd ed.). doi:10.1002/9781118256060

Wells, S.J. (2009). Tending talent. *HR Magazine, 54,* 53–57. Retrieved from https://www.shrm.org/hr-today/news/hr-magazine/pages/0509wells.aspx

Yoder, L.H. (2002). *Psychometric testing of a coaching survey* (Triservice Nursing Research. No. 905-97-Z-0014). Tacoma, WA: Geneva Foundation.

Young, L. (2016). Mentoring and the 6Cs. *Nursing Standard, 30*(24), 61–62. doi:10.7748/ns.30.24.61.s48

Zachary, L.J. (with Fischler, L.A.). (2009). *The mentee's guide: Making mentoring work for you.* San Francisco, CA: Jossey-Bass.

Zachary, L.J., & Fischler, L.A. (2012). *Feedback and facilitation for mentors* (Mentoring excellence: Pocket toolkit #2). San Francisco, CA: Jossey-Bass.

Zachary, L.J., & Fischler, L.A. (2013). Facilitating mentee-driven goal setting. *TD, 67*(5), 76–77. Retrieved from https://www.td.org/Publications/Magazines/TD/TD-Archive/2013/05/Facilitating-Mentee-Driven-Goal-Setting

Zanchetta, M., & Maheu, C. (2015). Research mentoring for oncology nurses in clinical settings: For whom, why, and how? *Canadian Oncology Nursing Journal, 25,* 476–479.

CHAPTER 23

Reinventing Yourself for Future Leadership

Mary Magee Gullatte, PhD, RN, ANP-BC, AOCN®, FAAN

Reinvention involves growing up. Growing above and beyond the hurts and memories of the past.

—Steve Chandler (2017, p. 120)

Introduction

As changes occur in health care, they often spell changes for individuals in the workplace. When change occurs, it often leaves people uncertain of their position or future in the organization. Concerns swirl around scope of work and practice, as well as around change and job security. The other driving force for a change could be from within the individual. Perhaps a person has reached a time and place in their career or life that finds them no longer fulfilled. Perhaps they find themselves imagining and thinking of a different personal and professional path. Perhaps they have reached a time and place where they want to reinvent themselves. The call to reinvent oneself may not be driven by an organizational change but by a personal need to allow oneself to be the person he or she really wants to be. This may take the form of academic pursuits for an advanced degree, a change in location or living arrangements, or a new direction in life (personal or professional career choice).

If you have been thinking of a change in your life, consider the following. When was the last time you updated your curriculum vitae or résumé? If it has been more than a year, you need to do so now. You should update your résumé at least annually or each time you have achieved a new accomplishment: finished a presentation, publication, award, or other recognition, or even a time when you have extended yourself to mentor or precept a colleague. When was the last time you spent some focused time to think of what you want to do or to be for yourself, just for you? Have you thought about your personal or professional dreams and what you want to accomplish? Do you have a desire to lead a professional organization? Do you have a desire to increase your legislative advocacy? Have you considered running for elected office in your local, state, or national government? If so, what actions have you taken to actualize those dreams and thoughts? Have you become complacent in your current job, position, or life? Are you just going along in your current state, year after year, because it is easy and offers no real challenge to take a risk and do something different? If you answered in the affirmative to any of these questions, here are some strategies and tactics for you to consider to reinvent your personal or professional self. These are all questions you should ask yourself before you are faced with an imperative to do so.

Taking a Risk to Secure Your Future

> *Whatever you can do, or dream you can, begin it. Boldness has genius, power and magic in it.*
>
> —a paraphrase of Johann Wolfgang von Goethe, *Faust*, in a translation by John Anster

Change often requires taking a personal or professional risk. Making a change is about weighing your options and exploring the possibilities and then taking action toward achieving your dream. What do you wish to achieve? What will it take for you to achieve it? What resources, support, or changes will you need to make to begin? Map out your vision, including what you will need to achieve it and over how long a period. Do you consider yourself a risk taker or risk adverse? Eleanor Roosevelt was once quoted as saying, "Do one thing every day that scares you."

Fear often keeps us from taking risk. According to Eleanor Roosevelt, though, fear should be a force to drive us. Taking a risk makes us uneasy, because of the uncertainty of the personal or professional outcome. Nurse leaders cannot be paralyzed by fear of action. Thoughtfully consider the risk you plan to take and weigh your options. General George Patton was quoted as saying, "Take calculated risks; that is quite different from being rash." When you want to do something, do not let fear keep you from doing what you believe is the right thing to do for the right reason.

Inherent to taking a risk is courage. Courage is the ability to act in the face of uncertainty. As defined in *Merriam-Webster Online Dictionary*, courage is "mental or moral strength to venture, persevere, and withstand danger, fear, or difficulty" ("Courage," n.d.). It takes courage to lead and to follow. Often, fear can paralyze us—fear of the unknown outcome and even fear of success. Note the poem by Marianne Williamson (1992) in Figure 23-1. The last sentence in her poem is very profound: "As we're liberated from our fear, our presence automatically liberates others" (Williamson, 1992, p. 165).

Think of the power you have in who you are and what you can do that you may not have thought about in some time. You have power in your knowledge. You have power in your practice. You have power in your current and future leader competencies and contributions you have made personally and professionally. Think of the power in the relationships you have made over the course of your career and in your broader personal and professional community. Now is the time to leverage those strengths and relationships. Begin your personal journey to reinventing yourself by gaining insight into who you are. An alluring quote from H. Jackson Brown Jr. reads, "Never let the odds keep you from doing what you know in your heart you were meant to do."

Completing a Self-Assessment

Self-assessment may be defined as a process of gathering information about yourself with the intent to make an informed personal or professional choice. The first step in reinventing yourself

---

Figure 23-1. Our Deepest Fear

Our deepest fear is not that we are inadequate,
Our deepest fear is that we are powerful beyond measure.
It is our light, not our darkness that most frightens us.
We ask ourselves,
Who am I to be brilliant, gorgeous, talented, fabulous?
Actually, who are you not to be?
You are a child of God.
Your playing small does not serve the world.
There is nothing enlightened about shrinking so that other people won't feel insecure around you.
We are all meant to shine, as children do.
We were born to make manifest the glory of God that is within us.
It's not just in some of us; it's in everyone.
And as we let our own light shine, we unconsciously give other people permission to do the same.
As we are liberated from our own fear, our presence automatically liberates others.

Note. From *A Return to Love: Reflections on the Principles of "A Course in Miracles"* (p. 165), by M. Williamson, 1992, New York, NY: HarperCollins. Copyright 1992 by Marianne Williamson. Reprinted with permission.

---

should include a formal self-assessment. Many free online tools are available to get you started. The anatomy of self-assessment has three inventories that you should attend to for your assessment: values, interests, and personal. Take the opportunity to do a self-assessment. Some no-cost Internet resources are listed in Figure 23-2.

Figure 23-2. Online Self-Assessment Tools

- Big Five Project Personality Test: www.outofservice.com/bigfive
- CareerPerfect work preference and values inventories: www.careerperfect.com/tips/career-planning/free-tests
- CustomInsight Focal 360: www.custominsight.com/360-degree-feedback/developing
- Leadership Legacy Assessment: www.yourleadershiplegacy.com/assessment/assessment.php
- 16Personalities personality test: www.16personalities.com/free-personality-test
- *The Trusted Leader* Self-Assessment: www.thetrustedleader.com/self-assess-1.html

---

Values

Values embody what you deem important in your life and your career. *Merriam-Webster Online Dictionary* defines values as something of relative worth or importance ("Value," n.d.). Your values have major influence on behavior and attitude and serve as broad guidelines in all situations. Some common healthcare values include integrity, truth, caring, fairness, discovery, excellence, innovation, and community engagement (see Figure 23-3). These values often intersect with personal and professional values. When there is misalignment of personal and organizational values, a philosophical shift exists. This is a defining moment in your career. If alignment cannot be reconciled, then you have a decision to make about your future.

Interests

Our interests also shape thought, direction, and actions. Your interests may also be your passion. What are your personal and professional interests? In which direction do you want to take your leadership? If you are interested in furthering your education, to what aim? What do you want

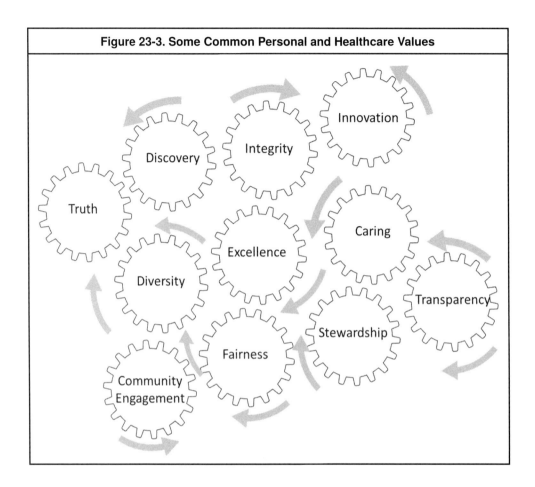

Figure 23-3. Some Common Personal and Healthcare Values

to accomplish with your master's or doctoral degree? Are you currently in the right place clinically? Is your passion pulling you in another direction than where you were five or even two years ago? What do you want to do, and where do you see yourself in the future? It is all about a "selfie" (a look inside yourself) question. Reinventing yourself is all about you. Do not be limited by your current state. Change your reality. As Albert Einstein once said, "The true value of a human being is determined primarily by the measure and the sense in which he has attained liberation from the self."

Personal

The personal inventory is about who you are as a person and who you want to be. Remember, it is not about where we come from or start, but where we end up. In other words, it is about envisioning your personal destiny and setting your goals and actions to get there. The next section dives deeper into the values and personal aspects in the anatomy of self-appraisal.

Anatomy of Self-Appraisal/Assessment

A plethora of leadership and personal self-assessment tools are available. Such tools are familiar to most leaders and include the Myers-Briggs Type Indicator® and various 360° assessment tools. Often, these tools are offered by employers for individual and professional leader development.

How do you appraise your own performance, leader strengths, and accomplishments? Jones (2013) identified six steps to writing your individual self-appraisal, which are outlined in Figure 23-4.

Figure 23-4. Six Steps to Developing a Self-Appraisal

1. **Share your brilliant successes.** Look at previous feedback received, projects you've completed and initiatives you've launched—all excellent fodder. If you haven't done so in the past, start keeping a performance journal. It will make your next self-appraisal that much easier to complete.
2. **Share what you've learned.** What have you learned in the past year? Look to identify the ways in which you've been able to enhance your skills; describe the new skills you've mastered and how they've helped you in your career development. Describe how you've applied these new skills to your job and how they support the goals of your department and organization.
3. **Share your challenges.** This isn't an annual opportunity for shameless self-promotion. It's an opportunity for some humility. Be candid about your challenges in the year. Describe how you overcame them or the steps you will take in the year ahead to address them.
4. **Be honest.** Don't embellish your accomplishments. Think hard about how you choose your ratings for yourself. Your manager will likely want you to support your ratings so be prepared to provide examples of your successes (why you deserve that high rating) and examples of your not-so-great performance (why you may deserve a weaker rating).
5. **Take time to do it well.** Your manager can tell if you rushed your self-appraisal. So take the time needed to do it justice (schedule time for it in your calendar!). After all, your self-appraisal is all about you, and you're worth it! Use all the space/features provided in the form to tell your story.
6. **Don't attempt to complete it in one go.** Treat your self-appraisal like a work of art that builds over time. You'll be much happier with the end result if you give yourself time to reflect and carefully support your self-assessment. As I mention above, use examples to support your assertions, and please, *please* make sure that you spell- and grammar-check your documents. These are all signs of how seriously you take the process and its importance to you.

Note. From "How to Write a Great Self Appraisal in Six Steps," by D. Jones, December 3, 2013, *Halogen Talent-Space Blog.* Retrieved from http://www.halogensoftware.com/blog/how-to-write-a-great-self-appraisal-in-six-steps. Copyright 2013 by Halogen Software Inc. Reprinted with permission.

Manifesting Personal Values

In empowering yourself and leading others, your personal values become a most important consideration. Every choice and every communication exchange is guided by values—your conscious or unconscious beliefs about how the world works or how it should work. Where do these values come from? The first set of values is formed in childhood. These usually are the same as your parents' or primary caregivers', including teachers, and, in some cases, those you have seen on television, in the movies, in popular culture, or shared from your local community. Later, as you grow into adulthood, you might challenge or change your values, but those childhood values will remain with you for life, serving as organizing principles as you make decisions and form relationships. These core beliefs shape your perceptions of what is important and serve as perceptual filters from one situation and one interaction to the next.

As individuals (and by extension, as organizations), we perceive, experience, and live out our values in multifaceted ways. Figure 23-5 summarizes ways our values, which are inherent in each of us, come into play as we interact with others and make behavioral choices.

Figure 23-5. Personal Values

1. As *beliefs* or a core "worldview": We would never give up, no matter what.
2. As *thought patterns* or filters: We use them to interpret events and people's behaviors.
3. As our *priorities* that show up in the day-to-day choices we make
4. As our *self-concept*: How we see ourselves and how we ideally would like to be seen by others
5. As our *self-esteem*: How we positively regard ourselves
6. As the *state of being* we strive for (e.g., love, happiness, freedom, peace, security)
7. As the *motives* that drive our choices (e.g., control, power, creativity, fame, wealth, service to humanity)
8. As the things we *fear* (e.g., loss, being bored, criticism, abandonment, loneliness)

Note. From "Inspiring Self and Others to Leadership" (p. 5), by D. Ambrose and M.M. Gullatte in M.M. Gullatte (Ed.), *Nursing Management: Principles and Practice* (2nd ed.), 2011, Pittsburgh, PA: Oncology Nursing Society. Copyright 2011 by Oncology Nursing Society. Reprinted with permission.

Leveraging Your Strengths and Living Your Values

Clarify your values and value your own style, strengths, and life experiences. What works for one leader may be different from what works for you. Once you are clear about your values, share them with the people who report to you and others you trust, and invite them to give you honest feedback when you are not living your values. This is important because to model integrity in your life and as a leader, your walk (how you act and how you behave) must match your talk (what you say you believe in and do).

Be aware, too, that situations will arise where your values differ from those of your coworkers or the organization itself. Learn to discuss these differences openly and honestly without judging yourself or others. The goal here is to foster mutual respect and understanding. At times, this may prove a risky proposition. This is the time to weigh your options and determine if the potential benefit outweighs the risk.

Some values are said to be *terminal*, whereas others are described as *instrumental*. *Terminal* values determine how you want to be seen or remembered by others—the type of person you would like to become. Do you want to be seen, for example, as a manager who cares deeply about people? Do you want to be remembered as engaging and likeable, or do you think it is enough that people respect you and do as you ask?

Instrumental values govern your daily behavioral choices from situation to situation. Do you go the extra mile regardless of the level of your compensation? Do you treat people as though they are basically trustworthy, or do you act as though most are untrustworthy? Are you extremely frugal, or do you believe in spending whatever it takes to get the results you want?

Of course, the two types of values always intersect. For example, if one of your terminal values is to be someone who has a great deal of integrity, instrumentally, you would choose behaviors such as keeping your word or "walking your talk."

As you work with and lead others, you will notice the elaborate interplay between personal, social, and organizational values governing your behaviors. Consider, for example, how values related to power, authority, inclusion, security, competition, well-being, safety, teamwork, and autonomy coincide or collide in your workplace, dictating behaviors and creating harmony or conflict. Likewise, consider how the values held by those in leadership roles ultimately shape the organization's culture and climate. Clearly, if you are in a leadership role, you must be grounded on a solid platform of values that will steer your actions in the right direction for yourself and for the organization. To define who you are as an aspiring leader will require the same.

In reinventing yourself, you must work on value alignment. This means your espoused values (what you say you believe in and desire) must consistently match your lived values (how you act in each situation). What might you need to let go? Unfortunately, value alignment often is difficult to achieve, but not impossible. Life's obligations, fears, habits, and the challenges of working in a stressful healthcare environment can compromise your ability to act in ways that align with your intrinsic and extrinsic values. Yet, you must find the courage and support to align, or to make decisions about what you will do when you cannot align. At times like this, you may need to engage a confidant or mentor, who may or may not be a member of your current workplace or immediate inner circle. This person can perhaps guide you or at least offer a listening ear as you work through any given situation.

Believing in Yourself

As a future nurse leader, how do you acquire the knowledge and skills you will need for current and future success? This question embodies the personal "selfie." First things first, you must begin by believing in yourself. Believe in the talents and skills you bring to the situation. Believe in the current leader competencies you possess and be true to yourself in recognizing the competencies you need to acquire. Believe that you can achieve and accomplish anything you desire to do. The popular children's book *The Little Engine That Could* (Piper, 1930) recounts the story of a small engine persevering to pull a long train over a mountain. Be the "engine" and, like in the story, not only believe you can but believe you will. It is within you and for you!

Do not dwell on past mistakes or missteps in your career or your personal life; move on, move up, and move out of your past. Conrad Hilton has been quoted as saying, "Successful people keep moving. They make mistakes, but they don't quit" (Feather, 2004). There is a new future waiting for you. To realize your new future, you must take action to secure your future by reinventing yourself. Think of this thought-provoking quote by Henry Ford: "If you believe you can, or if you believe you can't, you are probably right." Review the eight personal actions to reinventing yourself found in Figure 23-6 and personalize them to your own situation. How close are you to these actions? What steps do you need to close your personal gap to these actions? Begin your journey of reinvention today. Take the steps to open up a new and better future for yourself.

Summary

There comes a time when the need arises to make a change in personal or professional direction—a time to make a personal or professional change. Whether that is a life change or career change requires the same assessment strategies to accomplish the desired outcome. Sometimes making a change in your life or career can be daunting to say the least. Will the change involve new relationships or relocation? Will the change involve acquiring new knowledge, training, or skills? Has it been a decade or more since you were faced with such a required change? Do you have the required competencies to embark on a new direction, or will you need to pause and acquire them? From a professional perspective, when was the last time you updated your curriculum vitae or résumé? Have you been so immersed in the present that you have not envisioned or prepared for a different future for yourself? The reality is that today's healthcare environ-

Figure 23-6. Eight Personal Actions to Reinventing Yourself

Complete a Self-Assessment
- Objectively assess and identify your strengths and growth opportunities.

Surround Yourself With Positive People
- Distance yourself from colleagues, friends, and even family who do not support your dreams and aspirations. If they are asking negative questions, such as, "Why would you want to do that at your age?" or feeding you negative energy about what you want to do, find some people who are more supportive and who listen to your dreams with enthusiasm and willing support.

Believe in Yourself
- Respond that you will need some time to think over the idea/work. Then take the time to think it through before you reply.

Believe in Your Dreams
- When you believe in your dreams and start taking the necessary actions to actualize them, then others will begin to believe in you as well.

Set Goals
- Set progressive and realistic goals, with achievable milestones along the way. Remember goals should be SMART—specific, measurable, achievable, realistic (in whatever time frame you set), and, lastly, time bound. Setting a time will help you keep focus on your goals with touchpoints to achieving them.

Believe in Possibilities
- See the possibilities in what you can and want to achieve both personally and professionally.

Believe That You Will
- Know that you will be successful in achieving your goals and reinventing yourself.

Be Prepared
- Expect the unexpected. Be prepared for ups and downs on your journey, but persevere. Do not give up on your dreams for a better and bolder future.

ment, which is driven to improve efficiency and effectiveness of care, may lead to administrators realigning their work. At times, this realignment may mean reduction in workforce or a change in work. If or when that happens, does that affect your employment status? If it does, what do you do now? First things first, do not despair. Consider your talents and strengths and weigh your options, then act on them.

Now is the time to reflect on your next steps. Take a few days and inventory your skills and competencies. What do you want to do with this new opportunity to change direction in your life or career? Consider the possibilities for yourself. Make a few calls to colleagues you consider mentors and seek their counsel. Think positive and be optimistic about your future. You did not get to this level of achievement without talent and valuable competencies that make you an exemplary leader. When you are faced with your deepest fear, what should you do? Face that fear boldly and confidently, knowing that you will emerge on the other side victorious and often in a better place. Trust and believe in yourself. Trust your skill. Trust who you are as a person and as a professional. You can meet this new opportunity that life has offered you and be better for it. You will explore and embrace this change. It is time to discover a stronger and more resilient you.

All the best to you and your new and better future. Evaluate your inner and professional strengths and complete a self-competency assessment. Do it before you are faced with a tough decision and forced to make a change. This strategy will position you for success regardless of what life offers you in the future. Consider that change is not always negative, nor in many cases is it out of your control. See yourself being successful in whatever you endeavor to achieve. Imagine the positive possibilities! Partner with others who can help make your vision a reality—positive people, not dream killers.

Honor the dreams and aspirations you have for your career and your future. Consider what you need to do to prepare yourself for success. See your future as you would like it to be and not as it is now. Envision the glass as half full rather than half empty. Be an optimist, especially as it relates to you and your future. Our beliefs shape our future based on our thoughts and actions. Be kind to yourself through the process and enjoy the journey! You will be pleased with the new you.

References

Chandler, S. (2017). *Reinventing yourself: How to become the person you've always wanted to be* (20th anniversary ed.). Wayne, NJ: Career Press.

Courage. (n.d.). In *Merriam-Webster online dictionary*. Retrieved from http://www.merriam-webster.com/dictionary/courage

Feather, F. (2004). *Futuristic leadership A-Z*. Toronto, Canada: Motivated Publishing Ventures.

Jones, D. (2013, December 3). How to write a great self-appraisal in six steps. *Halogen TalentSpace Blog*. Retrieved from http://www.halogensoftware.com/blog/how-to-write-a-great-self-appraisal-in-six-steps

Piper, W. (1930). *The little engine that could*. New York, NY: Platt & Munk.

Value. (n.d.). In *Merriam-Webster online dictionary*. Retrieved from https://www.merriam-webster.com/dictionary/value

Williamson, M. (1992). *A return to love: Reflections on the principles of "A Course in Miracles."* New York, NY: HarperCollins.

Index

The letter f after a page number indicates that relevant content appears in a figure; the letter t, in a table.